D1194213

The Political Writings of Rufus Choate

The Political Writings of Rufus Choate
edited with an introduction and headnotes by
Thomas E. Woods, Jr.

Since 1947
REGNERY
PUBLISHING, INC.
An Eagle Publishing Company • Washington, DC

Unless otherwise indicated, the selections in this volume are taken from Samuel Gilman Brown, ed. *The Works of Rufus Choate, with a Memoir of His Life.* 2 vols. Boston: Little, Brown, 1862.

ISBN: 0-89526-154-5

Published in the United States by
Regnery Publishing, Inc.
An Eagle Publishing Company
One Massachusetts Avenue, NW
Washington, DC 20001

Distributed to the trade by
National Book Network
4720-A Boston Way
Lanham, MD 20706

Printed on acid-free paper
Manufactured in the United States of America

10 9 8 7 6 5 4 3 2 1

Books are available in quantity for promotional or premium use. Write to Director of Special Sales, Regnery Publishing, Inc., One Massachusetts Avenue, NW, Washington, DC 20001, for information on discounts and terms or call (202) 216-0600.

CONTENTS

CHAPTER

APPENDICES

INTRODUCTION

I T IS only in specialized studies of the American Whigs that one is likely to encounter Rufus Choate. Apart from the occasional passing reference, this orator of great renown, a congressman, senator, and colleague of Daniel Webster, has all but dropped out of American historical consciousness.

It was not always so. His pastor, the Rev. Nehemiah Adams, in a Sabbath discourse on Choate's death, could ask in all seriousness, "Who will undertake to analyze the character of this great product of the Divine workmanship?"[1] At the unveiling of a statue of Choate at the Boston Court House in 1898, Joseph H. Choate predicted that the great statesman and orator would one day be "enshrined in fame's temple with Cicero and Burke, with Otis and Hamilton and Webster." "I venture to believe," he went on to add, "that the Bar of Suffolk, aye, the whole Bar of America, and the people of Massachusetts, have kept the memory of no other man alive and green so long, so vividly and so lovingly, as that of Rufus Choate."[2] Choate's most recent biographer reminds us of the outpouring of published recollections and memories of the once-celebrated Massachusetts lawyer and congressman by his friends and contemporaries that followed closely upon his death. He was only narrowly passed over for inclusion in the legal category of New York University's Hall of Fame, and he soundly defeated many of the top legal minds of his day. The *Commonwealth History of Massachusetts* (1930) described him as "the Massachusetts lawyer who still attracts more interest than any other, with the exception of Webster."[3]

1. Nehemiah Adams, D.D., *A Sabbath Discourse on the Death of Hon. Rufus Choate, Together with the Address at His Funeral* (Boston: J.E. Tilton and Company, 1859), p. 7.
2. Joseph H. Choate, *An Address Delivered at the Unveiling of the Statue of Rufus Choate in the Court House in Boston, October 15, 1898* (Boston: 1898), p. 5.
3. Jean V. Matthews, *Rufus Choate: The Law and Civic Virtue* (Philadelphia: Temple University Press, 1980), p. 3.

Although himself an acclaimed orator and legal thinker, Choate never gained the notoriety and lasting recognition of his illustrious Massachusetts colleague Daniel Webster. He remains, however, an outstanding spokesman of a native conservative tradition which, though influenced by Edmund Burke, has its roots deep within American soil. A collection of his work thus fills a conspicuous gap in the history of American thought.

Rufus Choate was born on October 1, 1799, in Ipswich, Massachusetts, the fourth of six children.[4] From his earliest years he is reported to have been a voracious reader, devouring *Pilgrim's Progress* at age six and endlessly fascinated by the Bible. He had intimate contact with some of the most critical historical episodes of his childhood. The *Chesapeake-Leopard* affair of 1807 created a war frenzy in the United States unlike anything Thomas Jefferson had seen before; American opinion was outraged when a British ship, rebuffed by the *Chesapeake*'s captain when ordered to stop for inspection, opened fire on the Americans, killing two. Still a boy, Choate attended the ceremony in Salem when their bodies were reinterred (they had originally been buried in Halifax). The War of 1812, which arose out of some of the unresolved issues of that incident, fascinated young Rufus. English and American vessels could frequently be seen in Ipswich Bay; his first chronicler reports that while such ships "were watched from the shore with great interest," they were observed "by none with more concentrated gaze than Rufus."[5] As if this were not enough, Choate spent his undergraduate term at Dartmouth College in the midst of the dramatic events that led to *Dartmouth College v. Woodward* (1819), one of the landmark cases of John Marshall's tenure as Chief Justice of the Supreme Court.

After establishing his legal career in the 1820s, he ventured into state politics, serving several terms in the state legislature. Politics at this stage was for Choate not a matter of great urgency; his colleague Caleb Cushing wrote disparagingly in his diary about Choate and his neglect of the ordinary duties of his office. When he took his position in the United States Congress in December 1831, however, he was determined to be a diligent and conscientious legislator. He served two terms in that office, and from 1841 until 1845 occupied the U.S. Senate seat vacated when Daniel Webster was named secretary of state. In the years following his political career he would address some of New England's most important gatherings, exhorting his fellow Americans to follow

4. This brief account of Choate's early years relies heavily on Matthews, *Rufus Choate: The Law and Civic Virtue*, pp. 5ff.
5. Samuel Gilman Brown, ed., *The Works of Rufus Choate, with a Memoir of His Life* (Boston: Little, Brown, 1862), p. 3.

his brand of conservatism and civic virtue, until the last breath went out of him in 1859.

That he was a superb orator is disputed by no one. Although not quite of the caliber of Daniel Webster, Henry Clay, and John C. Calhoun, widely considered to have been the nation's top three speakers, Choate held a prominent place in the second tier of American orators.[6] He had an enormous vocabulary, so much so that when Chief Justice Shaw learned that a new dictionary had come out, he replied immediately: "For Heaven's sake don't let Choate hear of it."[7] Calhoun himself was stunned by Choate's eloquence, at one point wondering aloud to a group of senators, "Massachusetts sent us a Webster, but, in the name of heaven, whom have they sent us now?"[8] Oratory is, as Jean Matthews points out, "a mode of communication which the modern feels unable to take entirely seriously or even to cope with," which may help explain why Choate's widely acclaimed skills have done little in the twentieth century to secure him more than a passing reference in most history books.[9]

There can be no question that Choate was vindicating the opinions of virtually all Americans when he spoke, with his usual eloquence, of the need to maintain a policy of nonintervention in foreign conflicts. As reflected in George Washington's Farewell Address, the need for maintaining such a posture was one of the few issues on which Hamilton and Jefferson, Federalist and Republican, could agree during the first decades of the republic's existence. A front-page story for the *New York Daily Times*, reproduced here, describes an 1852 speech that Choate delivered at the University of Vermont on the subject of American sympathies in Europe as well as the limitations that must be observed in translating those sympathies into action. The United States, he said, echoing the famous observations of John Quincy Adams, would always sympathize with victims of unjust oppression. Americans would always be prepared to respond to natural or man-made disasters with sympathetic hearts and with an outpouring of humanitarian assistance appropriate to a nation of such great natural generosity. Choate reminded his listeners, however, that any kind of benevolence must be tempered by the prior responsibilities that the giver has toward himself and those under his charge. Such considerations must also inform the benevolence of nations. According to the *Times*, Choate told his audience that "the same sentiment which prescribes this form of love to man prescribes with equal authority that a nation

6. Matthews, *Rufus Choate: The Law and Civic Virtue*, p. 44.
7. Ibid., p. 45.
8. Joseph Neilson, *Memories of Rufus Choate* (Boston: Houghton, Mifflin and Co., 1884), p. 260.
9. Matthews, *Rufus Choate: The Law and Civic Virtue*, p. 4.

shall exercise it towards another only in strict subordination to its own interests, estimated by a wise statesmanship and a well-instructed public conscience." Choate gave a lively echo to Plato's insight that the virtues are one, and that the exaggeration of any particular virtue is a perversion of morality itself. Even individual benevolence "is to be controlled by reason, by respect to times, opportunities and circumstances; and must be proportioned among its objects, according to remoteness or proximity—waking warmest, bearing richest life in the nearer circles of the heart, the family, the vicinage, the country." When we reflect, however, on the differences between a nation and an individual, paying particular attention to the vast diversity of its composition and interests, it becomes clear that "the same Sovereign Disposer who has distributed the race into nations, wills also that the happiness of each nation shall form to itself the chief aim of its being, the sole or chief end of its policy." Any sane charity, then, must begin at home.[10]

Although on occasion he thus expressed the unanimous sentiments of his countrymen, Choate was a party man. For nearly all of his political life he was a member and staunch supporter of the Whigs, a political party that came into existence in the wake of a censure vote in the Senate to castigate President Andrew Jackson for "executive usurpation" in his handling of the question of the national bank and federal deposits. The party included members of the National Republicans, headed by Henry Clay, as well as ex-Federalists from New England led by Webster. For a time it even included Calhoun and other states' rights men looking for an outlet for anti-Jackson sentiment and activity. With the exception of this latter segment, the party favored the so-called "American System"—a program consisting of internal improvements, protective tariffs, and a national bank—that had been promoted by Henry Clay and his supporters since 1816.

On the subject of the American System, this volume contains several of Choate's speeches on the federal government's duty to protect domestic manufacturing by means of a systematic program of protective tariffs. He considered it the task of the enlightened statesman to formulate a trade policy that protected his country's manufacturing sector and the laboring classes whose livelihoods depended on it. This responsibility struck him as so obvious as almost to require no systematic proof. The usefulness and importance of a vigorous and thriving manufacturing base, disputed by no serious observer, implied the corresponding duty on the legislator to provide whatever reasonable conditions it should need to prosper. A protective system was such a policy. If the object of public

10. "Mr. Choate's Address on Kossuth and Non-Intervention," *New York Daily Times*, August 9, 1852, p. 1, reprinted here at p. 225.

policy were "to drive them [manufacturers] out of their business, or to reduce the wages of free labor to a level with the wages of European pauperism," then abandoning protection could be considered. But if the object is to encourage manufacturing, the course is clear: a consistent policy of tariff protection.[11]

The imperative of defending, through appropriate federal measures, the country's manufacturing base was simply a corollary of Choate's insistence on the centrality of the virtue of patriotism. The interests and well-being of one's own country, in whose soil his ancestors are buried, demands that he look to its interests first. Already in Choate's day there were voices being raised against patriotism as a virtue; in certain intellectual circles it was being portrayed as an uncivilized, atavistic sentiment that should have no place in the heart of the truly enlightened citizen. In an 1851 address on George Washington, Choate took note of what from his point of view was an extremely peculiar trend:

> It is among the strangest of all the strange things we see and hear, that there is, so early in our history, a class of moralists among us, by whom that duty, once held so sacred, which takes so permanent a place in the practical teachings of the Bible, which Christianity—as the Christian world has all but universally understood its own religion—not tolerates alone, but enjoins by all its sanctions, and over which it sheds its selectest influences, while it ennobles and limits it; which literature, art, history, the concurrent precepts of the wisest and purest of the race in all eras, have done so much to adorn and regulate—I mean, the duty of loving, with a specific and peculiar love, our own country; of preferring it to all others, into which the will of God has divided man; of guarding the integrity of its actual territory; of advancing its power, eminence, and consideration; of molding it into a vast and indestructible whole, obeying a common will, vivified by a common life, identified by a single soul; strangest it is, I say, of all that is strange, we have moralists, sophists, rather, of the dark or purple robe, by whom this master-duty of social man, is virtually and practically questioned, yea, disparaged. They deal with it as if it were an old-fashioned and half-barbarous and vulgar and contracted animalism, rather than a virtue. This love of country of yours, they say, what is it, at last, but an immoral and unphilosophical limitation and counteraction of the godlike principle of universal Benevolence?[12]

---

11. Rufus Choate, "Speech on the Bill to Alter and Amend the Several Acts Imposing Duties on Imports," p. 13 in this volume.
12. Brown, ed., *Works of Rufus Choate*, pp. 163–64.

Whatever fashionable opinion might say, however, it was the nation itself, in Choate's view an arrangement of human life ordained by God, that made civilized life possible. It was in the context of the rootedness that one found in his own country and its traditions that the ideal man was reared. The accomplishment of revolutionary America concerned America alone, it is true, but did that make it any less glorious? "Was that patriotism selfish or vain or bloody or contracted?" Choate demands. "Was it the less sublime because it was practical and because it was American?" An act of mature and sober statesmanship can be the greatest philanthropic work of all. "This making of a new nation in a new world, this devising of instrumentalities, this inspiration of a spirit, whereby millions of men, through many generations and ages, will come one after another to the great gift of social being—shall be born and live and die in a vast brotherhood of peace—mental and moral advancement, and reciprocation of succor and consolation, in life and death—what attribute of grandeur, what element of supreme and transcendent beneficence and benevolence does it lack?"[13]

Thus there was more to Whiggery than attachment to an economic program that had existed in germ in the minds of Alexander Hamilton and the Federalists as early as the 1790s. For one thing, as Daniel Walker Howe points out in his seminal study of the American Whigs, they spoke the language of morality more often and more self-consciously than did their Federalist forebears. Beyond that, the Whigs were much more likely than their Democratic counterparts to emphasize standard Burkean themes such as the importance of tradition and a deference to the past that recognizes the wisdom of previous generations. In an implicit rebuke of Jefferson and his insistence that the earth belonged in usufruct to the living, Choate called on Americans to "withstand the pernicious sophism that the successive generations, as they come to life, are but as so many successive flights of summer flies, without relations to the past or duties to the future."[14]

Choate, like many of the Whigs, was in fact an outspoken admirer of Edmund Burke. In a personal letter to a student who had written him seeking advice on a course of reading appropriate to a young man about to study law, Choate had this to say: "Aristotle's *Politics*, and all of Edmund Burke's works, and all of Cicero's works, would form an admirable course of reading, 'a library of eloquence and reason,' to form the sentiments and polish the tastes, and fertilize and enlarge the

---

13. Ibid., pp. 164–65.
14. Daniel Walker Howe, *The Political Culture of the American Whigs* (Chicago: University of Chicago Press, 1979), p. 229.

mind of a young man aspiring to be a lawyer and statesman. Cicero and Burke I would know by heart; both superlatively great—the latter the greatest, living in a later age, belonging to the modern mind and genius, though the former had more power over an audience,—both knew everything."[15] On another occasion he remarked that out of Burke "might be cut 50 Mackintoshes, 175 Macaulays, 40 Jeffreys, and 250 Sir Robert Peels, and leave him greater than Pitt and Fox together."[16]

There is a certain paradox to American Burkeanism. Burke's arguments against the French Revolution centered on the fidelity that a people owed to political arrangements hallowed by tradition and tested by experience. But the United States was itself an artificial construct, having been given life by the ratification of the Constitution, which had officially gone into effect only in 1788. Choate himself acknowledged that the Union was an "artificial aggregation."[17] Aware of this, he and his fellow Whigs naturally emphasized the continuity over time of the American experience, beginning with the colonial period, and portrayed the Constitution as merely the culmination of an evolving, organic order. Still, Choate knew that while a certain political, legal, and social continuity might be identifiable from the days of the colonies through the early republic, the Union itself was indeed a recent construct. Sincere and profound attachment to something so abstract would not come automatically. If this political order were to survive and flourish, attachment to the Union would have to be deliberately encouraged and cultivated. (During the debates over the tariff, he warned his countrymen against summary dismissal of Southern constitutional arguments, however absurd he himself considered them, because the Union could not survive if an entire section believed that its position had not been given its due.)

It must be said that for all of Choate's brilliance, his rhetorical flourish when discussing the Union sounds almost ludicrous to modern ears. The Union was a thing so sublime to Choate and the Constitution so stupendous as almost to defy belief that they could really have been the work of mere mortals. Choate removed the Union from the realm of practical, earthly things, refusing to view it as a merely utilitarian political arrangement to stand or fall with the test of time and experience. One historian argues that Choate attempted to raise the

15. Choate to Richard S. Storrs, Jr., January 2, 1841, in Brown, ed., *Works of Rufus Choate*, p. 47.
16. Howe, *Political Culture of the American Whigs*, p. 227.
17. Rufus Choate, "Speech Delivered Before the Constitutional Meeting in Faneuil Hall," p. 211 in this volume.

common law and the Constitution to the level of "sacred doctrine."[18] In seeking to inspire respect and even reverence for the Union, Choate declined to appeal to the self-interest of the states, rarely advancing as his chief argument the suggestion that a smoothly functioning central government would redound to all of the confederation's constituent parts. Instead, he insisted on attempting to cultivate a real affection for the Union. "To form and uphold a State," he once said, "it is not enough that our judgments believe it to be useful; the better part of our affections must feel it to be lovely. It is not enough that our arithmetic can compute its value, and find it high; our hearts must hold it priceless, above all things rich or rare, dearer than health or beauty, brighter than all the order of the stars."[19] Although necessarily more distant than state and local governments from the consciousness of the ordinary citizen, the Union was so rare and exquisite a political edifice for Choate that its grandeur needed to be emphasized again and again lest its proper appreciation and cultivation be neglected by the thoughtless and otiose.

It was this recognition of the importance of the Union that informed Choate's opinions regarding how best to address the problem of slavery. Choate, like Daniel Webster, was an opponent of slavery. He repeated his opposition to the institution many times over the course of his career, but it was during his work on an 1836 case before the Supreme Court of Massachusetts that he established himself on the issue. An organization called the Boston Female Anti-Slavery Society had brought before the Court the case of a six-year-old slave girl who had been brought to Boston for a visit by her mistress. The Society argued that the girl, by virtue of having been brought to a state where slavery had been abolished, was thereby free. The case was not a commentary on the fugitive slave clause of the Constitution, since the girl, having been brought to Boston simply for a visit, was not a fugitive. But it made a crucial point, on the basis of which many slaves subsequently sued for their freedom in Massachusetts courts: "Comity," Choate argued, "is only policy and courtesy—and is never to be indulged, at the expense of what the State, as a State, by its public law, declared to be justice."[20] That is, the understanding whereby sister states of the Union honor one another's laws was a matter of courtesy and convenience, not of unbending principle. The rule of comity thus could not be invoked to challenge Massachusetts's ability to declare free those

---

18. Howe, *Political Culture of the American Whigs*, p. 227.
19. Brown, ed., *Works of Rufus Choate*, p. 166.
20. Matthews, *Rufus Choate: The Law and Civic Virtue*, p. 41.

nonfugitive slaves who in one way or another managed to reach her territory. The Court, concurring with Choate, declared that "an owner of a slave in another State where slavery is warranted by law, voluntarily bringing such slave into this State, has no authority to retain him against his will, or carry him out of the State against his consent, for the purpose of being held in slavery."[21] The antislavery movement could well cheer the outcome.

At the same time, again imitating Webster, Choate believed that the tone of abolitionist writing and oratory reflected a hatred and bitterness that could only lead to sectional strife. Webster, of course, in his famous Seventh of March speech in 1850, had argued among other things that the extremism of abolitionist agitation had had the opposite of its intended effect. Indeed there can be little question that the abolitionists' stridency and radicalism, which raised the terrible specter of race war in the slave states, hardened the South in its proslavery position, at the same time undermining and discrediting native antislavery sentiment there. (Such antislavery sentiment prior to the 1830s was not inconsiderable in the South; in 1827 Ohio's Benjamin Lundy counted 106 emancipation societies in the slave states and only twenty-four in the free states.[22]) "Public opinion, which in Virginia had begun to be exhibited against slavery, and was opening out for the discussion of the question, drew back and shut itself up in its castle.... [E]very thing that these agitating people have done has been not to enlarge but to restrain, not to set free but to bind faster, the slave population of the South."[23] He also said of such people that they were apt "to think that nothing is good but what is perfect, and that there are no compromises or modifications to be made in consideration of difference of opinion or in deference to other men's judgment. If their perspicacious vision enables them to detect a spot on the face of the sun, they think that a good reason why the sun should be struck down from heaven."[24] This was precisely Choate's view. Compromise lay at the very heart of politics. Ending slavery was doubtless a desirable goal, but it must be accomplished in such a way that the great political order that made American liberty possible would not be destroyed in the process. "Do no evil that good may come," he warned. "Perform your share, for you have a share, in the abolition of slavery; perform

---

21. Neilson, *Memories of Rufus Choate*, pp. 406–7.
22. George Brown Tindall and David E. Shi, *America: A Narrative History*, 4th ed. (New York: W.W. Norton, 1996), p. 631.
23. Daniel Webster, "The Constitution and the Union," in *The Great Speeches and Orations of Daniel Webster*, ed. Edwin P. Whipple (Boston: Little, Brown, 1894), p. 619.
24. Ibid., p. 604.

your share, for you have a share, in the noble and generous strife of the sections—but perform it by keeping, by transmitting, a UNITED, LOVING
AND CHRISTIAN AMERICA."[25]

For the Burkean Choate it was the French Revolution all over again, with
the Republicans playing the role of the Jacobins. Burke, of course, had excori-
ated the French revolutionaries for violently attempting to replace the legiti-
mately constituted government of Louis XVI (a monarch whose tendencies
were, in fact, moderately in the direction of reform), whose roots went deep
within the French nation, with a radically new model of the state based not on
time, experience, and the peculiar temperament of the French nation, but simply on abstract philosophical speculation. In the United States of the 1850s, too,
as sectional conflict seemed to grow more and more imminent, Choate saw
the same culprit: an impatience with traditional channels of redress and an un-
reflective instinct to have done with the matter by force. Choate, again, was no
friend of slavery, but he believed that to proceed as though no other consideration of statecraft could trump the need for the immediate abolition of the slave
system would lead to tragedies that a true statesman must avoid. Gradualism and
compromise measures may not satisfy the ideological purist, but statecraft is not
the proper arena for ideological vindication. Again, abstract speculation was to
blame. The conviction that the slaves ought to be free was one with which many
civilized men could agree, but to demand immediate emancipation without due
consideration of the practical issues at stake in an undertaking so staggeringly
immense in scope was sheer foolishness.

The real tragedy from Choate's point of view was that the antislavery agitation that was creating such tension throughout the Union was not even really
necessary. Was the purpose of the new Republican Party "to keep slavery out
of the territories"? Then simply let nature take its course:

> There is not one but Kansas in which slavery is possible. No man
> fears, no man hopes, for slavery in Utah, New Mexico, Washington, or
> Minnesota. A national party to give them freedom is about as needful and
> about as feasible as a national party to keep Maine for freedom. And
> Kansas! Let that abused and profaned soil have calm within its borders;
> deliver it over to the natural law of peaceful and spontaneous immigra-
> tion; take off the ruffian hands; strike down the rifle and the bowie-knife;

---

25. Rufus Choate, "American Nationality," p. 373 in this volume. Emphasis in original.

guard its strenuous infancy and youth till it comes of age to choose for itself, and it will choose freedom for itself, and it will have forever what it chooses.[26]

It was with profound sorrow and anguish that toward the end of his life Choate felt compelled to change his political allegiance. In the election of 1856 he supported the Democrat, James Buchanan, for president. His decision startled and angered many of his fellow Whigs—"I don't recollect anything that has grieved me so much for years," said Francis Lieber—but he felt he had no choice.[27] The Whig Party had been destroyed by the Kansas-Nebraska controversy. He could not, of course, bring himself to support the Republicans, the "geographical party" against which he had declaimed since its inception; and his other option, the American or "Know Nothing" Party, with which he was not entirely comfortable, was no real option either. That left Buchanan as the only alternative. The Democratic Party, whatever its faults, "had burned ever with that great master-passion this hour demands—a youthful, vehement, exultant, and progressive nationality."[28] Buchanan was victorious, of course, but Choate remained pessimistic about the Union. Providence spared him from having to see that splendid constellation of states he so loved transformed into a spectacle of recrimination and blood, taking him from this earthly life on July 13, 1859.

Choate's legacy is difficult to assess. On the subject of federalism, he was a poor prophet. Although in many ways a nationalist, Choate did believe in federalism and unlike Hamilton was not anxious to reduce the state governments to a condition of utter subordination. But he discounted fears of "consolidation," which of course turned out to be all too justified, as utterly without foundation. "My dear friend," he wrote in a letter dated January 1833, "there is no more danger of consolidation. . .than there is of an invasion by the real Xerxes of Herodotus."[29] Just over a hundred years after these remarks, Franklin D. Roosevelt's Supreme Court would describe the Tenth Amendment, the guarantee against consolidation that Jefferson had described as the foundation stone of the entire Constitution, as a mere tautology. Choate could hardly be expected to anticipate so bizarre a development, but in making allegiance to the Union the central theme of his political life and in discounting threats of centralization that

26. Rufus Choate to Maine Whig State Central Committee, August 9, 1856, in Brown, ed., *Works of Rufus Choate*, pp. 215–16.
27. Matthews, *Rufus Choate: The Law and Civic Virtue*, p. 221; Howe, *Political Culture of the American Whigs*, p. 234.
28. Matthews, *Rufus Choate: The Law and Civic Virtue*, p. 224.
29. Brown, ed., *Works of Rufus Choate*, p. 39.

the states attempted to thwart by means of strict construction and even nullification, he reveals one of the tragic blind spots of Whig conservatism.

When he died in 1859 he was a man without a party, and a voice of moderation drowned out in a climate of agitation. President James Buchanan wrote
of him:

> I deeply regret the death of Mr. Choate. I consider his loss, at the pres-
> ent time, to be a great public misfortune. He was an unselfish patriot,
> devoted to the Constitution and the Union; and the more influence of his
> precept and his example would have contributed much to restore the
> ancient peace and harmony among the different members of the Confed-
> eracy. In him 'the elements were so combined,' that all his acquaintances
> became his devoted friends. So far as I know, even party malevolence spared
> him. He was pure and incorruptible; and in all our intercourse I have never
> known him to utter or insinuate a sentiment respecting public affairs which
> was not of a high tone and elevated character.[30]

Although his program for national economic development would indeed
come to pass (the protective aspect would triumph during his lifetime), Choate's
more profound thought would be largely ignored. Indeed his philosophy suffered the fate of that of any Burkean, in that its calls to sober reflection and calm
reason, of deference to ages and generations past, were rarely sufficient to temper the passions of deeply rooted conflict. Successful or not, Choate played an
important role in establishing a venerable tradition of conservatism within the
American tradition, an intelligent and consistent conservatism based on a proper
deference to generations past and in particular to the political achievements of
the founding era. Based as it was on serious historical reflection, Choate's conservatism cautioned against the careless supposition that all evils are easily
amenable to political amelioration. Finally, it rejected a practical internationalism, which required the United States to intervene in the affairs of other nations,
as well as the increasingly fashionable philosophical internationalism that condemned patriotism per se as a blight on civilization. It made no apologies for
defending America first, a position grounded firmly both in prudence and morality. It was, in short, a philosophy of American sovereignty and independence,
of respect for the Constitution, and of a Union stitched together by brotherhood and charity—developed by a man whose work, though until now nearly
forgotten, always repays careful study.

30. Letter of James Buchanan, July 18, 1859, in Brown, ed., *Works of Rufus Choate*, p. 249.

Chapter I.

SPEECH ON THE BILL TO ALTER AND AMEND THE SEVERAL ACTS IMPOSING DUTIES ON IMPORTS.★
Delivered before the United States House of Representatives, June 13, 1832.

One of the few legislative achievements of President John Quincy Adams was the protective Tariff of 1828, known to its opponents as the "tariff of abominations." His successor, Andrew Jackson, favored tariff reduction, and rates were indeed reduced in 1830 and 1832, but not enough to satisfy Southern free traders who feared that the policy of protection was becoming entrenched as a permanent program. With the specter of nullification having been raised by John C. Calhoun's anonymously released Exposition and Protest *in 1828, the increasing disaffection of the South, and of South Carolina in particular, over the course of Jackson's first term cast a certain foreboding over the congressional debates on the matter in 1832.*

Choate's speech on the tariff during that fateful year reveals the voice of a practical statesman. He concedes that most national measures are likely to have some disparate sectional impact, but adds that while the federal government should do what it can to mitigate the severity of that impact, in the final analysis it must take into account "the greatest good of the greatest number." (This, of course, is precisely the reasoning that Calhoun sought to counter with his theory of the "concurrent majority.")

The federal government, Choate maintains, entered into a solemn compact with the nation's manufacturing interests when it adopted a protective policy in 1816, following the War of 1812. If the object of the government of the United States is to "retain the manufacturers in their business, and keep up the wages of labor," which he thinks it reasonable to suppose, then the necessity of continuing the protective policy is obvious. But if "the object be to drive them out of their business, or to reduce the wages of free labor to a level with the wages of European pauperism, it is a different thing." Whatever hardship South Carolina might have to endure at the hands of protectionism—and Choate believes that such hardship had been greatly exaggerated—would be more than offset by the suffering that would attend American workers upon its repeal.

★ Taken from Gales and Seaton's Register [Ed.].

I WISH only, sir, said Mr. C., to submit some considerations upon a single one of all the topics which belong to this delicate and complex deliberation. I wish to present one reason only why you should not abolish, or substantially alter, the existing national protective system. Much has been said for the producers of cotton, rice, and tobacco, and the consumers of imported British goods. I beg your indulgence while I say something in behalf of that portion of the American people whom your legislation and word of honor have invited or compelled to become manufacturers, or to connect their labor, their capital, their fortunes, their calculations for life, for themselves and for their children, remotely or directly with manufactures, and who are now menaced by an abandonment of that policy which has made them what they are, and placed them where they are.

The question at this moment pending before the committee, upon the amendment offered by my colleague [Mr. J. DAVIS] to the bill reported by the Committee on Manufactures, is, perhaps, a decisive question. If you adopt it with such modifications, and such further less important amendments as are understood to be matured, and in readiness to be presented, you decide to preserve, substantially unimpaired, the American system as now established. Something you will also do, I hope it may be thought to be much, for conciliation and concession. You reduce the revenue to the needs of the Government, or at least you efficiently, and in good faith, begin the business of reduction. From one, perhaps from two articles, exclusively of Southern consumption, and of great importance to the South, negro clothing and cotton bagging, the protecting duty will, by exemption or drawback, be taken wholly away: But the general system of protection will remain untouched.

If, on the other hand, you reject this amendment, and pass the bill submitted by the Secretary of the Treasury, or that submitted by the Committee of Ways and Means, you prostrate that system. Looking at the rate of duties, and the mode and place of valuation therein prescribed, consulting with men in whose practical opinions I ought to have confidence, and judging as well as I may for myself, I am compelled to believe that each of those bills withdraws, and intends to withdraw, from our immature and springing manufactures, whatever of certain and substantial protection they now enjoy. The real question pending, therefore, is the broad one which gentlemen have discussed—Shall the existing protective system be maintained, or shall it be overthrown, either by direct abolition, or by compromise?

I have listened, sir, to this discussion with great interest. The magnitude of the consequences which all admit depend on it, and the ability with which it has been sustained, have made it to me a memorable and instructive occasion.

But in all that I have heard there has been only one plausible reason suggested for the abandonment of the protective system. That reason is, that the system operates with a local and partial severity upon the planting States. It is true that other considerations are pressed in argument. The gentleman from Georgia, who has just resumed his seat, [Mr. WILDE,] does not confine himself exclusively to the sectional objection. Elsewhere, as well as in the South, there is hostility to the system. Elsewhere, as well as there, there are political economists and politicians who maintain that it rests upon an unsound theory of the wealth of nations; that it unduly depresses and unduly fosters individual interests; that it is aristocratical and anti-republican in its tendencies, and that it produces, in the long run, national loss and national immorality. Elsewhere, as well as there, there are pursuits on which some of its provisions do press with unquestionable severity. Every where, as well as there, it produces some good and some evil, like all other contrivances of man; and it divides public opinion, to some extent, like every other subject which addresses itself to the reason and passions of man. But I am sure I speak the sentiment of nine in ten of the committee when I say that, were it not for its alleged severity of pressure upon the South, there would be no plausibility whatsoever in this formidable attack upon it. But for this we should utterly reject the suggestion so often reiterated here and elsewhere, that the extinguishment of the national debt affords a fit opportunity for overthrowing it. We should see nothing at all of that crisis which inspires so much newspaper eloquence. What, but for this, should we do? Why, as a matter of course, as fast as we could, we should reduce the revenue to the wants of Government, but we should do this without so much as touching the principle of the protective portion of the tariff. Its details we might, now or hereafter, no doubt, re-examine. We might insert an item here, or strike out another there; we might restore the true value of the pound sterling; abolish the mysteries and abominations of minimums; alter the place and mode of appraising goods; substitute cash payments of duties for credits; and if any interest affected by the general system should be found to suffer more or gain less than others, we might relieve it by exemption or drawback; but the system itself, in its general principle, grand outlines, and substantial construction, nobody would dream of tampering with.

I repeat it, then, the only plausible ground of attack on this policy, here assumed, is this, that it oppresses the States of the South; that it blights their harvests, blasts their fields, and causes the grass to grow on the wharves, and in the great thoroughfares of their commercial cities; that it enhances the prices of all they buy, and depresses the prices of all they sell.

To this argument of the South, various answers may be given. I shall confine myself, as I have said, to one, and that a plain, practical, and intelligible answer. It is this: that the injury which the abandonment of this policy will do to the individuals, and to the interests and sections remotely or directly connected with, and dependent on, manufacturing and mechanical industry, and to the country, will outweigh, immeasurably, any rational estimate of the good which it will do to the South.

I take it, sir, if the fact be so, this is a proper argument to be addressed to the committee. It is a question of expediency we are debating. "The greatest good of the greatest number" is the turning consideration, is it not! If the act to which gentlemen urge you so zealously will occasion more evil than good, in a large and comprehensive estimate of its consequences, will you be persuaded into it?

It is true, certainly, that a different doctrine has been insinuated, if not openly pressed, in this discussion. It has been argued that this is not a question of expediency, but of right, justice, and principle. It has been argued that, no matter how great may be the amount of the pecuniary, economical, individual and national sacrifice on the one side, occasioned by the subversion of the protective policy, or how trivial the compensation on the other, our Southern brethren may demand its subversion as a matter of clear right and justice. It is argued, or it follows from what is argued, that they may put a cotton plantation, or a tobacco field, against a thousand millions of dollars of manufacturing values, against the occupations and property of seventeen States, and against the wealth, power, enjoyments, and hopes of a whole nation; and demand, as a claim of mere right, that the greater should be sacrificed, not for the benefit of the less, but on a groundless expectation of such a benefit. That "great interests" on which the gentleman from Virginia [Mr. BOULDIN] laid such significant emphasis, should prevail against small interests, and that the majority, in a matter within their constitutional competence, should prescribe rule to the minority, is vehemently denounced as unjust and intolerable.

Sir, I am afraid that this language conveys no useful meaning, nor any meaning at all, for the direction of our duty as legislators in this exigency. Observe that it is not the constitutional power of the majority in Congress to make a protecting tariff which gentlemen deny. They mean something more and something else than this. Probably they do not doubt that you have the constitutional power to collect a necessary and given amount of revenue, in such manner as incidentally to extend protection to domestic industry. At least they do not very distinctly deny it. Observe, too, that they do not condescend to say that the majority ought to weigh this question deliberately and dispassionately, as a grave and difficult question of policy, with a liberal indulgence towards the opinions of the minority, and with a determination if possible to reconcile rather than sacrifice the smaller interests, and the subordinate good to the greater. This is not the language of the gentlemen. They go a great way beyond and above this. They mean to say, or they say nothing to the purpose, that, in this particular case, the majority of this nation, acting according to the forms of the constitution, upon a subject within the jurisdiction of the General Government, have no right to determine the national policy, or have no right to determine it as the greatest good of the greatest number shall in the judgment of the majority require, but as the minority shall dictate. They assert a moral right, or some sort of right, not a constitutional one, to have the protecting system forthwith abandoned without reference to consequences. *Fiat justitia, ruat colum,* say they. Sir, the ardor of debate has hurried gentlemen into exaggerated expression or confusion of thought. Let us, to use the language of a distinguished individual, one of that Congress of which the gentleman from Georgia [Mr. WILDE] has just furnished us so many interesting recollections, and whose great names he has praised with so much candor and discrimination—"let us seek for clear ideas." I suppose myself, upon the general question of continuing or withdrawing protection, to be one of the majority of this Legislature. The constitutional power to continue or withdraw protection is conceded to us. By what principle of political morality ought we to regulate the exercise of this power? For all legislation which is admitted to be authorized by the constitution, the people of the United States are one people. The confederated character of the Government and the separate existence of the States, for all such legislation, are of no importance. The power of the majority, and the rule of political morality which should control its exercise, are precisely the same for such legislation, as if the Government were consolidated, and our people "one, indivisible, and homogeneous," as the report of the Committee of Ways and Means describes the Government and the people of England. Local interests, pursuits, and opinions there are, of course, different, conflicting, almost irreconcilable. The South, the North, the West, have each their own. We are called to deliberate upon a policy which affects them all, some favorably, others unfavorably, or less favorably. What is the rule of our right and our duty? Sir, we ought, if we could do so, to adopt a policy which shall reconcile and harmonize all these interests, and promote the good of all, and of all equally. But that is impossible. What then are we to do? Consult the greatest good of the greatest number; regardless where or on whom the particular hardship which all general policy must produce shall fall, but regretting that it should fall on any body, and lightening it as well as we may. The moral right of the minority is that the majority shall exercise a sound discretion in good faith. The moral duty of the minority is acquiescence. If they are subjected to loss and hardship, and it be direct, specific, measurable in money, or such as the customs of civil societies recognise as a fit subject of compensation, they must be compensated. If not so, it is what the gentleman from South Carolina calls *damnum absque injuria*. Extreme cases provide for themselves, and are a law unto themselves. All this, Jeremy Bentham and the Westminster Review, to which we have been sent, in the course of this discussion, to learn political economy, would say is too clear for argument. I agree, certainly, that it is a very grave question of expediency, whether we shall perpetuate a system which is supposed to distribute its good and its evil sectionally; its good over one region, and its evil over another. I should hesitate a little longer perhaps upon a measure which was opposed by the entire people of a single State, than upon one which was opposed by an equal number of persons scattered through the twenty-four States. If the navigating interest of this country were confined to South Carolina, and her whole population were concerned in that interest, gentlemen might not think it expedient perhaps to burden it as they burden it now. The power and right of the majority, and the duty of the minority, would, however, remain the same.

Then, sir, to pass on. If the injury to other sections, interests, and individuals, and to the nation, will exceed the benefit to the South, the measure recommended is inexpedient, and must be rejected. Take, then, as well as you can, the dimensions of the evil of all sorts, which you will do if you overturn this system. Consider first the magnitude and character of the interests which it shelters, and their claims upon your care. I could not, in an hour, enumerate the various agricultural products and branches of mechanical and manufacturing industry, which make up the vast aggregate and *congeries,* so to speak, of your protected interests. It would be still less easy to express their value in "moneys numbered," or to gauge the height, depth, length, and breadth of the mischief which is meditated. You know, in general, that this interest has swollen to many hundred millions of dollars. You know that it comprehends many agricultural products to which the wisdom of all civilized nations has ascribed the first importance, and the whole circle of the plain, substantial, and useful arts, trades, and branches of manufacture, which characterize the judicious and practical industry of the Anglo-Saxon race of men, wheresoever upon earth they are found. You know that it is no local or subordinate interest. Viewing it merely as a business which is pursued, and a property which is holden by individuals, it is pursued and holden in the East, in the central States, in the West, in the South, and in the Southwest; and thousands of those classes of our citizens whom the legislator would most wish to favor, laborers, mechanics, farmers, capitalists of middling fortunes, their own acquisition, have connected themselves inseparably with its prosperity and its decline. I might impress perhaps a more vivid and just conception of its importance and character, by entering into some details. But it is needless. I speak to statesmen who hold the fate of the whole national industry in their hands, who are now deliberating upon a measure pregnant with its fate, and they have surely prepared themselves for such a duty by a careful survey of its particular employments, as well as its grand aggregate and magnitude.

Remember now the claims which this industry has upon you. Sir, had these interests sprung spontaneously up amongst us, had they grown by your neglect, instead of having flourished by your care, no statesman would sacrifice or tamper with them. They are too vast and precious to be thrown away, "as a drunkard flings his treasure from him," and too complex and delicate to be subjected to bold theories and untried experiments. But to pass a bill in two sections, such as this of the Committee of Ways and Means, dooming the whole body of them to ruin, utter and immediate, no Government which God ever suffered to stand one hundred years upon the earth ever did such a deed. However they may have grown up, whencesoever they came, every Government deserving the name of a Government, every statesman aspiring to the character of a statesman, would regard them as a vast addition to the wealth, capacities, enjoyment, and power of the nation, and would cultivate them accordingly.

I had almost forgotten what fell from the gentleman from Tennessee, [Mr. BELL.] He said, I think, that these interests were only a low concern of property and wealth, almost beneath the transcendental dignity of American statesmanship. He told us that the solicitude which the people of the Eastern and central States feel on this subject, springs only from their avarice. The anxiety which shakes the cold, calm, and iron frame of Pennsylvania like an ague, is only a convulsive spasm of alarmed rapacity. When your free citizens come up hither by thousands, (I have myself presented petitions of a thousand,) as in a great procession of trades, and remonstrate against this measure of comprehensive terror and desolation, why, it is the lowest and basest of all the human passions which moves them! Labor cannot ask you to leave him undisturbed the occupation which is all he has to bequeath to his child, but he is rebuked on this floor, by statesmen and gentlemen, for his avarice! Sir, repressing altogether what I was about to say, I submit that South Carolina on one side, and the mechanical, and manufacturing, and free agricultural industry of the country on the other, have a right to move this great question here or elsewhere, without being subjected to such injurious imputations as these. I do not admit that the sentiment which excites these large masses of the community upon a subject so engrossing as that of their occupations and property, is a low or degrading sentiment. Let me tell the gentleman from Tennessee, too, that the wealth of this nation, its safe tenure, its undisturbed enjoyment, its steady and honest accumulation, are beneath the notice of no American statesman, in any crisis. Let me remind him that civil government is instituted mainly for the care of property. He remembers how broadly this sentiment is asserted by Cicero, in the best treatise of morality that was ever written. *"Hanc ob causam maxime, ut sua tenerent, respublicë civitatesque constitutë sunt."* The promotion of a property interest, commerce, and public credit, we know historically was a leading inducement to the formation of this constitution itself. While, therefore, I would fain deem as highly as the gentleman from Tennessee, of the office and duties of an American statesman, and appreciate fully the beauty and eloquence of his appeal to us to raise ourselves above avarice and ambition to patriotism and union, I say still that this great question is substantially a question of individual occupation, and property, and national wealth, and as such is to be discussed and settled. I resume, then, and repeat, had these mechanical and manufacturing interests, and associated agricultural interests, grown up without any agency of yours, their preservation and prosperity would be now, in all the circumstances of this time, a leading object with every American statesman.

But their claims upon you stand on stronger ground than this. Sir, the relation of this Government to these interests is peculiar and responsible. It is a parental relation. Your legislation created them. You invited this property into this investment. You enticed these laborers into this vineyard. You called this capital from the land and the sea; you sought it out, and found it where it lay safe, diffused, and dormant, and embodied and fixed it in establishments and occupations from which it cannot be extricated without ruin to its confiding owners. This consideration, in a great degree, determines the duty of this Government. You have plighted your faith, and the people have trusted in it. Henceforward your original perfect freedom of choice is in some sort taken away. You may have doubted about the political economy of this question at first, and you may doubt now. You may have doubted about its constitutionality and expediency, then and now. The difficulty is, you heard all this matter fully debated; it was discussed by the press; in the primary meetings of the people all over the country, and on this floor by the first talents and the purest patriotism. You heard all, deliberated long, weighed carefully, and decided to adopt a permanent protective policy, and the whole people have acted upon your decision. You have put your hand to the plough, and how can you turn back?

Sir, this conduct of this Government, coupled with the subsequent investment of capital, or the continued employment of capital before invested, constitutes a sort of legislative pledge to those who have relied on it. It is a reasonable assurance of the permanence of this system, holden out by the Government, on which confiding and intelligent men have embarked all their fortunes and all their hopes, and might judiciously do so. The distinguished author, however, of the report of the memorial of the Free Trade Convention, holden in Philadelphia in September last, denies this. He observes, "after having given the fullest consideration to this important subject, your memorialists have not been able to perceive any other objection to the immediate adoption of their plan, than that which arises from vested interests; these are entitled to respect only because they do exist, and not on account of any presumed legislative pledge, which no Legislature could give, and which, if so intended, your memorialists altogether deny to be in any degree binding upon subsequent Legislatures." Sir, without intending any disrespect to the distinguished author whose abilities and services are fully appreciated, this doctrine seems to be as unsound as it is cold and severe. Properly explained and properly qualified, the protective legislation of this Government is a pledge to the people, which is sacred, and which ought to be redeemed at the hazard of all things but honor and union.

But attend to the nature and limitations of this pledge. What was the extent of the assurance given to the capital and labor of the country, by the passage of your various tariffs of protection? Why, you undertook, to those who acted on it, to continue to afford them such and so much protection against foreigners as you can afford by any practicable assessment of duties of revenue. You are not to raise revenue for protection. You raise it to defray the expenses of the Government, the army, the navy, civil list, pensions, and miscellanies, and you are to raise no more than is necessary for those purposes. The amount to be raised is first to be fixed by reference to those purposes, and then that amount is to be so distributed upon the objects of importation, as to afford the utmost practicable incidental protection to domestic manufactures, if so much is necessary. If that blessed consummation so devoutly wished by the report of the Committee of Ways and Means should ever be realized, and the Government should come to be administered for nothing, the manufacturer gets no more protection in this form. If five millions should ever suffice to defray the expenses of administering it, that sum measures the limits of protection. So far the manufacturer takes his risk, because he reposes upon a system which couples protection with revenue, and makes protection subordinate to revenue.

Sir, I limit and qualify this legislative pledge still more strictly. I agree that, if after the adoption of the protective policy by this Government, after capital had been invested, and manufactures had begun to spring up beneath that policy; if, after all this, a new state of facts substantially should present itself; if it should be ascertained either that no further protection was necessary, the manufactures having outgrown that necessity, or that all further protection was unavailing and inexpedient, it being discovered to be impossible to introduce or sustain them by such means, or that unforeseen and great mischiefs to other paramount interests would attend their successful introduction by such means, then the pledge would be no longer obligatory, and Government might abandon the policy of protection without staining its honor, or impairing confidence in its justice. To this extent also the manufacturer takes his risk.

This brings us, sir, to the great question upon which this deliberation, in the view of a practical statesman, mainly turns. Has a state of facts, substantially new and material, arisen since the year 1824, or the year 1828, which discharges you of your pledge, and renders it honorable, expedient, and honest to abandon the protected interests, and change the policy then deliberately adopted? Sir, the Congress of 1824, and that of 1828, had their duty to do, and we have ours. They had their responsibilities, and we have ours. In the discharge of that duty, under the whole weight of that responsibility, they settled this policy, and, in view of the vast interests now embarked in it, we are to assume that it was rightly settled. Our business is to inquire whether, in the eight years which have since elapsed, matter *ex post facto* has arisen, requiring us to undo what they have done. Has it been ascertained, then, that no further protection is necessary, manufactures having outgrown such necessity? Nobody pretends this. It is admitted by every one who has debated this question here, and by the whole anti-tariff press, that continued protection to some extent is indispensable, if the object be to retain the manufacturers in their business, and keep up the wages of labor. If the object be to drive them out of their business, or to reduce the wages of free labor to a level with the wages of European pauperism, it is a different thing. Has it been ascertained, however, let it be further demanded, that the protected manufactures have reached such a point that the rate of duties proposed by the bill submitted by the Secretary of the Treasury will afford them adequate protection? In other words, is it ascertained that the proposed duties are as accurately adapted and adjusted to the present condition of domestic manufactures, as the existing duties were adapted to their condition when they were laid on?

In 1824 and 1828 certain protecting duties were imposed. This was done upon great consideration, and a careful study of this most complex subject in all its parts and all its bearings. It has not been intimated by any gentleman, and not a title of proof has been adduced on this occasion to show that those duties, taking into consideration the state of our manufactures then, were too high for their object—effectual protection. But it is a common and plausible thing to say that as a manufacture grows, and strikes its root deeper, and acquires hardihood and a self-sustaining capacity, as skill is improved, and capital flows into the employment, and domestic competition becomes adventurous and fortunate, that, then, less than the original degree of protection is necessary, and duties may come down somewhat. This is the argument from which there is most to dread. Sir, this project of reducing duties of protection, to keep pace with a supposed advancement of the manufacture, is the most delicate business that ever was undertaken. The problem is this: if sixty per cent. was only adequate protection in 1828, what rate per cent. is adequate protection in 1832? Nay, the problem is still more complicated. You propose to abolish minimums; and therefore the question is, what ad valorem duty now will be an exact equivalent for the artificial specific duty of the existing tariff? Here, precision, certainty, proof, accurate calculation, are every thing. Five per cent. more or less may make all the difference between a protecting duty and a duty which yields no protection. The loose, indolent, and mischievous suggestion so often repeated, with so little meaning, that manufactures can now to a great degree take care of themselves, is an unsafe guide of practical legislation. Where are the proofs on which you assert that this industry can sustain this reduction? Show your estimates. Work out the sum. Take the complex and careful calculation upon which the Congress of 1828 proceeded; go over it item by item, and let us see upon what supposed alteration of circumstances you ground this perilous experiment. The cost of foreign production, the cost of domestic production, the dangers from fluctuations of foreign markets and business, and from frauds upon your own custom-houses, is there any new light upon these subjects? Have you examined witnesses? Have you so much as read an affidavit? Have you taken an observation? or do you go by dead reckoning? And, either way, do let us look over your day's work! Sir, they who are striving to overturn the system of protection, act intelligently and consistently in voting for this reduction of duty, if they can obtain no more, regardless of its extent and consequences. But I entreat the majority of this House, the friends and framers of the system, to be cautious how they receive the delusive, or, at the best, doubtful proposition, that a duty of one-half will as effectually protect the interests to which they are devoted, now, as the whole duty protected them when it was first imposed. They may voluntarily renounce protection, if they think the times demand the sacrifice. But let them not be deluded out of it; nor attempt to sooth the country by the pretence that it has been preserved, when they know it has not, or do not know that it has.

Upon the whole, sir, I submit that it has not been ascertained, since 1824 or 1828, that no further protection is necessary, nor that the proposed degree of reduced protection is all which is necessary.

Well, sir, has it been ascertained that protection is unavailing and inexpedient, it being now discovered to be impossible to introduce domestic manufactures by such means at all, or at least without great and disproportionate expense? Let it be premised that it is only four years since the system was consummated. Even if you date back from 1824, it is quite too short a time to develop the fair action of a complex policy like this. He is a bold statesman, and that is a bold party and a bold administration which will say that the result of such an experiment has demonstrated that this kind of industry cannot be engrafted upon the stock of the masculine morality, energetic habits, the skill, perseverance, and frugality of this people. However the system had operated, nobody could say it had failed on a fair trial, and therefore should be abandoned. But I go further. I ask every member of this committee, if even the brief, and in some respects unfavorable experiment which has been made, does not prove conclusively that this seed is sown on good ground, and that, although it is yet but in the blade and the green ear, it will shoot higher, and bring forth of full corn in the ear a hundred fold. You have not overrated the capacities of your country, nor erred in your vision of her greatness. We see far enough to know that whatever of wealth, power, enjoyment, and aggrandizement, a diversified, persevering, rewarded, intellectual industry will bestow upon a nation, is already within our grasp. We see far enough to know that the same great power of the social world, which reared and which upholds the strong columns of England's ocean throne, will carry us up also to the same dazzling elevation, and cover us over, in the fulness of time, with the same brightness of glory. *Sic tibi etiam itur ad astra!*

Gentlemen say, however, that they admit you can introduce and establish manufactures by a protective policy, but it will cost too much. The price paid by the consumers of the country is too high, and the remuneration which we anticipate is too remote and too inadequate. Sir, this does not come to the point. You expected it would cost something thus to introduce manufactures, when you adopted this policy. You expected a temporary enhancement of prices to the consumers, and you looked forward to a great ultimate national compensation, overbalancing this sacrifice, "casting your bread upon the waters to receive it again after many days."

The true question is this: Has it been proved, by the experiment of these eight years, that it will cost more than you expected to establish manufactures by a protective policy? Do prices stand higher, or is domestic competition less enterpris-

ing and successful, or have manufactures thriven more feebly than you anticipated, rendering it probable that you will be forced to give, not too much for the
whistle, but more than you meant to give? Sir, the reverse of all this has happened.
The friends and foes of the system have been alike disappointed by its splendid
and quick success. Prices have fallen, from some cause, competition is crowded
and bold, and manufactures have multiplied themselves, if it so pleases the gentleman from Tennessee, "beyond the dreams of avarice," or of enthusiasm.

Has the experiment proved that the successful introduction of manufactures,
by aid of this kind of legislation, works out in any way an overbalance of
national injury? Does it operate to diminish revenue, or to depress trade, navigation, commerce, and agriculture, and the wages of labor? Do the great cities
wither under this curse? Does the country wither under it? Does it begin to
develop anti-republican and aristocratical influences in our society? No, sir, the
gentleman from Tennessee himself admits that the eye of man never reposed
upon a more soothing spectacle of general enjoyment and prosperity than that
which this whole land—excepting only, what I do not except, the Southern
region of misery—this moment presents. "Thrice happy, if we but knew our
happiness!"

Will it be said, however, that public sentiment has at length declared against
the system, and that this is a new fact, relieving you of your pledge, and requiring you to retrace your steps? Sir, it should be borne in mind that the Government settled this policy against a very divided public opinion, and therefore the
continuance of such a divided opinion ought to be cautiously received, as a reason for receding from it. I do not know that in 1824 the weight of opinion was
not against the protecting tariff. The literary press of this country and of England, the professed and perhaps sincere sentiments of British statesmen given
out in Parliament about that time, the whole navigating and commercial interests, the united East and South, some of the first abilities of the day in Congress,
encountered by great abilities, it is true, on the other side; these were against it,
and yet it was adopted. Was any body so weak as to suppose that a trial of eight
years would convert all this body of opposition over to the tariff? Can you then
honorably urge this anticipated continuance of hostility, supposing it were un-
diminished, as a reason for giving up a system with which so many interests have
since been intertwined, and which you adopted in defiance of that hostility?
But, sir, this is not all. Every candid man who hears me, will admit that public
sentiment is more favorable to the preservation of the tariff, than it was to its
passage. The press, the elections, the voice of the Northern States, Maryland,
of East Tennessee, every thing proves it.

Will it be said, finally, that although opposition has diminished upon the whole, it has however assumed an anomalous, organized, semi-belligerent form in one State; that South Carolina will secede from the Union in five months, if you do not abandon the protected interests? Is this a new and material fact, which requires us to abandon them?

This is a topic of great delicacy. The less perhaps I say about it, the better. It may appear presumptuous in me, after the solemn asseveration of the gentleman from South Carolina, [Mr. MCDUFFIE,] whose great talents and energetic and persevering character so well fit him for fulfilling his own prediction, if he should be so minded, (I do not think he will,) to express the opinion that South Carolina will neither nullify nor secede; yet such is nevertheless my prevailing opinion, and certainly my hope. One thing I take leave to say, with the freedom which is the privilege and duty of the humblest in this body. She has no more right, and no fairer pretest, to leave the Union, if you continue this policy, than Massachusetts has to go, if you abandon it. No casuistry can distinguish between the two cases. In 1816, Massachusetts resisted the adoption of the policy, and South Carolina favored it. In 1824 and 1828, they stood together in opposition. It was adopted. Massachusetts acquiesced in the declared and constitutional general will, withdrew her capital from the sea, and with no good grace at first began to manufacture. South Carolina stood out against the law. She asks you to repeal it to-day, because it does her a great injury. Massachusetts asks you not to repeal it, because that will do her a great injury. Where is the difference? But the gentleman said that it is a great principle South Carolina contends for; that her cause is glorious, commending her, whether she succeed or fail, to the approbation of the world and posterity.

Sir, there is no more principle on the South Carolina side of this controversy, than there is on the Massachusetts side of it. She would repeal the law, to benefit her cotton planters. We would retain it, to benefit our cotton, woollen, and glass manufacturers, and keep up the wages of free labor. It does no discredit to either State to admit that it is a matter of property and interest which is in dispute. I think Burke says that all the great contests for liberty in modern times have turned chiefly upon questions of taxing. But I cannot allow that one State has, in this particular, any advantage over the other.

Now, sir, I will judge other States by my own State. When I return to my constituents, and they ask me if this vote which I am to give will not help to drive South Carolina out of the Union, I shall answer no; that South Carolina is as patriotic as Massachusetts. I shall remind them that if this great question had gone against us; had Congress in good faith, and in the exercise of its best discretion, decided to abandon the protective system altogether, and thus had swept the "sweet and cheerful surface" of Massachusetts as by the fire of judgment; I shall remind them that she would not secede, and that South Carolina is no less nor more patriotic than Massachusetts. Of course the press will be, as it is, inflammatory; turbulent conventions will be holden; lofty, passionate language will be uttered; rash overt acts even may be done. But I trust still that her statesmen, and men of lead, talent, and education; her moral and religious men; her men of weight, property, and character; and, above all, the old South Carolina rank and file, will stand steadfast for union, as they were once foremost and first for independence. In this all of us may be mistaken. But, at all events, I do not recognise, in the position of South Carolina, that new and unexpected fact which I demand as the condition upon which this pledge may be disregarded, and these interests sacrificed.

Look then, sir, at the evil which you will do. You violate in some sort the plighted faith of the nation. You inflict an injury upon those who have expected every thing from your honor, beyond estimate and beyond compensation. Sir, nobody can certainly foretell the manner or the degree of the effect which the bill reported by the Committee of Ways and Means will produce. The deluge will sweep over the whole land, and swell up to the tops of the mountains. How many may escape drowning, what new formations may grow, and after what interval, upon the ruins of that old and fair creation that will have perished in the flood? Sir, this is a speculation into which I have no means or spirit to enter. Some consequences, however, of passing such a bill as that, are manifest. That vast mass of property in manufactures on hand; buildings, machinery, stock in all stages of the process, fabrics unsold, wool, sheep, and the rest, would fall at once, and irrecoverably and incalculably in value. Wheels will stop; operatives will be dismissed; bankruptcy will follow; and sudden and violent transfers of property, and great speculations on great sacrifices. A shock will be given to industry through all its thousand employments. After some interval, perhaps, of depression and apprehension, capitalists would resume the business with diminished confidence, reduced and unsteady profits, and the wages of free labor at nine pence a day. Sir, whether manufacturing industry does or does not survive this blow, the statesman, the party, the administration, which inflicts it, has a great deal to answer for in this world.

But this is not half the evil. The statesman who does this deed, is guilty of prodigally squandering away a national property worth more than the public domain. He flings from him, like a spendthrift heir, all that has yet been done for the establishment of domestic manufactures. He turns the shadow upon the dial many degrees backwards: and now, after so much skill has been acquired, and so much capital turned in; just when the first evils and sacrifices which attend the introduction of this industry by legislative aid, are beginning to be compensated; just when prices and profits are fallen to their lowest desirable point, and wages are steady and reasonable, and competition eager; just when that which was sown in weakness is rising in strength, he throws it all as a useless thing away. Sir, I do not believe that Adam Smith or Mr. Huskisson, if they were alive and here to-day, would give you such counsel. All men admit, and free trade theorists as fully as any, that manufactures are indispensable to the higher attainments of national greatness, and consideration, and wealth, and enjoyment. Nobody has demonstrated this proposition so well as Adam Smith. What they contend for is, that you shall not force manufactures upon your people by commercial regulation. They are a great good, only you may give too much for it. But they all admit that manufactures, however unphilosophically introduced and sustained, when established, are a perennial spring of resource and energy to a State. They all admit that it is the industry of England, helped forward perhaps by a hundred foolish laws of Edward or Elizabeth, which has placed her at the head of modern civilization, and put into her hands more than the sceptre of the sea. Why, the gentleman from Virginia himself [Mr. BOULDIN] agrees with Alexander Hamilton in his estimate of the national importance of manufacturing industry. Now you choose to begin by forcing this species of industry by a protecting tariff. Grant that you started wrong. It is better to go through than to go back. It is more economical to do so. Do you not see that the country has grown to your laws? Occupation, capital, hope, which is the life of the world, are they not rapidly accommodating themselves to this policy? The first bad effects, the disturbance and derangement which mark the moment of its introduction, are disappearing. Consumers of all classes feel the benefits of a full domestic competition. A great body of skill is generated, worth more, in the contemplation of philosophical statesmanship, than a thousand mines of barbaric gold. I suspect, therefore, that if Adam Smith were to come into this Hall at this moment, he would tell us that to be sure we had started foolishly; that we had set at naught his wisest counsels, and were rather an unmanageable set of pupils in political economy; but that we had gone so far in, that it was better to wade through than to wade back. He would say, I imagine, that although it was a bad calculation to prepare this ground and sow this seed, at so much expense of time and money, and against all the theories of husbandry, it would be a still worse one, now that the season is so far advanced, and the crop is half leg high, to throw down the fence, and turn the cattle in, and wait through another long and dreary winter, in the dream of witnessing a spontaneous crop of American wheat. But whatever he might say, sure I am the strong common sense of the people of this country will tell you this.

I observed just now that all men admit the value of manufactures to a nation, although they do not admit that it is expedient to force their growth by legislative stimulants. It escaped my recollection at the moment, that the gentleman from Tennessee [Mr. BELL] seemed to argue not merely against the protective system, but against manufacturing industry itself, as dangerous or undesirable. He argued that European, feudal policy regarded it with favor, because it threw great masses of property into few hands, depressing and impoverishing the body of the people; an aristocratical arrangement, having a tendency to uphold a privileged order, and furnishing reservoirs and cisterns, whence princes and barons might draw the pecuniary means of foreign or domestic war. Our policy was different, he argued, and would regard manufacturing industry differently. Sir, without intending to go out of my way to discuss this interesting topic, I will say that the gentleman's theory, however ingeniously supported, contradicts the whole history of the middle ages, and the whole history of European politics and industry. That history tells us that the small commercial and manufacturing corporations which grew up by the seashores of all the feudal kingdoms of Europe, from Italy to England, and from Spain to the Hanse Towns, were the first seats of popular liberty in modern times. They were the first, and they were long the only spots where any thing like a free people existed, after the wane of the republican glory of Greece and Rome; and it was the intelligence and spirit of this very population which rent the gorgeous and bloody trappings, and beat down the castle walls of feudal aristocracy, and gave to the world its first idea of representative, popular Government. Modern European liberty was literally the daughter of manufacturing and commercial industry and riches. "These pursuits gave men wealth, and wealth gave them leisure, and leisure reflection, and reflection taught them the knowledge and the worth of social right." The manufacturers and merchants of Europe, two hundred years before America was discovered, almost in every feudal State, had compelled the prince and the nobles to erect them and their representatives into a third branch of the national Parliament; and Robertson observes "that all the efforts for liberty, in every country in Europe, have been made by this new power of the Legislature." It is quite remarkable, that in the time of James I, as the accomplished historian of his reign informs us, "the puritans of England, the framers of the English constitution, and the founders of the free republics, and undefiled religion of the new world, were of the middle class, wealthy traders, substantial shopkeepers, mechanics, journeymen, and manufacturers, and that they resided chiefly in the counties of Norfolk, Suffolk, and Essex, in London, and the clothing towns of Gloucester, the most populous and most civilized quarters of England, the principal seat of manufactures, the asylum of foreign protestants, and the scene of a large proportion of the martyrdoms of Mary." Let me read to the gentleman a sentence or two from an article, in perhaps the ablest of the British tory journals, Blackwood's Magazine. It was written in 1831; and the writer is attempting to trace the origin and causes of that spirit of reform which at this moment shakes all England like an earthquake: "The two great powers operating on human affairs, which are producing this progressive increase of democratic influence, are the extension of manufactures, and the influence of the daily press. Manufactures, in every age and quarter of the globe, have been the fruitful source of democratic feeling. We need not appeal to history for this eternal truth; its exemplification is too manifest in the present time to admit a moment's doubt. The manufacturers reside in small towns. The members whom they return to Parliament will be the faithful mirror of their democratic opinions. Every successive year brings one of the rural boroughs within the vortex of manufacturing wealth, and the contagion of manufacturing democracy. Look at Preston and others, and an idea may be formed of the democratic tendency of small manufacturing towns." I really do not think it necessary to say more to prove that the industry which we ask you to protect is not hostile to the genius of our institutions, and the spirit of our civil policy.

You see the evil which you will do. Who now will show us any good to compensate for so much evil? This brings me to the interesting question: is the tariff productive of real, considerable, uncompensated injury to the South? I do not intend to discuss the question at length. I have examined it as well as I could; not for the purpose of debating it here, because I thought my duty to the South, my own constituents, and to the country, required it. The opinion which I have formed, and on which I shall act, I ask leave briefly to declare, without troubling you with the grounds of it at large.

I do not think, then, that it is made out, either as a doctrine of political economy by reasoning, or as a proposition of fact by proof, that the existing protective system does produce evil in the South. Four of the seven Southern States, Georgia, Tennessee, Alabama, and Mississippi, are as prosperous as any States in the Union. In the other three, Virginia, North Carolina, and South Carolina, there is no decline, or distress, or decay, but there is probably a diminished or retarded growth of prosperity. Even there, population advances more rapidly than in the tariff States of New Hampshire, Connecticut, New Jersey, or

Delaware, and very nearly as rapidly in the tariff State of Massachusetts. The attempt to trace the cause of this diminished prosperity, whatever may be the degree of it, to the tariff, has been a total failure. Other facts, notorious, and admitted, explain all the appearances. The over-production of the great staple of cotton, and its consequent fall in price; the superior ease and cheapness with which it can be raised in Alabama and Louisiana, compared with South Carolina; the advantage for commerce possessed by New York over Charleston; the fall of all prices and profits, and the wages of labor all over the world; the great change of times within a few years requiring to be met, but not yet met, by a corresponding change of economy, and the habits of the South: these causes, and others, including the peculiar character of the great body of Southern labor, explain every thing which is here relied on as indicating the bad effects of the tariff. To the argument, that the tariff enhances prices to the consumer, there are three answers. The first is, that if this be so, the evil is not sectional, but thrown impartially upon the whole consumption of the United States. The second is, that there is no proof, and no reason to believe, that prices would stand permanently lower if the protective policy were now abandoned, than they will permanently stand under the steady operation of that policy. And the third is, that if there is sectional grievance, there is sectional compensation also. The enhanced value of slaves as a marketable article to supply the growing demand in the Southwest, the withdrawal of capital from cotton to sugar in Louisiana, the increasing demand for cotton and flour in the North, the increasing ability of the Northern population to consume generally, creating an enlarging demand for all sorts of foreign goods, and an enlarging correspondent demand for Southern exports to pay for those goods; in all these ways, if there is sectional grievance, there is sectional compensation too. To the other argument, that the tariff affects the producer of Southern staples, over and above its effect on him as a consumer, I cannot yield assent. It is said, by Voltaire, I think, that no man is obliged to believe what he does not understand; and I confess I do not comprehend how the tariff lessens the price or the demand for cotton; and whether its proceeds come home in goods or specie, and whoever brings them, I see no clear and certain unfavorable effect upon Southern productive labor or capital. But having said this, I am willing to admit that it does not fully meet the difficulty. Be it that there is no ground of complaint on the part of our brethren of the South. Be it that there is no real evil produced by the tariff, and removable by its repeal. There is evil, nevertheless, occasioned by it, which it is most desirable to remove. There is excitement which one would wish to allay. There is alienation which one would wish to win back to its first love. It is not quite enough to refute the reasoning, and explain away the evidence of the South. It is not enough to taunt her with the recollection of that long series of hostile policy with which she pursued the industry of New England when she held the power. It is not enough to show, as surely it can be shown, that she was herself the author of the very policy which she now reprobates. Still the difficulty recurs. There is a great sectional excitement; and that, whether groundless or not, is, perhaps, *per se,* a case to act on. It is desirable to allay the excitement. Yes, certainly. But how? Sir, my humble scheme is this: I think, in the language of medical men, that the case requires topical treatment, local applications. Search out the sectional grievance, if you can find it. Find what are the articles exclusively of Southern consumption, and important in the economy of the South, and relieve them of all protecting duty. Strike them out of the statute. For so much let there be no tariff, and let them be fabricated in England, that the American Union may be preserved and let all others be; as they now are, effectually protected. There is negro clothing: gentlemen intimate that this is an unimportant concession. Why, sir, a distinguished member of the other branch of this Legislature from Virginia, said these words in debate in that body during the present session: "I urged (he is relating a conversation with another United States' Senator) the abandonment of duties on negro clothing. I said it will be kindly taken at the South, and go far to produce harmony." Let it be given then to kind feeling and harmony.

There is cotton bagging, too. The duty on this article ought not to be yielded; but yet perhaps the same object may be differently effected. Perhaps a drawback of the amount of the duty on all foreign and all domestic cotton bagging actually exported might adjust and harmonize the interests of the South and the West. This proposition was made on this floor two years since by a gentleman from Massachusetts. If those interested in the manufacture should renew it, it shall have my vote. The gentleman from Alabama, [Mr. CLAY,] after the glowing representation which he has just given us of the importance of this article to the producers of cotton, will hardly deny the value of this concession.

In this way, by this mode of practice, perhaps something may be done. There is no hope in any other. I do not call that a proposition of compromise of the gentleman from Tennessee, [Mr. BELL,] which begins with an eloquent rebuke of both the contending parties, accusing one of avarice and the other of ambition, and both of want of patriotism, representing each as equally in the wrong, and ends with an elaborate argument to prove that the protective system ought to be rased to its foundations. And I do not call that a proposition of compromise which comes from the Executive; which reduces the duties on the whole circle of protected articles, leaving some, but not leaving enough for the great New England interests, (Pennsylvania fares better!) forgetting that inadequate protection is no protection; and forgetting, too, that a duty may be too high to be defended as a revenue duty, and yet not high enough to avail for protection. That is not a compromise; or if so, it is inadmissible.

One remark, sir, suggested by the impressive concluding observations of the gentleman from Georgia, [Mr. WILDE,] who has just resumed his seat, and I will relieve the committee. I confess that I have more than once during this discussion been led to fear, with the gentleman from Georgia, in a moment of despondency, that the diversity of employment growing up in the opposite extremities of this country: manufactures, and what you may call the agriculture of manufactures in the East, and that which may be called the agriculture of commerce in the South; the consequent diversity of habits, opinions, and supposed or real interests which this may produce; the occasional struggles in which the two parties may be involved to get control of the national policy, and wield that to their several advantage; the eternal and inherent hostility which exists between free trade doctrine and measures and protective doctrine and measures; and that still deeper, still more unappeasable hostility which the gentleman fears may grow up between free labor and the employers of slave labor—I say, sir, I have thought it possible, as he has, that these causes may sever this Union. There seems to be, I have feared, ground laid for a separation of the States, not so much in the faults of man, as in the nature of things.

But this feeling is all allayed and rebuked by the recollection (I hope the gentleman from Georgia may derive consolation in the same way) that Washington long ago foresaw all these imaginary causes of disunion, and regarded them very differently. He foresaw, in his lifetime, that the East would be the seat of manufactures, and the South the region of agriculture, to the end of the world. He foresaw, too, that national legislation would be occasionally invoked to protect the domestic industry of the East against foreign regulation and foreign competition; and thus be made to press, perhaps with severity, upon the agriculture and commerce of the South. But he contemplated all this with exultation, not fear. He saw in this diversity of pursuits and interests, not the seeds of dissolution, but the ties of union, "stronger than links of iron"—"a triple cord which no man can break." In his farewell address, written in 1796, after these different, not adverse tendencies of labor and capital had developed themselves; after it was plain that the East would manufacture, and the South raise cotton, rice, and tobacco, through all time; after Alexander Hamilton, his bosom friend, had unfolded the national uses and value of manufacturing industry, and had recommended all sorts of protection, and prohibition, and bounty, to introduce and sustain it; after Congress had passed one act expressly for the encouragement of domestic manufactures, thus making it plain to his foresight that national legislation would be brought in aid of the great object; after all this, he expresses himself, not with apprehension, but with confidence, or, rather let me say, with joy. He says: "In your interest, every portion of our country finds the most commanding motive for carefully guarding and preserving the union of the whole. The North, in an unrestrained intercourse with the South, protected by the equal laws of a friendly Government, finds in the production of the latter great additional resources of maritime and commercial enterprise, and precious materials of manufacturing industry. The South, in the same intercourse, benefiting by the same agency of the North, sees its agriculture grow, and its commerce expand." Sir, the condition of our coasting trade and internal commerce, at this moment, is the best possible commentary on the wisdom of this scripture.

What then is there, sir, so very terrible in the signs of these times? What is this great crisis upon which gentlemen are so eloquent? What if there be some excitement of feeling, some harsh words, and some lowering looks between the brethren of this wide household? What if South Carolina, and Pennsylvania, and Massachusetts, do feel strongly, and express themselves strongly, on this question? All these things must needs be, and may very safely be. They are only part of the price—how inadequate the price!—which every nation pays for greatness and liberty. All signal and durable national fame and empire are reached, if they ever are reached, through such occasional and temporary tribulation as this. The history of every free State which ever existed, filling space enough to leave a history, is an unbroken record of internal strife, and sharp civil contention, and the collision of interests and feelings which the good men of the time thought utterly irreconcilable, but which were yet harmoniously reconciled; the appointed discipline, by means of which they severally ascended to their places in the system of the world. Instead, then, sir, of anticipating with the gentleman from Georgia the time when, in pursuance of the pathetic suggestion of the patriarch which he has just repeated, we shall divide our flocks and herds, and take each our several way, "that there be no more strife between us;" instead of looking with so much apprehension upon this diversity of pursuits and interests, let us adopt a more cheerful theory. Let us agree to see in it, as long as we can, "merely that combination and that opposition of interests, that action and that counteraction which, in the natural and the political world, from the reciprocal struggle of discordant powers, draws out the harmony of the universe." This is the language of one of the wisest men and most accomplished minds that ever lived, I hope our example may illustrate its truth.

Chapter II.

THE COLONIAL AGE OF NEW ENGLAND.
An Address Delivered at the Centennial Celebration of the Settlement of the Town of Ipswich, Mass., August 16, 1834.

On the occasion of the two hundredth anniversary of the founding of Ipswich, Massachusetts, Choate delivered a speech on the contributions of colonial New England to the tradition of American liberty. He notes with great satisfaction that Ipswich earned for itself "an honorable place in the universal history of liberty" when it resisted the arbitrary power of Sir Edmund Andros, the British official appointed to head the so-called Dominion of New England during the 1680s. At least as important, in his opinion, was that these colonists were, unlike the French revolutionaries, especially fit to exercise their liberty and independence properly. Even during the fervor of the revolutionary period we see among them "no impious dream of human perfectibility" and "no unloosing of the hoarded-up passions of ages from the restraints of law, order, morality, and religion, such as shamed and frightened away the new-born liberty of revolutionary France." That New England would, within Choate's lifetime, become the chief source in America of theological liberalism, confidence in human perfectibility, and various kinds of experimental living, was an irony regarding which the great orator does not appear to have commented on the record.

Choate's sincere and profound affection for his native New England serves as an important reminder that the nationalism of his party was not incompatible with, and indeed was informed by, a firm attachment to the regions in which their members had been reared.

It is a fact which a native of this old, fertile, and beautiful town may learn with pleasure, but without surprise, that it was always the most fertile or among the most fertile and most beautiful portions of the coast of New England. John Smith, who in 1614 explored that coast from Penobscot to Cape Cod, admires and praises "the many rising hills of Agawam," whose tops and descents are grown over with numerous corn-fields and delightful groves, the island to the east, with its "fair high woods of mulberry trees," and the luxuriant growth of oaks, pines, and walnuts, "which make the place," he says, "an excellent habitation;" while the Pilgrim Fathers in December 1620, when deliberating on the choice of a spot for their settlement, some of them "urged greatly to Anguan or Angoan, a place twenty leagues off to the northward, which they heard to be an excellent harbor for ships, better ground, and better fishing." As early as January, 1632, the first governor of Massachusetts, John Winthrop, declared Agawam to be "the best place for tillage and cattle *in the land;*" others described its great meadows, marshes, and plain ploughing grounds; and that the government of the infant colony, Massachusetts, at the time resolved that it should be occupied forthwith by a sort of garrison, in advance and in anticipation of its more formal and numerous settlement, for the express purpose of keeping so choice a spot out of the hands of the French. In March, 1633, accordingly, there was sent hither a company of thirteen men to acquire and to preserve rather for the future than the present uses of the Colony, as much as they might of that fair variety of hill, plain, wood, meadow, marsh, and seashore, whose fame had spread so widely. The leader of the little band was John Winthrop, the son of the Governor. They arrived in that month—the dreariest of the New England year—on the banks of the river which washes in his sweet and cheerful course the foot of the hill on which we are assembled. They proceeded to purchase of Masconomo, the Sagamore of Agawam, by a deed to him, Winthrop, a portion of the territory which composes the present corporation of Ipswich; and there remained without, I imagine, any considerable addition to their number, without any regularly organized church, or stated preaching, or municipal character, until May, 1634. At that time the Rev. Thomas Parker, the pupil of the learned Archbishop Usher of Dublin, and about one hundred more, men, women, and children, came over from "the Bay" and took up their abode on the spot thus made ready for them. In August, 1634, the first church was organized; and on this day two hundred years ago the town was incorporated. With that deep filial love of England and the English, which neither persecution, nor exile, nor distance, nor the choice of another and dearer home, nor the contemplation of the rapidly revealing and proud destinies of the New World, ever entirely plucked from the hearts of all the Colonists down to the war of Independence, they took the name of Ipswich from the Ipswich of the east coast of England, the capital of the county of Suffolk, and the birthplace of Cardinal Wolsey.

And thus and by these was begun the civil and ecclesiastical establishment and history of Ipswich. You have done well in this way to commemorate an event of so much interest to you. It is well thus filially, thus piously, to wipe away the dust, if you may, which two hundred years have gathered upon the tombs of the fathers. It is well that you have gathered yourselves together on this height; that as you stand here and look abroad upon as various and inspiring a view as the sun

shines upon; as you see fields of grain bending before the light summer wind,—
one harvest just now ready for the sickle, and another and a richer preparing; as
you see your own flocks upon the tops and descents of the many rising hills;
mowing-lands shaven by the scythe; the slow river winding between still meadows, ministering in his way to the processes of nature and of art,—losing himself at last under your eye in the sea, as life, busy or quiet, glides into immortality;
as you hear peace and plenty proclaiming with a thousand voices the reign of
freedom, law, order, morality, and religion; as you look upon these charities of
God, these schools of useful learning and graceful accomplishment, these great
workshops of your manufacturers, in which are witnessed—performed every
day—achievements of art and science to which the whole genius of the ancient
world presents nothing equal; as you dwell on all this various, touching, inspiring picture in miniature of a busy, prosperous, free, happy, thrice and four times
happy, and blessed people,—it is well that standing here you should look backwards as well as around you and forward,—that you should call to mind, to
whom under God you owe all these things; whose weakness has grown into this
strength; whose sorrows have brought this exceeding great joy; whose tears and
blood, as they scattered the seed of that cold, late, ungenial, and uncertain spring,
have fertilized this natural and moral harvest which is rolled out at your feet as
one unbounded flood.

The more particular history of Ipswich from its settlement to this day, and of
the towns of Hamilton and Essex—shoots successively from the parent stock—
has been written so minutely and with such general accuracy, by a learned clergyman of this county, that I may be spared the repetition of details with which
he has made you familiar. This occasion, too, I think, prescribes topics somewhat
more general. That long line of learned ministers, upright magistrates, and valiant
men of whom we are justly proud—our municipal fathers—were something
more and other than the mere founders of Ipswich; and we must remember their
entire character and all their relations to their own times and to ours, or we cannot do them adequate honor. It is a boast of our local annals that they do not
flow in a separate and solitary stream, but blend themselves with that broader and
deeper current of events, the universal ante-revolutionary history of North
America. It is the foundation of an empire, and not merely the purchase and
plantation of Agawam, which we commemorate,—whether we will or not; and
I do not fear that we shall enlarge our contemplations too far, or elevate them
too high, for the service to which we have devoted this day.

The history of the Colonies which were planted one after another along our
coast in the seventeenth century, and which grew up in the fulness of time into
thirteen and at last into twenty-four States, from their respective beginnings to

the war of Independence, is full of interest and instruction, for whatever purpose or in whatever way you choose to read it. But there is one point of view in which, if you will look at the events which furnished the matter of that colonial history, I think you will agree with me that they assume a character of peculiar interest, and entitle themselves to distinct and profound consideration. I regard those events altogether as forming a vast and various series of influences,—a long, austere, effective course of discipline and instruction,—by which the settlers and their children were slowly and painfully trained to achieve their independence, to form their constitutions of State governments and of federal government, and to act usefully and greatly their part as a separate political community on the high places of the world.

The Colonial period, as I regard it, was the charmed, eventful infancy and youth of our national life. The revolutionary and constitutional age, from 1775 to 1789, was the beginning of its manhood. The Declaration of Independence, the succeeding conduct of the war of Independence, the establishment of our local and general governments and the splendid national career since run,—these are only effects, fruits, outward manifestations! The seed was sown, the salient living spring of great action sunk deep in that long, remote, less brilliant, less regarded season,—the heroic age of America that preceded. The Revolution was the meeting of the rivers at the mountain. You may look there, to see them rend it asunder, tear it down from its summit to its base, and pass off to the sea.

But the Colonial period is the country above, where the rivers were created. You must explore that region if you would find the secret fountains where they began their course, the contributory streams by which they grew, the high lands covered with woods, which, attracting the vapors as they floated about them, poured down rain and melted snow to swell their currents, and helped onward the momentum by which they broke through the walls of nature and shook the earth itself to its centre! One of our most accomplished scholars and distinguished public men speaks somewhere of the "Miracle of the Revolution." I would say rather that the *true* miracle was the character of the people who *made* the Revolution; and I have thought that an attempt to unfold some of the great traits of that character, and to point out the manner in which the events of the preceding Colonial Age contributed to form and impress those traits, imperfect as it must be, would be entirely applicable to this occasion.

The leading feature, then, in the character of the American people in the age of the Revolution was what Burke called in Parliament their "fierce spirit of liberty." "It is stronger in them," said he, "than in any other people on the earth." "I am convinced," said our youthful and glorious Warren,—in a letter to Quincy, little more than six months before he fell on the heights of Charlestown,—

"I am convinced that the true spirit of liberty was never so universally diffused through all ranks and orders of men on the face of the earth, as it now is through all North America. It is the united voice of America to preserve their freedom or lose their lives in defence of it." Whoever overlooks, whoever underestimates this trait in the character of that generation of our fathers,—whoever has not carefully followed it upwards to its remote and deep springs, may wonder at, but never can comprehend, the "Miracle of the Revolution." Whence, then, did they derive it? Let us return to the history of the Colonists before they came, and after they came, for the answer; and for distinctness and brevity let us confine ourselves to the Northern Colonists, our immediate ancestors.

The people of New England, at the beginning of the Revolutionary War, to describe them in a word, were the Puritans of Old England as they existed in that country in the first half of the seventeenth century; but changed,—somewhat improved, let me say,—by the various influences which acted upon them here for a hundred and fifty years after they came over.

The original stock was the Puritan character of the age of Elizabeth, of James I., and of Charles I. It was transplanted to another soil; another sun shone on it; other winds fanned and shook it; the seasons of another heaven for a century and a half circled round it; and there it stood at length, the joint product of the old and the new, deep-rooted, healthful, its trunk massive, compact, and of rough and gnarled exterior, but bearing to the sky the glory of the wood.

Turn first now, for a moment, to the Old English Puritans, the fathers of our fathers, of whom came, of whom were, planters of Ipswich, of Massachusetts, of New England,—of whom came, of whom were, our own Ward, Parker, and Saltonstall, and Wise, Norton, and Rogers, and Appleton, and Cobbet, and Winthrop,—and see whether they were likely to be the founders of a race of freemen or slaves. Remember, then, the true, noblest, the least questioned, least questionable, praise of these men is this: that for a hundred years they were the sole depositaries of the sacred fire of liberty in England, after it had gone out in every other bosom,—that they saved at its last gasp the English constitution, which the Tudors and the first two Stuarts were rapidly changing into just such a gloomy despotism as they saw in France and Spain, and wrought into it every particle of freedom which it now possesses,—that when they first took their seats in the House of Commons, in the early part of the reign of Elizabeth, they found it the cringing and ready tool of the throne, and that they reanimated it, remodelled it, reasserted its privileges, restored it to its constitutional rank, drew back to it the old power of making laws, redressing wrongs, and imposing taxes, and thus again rebuilt and opened what an Englishman called "the chosen temple of liberty," an English House of Commons,—that they abridged the tremendous power of the crown and defined it,—and when at last Charles Stuart resorted to arms to restore the despotism they had partially overthrown, that they met him on a hundred fields of battle, and buried, after a sharp and long struggle, crown and mitre and the headless trunk of the king himself beneath the foundations of a civil and religious commonwealth. This praise all the historians of England— Whig and Tory, Protestant and Catholic, Hume, Hallam, Lingard, and all— award to the Puritans. By what causes this spirit of liberty had been breathed into the masculine, enthusiastic, austere, resolute character of this extraordinary body of men, in such intensity as to mark them off from all the rest of the people of England, I cannot here and now particularly consider. It is a thrilling and awful history of the Puritans in England, from their first emerging above the general level of Protestants, in the time of Henry VIII. and Edward VI., until they were driven by hundreds and thousands to these shores; but I must pass it over. It was just when the nobler and grander traits—the enthusiasm and piety and hardihood and energy—of Puritanism had attained the highest point of exaltation to which, in England, it ever mounted up, and the love of liberty had grown to be the great master-passion that fired and guided all the rest,—it was just then that our portion of its disciples, filled with the undiluted spirit, glowing with the intensest fervors of Protestantism and republicanism together, came hither, and in that elevated and holy and resolved frame, began to build the civil and religious structures which you see around you.

Trace, now, their story a little farther onward through the Colonial period to the War of Independence, to admire with me the providential arrangement of circumstances by which that spirit of liberty, which brought them hither, was strengthened and reinforced, until at length, instructed by wisdom, tempered by virtue, and influenced by injuries, by anger and grief and conscious worth and the sense of violated right, it burst forth here and wrought the wonders of the Revolution. I have thought that if one had the power to place a youthful and forming people, like the northern colonists, in whom the love of freedom was already vehement and healthful, in a situation the most propitious for the growth and perfection of that sacred sentiment, he could hardly select a fairer field for so interesting an experiment than the actual condition of our fathers for the hundred and fifty years after their arrival, to the War of the Revolution.

They had freedom enough to teach them its value, and to refresh and elevate their spirits, wearied, not despondent, from the contentions and trials of England. They were just so far short of perfect freedom, that, instead of reposing for a moment in the mere fruition of what they had, they were kept emulous and eager for more, looking all the while up and aspiring to rise to a loftier height, to breathe a purer air, and bask in a brighter beam. Compared with the condition of England down to 1688,—compared with that of the larger part of the continent of Europe down to our Revolution,—theirs was a privileged and liberal condition. The necessaries of freedom, if I may say so,—its plainer food and homelier garments and humbler habitations,—were theirs. Its luxuries and refinements, its festivals, its lettered and social glory, its loftier port and prouder look and richer graces, were the growth of a later day; these came in with independence. Here was liberty enough to make them love it for itself, and to fill them with those lofty and kindred sentiments which are at once its fruit and its nutriment and safeguard in the soul of man. But their liberty was still incomplete, and it was constantly in danger from England; and these two circumstances had a powerful effect in increasing that love and confirming those sentiments. It was a condition precisely adapted to keep liberty, as a subject of thought and feeling and desire, every moment in mind. Every moment they were comparing what they had possessed with what they wanted and had a right to; they calculated by the rule of three, if a fractional part of freedom came to so much, what would express the power and value of the whole number! They were restive and impatient and ill at ease; a galling wakefulness possessed their faculties like a spell. Had they been wholly slaves, they had lain still and slept. Had they been wholly free, that eager hope, that fond desire, that longing after a great, distant, yet practicable good, would have given way to the placidity and luxury and carelessness of complete enjoyment; and that energy and wholesome agitation of mind would have gone down like an ebb-tide. As it was, the whole vast body of waters all over its surface, down to its sunless, utmost depths, was heaved and shaken and purified by a spirit that moved above it and through it, and gave it no rest, though the moon waned and the winds were in their caves; they were like the disciples of the old and bitter philosophy of Paganism, who had been initiated into one stage of the greater mysteries, and who had come to the door, closed, and written over with strange characters, which led up to another. They had tasted of truth, and they burned for a fuller draught; a partial revelation of that which shall be hereafter, had dawned; and their hearts throbbed eager, yet not without apprehension, to look upon the glories of the perfect day. Some of the mystery of God, of Nature, of Man, of the Universe, had been unfolded; might they, by prayer, by abstinence, by virtue, by retirement, by contemplation, entitle themselves to read another page in the clasped and awful volume?

Sparing and inadequate as their supply of liberty was, it was all the while in danger from the Crown and Parliament of England, and the whole ante-revolutionary period was one unintermitted struggle to preserve it, and to wrest it away. You sometimes hear the Stamp Act spoken of as the first invasion of the rights of the colonists by the mother-country. In truth, it was about the last; the most flagrant, perhaps, the most dreadful and startling to an Englishman's idea of liberty, but not the first,—no, by a hundred and fifty years not the first. From the day that the Pilgrims on board The Mayflower at Plymouth, before they landed, drew up that simple, but pregnant and comprehensive, form of democracy, and subscribed their names, and came out a colony of republicans, to the battle of Lexington, there were not ten years together,—I hardly exempt the Protectorate of Cromwell,—in which some right—some great and sacred right, as the colonists regarded it—was not assailed or menaced by the government of England, in one form or another. From the first, the mother-country complained that we had brought from England, or had found here, *too much liberty,*—liberty inconsistent with prerogatives of the Crown, inconsistent with supremacy of Parliament, inconsistent with the immemorial relations of all colonies to the country they sprang from,—and she set herself to abridge it. We answered with great submission that we did not honestly think that we had brought or had found much more than half liberty enough; and we braced ourselves to keep what we had, and obtain more when we could;—and so, with one kind of weapon or another, on one field or another, on one class of questions or another, a struggle was kept up from the landing at Plymouth to the surrender at Yorktown. It was all one single struggle from beginning to end; the parties, the objects, the principles, are the same;—one sharp, long, glorious, triumphant struggle for liberty. The topics, the heads of dispute, various from reign to reign; but though the subjects were various, the question was *one,*— shall the colonists be free, or shall they be slaves?

And that question was pronounced by everybody, understood by everybody, debated by everybody,—in the colonial assemblies; by the clergy on the days of thanksgiving, on fast-days, and quarterly fast-days; and by the agents of the colonies in England; and at last, and more and more, through the press. I say nothing here of the effect of such a controversy so long continued, in sharpening the faculties of the colonists, in making them acute, prompt, ingenious, full of resource, familiar with the grounds of their liberties, their history, revolutions, extent, nature, and the best methods of defending them argumentatively. These were important effects; but I rather choose to ask you to consider how the *love* of liberty would be inflamed; how ardent, jealous, irresistible it would be made; with what new and what exaggerated value even, it would learn to invest its object, by being thus obliged to struggle so unceasingly to preserve it; and by coming so many times so near to lose it; and by being thus obliged to bear it away like another Palladium, at the hazard of blindness, from the flames of its temple which would have consumed it,—across seas gaping wide to swallow it up,— through serried ranks of armed men who had marked it for a prey.

There was one time during this long contest when it might have seemed to any race of men less resolved than our fathers, that liberty had at last returned from earth to the heavens from which she descended. A few years before 1688— the year of the glorious revolution in England—the British king succeeded, after a struggle of more than half a century, in wresting from Massachusetts her first charter. From that time, or rather from December, 1685, to April, 1689, the government of all New England was an undisguised and intolerable despotism. A governor, Sir Edmund Andros,—not chosen by the people as every former governor had been, but appointed by James II.,—worthy to serve such a master,— and a few members, less than the majority, of the council, also appointed by the king, and very fit to advise such a governor, grasped and held the whole civil power. And they exercised it in the very spirit of the worst of the Stuarts. The old, known body of colonial laws and customs which had been adopted by the people, was silently and totally abolished. New laws were made; taxes assessed; an administration all new and all vexatious was introduced, not by the people in general court, but by the governor and a small, low faction of his council, in whose election they had no vote; over whose proceedings they had no control; to whom their rights and interests and lives were all as nothing compared with the lightest wish of the Papist and tyrant James whom they served. A majority of the council, although appointed by the king, wore yet true hearts of New England in their bosoms, and resisted with all their might the tyranny which the government was riveting upon her. One of these, Major Samuel Appleton, was an inhabitant of Ipswich, a son of one of the earliest settlers of the town, the ancestor of a long line of learned, energetic, and most respectable descendants. He had the high honor to be arrested in October, 1689, by Andros and his faction in the council, as being a factious member of the board and disaffected to the government, and was obliged to give bonds in the sum of £1000 to be of good political behavior. But the efforts of this gentleman, and of such as he in the council, could avail nothing; and the arbitrary tyranny of the creatures of the Stuarts became the only government of Massachusetts.

In this the darkest day that New England ever saw, it is grateful to pause and commemorate an act of this town of Ipswich which deserves, I think, an honorable place in the universal history of liberty. Sir Edmund Andros and his faction had, without the intention of the colonial legislature, or any representatives of the people, made a decree imposing a State tax on the people, against that fundamental principle of liberty, that the people alone can tax themselves. They had assessed in several towns quotas of it, and had commanded them to choose each a commissioner, who, with the boards of the selectmen, should assess the quota of the town on its inhabitants and estates respectively. A meeting of the inhabitants of Ipswich was warned to be holden on the 23d August, 1687, to choose a commissioner to aid the selectmen in assessing the tax. The evening before the meeting the Rev. John Wise, the minister of the parish now Essex, a learned, able, resolute, and honest man,—worthy to preach to the children of Puritans,—Robert Kinsman, William Goodhue, Jr., and several other principal inhabitants of Ipswich, held a preparatory caucus at the house of John Appleton, brother of Major Samuel Appleton, which stood, or stands, on the road to Topsfield, and there "discoursed, and concluded that it was not the town's duty *any way* to assist that *ill method* of raising money without a general assembly." The next day they attended the town-meeting, and Mr. Wise made a speech, enforcing this opinion of his friends, and said, "We have a good God, and a good king, and should do well to stand on our privileges." And by their privileges they concluded to stand. I cannot read the simple, manly, and noble vote of Ipswich on that day without a thrill of pride,—that then, when the hearts of the pious and brave children in Massachusetts seemed almost sunk within them,—our charter gone, James Stuart the Second on the throne, (I suspect it was irony or policy of Mr. Wise to call him a good king)—just when the long-cherished, long-dreaded design of the English Crown to reduce the colonies into immediate dependence on itself, and to give them, unconcealed, slavery for substantial freedom, seemed about to be consummated,—that we here and then, with full knowledge of the power and temper of Andros and his council, dared to assert and to spread out upon our humble record the great principle of English liberty and of the American Revolution. The record declares "that considering the said act" (referring to the order of the governor and council imposing the tax) "doth infringe *their liberty as free-born English subjects* of His Majesty, and by interfering with the statute laws of the land by which it was enacted that no taxes should be levied upon the subjects *without the consent of an assembly chosen by the free men for assessing the same,*— they do, therefore, vote that they are not willing to choose a commissioner for such an end without such a privilege;—and they, moreover, consent not that the selectmen do proceed to levy any such rate, until it be appointed by a general assembly, concurring with the Governor and Council."

For the share they had taken in the proceedings of that memorable day, Mr. Wise and five others, probably those who met with him, and Mr. Appleton himself, were arrested, by order of the Governor, as for a contempt and misdemeanor, and carried beyond the limits of the county, imprisoned in jail at Boston, denied the writ of habeas corpus, tried by a packed jury—principally strangers and foreigners, I rejoice to read—and a subservient court, and of course found guilty. They were all fined more or less heavily, from £15 to £50, compelled to enter into bonds of from £500 to £1000 each to keep the peace, and Mr. Wise was suspended from the ministerial function, and the others disqualified to bear office.

The whole expense of time and money to which they were subjected was estimated to exceed £400,—a sum equivalent to perhaps $5000 of our money,— enough to build the Ipswich part of Warner's Bridge more than three times over; which the town shortly after nobly and justly, yet gratuitously, refunded to the sufferers.

These men, says Pitkin, who is not remarkable for enthusiasm, may justly claim a distinguished rank among the patriots of America. You, their townsmen— their children—may well be proud of them; prouder still, but more grateful than proud, that a full town-meeting of the freemen of Ipswich adopted unanimously that declaration of right, and refused to collect or pay the tax which would have made them slaves. The principle of that vote was precisely the same on which Hampden resisted an imposition of Charles I., and on which Samuel Adams and Hancock and Warren resisted the Stamp Act,—the principle that if any power but the people can tax the people, there is an end of liberty.

The later and more showy spectacles and brighter glories and visible results of the age of the Revolution, have elsewhere cast into the shade and almost covered with oblivion the actors on that interesting day, and the act itself,—its hazards, its intrepidity, its merits, its singularity and consequences. But you will remember them, and teach them to your children. The graves of those plain, venerable, and sturdy men of the old, old time, who thus set their lives on the hazard of a die for the perishing liberties of Massachusetts; the site of the house where they assembled—they, the fathers of the town—the day before the meeting, to consider what advice they should give to their children in that great crisis, so full of responsibility and danger; the spot on which that building stood where the meeting was holden and the declaration recorded,—these are among you yet; your honor, your treasure, the memorials and incentives of virtue and patriotism and courage, which feared God and knew no other fear! Go sometimes to those graves, and give an hour of the summer evening to the brave and pious dead. Go there, and thank God for pouring out upon them the spirit of liberty, and humbly ask Him to transmit it, as it breathed in them, their children, and their children's children, to the thousandth generation!

I have said part of what I intended of one trait in the character of our fathers of the revolutionary age,—their spirit of liberty. But something more than the love of liberty is needful to fit a people for the enjoyment of it. Other men, other nations, have loved liberty as well as our fathers. The sentiment is innate, and it is indestructible, and immortal. Yet of the wide-spread families of the earth, in the long procession of the generations, that stretches backward to the birth of the world, how few have been free at all; how few have been long free; how imperfect was their liberty while they possessed it; how speedily it flitted away; how hard to woo it to return! In all Asia and Africa—continents whose population is more than four sevenths of the human race on earth, whose history begins ages before a ray of the original civilization of the East had reached to Europe—there was never a free nation. And how has it been in Europe, that proud seat of power, art, civilization, enterprise, and mind? Alas for the destiny of social man! Here and there in ancient and in later times, in Greece, in Rome, in Venice, in France, men have called on the Goddess of Liberty in a passionate and ignorant idolatry; they have embodied her angelical brightness and unclouded serenity in marble; they have performed dazzling actions, they have committed great crimes in her name; they have built for her the altars where she best loves to be worshipped,—republican forms of government; they have found energy, genius, the love of glory, the mad dream of power and pride in her inspiration. But they were not wise enough, they were not virtuous enough for diffused, steady, lasting freedom. Their heads were not strong enough to bear a draught so stimulating. They perished of raging fever, kindled by drinking of the very waters of social life! These stars one after another burned out, and fell from their throne on high!

England guarded by the sea; Holland behind her dikes; a dozen Swiss Cantons breathing the difficult air of the iced mountain tops,—these, in spite of revolutions, all were free governments. And in the whole of the Old World there was not another. The love of liberty there was; but a government founded in liberty there was not one besides. Some things other than the love of freedom are needful to form a great and free nation. Let us go farther then, and observe the wisdom and prudence by which, after a long and painful process, our fathers were prepared, in mind and heart, for the permanent possession, tempered enjoyment, and true use of that freedom, the love of which was rooted in their souls; the process by which, in the words of Milton, they were made into a "right pious, right honest, right holy nation," as well as a nation loving liberty. In running over that process, I am inclined to attach the most importance to the fact that they who planted New England, and all the generations of successors, to the war of Independence, were engaged in a succession of the severest and gravest trials and labors and difficulties which ever tasked the spirit of a man or a nation.

It has been said that there was never a great character,—never a truly strong, masculine, commanding character,—which was not made so by successive struggles with great difficulties. Such is the general rule of the moral world, undoubtedly. All history, all biography verify and illustrate it, and none more remarkably than our own.

It has seemed to me probable that if the Puritans, on their arrival here, had found a home like that they left, and a social system made ready for them,— if they had found the forest felled, roads constructed, rivers bridged, fields sown, houses built, a rich soil, a bright sun, and a balmy air,—if they had come into a country which for a hundred and fifty years was never to hear the war-whoop of a savage, or the tap of a French drum,—if they had found a commonwealth civil and religious, a jurisprudence, a system of police, administration, and policy, all to their hands, churches scattered, districts, parishes, towns, and counties, widening one around the other,—if England had covered over their infancy with her mighty wing, spared charters, widened trade, and knit child to mother by parental policy,—it is probable that that impulse of high mind, and that unconquerable constancy of the first emigrants, might have subsided before the epoch of the drama of the Revolution. Their children might have grown light, luxurious, vain, and the sacred fire of liberty, cherished by the fathers in the times of the Tudors and Stuarts, might have died away in the hearts of a feeble posterity.

Ours was a different destiny. I do not mean to say that the whole Colonial Age was a scene of universal and constant suffering and labor, and that there was no repose; of peril pressing at every turn, and every moment, on everybody. But in its general course it was a time of suffering and of privation, of poverty or mediocrity of fortune, of sleepless nights, grave duties, serious aims; and I say it was a trial better fitted to train up a nation "in true wisdom, virtue, magnanimity, and the likeness of God,"—better fitted to form temperate habits, strong character, resolute spirits, and all the radiant train of public and private virtues which stand before the stars of the throne of liberty,—than any similar period in the history of any nation, or of any but one, that ever existed.

Some seasons there were of sufferings so sharp and strange, that they might seem designed to test the energy of Puritan principles. Such was the summer and winter after Governor Winthrop's arrival in New England, 1630–1631. Such the winter and spring after the arrival of the Puritans at Plymouth, 1620–1621. They wasted away—young and old of the little flock—of consumption and fever of lungs; the living scarcely able to bury the dead; the well not enough to tend the sick; men who landed a few weeks before in full strength, their bones moistened with marrow, were seen to stagger and fall from faintness for want of food. In a country abounding in secret springs, they perished for want of a draught of good water. Childhood drooped and died away, like a field-flower turned up by the ploughshare. Old age was glad to gather himself to his last sleep. Some sank down, broken-hearted, by the graves of beloved wives and sons. Of the whole one hundred and one who landed at Plymouth, there were once only seven able to render assistance to the dying and the sick.

A brilliant English writer, speaking of the Jews, exclaims, with surprise and indignation, that even a desert did not make them wise. Our fathers, let me say, not vaingloriously, were readier learned of wisdom. Their sufferings chastened, purified, and elevated them; and led them to repose their weary and stricken spirits upon the strength which upholds the world. Thus to be afflicted, thus to profit by affliction, is good for a nation as it is good for a man. To neither is it joyous, but grievous; to both it is all made up over and over again by a more exceeding weight of glory.

Look now, passing from the sufferings, to the gigantic labors of our Colonial Age, and calculate their influence on those who performed them.

The first great work of the earlier generations of New England was to reclaim the country, to fit it for the sustentation of life from day to day, from season to season, and thus to become the abode of an intellectual and social civilization advancing indefinitely. This is the first great work of all nations, who begin their existence in a country not before the residence of cultivated man. The nature of this work,—the ease and difficulty of performing it depending of course on the great natural characteristics of the region,—its fertility, its even or uneven surface, the quality, as well as the abundance or scarcity of its products, the brightness and dryness, or gloom and moisture of its skies, its cold or hot temperature, and the like,—the nature of this first and severest of the herculean labors of nations, perhaps quite as much as any other cause, perhaps as much as all other causes, affects the moral and mental character and habits of the people which have it to do. It has been maintained, and with great ingenuity, that the whole subsequent career of a nation has taken impulse and direction, from the circumstances of physical condition in which it came first into life. The children of the luxurious East opened their eyes on plains, whose fertility a thousand harvests could not exhaust, renewing itself perpetually from the bounty of a prodigal nature, beneath bright suns, in a warm, balmy air, which floated around them like music and perfumes from revels on the banks of rivers by moonlight. "Every blast shook spices from the leaves, and every month dropped fruits upon the ground." "The blessings of nature were collected, and its evils extracted and excluded." Hence the immemorial character of a part of the tribes of Asia. They became indolent, effeminate, and timorous. Steeped in sensual enjoyments, the mind slept with the body; or if it awoke, unlike the reasoning, speculative, curious, and energetic intellect of Europe, it reposed in reverie; it diffused itself in long contemplation, musing rather than thinking, reading human destiny in the stars, but making no effort to comprehend the system of the world. Life itself there, is but a fine dream; and death is only a scattering of the garlands, a hushing of the music, a putting out of the lights of a midsummer night's feast. You would not look there for freedom, for morality, for true religion, for serious reflections.

The destiny of the most of Europe was different. Vast forests covering half a continent, rapid and broad rivers, cold winds, long winters, large tracts unsusceptible of cultivation, snow-clad mountains on whose tops the lightning plays impassive,—this was the world that fell to their lot. And hence partly, that race is active, laborious, curious, intellectual, full of energy, tending to freedom, destined to freedom, but not yet all free.

I cannot now pause to qualify this view, and make the requisite discriminations between the different States of that quarter of the world.

To the tempest-tossed and weather-beaten, yet sanguine and enthusiastic spirits who came hither, New England hardly presented herself at first in all that ruggedness and sternest wildness which nature has impressed indelibly upon her. But a few summers and winters revealed the whole truth. They had come to a country fresh from the hand of nature, almost as on the day of creation, covered with primeval woods, which concealed a soil not very fruitful and bearing only the hardier and coarser grains and grasses, broken into rocky hills and mountains sending their gray summits to the skies, the upland levels, with here and there a strip of interval along a pleasant river, and a patch of salt-marsh by the side of the sea,—a country possessing and producing neither gold, nor diamonds, nor pearls, nor spices, nor opium, nor bread-fruit, nor silks, nor the true vine,—to a long and cold winter, an uncertain spring, a burning summer, and autumn with his fleecy clouds and bland south-west, red and yellow leaf and insidious disease;—such was the ungenial heaven beneath which their lot was cast; such was New England, yielding nothing to idleness, nothing to luxury, but yet holding out to faith and patience and labor, freedom and skill, and public and private virtue,—holding out to these the promise of a latter day afar off, of glory and honor and rational and sober enjoyment. Such was the country in which the rugged infancy of New England was raised. Such was the country which the Puritans were appointed to transpose into a meet residence of refinement and liberty. You know how they performed that duty. Your fathers have told you. From this hill, westward and southward, and eastward and northward, your eyes may see how they performed it. The wilderness and the solitary place were glad for them, and the desert rejoiced and blossomed as the rose. The land was a desolate wilderness before them; behind them, as the garden of Eden. How glorious a triumph of patience, energy, perseverance, intelligence, and faith! And then how powerfully and in how many ways must the fatigues, privations, interruptions, and steady advance and ultimate completion of that long day's work have reacted on the character and the mind of those who performed it! How could such a people ever again, if ever they had been, be idle, or frivolous, or giddy, or luxurious! With what a resistless accession of momentum must they turn to every new, manly, honest, and worthy labor! How truly must they love the land for which they had done so much! How ardently must they desire to see it covered over with the beauty of holiness and the glory of freedom as with a garment! With what a just and manly self-approbation must they look back on such labors and such success; and how great will such pride make any people!

There was another great work, different from this, and more difficult, more glorious, more improving, which they had to do, and that was to establish their system of colonial government, to frame their code of internal law, and to administer the vast and perplexing political business of the colonies in their novel and trying relations to England, through the whole Colonial Age. Of all their labors this was the grandest, the most intellectual, the best calculated to fit them for independence. Consider how much patient thought, how much observation of man and life, how much sagacity, how much communication of mind with mind, how many general councils, plots, and marshalling of affairs, how much slow accumulation, how much careful transmission of wisdom, that labor demanded. And what a school of civil capacity this must have proved to them who partook in it! Hence, I think, the sober, rational, and practical views and conduct which distinguished even the first fervid years of the Revolutionary age. How little giddiness, rant, and foolery do you see there! No riotous and shouting processions,—no grand festivals of the goddess of reason,—no impious dream of human perfectibility,—no unloosing of the hoarded-up passions of ages from the restraints of law, order, morality, and religion, such as shamed and frightened away the new-born liberty of revolutionary France. Hence our victories of peace were more brilliant, more beneficial, than our victories of war.

Hence those fair, I hope everlasting, monuments of civil wisdom, our State and Federal Constitutions. Hence the coolness, the practised facility, the splendid success, with which they took up and held the whip and reins of the fiery chariot flying through the zodiac, after the first driver had been stricken by the thunder from his seat.

Do you not think it was a merciful appointment that our fathers did not come to the possession of independence, and the more perfect freedom which it brought with it, as to a great prize drawn in a lottery,—an independent fortune left unexpectedly by the death of a distant relative of whom they had never heard before,—a mine of gold opened just below the surface on the side of the hill by a flash of lightning? If they had, it would have turned their heads or corrupted their habits. They were rather in the condition of one of the husbandment of old Ipswich, a little turned of one-and-twenty, who has just paid off the last legacy, or the last gage upon the estate left him by his father,—an estate where his childhood played with brothers and sisters now resting in early graves, in which the first little labors of his young hands were done, from which he can see the meeting-house spire above the old intervening elms, to which his own toil, mingled with that of his ancestors of many generations, has given all its value, which, before he had owned, he had learned how to keep, how to till, how to transmit to his heirs enlarged and enriched with a more scientific and tasteful cultivation.

I can only allude to one other labor, one other trial of the Colonial Age,— the wars in which for one hundred and fifty years our fathers were every moment engaged, or to which they were every moment exposed, and leave you to estimate the influence which these must have had on the mind and character, and at last on the grand destinies of New England and of North America.

It is dreadful that nations must learn war; but since they must, it is a mercy to be taught it seasonably and thoroughly. It had been appointed by the Infinite Disposer, that the liberties, the independence of the States of America should depend on the manner in which we should fight for them; and who can imagine what the issue of the awful experiment would have been, had they never before seen the gleam of an enemy's bayonets, or heard the beat of his drum?

I hold it to have been a great thing, in the first place, that we had among us, at that awful moment when the public mind was meditating the question of submission to the tea-tax, or resistance by arms, and at the more awful moment of the first appeal to arms,—that we had some among us who personally knew what war was. Washington, Putnam, Stark, Gates, Prescott, Montgomery, were soldiers already. So were hundreds of others of humbler rank, but not yet forgotten by the people whom they helped to save, who mustered to the camp of our first revolutionary armies. These all had tasted a soldier's life. They had seen fire, they had felt the thrilling sensations, the quickened flow of blood to and from the heart, the mingled apprehension and hope, the hot haste, the burning thirst, the feverish rapture of battle, which he who has not felt is unconscious of one half of the capacities and energies of his nature, which he who has felt, I am told, never forgets. They had slept in the woods on the withered leaves or the snow, and awoke to breakfast upon birch bark and the tender tops of willow trees. They had kept guard on the outposts on many a stormy night, knowing perfectly that the thicket half a pistol-shot off, was full of French and Indian riflemen.

I say it was something that we had such men among us. They helped discipline our raw first levies. They knew what an army is, and what it needs, and how to provide for it. They could take that young volunteer of sixteen by the hand, sent by an Ipswich mother, who, after looking upon her son equipped for battle from which he might not return, Spartan-like, bid him go and behave like a man—and many, many such shouldered a musket for Lexington and Bunker Hill—and assure him, from their own personal knowledge, that after the first fire he never would know fear again, even that of the last onset. But the long and peculiar wars of New England had done more than to furnish a few such officers and soldiers as these. They had formed that public sentiment upon the subject of war which reunited all the armies, fought all the battles, and won all the glory of the Revolution. The truth is that war, in some form or another, had been, from the first, one of the usages, one of the habits, of colonial life. It had been felt, from the first, to be just as necessary as planting or reaping,—to be as likely to break out every day and every night as a thunder-shower in summer, and to break out as suddenly. There have been nations who boasted that their rivers or mountains never saw the smoke of an enemy's camp. Here the war-whoop awoke the sleep of the cradle; it startled the dying man on his pillow; it summoned young and old from the meeting-house, from the burial, and from the bridal ceremony, to the strife of death. The consequence was, that that steady, composed, and reflecting courage which belongs to all the English race grew into a leading characteristic of New England; and a public sentiment was formed, pervading young and old, and both sexes, which declared it lawful, necessary, and honorable to risk life, and to shed blood for a great cause,—for our family, for our fires, for our God, for our country, for our religion. In such a cause it declared that the voice of God Himself commanded to the field. The courage of New England was the "courage of conscience." It did not rise to that insane and awful passion,—the love of war for itself. It would not have hurried her sons to the Nile, or the foot of the pyramids, or across the great raging sea of snows which rolled from Smolensko to Moscow, to set the stars of glory upon the glowing brow of ambition. But it was a courage which at Lexington, at Bunker Hill, at Bennington, and at Saratoga, had power to brace the spirit for the patriots' fight,—and gloriously roll back the tide of menaced war from their homes, the soil of their birth, the graves of their fathers, and the everlasting hills of their freedom.

But I cannot any farther pursue this sketch of the life which tasked the youthful spirit of New England. Other labors there were to be done; other trials to pass through; other influences to discipline them and make them fit for the rest which remains to the heirs of liberty.

> "So true it is—for such holy rest,
> Strong hands must toil—strong hearts endure."

It was a people thus schooled to the love and attainments and championship of freedom—its season of infant helplessness now long past, the strength and generosity and fire of a mighty youth, moving its limbs, and burning in its eye— a people, whose bright spirit had been fed midst the crowned heights, with hope and liberty and thoughts of power—this was the people whom our Revolution summoned to the grandest destiny in the history of nations. They were summoned, and a choice put before them: slavery, with present ease and rest and enjoyment, but all inglorious—the death of the nation's soul; and liberty, with battle and bloodshed, but the spring of all national good, of art, of plenty, of genius. Liberty born of the skies! breathing of all their odors, and radiant with all their hues! They were bidden to choose, and they chose wisely and greatly.

> "They linked their hands—they pledged their stainless faith
> In the dread presence of attesting Heaven—
> They bound their hearts to sufferings and death
> With the severe and solemn transport given
> To bless such vows. How man had striven,
> How man might strive, and vainly strive they knew,
> And called upon their God.
> They knelt, and rose in strength."

I have no need to tell you the story of the Revolution, if the occasion were to justify it. Some of you shared in its strife; for to that, as to every other great duty, Ipswich was more than equal. Some who have not yet tasted of death, some perhaps even now here, and others who have followed or who went before their illustrious La Fayette. All of you partake of its fruits. All of you are encompassed about by its glory!

But now that our service of commemoration is ended, let us go hence and meditate on all that it has taught us. You see how long the holy and beautiful city of our liberty and our power has been in building, and by how many hands, and at what cost. You see the towering and steadfast height to which it has gone up, and how its turrets and spires gleam in the rising and setting sun. You stand among the graves of some—your townsmen, your fathers by blood, whose names you bear, whose portraits hang up in your homes, of whose memory you are justly proud—who helped in their day to sink those walls deep in their beds, where neither frost nor earthquake might heave them,—to raise aloft those great arches of stone,—to send up those turrets and spires into the sky. It was theirs to build; remember it is yours, under Providence, to keep the city,—to keep it from the sword of the invader,—to keep it from licentiousness and crime and irreligion, and all that would make it unsafe or unfit to live in,—to keep it from the fires of faction, of civil strife, of party spirit, that might burn up in a day the slow work of a thousand years of glory. Happy, if we shall so perform our duty that they who centuries hence shall dwell among our graves may be able to remember, on some such day as this, in one common service of grateful commemoration, their fathers of the *first* and of the *second* age of America,—those who through martyrdom and tempest and battle sought liberty, and made her their own,—and those whom neither ease nor luxury, nor the fear of man, nor the worship of man, could prevail on to barter her away!

CHAPTER III.

SPEECH ON THE POWER AND DUTY OF CONGRESS TO
CONTINUE THE POLICY OF PROTECTING AMERICAN LABOR.
DELIVERED IN THE SENATE OF THE UNITED STATES, March 14, 1842.

In early 1833, Andrew Jackson's federal government appeared to be on a collision course with a rebellious South Carolina, where a special convention held the previous year had put the theory of nullification into practice by declaring the Tariffs of 1828 and 1832 null and void. Hostilities never actually broke out, of course, thanks to a compromise measure introduced by Kentucky's Henry Clay that would lower the tariff gradually over the next ten years.

Thus as the 1840s opened, the tariff was destined to become an important national issue once again. Choate's 1842 speech on the subject, reproduced below, is interesting for a number of reasons, not least of which is that it reveals the continuing centrality of the Constitution in policy debates. Speaking in 1832, Choate had scarcely appealed to the Constitution at all, portraying the dispute instead as a clash of material interests among the sections. Here, however, he feels obligated to address at some length the ongoing claims of opponents of protection that the Constitution had envisioned the tariff as a revenue measure only and not as the basis of a protective program. The "tendency of the time," he observed, "is to regard this protecting power as stricken out of the Constitution." That most of Choate's arguments had been anticipated and answered by John C. Calhoun during the 1830s weakens but by no means nullifies the points raised here. Later that year, President John Tyler signed the protective Tariff of 1842 into law.

[THE resolutions of Mr. CLAY being under consideration, one of which was in the FOLLOWING TERMS:

"*Resolved*, That, in the adjustment of a tariff to raise an amount of twenty-six millions of revenue, the principles of the Compromise Act generally should be adhered to, and that especially a maximum rate of ad valorem duties should be established, from which there ought to be as little departure as possible," Mr. Choate spoke as follows:]

MR. PRESIDENT,—

I HAD wished to say something on one branch of one of the subjects to which the resolutions extend; I mean that of the readjustment of the tariff, as it may affect domestic industry. In my view, it is the great subject of the session and of the day. I agree with the Pennsylvania memorialists, whose petition has just been read, that the subject of the currency—difficult, delicate, and important as it is, and creditable as it will be to my friend from New York, [Mr. Tallmadge,] and useful to the country to adjust it—bears no comparison, in point of importance, with this. We are coming, whether we will or not, by the progress of the Compromise Act, to an era in the history of the national industry and the national prosperity. We have it in our power to mark this era by the commission of a stupendous mistake, or by the realization of a splendid felicity and wisdom of policy. This very tariff which we are about to construct may, on the one hand, paralyze American labor, drive it from many of its best fields of employment, arrest the development of our resources of growth and wealth, and even the development of the mind and genius of America, our main resource, turning back the current of our national fortunes for an age; or it may, on the other hand, communicate an impulse, that shall be felt after we are in our graves, to that harmonized agricultural, manufacturing, and commercial industry, which alone can fill the measure of this or of any country's glory.

Under this impression of the importance of the subject, I have wished to take part in the discussion of it. In the present stage, however, of this business of arranging the tariff in the two houses of congress,—with no bill before us, with no report of either of the committees on manufactures, although we have had a very able speech from the chairman of our own committee, [Mr. Simmons,] unaided to any considerable and useful extent by the voice of the country, which, if I do not misunderstand the country, will come up, peremptory and unequivocal, the moment you have a bill reported, and before, if that is delayed much longer,—I do not think it expedient, or even practicable, to go far into the consideration of details. I mean to abstain from them altogether at this time. I move no question now about the amount of annual revenue which you will require for the wants of government, nor whether you should raise it from duties on imports alone, or partly from the proceeds of the public lands. I have nothing now to say about specific duties or ad valorem duties, horizontal or discriminating tariffs, home valuation or foreign valuation. The actual state of information before us, in parliamentary and authentic form, is not such as to make it worth while to anticipate that kind of discussion. But there is one preliminary and general principle upon which I shall consider myself obliged to stand; by which I shall consider myself obliged to try every question of detail that shall present itself;

and which it may be as fair and proper to announce at this moment as at any other; and that is, that congress has the constitutional power so to provide for the collection of the necessary revenues of government as to afford reasonable and adequate protection to the whole labor of the country, agricultural, navigating, mechanical, and manufacturing, and *ought to afford that protection*. This general principle I shall take with me through all this investigation; and it is the only one which it is necessary now to declare. I mean by this to say, that I shall enter on this business of the tariff with no unalterable predetermination as to the precise mode of effecting the grand object in view; although I certainly hold a very confident opinion that discriminating and specific duties will be found indispensable. But this I am ready to avow: that the protection of American labor, on all its fields and in all its forms, is to be kept constantly and anxiously in view in all our arrangements; that you have the constitutional power to secure that protection; and that you are bound to do so, regardless of everything and everybody but the Constitution, justice, and a true and large American policy.

There can be no doubt then, it would seem, in the first place, on the constitutional power of congress, in the assessment of duties of revenue, so to discriminate among objects of duty as to bring to life and to keep alive the whole multiform, agricultural, manufacturing, and commercial industry of the country. To state the immediate proposition which I mean to examine more precisely: You are about determining to raise a certain annual amount of revenue,— twenty-six millions of dollars, if you please. The wants of government require at least so much, whatever becomes of the land bill. The amount is fixed by reference to those wants. Now, without intending by any means to concede that this is the extent of your constitutional power,—for certainly, in my judgment, it goes a great deal further,—what I would say is, that, in assessing the duties which are to yield the amount thus determined on, you may discriminate for the protection of labor. You may admit some articles free, and just as many of them as you please, without any regard to the enumeration in the Compromise Act. You may prohibit the importation of others. You may admit some under specific, and some under ad valorem duties,—some under a low rate, and some under a high one,—some under a foreign valuation, others under a valuation at home,—and others, or all, under that legislative preëstablishment of value which the Senator from Rhode Island [Mr. Simmons] proposes to substitute for fraudulent or mistaken estimates of actual and changeable value made abroad or at home. All this you may do; these varieties of proceeding you may choose between, with intent to bring out and sustain the domestic labor of America against the capital, the necessities, or the policy of foreigners, whether individuals or governments. Upon the words of the Constitution, if it were an open question to-day, this is clear. The history of the origin, construction, and adoption of that instrument demonstrates it. And, then, there is a weight of opinion, and a series of practical interpretation, which should put the matter forever at rest.

Mr. President, the senate would hardly excuse me for assuming to offer a formal and laborious argument as an original one, in proof of this matter. Delicacy, honor, and good sense would forbid such an attempt to appropriate borrowed plumes. No man's ability or research could clothe the subject with any useful novelty; how much less can mine! I desire, therefore, only to recall to your mind the general nature and main points of an argument already and long ago familiar to you. And even this I should not venture on, if the state of opinion in the country and in congress did not appear to render such a discussion seasonable and useful. Sir, the tendency of the time is to regard this protecting power as stricken out of the Constitution. I have even heard judicious men speak of it as an *exploded* thing. We reason, some reason—certainly not the honorable mover of these resolutions—but some reason as if it had been agreed somewhere, at some time, and by somebody or another, that the power should never again be asserted, or never again be exercised. They would persuade you that the people, nine years ago, to secure to themselves the peaceable enjoyment of their rights for nine years longer, had stipulated that, at the end of the time, they would surrender the principle of constitutional protection forever. For a fleeting term of possession,—nothing in the life of a nation; nothing in the life of a man,—they agreed to squander away the inheritance itself!

Now, Sir, without pausing to inquire into the origin of this opinion, without pausing to inquire how far it may be attributable to the silent influence of the Compromise Act in unsettling the tone of the public mind, still less to debate the merits of that celebrated arrangement, or to judge between the sagacity, patriotism, and firmness of those who suggested and those who opposed it, I think it may not be unseasonable to ascend from that act to the contemplation of first principles. Let us turn from the stormy passions, and unconstitutional organizations, and extorted expedients of 1833, and breathe the pure and invigorating air of 1789! Let us see what our fathers framed the government for, and what they expected of it.

I find your authority then, Sir, to pass laws of protection, where the calm and capacious intelligence of Mr. Madison found it in 1789, in 1810, and 1828. That great man, among our greatest of the dead or the living; who had helped so much to frame the Constitution and procure its adoption, defending and expounding it with his tongue and pen to his own Virginia, and to the whole country; who had weighed, aye, Sir, and helped to coin and stamp, every word in it; and who knew the evils, the wants, the hopes, the opinions in which it had its origin, as well as any man ever knew why he removed from an old house to a new one; Mr. Madison, in 1789 sustaining in congress that celebrated law laying impost duties for the support of government, the discharge of the public debt, and the encouragement and protection of manufactures, in 1810, in a message to congress, and in 1828, in his letter to Mr. Cabell,—at the beginning, in the midst, and at the close of his career; first when his faculties were at their best, his memory of events recent, his ambition high; again with the utmost weight of his official responsibilities upon him; and again in old age, when his passions were calmed, the measure of his fame full, and he looked round upon the widespread tribes of the people whom he had served, and who had honored him so long, and upon their diversities of interest and of sentiment with a parental and patriarchal eye,—he found your authority always in the Constitution, and he found it in your "power to regulate commerce with foreign nations, among the several States, and with the Indian tribes." Let me read a passage from his speech in congress in 1789, upon Mr. Fitzsimons's proposition to combine the objects of protection and revenue in the bill laying duties on imports:—

"The States that are most advanced in population, and ripe for manufactures, ought to have their particular interests attended to in some degree. While these States retained the power of making regulations of trade, they had the power to protect and cherish such institutions. By adopting the present Constitution, they have thrown the exercise of this power into other hands; they must have done this with an expectation that those interests would not be neglected here."—*James Madison, Gales and Seaton's Debates, old series,* vol. i. p. 116.

In his message of the fifth of December, 1810, after adverting to a "highly interesting extension of useful manufactures, the combined product of professional occupations and of household industry," he observes, "how far it may be expedient to guard the infancy of this improvement in the distribution of labor, by *regulations of the commercial tariff,* is a subject which cannot fail to suggest itself to your patriotic reflections." His letter to Mr. Cabell, written in September, 1828, in which he defines his opinions upon the power more precisely, and produces a very strong argument in support of them, is known to everybody. "The question is," he says, "whether, under the Constitution of the United States, 'the power to regulate trade with foreign nations,' as a distinct and substantive item in the enumerated powers, embraces the object of encouraging, by duties, restrictions, and prohibitions, the manufactures and products of the country?

And the affirmative must be inferred from the following considerations;" which he proceeds to unfold and urge with that force of persuasive reason for which he was so remarkable.

I derive, then, your power to arrange duties, for the purpose of protection, from your power to regulate commerce. The "Congress shall have power to regulate commerce with foreign nations, and among the several States, and with the Indian tribes." What does this language mean? *How, and by what means,* does the Constitution authorize you to regulate commerce, and *for what ends* to regulate it? The answer is, it authorizes you to regulate it, among other means, by the imposition of discriminating duties, or prohibitory duties on imports of foreign manufactures, or other articles, for the purpose, among other purposes, of encouraging domestic manufactures, and any and every other form of domestic industry.

The presumption, certainly, in the first instance is, that these words of the Constitution mean to communicate the power to pass any law, to do any act, for any purpose, which, in the general and political language of the country in 1787, was deemed and called an ordinary and usual governmental commercial regulation. You may regulate commerce. Then you may do it by any and all such means, and for any and all such ends, as formed at that time the known and usual means and ends by and for which governments habitually regulated commerce. If you cannot do it by all such means, and for all such ends, you cannot by any, nor for any. All the known and usual modes, and all the known and usual ends, are committed to you; or none are so. This is the first and legal import, *primâ facie,* of so general a grant. The presumption in the first instance is, that this language was used in the sense which it was generally understood to bear when asserted of or applied to other governments in other writings, or in the current speech of the age of the Constitution. If, in the contemporaneous written and spoken vocabulary, a "commercial regulation" comprised and meant a certain act, or certain classes of acts, a certain act for a certain purpose; if a law of England, or of one of the States, laying duties on imports for the encouragement of domestic labor, mechanical, manufacturing, navigating, or agricultural, was, in that vocabulary, held and called a common commercial regulation; one of the recognized and familiar exercises of the power to regulate commerce; the presumption is, that the words here mean what they meant everywhere else. If you can control this presumption by inspection of other parts of the Constitution, or of its general structure, or by other legitimate evidence, do so; but the burden will be on you. It was upon this presumption that the discussion in this body, the other day, upon the bankrupt law proceeded. To determine the nature and limits of your power to pass such a law, you inquired what bankruptcy meant, and what laws upon the subject of bankruptcy were, in the legal language of the time? The senators from Delaware, [Mr. Bayard,] and from Missouri, [Mr. Benton,] who debated this subject so ably, in opposition to the bill, did not argue that, from the nature of this government, the phrase "laws upon the subject of bankruptcy" must be supposed to mean less or more than the same phrase anywhere else. They treated it as a question on the meaning of language; and, assuming that the words in the Constitution meant what the same words meant elsewhere, they sought that meaning in the contemporaneous, popular, and technical vocabulary of the States, and of England. Just so here. To determine the nature and limits of this power to regulate commerce, to determine whether it enables you to construct a protecting tariff, inquire whether in the political and popular vocabulary of 1787 such a tariff was an ordinary form and kind of commercial regulation. If it were, the doubt is resolved.

And now is it not indisputable that, at that day, what we now call a discriminating tariff for protection was universally known and described as one familiar and recognized kind of commercial regulation? and that a power of government to regulate commerce was universally understood to include the power to make such a tariff? Sir, nothing is more certain. Nothing is more certain than that, by a concurrence of extraordinary circumstances, the expressions, *commercial regulations, regulations of trade, the power to regulate commerce, the power to regulate trade,* and the like, had acquired, in the political and popular language of the day, a definite and uniform sense; and that, according to that sense, a protecting tariff was a form of commercial regulation, and the power to regulate commerce included the power to construct such a tariff.

Go back, for a moment, in the first place, to the close of the war in 1783, and inquire what this language meant then. No other words, or combination of words, had so settled, so precise, and so notorious a signification. You remember how this came to pass. The discussions and the events of the twenty years before had given them currency, and fixed their meaning. They had been burned and graven, as it were, into the memory of America. The disputes of England and her colonies, which brought on the Revolution, had turned on the extent of her power over them. She asserted in 1764 an enlarged and a menacing extent of claim; a claim not only to regulate their trade, but to lay internal and external taxes, and to bind them in all cases whatsoever. They admitted the right to regulate trade; they admitted the right to do it by the imposition of duties on imports into the colonies, and on their imports into England; they admitted the right to do it for the purpose of developing and sustaining the manufacturing, mechanical, and navigating industry of the mother-country; but they denied the right, for the first time asserted in the Stamp Act, to lay internal taxes. She asserted both rights; and from this conflict of the exactions of dominion and the resistance of liberty, arose the discussions which preceded the war, and the war itself. Now, what I ask you particularly to remark is, that, in all the stages and in all the forms of this controversy; a controversy extending over twenty years; a controversy which addressed the reason and exasperated the feelings of all America, and made everybody familiar with its topics and its vocabulary,—*all the disputants on both sides agreed exactly on the nature of a commercial regulation, and of the acts which might be done under the power to make such a regulation.* Grenville, Lord North, Lord Chatham, and Burke, in England; and in the colonies, John Dickinson the Pennsylvania farmer, Benjamin Franklin the Boston mechanic, John Adams the Massachusetts lawyer, whose energy and eloquence brought up a hesitating congress to the Declaration of Independence, Sewall, the champion of parliament and the crown, Jefferson, who first denied the right of England to exert either of the powers she claimed—these and a hundred others, some of whose names we know, while some have perished—*stant nominum umbræ!*—all who took part for you or against you in that, your "agony of glory," concur in this. All of them agreed that the long series of legislation by which England had laid duties on imports of the colonies, for the purpose of bringing out and sustaining her domestic industry of all kinds, were regulations of trade; all of them agreed that, if she had power to regulate the trade of the colonies, her protecting tariffs were clearly within the exercise of the power; and all of them at first, and most of them, even on the American side, down nearly to the Declaration of Independence, conceded to her that precise power. Taking their stand upon the nature of this power, and of the acts it authorized, those who sustained the claim of England argued that her right to lay internal taxes followed of course, while those who espoused the cause of liberty denied that it followed at all; but upon the nature of that power, and of the acts it authorized, if it existed, there was no diversity of opinion, and there was nearly a unanimous concession that it did exist. Every speech, every address, every public act, every essay, every pamphlet, all the written remains of that anxious and momentous controversy, which employed so many eloquent tongues and pens, and went, at last, to the arbitrament of war, prove this. It is wholly indisputable that if, in the year 1783, it were written or said that England, before the Revolution, and the States after it, had the power to regulate the trade of America, the writer or speaker meant to declare that England first, and subsequently the

States, had the power, among other things, *to tax imports in order to protect man-ufactures, the arts, navigation, and agriculture; and that he was understood to mean so by all England and all America.*

Mr. President, I could not exhibit in a day all the evidence of this which breaks forth from every page of our Revolutionary and ante-Revolutionary political literature. You know how considerable a body of writing it is. It is familiar to the earlier and the maturer studies of senators. You have not been inattentive to a class of compositions, some of which the masculine taste of Chatham did not refuse to rank with the best political writings of the master States of antiquity.

Let me read a few selections, however, in proof and illustration of the currency and the meaning of this language prior and down to 1783. Some of them, I know, have been accumulated and arranged for this purpose by others; and, indeed, the *principle* of this whole mode of argument, and the nature of the investigations by which it should be conducted, are suggested by Mr. Madison's letter. But I have not thought it proper to omit any for this reason; and some of them, I think, have not been adverted to at all.

In an anonymous pamphlet, published as early as August, 1765, entitled "Considerations on the propriety of imposing taxes in the British colonies, for the purpose of raising a revenue, by act of Parliament," of which I know only that it was one of the numerous and effective contributions of Virginia to the cause of colonial liberty, the writer, (page 33,) says:—

"It appears to me that there is a clear and necessary distinction between an act imposing a tax for *the single purpose of revenue,* and those acts which have been made *for the regulation of trade,* and have produced some revenue in *consequence of their effect* and operation as *regulations of trade.*" And again, (page 34): "It is a common, and frequently the most proper method, to regulate trade by duties on imports and exports. The authority of the mother-country to regulate the trade of the colonies being unquestionable, what regulations are the most proper are to be of course submitted to the determination of the Parliament; and, if an *incidental revenue* should be produced by such regulations, these are not, therefore, unwarrantable."

I ought to have reminded you that before this, in 1761, even James Otis, in that great argument upon the subject of writs of assistance which breathed (I may use the vivid expression of John Adams) "the breath of life into America," admitted, upon the ground of *necessity,* the power of England to pass her whole series of acts of trade "as regulations of commerce," while he utterly denied their validity as laws of revenue. Let me refer you to the glowing and remarkable analysis of that argument, contained in the letters of Mr. Adams to Mr. Tudor, written in 1818.

In October, 1765, the first congress of the colonies assembled at New York to confer on the means of preserving the liberties of America, menaced by that new system of imperial policy of which the Stamp Act was the most palpable, most alarming, but not the only manifestation. Of the proceedings of this congress we know little. Tradition has preserved something of the impression which the genius and eloquence of James Otis, and his profound knowledge of the interests, and his deep comprehension of the rights and unappeasable resentment for the wrongs of the colonies, produced on the assembly; but his words of fire are perished forever. There survive, however, of the labors of that body, a general declaration of rights, an address to the king, a petition to each house of parliament, and a report of a committee on the subject of the colonial rights. I read you a sentence from the address to the king, which is repeated, almost in the very same words, in the report of the committee. You may find it in Pitkins's "Civil and Political History," first volume, pages 185 and 453.

"It is also humbly submitted whether there be not a material distinction, in reason and sound policy at least, between the necessary exercises of parliamentary jurisdiction in general acts, for the amendment of the common law, *and the regulation of trade and commerce* through the whole empire, and the exercise of that jurisdiction by *imposing taxes on the colonies.*"

In February, 1766, Dr. Franklin underwent his celebrated examination "before an august assembly," as the colonial writers of the day called the house of commons; and to the question "was it an opinion of America, before 1763, that parliament had no right to lay duties and taxes there?" he answered, "I never heard an objection to the right to lay duties to regulate commerce." See how fully this is confirmed by John Dickinson, in the second of the "Farmer's Letters," written in 1767:—

"The Parliament," he observes, (page 4,) "unquestionably possesses a legal authority to regulate the trade of Great Britain and all her colonies. Such an authority is essential to the relation of a mother-country and her colonies, and necessary for the common good of all."

He then adverts to the legislation of England for the colonies before the Stamp Act, makes extracts from the several statutes, beginning with 12 Car. II., and then adds:—

> "All before the Stamp Act are calculated to regulate trade, although many of them imposed duties on it." "Great Britain," he proceeds in the same letter, (page 9,) "has prohibited the manufacturing iron and steel in these colonies without any objection being made to her right of doing it. The like right she must have to prohibit any other manufacture among us. Our great advocate, Mr. Pitt, in his speeches on the debate concerning the repeal of the *Stamp Act,* acknowledged that *Great Britain* could restrain our manufactures. His words are these: 'This kingdom, as the supreme governing and legislative power, has *always* bound the colonies by her regulations and *restrictions* in trade, in navigation, in *manufactures*—in everything, *except that of taking their money out of their pockets without their consent.*' Again he says: 'We may bind their trade, *confine their manufactures,* and exercise every power whatever, except that of taking their money out of their pockets without their consent.' " "External impositions, (this is Mr. Dickinson's language, letter 4, page 17,) *for the regulation of our trade,* do not grant to his Majesty the property of his colonies."

"There is a plain distinction," Lord Chatham had said the year before, in one of those glorious efforts of his eloquence which so much endeared him to our fathers, and stirred their hearts like the sound of a trumpet—"there is a plain distinction between taxes levied for the purpose of raising a revenue and duties imposed *for the regulation of trade,* although some revenue might arise from the latter." We may regulate trade,—such was his argument,—we may regulate it by the imposition of duties; we may do it for the purpose of giving direction and development to the whole industry of the empire. But we cannot levy an internal tax for revenue.

Burke, whose long series of exertions for the rights of the colonies do him as much honor as the marvellous affluence of his genius, proceeds everywhere upon the same distinction, and uses everywhere the same language. "Without idolizing the trade laws," he says, in his speech on conciliation with America in 1775, "I am sure they are still, in many ways, of great use to us. But my perfect conviction of this does not help me in the least to discern how the revenue laws form any security whatsoever to the *commercial regulations,* or that these *commercial regulations* are the true ground of quarrel." And the year before, in his speech on American taxation: "This is certainly true, that no act avowedly for the purpose of revenue, and with the ordinary title and recital, taken together, is found in the statute book till the year 1764. All before this period *stood on commercial regulation and restraint.*"

Nearly at the same time the congress which declared our independence, in a grave and lofty paper, in which they claimed for the colonies "the free and exclusive power in all cases of taxation and internal policy," avowed nevertheless,—

"That, from the necessity of the case, we cheerfully consent to the operation of such acts of the British Parliament as are *bonâ fide* restrained to the *regulation of commerce* for the purpose of securing the commercial advantages of the whole empire to the mother-country, and the commercial benefits of its respected members, excluding every idea of taxation for raising a revenue on the subjects of America without their consent."

In 1774 and 1775, John Adams, in a series of papers, under the signature of Novanglus, vindicated the cause of American liberty against the king's attorney-general, Sewall, with a vigor and ability which gave assurance of the future champion of independence. These papers and those of his antagonist discussed all the points of controversy between England and her colonies, and reviewed the whole history of their original and their altered relations; and, exasperated and soured as the colonists had become, clearly and far as the eagle glance of the orator of independence already saw into the future, it is remarkable that then, even almost down to the battle of Lexington, this distinction was still recognized and respected and reasoned on.

"And from that time to this, (i.e. for more than a hundred years,) the general sense of the colonies has been, that the authority of parliament was confined to the regulation of trade, and did not extend to taxation or internal legislation." "Duties for regulating trade we paid because we thought it just," &c. "As for duties for a revenue, none were ever laid by parliament for that purpose until 1764, when, and ever since, its authority to do it has been constantly denied."—*Letters of Novanglus and Massachusettensis,* pp. 38, 39. *Feb.* 13*th*, 1775.

The ministry at length perceived the expediency of admitting the justice of a distinction with which England and America had become so familiar. In 1778

Lord North, aroused to the realities of his situation, and seeking to win the insurgent colonies from independence and from France, procured the passage of a bill which offered a compromise upon the precise basis for which they had so long contended. "It is expedient," such was the language of the bill, "to declare that the King and Parliament of Great Britain will not impose any duty or tax for the purpose of raising a revenue in the colonies, except only such duties as may be expedient to impose for the *regulation of commerce*." (St. 18, Geo. III.) But, in the phrase of Paine, "the charm had been broken," and the tardy offer of conciliation was unheard, or distrusted, or distasteful, amid the voice of battle, by the hoarded up resentments of a whole people, to the spirit of liberty and to the passion of glory.

And now, what kind of regulations were those which the colonies so long and so universally conceded to England the right to make? Sir, they were, among others, what, in the language of this day, we call discriminating and protecting tariffs. They were laws imposing duties on imports, as you see by the passages I have selected, and imposing them for the purpose of encouraging the navigation and trade, and developing the manufacturing capacity and labor, that had seated England on the throne of the commercial world. "One thing at least is certain," says Mr. Madison in his letter to Mr. Cabell, "that the main and admitted object of the parliamentary *regulations of trade with the colonies* was the encouragement of the *manufactures* in Great Britain." They were designed, among other objects, expressly to secure to the English manufacturer the *home* market and the colonial market *for his fabrics,* and the *colonial* supply of his *raw materials,* against the competition which might reduce the price of the former and enhance the price of the latter. Other and broader objects they pursued, undoubtedly; but, for the purposes of this discussion, I speak only of this. For the accomplishment of this object they restrained, by heavy duties or by direct prohibition, the importation of foreign manufactures into the colonies; they discouraged the colonial manufacturers themselves; and they obliged them to send, in English ships, to English markets, and to English markets alone, the raw material, which English genius was to transfigure and refine into shapes of beauty and usefulness, to enrich and swell her commerce with the world. Read the titles and objects of that long succession of laws, in the argument of James Otis, to which I have alluded, and his burning commentary on them, and you will well comprehend the extent and energy of English governmental regulation. Read particularly pages 213 and 294 of the letters of Novanglus and Massachusettensis, and Pitkin's "Political and Civil History of the United States," first volume, page 401. Read the celebrated preamble of the act of navigation itself:—

> "In regard his Majesty's plantations beyond the seas are inhabited and peopled by his subjects of this his kingdom of *England, for the maintaining a greater correspondence and kindness between them,* and keeping them in a firmer dependence upon it, and rendering them yet more beneficial and advantageous unto it *in the further employment and increase of English shipping* and seamen, vent of *English woollens,* and other manufactures and commodities, *rendering the navigation to and from the same more safe and cheap,* and making this kingdom *a staple,* not only of the commodities of those plantations, but also of the commodities of other countries and places, *for the supplying of them;* and it being the *usage* of other nations to keep plantations trade to themselves," &c.

Upon the policy here so vigorously sketched, that whole series of regulations of trade reposed. They may all be summed up under the terms of this description; that they were a body of English law, designed by the regulation of the commerce of England and her colonies with each other, and the rest of the world, to develop, to its utmost capacity, the labor of the British empire, in all its forms, according to the discretion of the imperial parliament.

I hold it then, Sir, clear and indisputable, that, down to the close of the war with England in 1783, the phrase "commercial regulations," in the understanding of everybody, included discriminating protecting tariffs; and that when it was said that, before the Revolution, England had the power to regulate commerce, and that, after the declaration of independence, the States had it, it was meant, in the understanding of everybody, that she first, and then they, could make such tariffs. So much is certain.

And now, when you consider that the Constitution was made only four years later; that it was made by and for the generation which had gone through the war and the whole preparatory controversy; that many of those who shared in that controversy, and were most familiar with its topics and its terms, were still alive, in the Convention, or mingling with the people; the presumption undoubtedly is, that this language continued to bear the same sense down to the date of the Constitution, and that it means in that immortal production just what it means in all the other written and spoken speech of the day. But I do not leave this upon what I should have deemed a resistless presumption. To show you that such was the fact, that its meaning remained unaltered to 1787, and that it was inserted into the Constitution precisely *because that was its meaning,* I proceed now to lay before you another kind of evidence, and, as I think, a conclusive body of it.

It is not wholly unworthy of remark, that that which I may call the *colonial, controversial,* and *technical* use of this language,—that use of it which I have been illustrating,—was exactly in conformity with its literary, general, and popular use. Mr. Verplanck observes, in his letter to Colonel Drayton, that Adam Smith calls those restrictive tariffs to which he objects commercial regulations. This is true. He sets the system of free trade and that of commercial restraint in contrast; and that whole body of prohibitions, taxations, and general policy, designed to foster domestic labor, he assails under the name of "commercial regulations." And as his work was first published in 1779, it may be presumed, and indeed is known, to have begun to attract the notice of intelligent persons as early as the period immediately after the war, and thus to have contributed to diffuse, impress, and define the sense of the language we are considering.

It is a fact, which bears still more directly upon the point of inquiry to which I have arrived, that after the war several of the States imposed duties, more or less heavy, on imports of foreign manufactures, avowedly for the purpose of sustaining their own manufactures, and that these tariffs were commonly called, in the language of our politics between 1783 and 1789, *commercial regulations.* Massachusetts, New York, Pennsylvania, and I believe other States, had done this. "It is happy for the mechanics in America," (says a writer of Maryland, at some time between 1783 and 1787, "American Museum," first volume, page 215,) "that they have met with the protection and encouragement of government in several of the wisest States." I cannot resist the pleasure of referring to the act of the State of Pennsylvania on this subject, passed in 1785, and of marking the good sense and the forecast which it exemplifies. It recites that divers useful arts and manufactures had been gradually introduced into that State, which had been able, during the war, to supply in the hour of need weapons, ammunition, and clothing, without which the war could not have been carried on; and then proceeds in section two:—

> "And whereas, although the fabrics and manufactures of Europe and other foreign ports, imported into this country in times of peace, may be afforded at cheaper rates than they can be made here, yet good policy and a regard to the well-being of divers useful and industrious citizens, who were employed in the making of like goods in this State, demand of us that moderate duties be laid on certain fabrics and manu-

factures imported, which do not interfere with, and which (if no relief be given) will undermine and destroy, the useful manufactures of the like kind in this country."

A writer in the "American Museum," on American manufactures, to whom I will refer you more particularly before I have done, at some time before 1787, warmly commends the noble example of Massachusetts in this particular. (Am. Mus. first volume, page 23.) Now, these impositions of duties, for this purpose, by the States, all impositions of duties on imports of the States were called *commercial regulations* by our writers and speakers of the period after the Revolution and before the Constitution. "While the States," said Mr. Madison in the debate in 1789, to which I have referred, "retained the power of making regulations of trade," (referring palpably to these legislative taxations on imports,) "they had the power to protect and cherish manufactures." They were denominated *commercial acts, trade laws,* and *regulations of commerce,* indifferently and universally, in the current language of the time. Tench Coxe, in an inquiry into the principle of a commercial system for the United States, written before the adoption of the Constitution, describes and complains of them under all those appellations. (Am. Mus., first volume, 444.) I suppose it out of all doubt that if, at that time, it had been written or said that the States had the power to regulate commerce, as very frequently in those very words it was written and said, everybody would have understood it to be meant that this included, as one of its commonest exemplifications and exertions, a power to make a protecting tariff. When that precise form of speech was then embodied into the Constitution, did it not mean the same thing?

But, to put this matter at rest, let me ask you to look a little more at large into that considerable body of writings which appeared in the States, between the peace of 1783 and the adoption of the Constitution, upon the subject of a new Constitution. A word first on their general character.

You know how soon after the war an opinion began to prevail that the country needed a stronger government. Suggested at first, like the Revolution itself, by the intelligence of the community, it spread fast and far; the events of every day gave it diffusion and strength; it possessed itself at last of the general mind, and the Constitution was the result. During the progress of this opinion, it produced a great deal of discussion. These writings, into which I wish you now to look, are the fruits of that discussion, and embody its topics and its language. Less known than the more lofty and classical controversial literature of the more glorious revolutionary and ante-revolutionary time, they are to us the most interesting and most instructive writings in the world. No man, I could almost say, can understand the Constitution without the study of them. No man can understand the nature of the new remedial law until he has meditated the disease which it was made to cure, in these vivid pictures of it. No man can understand the vocabulary of the Constitution until he has familiarized himself, in these writings, with the current vocabulary of the people, by whom and for whom it was composed. The defects of the old confederation; its utter insufficiency for our greatness and our glory; the evils which bore the people to the earth, and made their newly acquired independence a dreary and useless thing; the disordered condition of the currency; our exhausting system of trade; the action of conflicting and inadequate commercial regulations of the States; the excessive importations of foreign manufactures; the drain of specie; the stagnation of labor, oppressed and disheartened by a competition with all the pauper labor of all the world; the depression of agriculture, sympathizing with other labor by an eternal law; the need of a system of divided and diversified employments, which should leave no one over-crowded, should leave no man's faculties undeveloped and unexcited, which should give a market and a reward to all industry; the wants, sufferings, fears, wishes; the universal stimulation of mind and fermentation of opinions in which the Constitution had its birth—you find them all there, and you find them nowhere else.

Looking with some labor into a collection of part of these writings in the "American Museum," a work embodying the general spirit of the press from 1783 to 1787, I think I find conclusive evidence of this fact, to wit: that a confident and sagacious and salutary conviction came to be generally adopted; First. That one capital source of the evils which oppressed us was the importation of too many foreign manufactures, and the use of too few domestic manufactures; too much encouragement of the foreign laborer, and too little encouragement of our own; Secondly. That a new and more perfect union and a stronger government were required, among other ends, very much for the cure and prevention of this precise evil; and Thirdly. That, in order to effect this end, the new government must be clothed with this *specific power of regulating trade, whereby it could check the import of foreign manufactures,* by duties and prohibitions, and thus bring to life and keep alive domestic manufactures, and with them the entire labor of America. If this is so, it will prove at once, *first,* that this language retained the same signification in 1787 which it had borne in 1764; and, *next,* that it means in the Constitution just what it meant everywhere else, and was inserted there *because* it bore that meaning. Let me ask your attention, then, to some evidence and illustrations of the fact, to which I might add a thousand.

In the first volume of the collection I have referred to is an article on American manufactures. It is continued through three months of the "Museum," and was written in Maryland at some time after 1783, and before 1787. The proposition which the essayist maintains is, that manufactures ought immediately to be established in the United States. In support of this, he reasons forcibly and zealously, and with much maturity and breadth of view, considering the time when he wrote; presents a vivid exhibition of the uses of manufactures and of manufacturing industry; of the rank they hold in all civilized States; of the division of labor which they render practicable, and the influence of that division in stimulating all the faculties of men and nations, and in supplying to each faculty and each mind its favorite employment and adequate reward; and, above all, he urges the actual evils which were weighing the country down; its foreign debt; its ruinous consumption; its expensive tastes; its incomplete development of industry; its deficiency in the means of self-reliance and self-support and self-regulation, as a decisive argument for his purpose. He goes on then to inquire how manufactures may be introduced and sustained; and his scheme is, *a government which should have power to regulate trade, and in the exercise of that power should, among other expedients, impose duties on imports of articles coming in competition with the domestic labor.* "I am convinced," he says, (page 212,) "that to begin at this juncture the establishment of manufactures will be the only way to lay the foundation for the future glory, greatness, and independence of America." "Well, how, then," he asks, "shall we make the beginning?" "Free trade," he argues, "in our situation, adopting the sentiment of Montesquieu, 'must necessarily lead us to poverty.' " "A State whose balance of trade is always to its disadvantage cannot grow rich." We must have regulated trade, then. "But, we are told by some," he proceeds, "that trade will regulate itself." Hear how he combats this proposition, and what is the precise *regulation of trade* which he urges upon the statesmen of America:—

"If trade will regulate itself, why do the wisest and most prosperous governments make laws in favor and support of their trade? Why does the British Parliament employ so much time and pains in regulating their trade, so as to render its advantages particularly useful to their own nation? Why so preposterous as to abide by and enforce their boasted navigation act? But so far is trade from regulating itself, that it continually needs the help of the legislation of every country, as a nursing father. If we Americans do not choose to regulate it, it will regulate us, till we have not a farthing left in our land. Trade, like a helpless infant, requires parental care, and to be well looked after; for, says the same excellent author: 'A country that constantly exports fewer manufactures or commodities than it receives will soon find the balance sinking; it will receive less and less, till, falling into extreme poverty, it will receive nothing at all.' The truth is, trade regulates or corrects itself just as everything else does that is left to itself. The manner the late war, for instance, would have corrected itself, had we supinely sat still and folded our arms together, would have been such a correction as I hope no person who makes use of this flimsy argument would wish to have taken place; *and unless we shortly regulate and correct the abuses of our trade by lopping off its useless branches and establishing manufactures,* we shall be corrected perhaps even to our very destruction."

"The mechanics," he continues, "hope the legislature will afford them that protection they are entitled to; for, as the present baleful *system of trade* and scarcity of cash occasion numbers of them to want employment, though they are able and ready to furnish many articles which are at present imported, and as many of their branches are fast declining, and some are likely to become totally extinct, they conceive *that duties ought to be laid on certain imported articles in* such a manner *as to place the American manufacturers on the same footing as the manufacturers* of Europe, and enable them to procure bread and support for their families." And then, in further explanation, he adds, "An excessive duty might be only an encouragement to the smuggler; on the other hand, let them be only so high as to enable the manufacturer to procure a decent subsistence for his family."

Mark two things in this argument and these extracts: *the advice to encourage domestic manufacture* by duties on foreign manufacture, *and the use of language* which calls such an impost, for such an object, *a regulation of trade.*

I should never have done, Sir, if I attempted to read all the proofs which I find in these papers, that the importance of establishing American manufactures seems, even then, to have been generally apprehended; and that a powerful and an immediate impulse was expected to be given to them, in some way, by the new Constitution. The concurrence of opinion upon that point is marvellous. It is still more marvellous, the maturity of the public judgment upon the nature and uses of manufacturing industry, and the very considerable extent to which that industry already had taken root, when you consider with what severity the austere and long dominion of England had pressed upon it; and how short and how unpropitious the time had been for the arts of peace to grow, after that dominion had passed away. But I must confine myself closely to selections which illustrate the meaning and objects of the constitutional phraseology. Let me, however, read a passage or two from a series of letters, by a North Carolinian, under the signature of Sylvius. I find them in the second volume of the "Museum," page 107, and they appeared in August, 1787. His cure, too, for the oppressive indebtment, depreciated currency, scarcity of money, exhausting importations, and, what he calls, luxurious appetites of the day, is the encouragement of American manufactures, and the substitution of a tax on imported manufactures for all other modes of taxation.

> "The more I consider" (says he, page 108) "the progress of credit and the increase of wealth in foreign nations, the more fully I am convinced that paper-money must prove hurtful to this country; that we cannot be relieved from our debts except by promoting domestic manufactures; and that during the prevailing scarcity of money the burdens of the poor may be relieved by altering the mode of taxation."

Addressing himself to the second of these propositions, he adverts to the appalling enlargement of the foreign debt since the peace; to the fact that it has been contracted for clothing; clothing for the master; clothing for the slave; furniture; "saws, hammers, hoes, and axes, as if," says he, "the wolf had made war against our iron as well as our sheep;" Irish butter and beef, and British ale, porter, and cheese, "as if our country did not produce barley, hops, or black cattle;" hazle and oak sprouts under the name of "walking sticks;" luxuries of all denominations, swelling it in three years to six millions of dollars; and then exclaims,—

> "Let us turn our attention to manufactures, and the staple of our country will soon rise to its proper value, for we have already glutted every foreign market. By this expedient, instead of using fictitious paper, we shall soon obtain hard money sufficient; instead of toiling in the field, and becoming poor, that we may enrich the manufacturers of other countries, we shall prosper by our own labor, and enrich our own citizens." "Every domestic manufacture is cheaper than a foreign one, for this plain reason: by the first, nothing is lost to the country—by the other, the whole value is lost; it is carried away, never to return. It is perfectly indifferent to this

State or to the United States, what may be the price of domestic manufactures, because that price remains in the country."

He proceeds then to recommend a substitution of an excise on foreign
manufactures sold in the State, for other modes of taxation; and, although I
do not find here an illustration of the meaning of the words which I am investigating, you will be struck with the confidence with which he presses the
grand elementary suggestion of a tax on foreign labor for the encouragement
of home labor.

"All wise governments" (such is his argument, page 124) "have
thought it their duty, on special occasions, to offer bounties for the
encouragement of domestic manufactures; but an excise on foreign goods
must operate as a bounty." "I have said that an excise is more favorable to
the poor than a land or poll tax. I will venture an additional sentiment:
there never was a government in which an excise could be of so much
use as in the United States of America. In all other countries, taxes are
considered as grievances. In the United States, an excise on foreign goods
would not be a grievance: like medicine to a sick man, it would give us
strength; it would close that wasteful drain by which our honor and our
wealth are consumed. What, though money was not wanted—though we
did not owe a florin to any foreign nation—though we had no domestic debt—and though the expenses of civil government could be supported for many years without a tax, still it may be questioned whether
an excise would not be desirable. It would certainly be the best expedient for promoting domestic manufactures; and the condition in which
we now live, our general dependence on a foreign country for arms and
clothing, is dishonorable—it is extremely dangerous."
    "It is the duty of the statesman either to check or to promote the sev-
eral streams of commerce by taxes or bounties, so as to render them profitable to the nation. Thus it happened in Massachusetts. A tax of twenty-five
per cent. was lately imposed on nails, and the poor of Taunton were immediately returned to life and vigor."
    "If any man has doubts concerning the effect of large taxes on foreign
manufactures, he should turn his eyes to the Eastern States. The mechanic
is generally the first who perceives the effects of a pernicious commerce;
for the support of his family depends on his daily labor." "Hence it is

that the merchant may be profited by a particular branch of commerce, and may promote it diligently, while his country is sinking into a deadly consumption."

You have heard the early and the mature good sense of North Carolina. Listen to a sentence or two from an essay, "on the advantages of trade and commerce," written at *Charleston* in South Carolina, in 1786, and consider what inferences it suggests upon the general subject of the public opinion of that eventful day. It is signed "*American,*" and breathes the very spirit of commercial, political, and industrial union; of union for defence against the arts as well as the arms of the world. "There are but two ways to national wealth," (he begins,) "conquest and the encouraging of agriculture, manufactures, and commerce." This he illustrates historically. England at first was poor; "but as soon as the spirit of manufacturing raised its head, *and commerce was regulated by good laws,*" (is it not palpable that he means the protecting tariff, behind which that intellectual industry has so splendidly developed itself?) "they rose superior to every obstacle." ("American Museum," second volume, pages 328 and 329).

"It is in vain" (he continues, page 330) "for any people to attempt to be rich, or have a sufficient circulating specie among them, whose imports exceed their exports; the hand of the manufacturer in a distant land seems to act upon gold and silver as the loadstone does on the needle."

Again, after adverting to a revenue of three millions and a half raised by England, and by monopolizing our trade, he proceeds (page 331):—

"A great part of this may be saved to these States by our becoming our own merchants and carriers; and a great part of the remaining sum may be saved in a few years by *encouraging* our own manufactors; and even this encouragement will be of service to our revenues—I mean laying a duty on our imports, and giving a small part in bounties to our own tradesmen."

By tradesmen he means mechanics. And to the suggestion to turn planters into manufacturers, he answers:—

"I by no means wish it. I only wish to encourage European tradesmen to come to reside here. I wish to see as much as possible exported, and as little imported. The planters that buy the manufactures of America stop so much money in this country, which must return again to the planters' hands as long as traders eat."

Duties of encouragement, let me observe in passing, he calls "restrictions on the British trade."

I must hurry away from the accumulations of proof before me, which bear on the general subject; the formation of associations to encourage manufactures, the resolutions of the patriotic society of Richmond, of the ladies of Halifax in North Carolina, and of Hartford in Connecticut, and of the legislature and executive of Massachusetts to effect this by individual and organized exertion, and all the other indications which break from the universal press of that stirring and anxious time, and which show you with how true an instinct the genius of America was turning itself to take hold on the golden key that opens the palace of national wealth and greatness; I must hurry from these to call your attention to some others more immediately applicable to the proposition which I am maintaining. Look, then, for a moment, into an address by a "Jerseyman," in November, 1787, to the citizens of New Jersey, on the new Constitution. Hear him, one of the people, appealing to the people with the open book in his hand, speaking the language of the people,—hear him on the clause which you are attempting to interpret:—

"The great advantages," ("Amer. Mus.," second volume, page 437,) "which would be the result of the adoption of the proposed Constitution, are almost innumerable. I will mention a few among the many. In the first place, the proper regulation of our commerce would be insured,—the imposts on all foreign merchandise imported into America would still effectually aid our continental treasury. This power has been heretofore held back by some States on narrow and mistaken principles. The amount of the duties since the peace would probably, by this time, have nearly paid our national debt. *By the proper regulation of our commerce* our own manufactures would be also much promoted and encouraged. Heavy duties would discourage the consumption of articles of foreign growth. This would induce us more to work up our raw materials, and prevent European manufacturers from dragging them from us, in order to bestow upon them their own labor and a high price before they are returned into our hands."

Just then, too, a Pennsylvania patriot, under the signature of "One of the People," was making a similar appeal to the intelligence of that great State on behalf of the new Constitution. And how does he interpret this grant of power?

"The people of Pennsylvania, in general, are composed of men of three occupations,—the farmer, the merchant, the mechanic. The interests of these three are intimately blended together. A government, then, which will be conducive to their happiness, and best promote their interest, is the government which these people should adopt. The Constitution now presented to them is such a one. Every person must long since have discovered the necessity of placing the exclusive power of regulating the commerce of America in the same body; without this it is impossible to regulate their trade. The same imposts, duties, and customs, must equally prevail over the whole, for no one State can carry into effect its impost laws. A neighboring State could always prevent it. *No State could effectually encourage its manufactories*—there can be no navigation act. Whence comes it that the trade of this State, which abounds with materials for ship-building, is carried on in foreign bottoms? Whence comes it that shoes, boots, made-up clothes, hats, nails, sheet-iron, hinges, and all other utensils of iron, are of British manufacture? Whence comes it that Spain can regulate our flour market? These evils proceed from a want of one supreme controlling power in these States. They will be all done away by adopting the present form of government. It will have energy and power *to regulate your trade and commerce*—to enforce the execution of your imposts, duties, and customs. Instead of the trade of this country being carried on in foreign bottoms, our ports will be crowded with our own ships, and we shall become the carriers of Europe. *Heavy duties will be laid on all foreign articles which can be manufactured in this country,* and bounties will be granted on the exportation of our commodities; *the manufactories of our country will flourish;* our mechanics will lift up their heads, and rise to opulence and wealth."

And a little after this, in July, 1788, I find a "Bostonian" (Am. Mus., 4th vol., 331st page) advising duties on English importations, under the name of regulations and restrictions of trade for the encouragement of our own manufactures.

"The ill policy of our *commercial arrangements* has served to impoverish us in our finances, by the enormous remittances of our currency, occasioned an almost general bankruptcy, and has had the pernicious tendency to discourage our enterprise in manufactures, and ruined many of those branches which, during the war, had arisen to a flourishing state." "Our trade with that nation has been the principal source of all our misfortunes. It has thrown a number of our best estates into the hands of

British merchants, has occasioned a most rapid decrease of our medium, has ruined our manufactures, and will, if pursued, sap the foundation of the best government that ever can be established in America. The first object, therefore, of the federal government must be to restrain our connection with Great Britain, unless on terms of reciprocity. While they continue their duties and prohibitions, *we must lay similar restrictions and embarrassments on their trade, and prevent, by excessive duties, the redundance of their manufactures.*"

Some time in the year 1783 or 1784, there were published in a Virginia newspaper, "Reflections on the policy and necessity of encouraging the commerce of the citizens of the United States," by St. George Tucker, of Petersburg. They are written with great vigor, good sense, and a true national spirit, and present a powerful argument for a discrimination in favor of American tonnage. Towards the close of the essay, (page 274, of the 2d vol. of the Am. Mus.,) he adverts to another subject, in the following terms:—

"Before I conclude, let me call the attention of my reader for a moment to the debt due from America to the subjects of Great Britain, which I have heard estimated at four or five millions of pounds. This debt was accumulated from a balance in trade annually accruing to Great Britain from the causes hereinbefore pointed out. That trade must be destructive where such a balance continually arises against us. Surely it is proper to guard against such an event in future. This might be effected, in part, perhaps, by laying heavy duties, if not actual prohibitions, on the importation of such articles as are the produce of the United States. Is it not surprising, for example, that bar-iron, lead, saltpetre, leather, train-oil, tallow, candles, soap, malt-liquors, butter, beef, pork, and potatoes, should constitute a part of the annual imports from Europe to America?"

Did not this writer understand that legislation, for the purpose of turning the balance of trade in our favor, was a "regulation of trade"? and is not the protecting tariff which he recommends exactly an instance of such legislation?

I spare you, Sir, the infliction of more of these superfluous proofs. And yet the nature of the fact to be proved—that a whole people, a whole generation of our fathers, had in view, as one grand end and purpose of their new government, the acquisition of the means of restraining, by governmental action, the importation of foreign manufactures, for the encouragement of manufactures and of all labor at home, and desired and meant to do this by clothing the new government with this specific power of regulating commerce—required and justified a pretty wide collection and display of their opinions, sufferings, expectations, and vocabulary, from sources the most numerous and the most scattered.

And now, from the bosom of the people holding these opinions, oppressed by these incommodities, nourishing these hopes, determined on this relief, and speaking this language, arose the Constitution,—immortal, unchangeable! In fulfilment of these hopes, it embodied the great governmental instrumentality which had been determined on, in the exact language which more than twenty years had made familiar. I say, then, sir, that when the country called the convention together which formed the Constitution, it was the *general design* to confer the protecting power upon the new government; that the governmental power to regulate trade was generally understood to embrace the protecting power; and it was inserted in the Constitution exactly because that was its meaning.

Before proceeding further in the accumulation of evidence, *ab extra,* of the meaning and objects of this power to regulate commerce, let me pause to attend to some of the reasoning by which the proposition which I maintain has been encountered.

I do not think, then, Sir, that anybody will deny that, in the commercial, political, and general vocabulary of 1787, and of all the period back to 1764, a discriminating tariff, a tariff discriminating for the protection of domestic industry, was universally called a commercial regulation. Everybody will agree that, if at that time it had been written or spoken that England, the States, or any other government upon earth, had the power to make a commercial regulation or to regulate commerce, it would have been universally understood (such was the settled form of speech) to include the power to make a strict protecting tariff, and that such a tariff would have been one of the most ordinary and most familiar acts in exercise of such power of regulation. But then it will be said that it does not follow that the same language means, in this Constitution, when applied to and asserted of this government, what it meant everywhere else, when applied to or asserted of any other government in the world. England, the States, under the power to regulate commerce, could make a strict and technical protecting tariff: Congress, under the same power, or rather under the same exact form of expression, the same enunciation *in terms* of power, can do no such thing.

Sir, he who asserts this has the burden of proof heavily upon him. Independently altogether of the evidence which I have already presented, to show that the country looked directly to this power of regulating commerce as the precise power under and by which the new government was to tax or prohibit imports for the encouragement of manufactures; independently of that, when you admit, as you must, that, for more than twenty years before the Constitution was formed, this language was universally current in the Colonies and States; that it had acquired, by force of circumstances, an unusually precise, definite, and well-understood sense; that it had all that time been employed to designate or to include a certain known governmental function; that when applied to England, the States, and all other governments, it had, in the understanding of everybody, embraced a certain species and exercise of power for a certain purpose;—when you admit this, and then find it here in the Constitution of this government, employed to confer a power on it, must you not admit that the presumption is, that it is used in the sense which everybody had understood it so long to bear, when applied to other governments,—neither larger nor narrower; that it means to include the same well-known function, and not to exclude it; that it means to communicate the same extent and the same purpose of power, and not less,—the same in quantity, the same in object?

How is this conclusion evaded? I have heard it attempted thus: The powers given by the Constitution to this government are given *in trust,* to accomplish the specific and few *objects of the Constitution.* The promotion of manufactures is not one of the objects of the Constitution; the promotion of commerce is. The power to regulate commerce, therefore, is given in trust, for the accommodation and promotion of commerce, technically and strictly so called. This, for substance, is the argument of a very able writer in the "Southern Review" of August, 1830.

Now, Sir, waiving for a moment the direct proof *aliunde* which I have produced, and shall produce, to show the exact meaning of this grant of the power of commercial regulation, I answer, that it is true that the powers of the Constitution are given in trust for its objects; that the powers are given in trust for the objects of those powers. But then arises the question, what are the objects of this particular power? What are the purposes which it was inserted in the Constitution to accomplish? You beg the whole proposition in dispute, when you assert that it is no part of the objects of the Constitution to develop the productive capacities of the country, by protecting it from an unpropitious and deleterious foreign commerce, and securing it a beneficial one. The precise question is, if this is not in part the object of this very power? It strikes me, Sir, that our opponents on this general question assume, that because commerce is the subject on which the constitutional regulations are to operate, therefore the end and purpose for which these regulations must be made, is the direct and immediate advancement or enlargement of commerce itself, without regard to its qualities or its adverse or propitious influence on the nation by which or with which it is carried on. What else they mean when they say that this power is given with a view to "commerce as an end," I confess I do not know; but surely this is pure assumption, and will not bear a moment's examination. In the first place, they forget that the unlimited terms of the constitutional grant, explained and defined by the historical deduction which I have exhibited, authorize the making of some such regulations as conclusively demonstrate that the object and purpose of the grant is not solely and directly the enlargement of commerce as an end, without regard to the question, what are its imports, or what its exports, or what its influence on the interior labors and prosperity of the country; but rather the *promotion of national prosperity by means of a judiciously regulated commercial intercourse.* The grant is of power to regulate commerce. The grant is general; it is exclusive as well as general. It is a power to prescribe rules by which commerce shall be conducted; it is a power to make commercial regulations. Unless, then, the extent of this grant is limited by other clauses of the Constitution, or by other evidence of an intent to limit it; unless, in some such way, it be shown that there are some commercial regulations which the Constitution did not mean to authorize you to make, taking the grant by itself, and construing it by the law of grant, it communicates power to make all commercial regulations. It is not a power to make some, but all. It is not a power to do some of the things, to pass some of the laws, which are acts in exercise of a general power to regulate commerce, but to do them all. It extends to all, or it reaches not one. Well, among them, among the most common and best known regulations of commerce, the most common and best known acts in exercise of a power to regulate commerce, as we have seen, was a discriminating and protecting tariff; a law moulding commercial intercourse in such manner as to invite to the development of domestic labor. The grant, then, communicates a power to make such a regulation among others. It stands precisely as if the constitutional language had been, congress shall have power to prescribe rules for the regulations of commerce, and among them protecting tariffs. The analysis of the whole complete aggregate of things authorized, reveals this act as one of them. We take, then, by the legal necessary construction of the grant, the power to make a protecting tariff; and the nature of the power itself involves and discloses the object of the power, to wit, protection. The nature of the operation authorized to be performed *on* commerce, evinces that there is an end and purpose in the contemplation of the Constitution *beyond* commerce itself as an end; and that is the national prosperity.

But, in the next place, these reasoners seem to forget that commerce is, from its nature, and was regarded by the people of this country, at the time of the adoption of the Constitution, and by all governments, and all people then or ever in the world, a mere vast *means* of prosperity, or of decay, to a nation by whom or with whom it is carried on; and therefore that the Constitution, when it clothed you with the general power of regulating it, intended that you should do so with a view to the attainment of those ends, of which, in its nature, and in the opinions of nations, it is capable of being made the instrument. The framers of the Constitution meant to clothe you with the power of disarming it of all the evil and extracting from it all the good to which the wisdom of government is equal. They could not have intended to do anything so absurd as simply to authorize and require you to promote, enlarge, or advance commerce, *per se,* and in the abstract, without regard to its quality; to its adverse or its propitious influence upon the prosperity, the morality, the health, and the industry of the people; to the goods it brought home; to the goods it carried away; the national character of the tonnage it employed, and of the labor it rewarded. They did not look to commerce, but to *beneficial commerce.* They saw the distinction perfectly. They regarded it, as did the country universally, and as all nations in all ages have done, as an agent of large and varied influence, sometimes of good and sometimes of evil, according to its nature, and according to the regulations under which it was conducted. They knew, or they believed, that in one form, under one system of regulations, it might strengthen, adorn, and enrich a State; might seat it on the throne of the sea; might raise its merchants to be princes, yet not impoverish and not depress its mechanics and its farmers; might stimulate the thousand hands of its labor by multiplying its occupations, enhancing its rewards, relieving it from oppressive competitions with the redundant capital, matured skill, and pauperism of older nations; might swell its exports with the products of its own skill; might turn in on it the golden stream of the metals, and make it the workshop, as well as the warehouse, of the world: while, in another form, and under another system of regulations, it might impoverish and enfeeble it; drain it of its specie; overstock its agriculture, yet deprive it of a market; plunge it beneath an insupportable foreign debt; and restrain the division of its labor and the development of its genius. This is the exact view taken of commerce, by the whole American press, from 1783 to 1787.

Commerce, then, in its nature, and the understanding of all, is a means. When, therefore, the general power of regulating it is given to the national government, according to what principles, for the accomplishment of what objects, are you to exert it? Are you not to do it for those ends, and for all of them, which, by the general theory and practice of governments, it is adapted to attain? And is not the relief of domestic labor, from the oppressive competitions of an unrestrained foreign trade, among these ends?

Well, now, Sir, to answer this reasoning, it must be shown, by inspection of other parts of the Constitution, by an analysis of its general structure, or by evidence *ab extra,* that this grant of power is not so broad. It must be shown, in some such way, that there were some well-known and important commercial regulations, some acts familiarly and notoriously done by all governments, in exercise of the power to regulate, which were not intended to be granted by the terms of this most comprehensive and most unlimited grant. It must be shown, in some such way, that this pretty important exception ought to be engrafted on the grant: the congress shall have power to regulate trade with foreign nations, provided, however, *that it shall aim at nothing but free trade;* that it shall have no power to make any, or no power to make all those commercial regulations by which other governments always endeavored, and the United States of America, since the Revolution, have endeavored, to increase their own tonnage; to make their exports exceed their imports, to avoid a drain of their specie; to preserve a favorable balance of trade; and to draw forth their own capacities of labor and of wealth, and their own means of independence. But can you thus qualify the unalterable and the unlimited terms of the Constitution? How do you do it? You say you reason from other parts, and from the general structure of the instrument; and that no other part of it displays any solicitude for the encouragement of domestic industry, nor does anything to enable you to promote it. But what is that argument worth, even if the fact were so? Does it abridge the clear and broad terms of this particular grant? Because the Constitution clothes you with no other means of developing the industrial capacities of the country than a discreet, wise, and customary commercial system, do you infer, against its positive terms, that it could not have intended to give you even that means? Might it not give you that, and yet give you no other? Might it not go so far, and no farther? Might it not clothe you with that large and imperial power, without going on to authorize you to prescribe the forms of apprentice' indentures, and determine how many hours in a day the operatives in a woollen-mill shall be held to labor? From the nature of the case, is not the selection of powers to be conferred on the general government, from the whole field of sovereign power, in some measure arbitrary,—arbitrary in what is given, arbitrary in what is left? The line must be drawn somewhere. How it is drawn, in fact, is a matter of pure interpretation. You cannot put your finger upon a granted power, and say, If the framers of the Constitution meant to give this, logical and political consistency would have led them to give another; but that they have not given, and therefore they have not given this. Such reasoning substitutes the fancies of sophists for the text of the Constitution, and turns the guide of life into foolishness and a stumbling-block.

And what is there in the general structure of the Constitution, what is there in the nature of the government established by it, which renders it so improbable that the power of regulating commerce, for the development of native capacity and industry, should be given to it, that you must abridge, by supposition, an apparently express grant of that very power? I say, Sir, that the Constitution, in conferring this power on this government, has been true to itself; it has acted like itself; it has acted in conformity with its peculiar structure, and its grand aims. What is the power, after all? Nothing more and nothing less than a means of defending American industry against foreign instruments of annoyance. Foreign governments, or foreign subjects, pour in upon us importations of articles which make us poor, or make us idle, or make us diseased, or make us vicious. No government that ever stood one hundred years on the earth but had the power of defending itself against aggression so deleterious, although in form pacific. To which of the governments in our system, the State or the National, should the power belong? Reasoning on the nature of our system, and *a priori,* which should possess it? Should it not be that which possesses the treaty-making power, the war- and peace-making power, the power of regulating all foreign intercourse? Should the States retain it? Was not the Constitution framed in great measure, because they were totally unequal to its effective administration?

In a still larger view, Sir, of the offices and the powers of the national government, under the Constitution, you ought to have this power of protecting the labor of your country. The means, the ends, the principles of determination, pertain appropriately to the imperial and grand trust with which you are clothed. The means is the regulation of foreign intercourse, which all belongs to you. The ends are the independence and the happiness of America. The principles of determination are the most interesting phenomena of the social and political world, the truths of the first of practical sciences, the loftiest and most comprehensive sentiments and aspirations of statesmanship and patriotism. What is it that you do when you exercise this power? Why, Sir, you determine by what system of foreign intercourse our vast capacities of growth and wealth may best be developed; the unsightly but precious elemental material that sleeps beneath our soil be transfigured into forms of beauty and use; the children of labor in all their fields be trained through labor to competence, comfort, and consideration; "our agriculture be made to grow, and our commerce to expand;" the golden chain of union be strengthened; our vast destinies unfolded and fulfilled. This is what you do.

And I say the means you work by, the ends you aim at, and the policy you proceed on, are just such as such a system as ours should commit to you.

But, Sir, to advance from these less certain reasonings to indisputable facts, which, indeed, I have partially anticipated. I hold it to be susceptible of as rigorous moral demonstration as any truth of history, first, that, before the Constitution was presented to them, the people of this country, generally, demanded a government which should have power to mould their whole foreign intercourse into the most beneficial form, and, among other things, should have power to mould it into such form as might bring out American labor, agricultural, mechanical, manufacturing, navigating, and commercial, into its completest development, and for that end to make discriminating tariffs; secondly, that when, at length, the doors of the convention were thrown open, and the Constitution, the object of so many hopes, of so much solicitude, was presented to their eager view, they believed that they found in it just the power they had looked for so long, and they adopted it in that confidence; thirdly, that every member of the convention itself supposed it to contain the power; and fourthly, that the new government, from its first organization, proceeded to execute it vigorously and usefully by a broad policy of protection openly avowed,— protection of agriculture, protection of navigation, protection of manufactures; and that, although particular exertions of the policy were vehemently resisted on grounds of expediency, and although other national legislation was denied to be authorized by the Constitution, the power to push this policy to the utmost limit of congressional discretion was never called in question for more than thirty, or certainly more than twenty years.

Sir, if this be so, and yet the Constitution contains no such power, vain is the search after moral truth; idle the attempt to embody the ideas of a people in the frame of their government, and in the language of their fundamental law. You were as wisely employed in writing them upon the clouds of the summer-evening western sky, in the dream of seeing them carried round the world in the train of the next day's sun.

Well, is it not so? I have shown you already that the country demanded, and expected beforehand, a government which should possess this power; that it had done so for years; that the events of every hour, from the peace to the rising of the convention, only increased the urgency of the demand, and the confidence of the expectation. I proceed to show, in the next place, that when at last the Constitution was given to the longing sight of the people, and they threw themselves upon it as a famished host upon miraculous bread, their faculties sharpened and prepared by so many years of discussions, and by the more instructive discipline of suffering, stimulated to read by hope and fear and jealousy and curiosity, then they thought they found in it this power. There it was, in the very language familiar to them from childhood; language associated, fast and imperishably, with the story of the long wrongs of England, the resistance of America, the great names of heroes and wise men, the living and the dead, with liberty and with glory.

See if the fact is not so, and then see how resistless it is as *evidence* that the power really was there. Look into the press of that day,—that day when men were great, and events were great,—look into the newspaper press, and tell me if you find, anywhere, a whisper of complaint of any deficiency *of power in this regard in the new Constitution.* You have heard, in the selections I have read, something of what the people *expected;* do you find, by looking farther into the same source of evidence, that they were *disappointed* in their expectations? Fears there were, sickly fears, patriotic fears, and loudly uttered, that the Constitution was too strong,— too strong for liberty. But who said that, in its protecting energy, it was too weak? Who complained that he did not find it clothed with the whole power of defense against other nations,—defence against their arms, their policy, their pernicious trade, their extorted and pauper labor? I can only say that I have found no trace of such an objection.

But see the affirmative evidence of a general belief that the Constitution did contain the power. Look at the long processions of the trades, where the whole mechanical and manufacturing industry of the country assembled to celebrate, as a jubilee, the establishment of a government by which their interests might at length hope to be cherished. Is it not as if the universal heart of the people was throbbing with the sudden acquisition of a second and a real independence? Hear the debates in the conventions of the States, deliberating upon the Constitution. In that of Massachusetts, one of its advocates, urging the importance of making the entire grant of power to congress which it contemplated, said:—

> "Our manufactures are another great subject which has received no encouragement by national duties on foreign manufactures, and they never can by any authority in the old confederation. Besides this, the very face of our country leads to manufactures; our numerous falls of water, and places for mills, where paper, snuff, gunpowder, iron-works, and numerous other articles are prepared,—these will save us immense sums of money that would otherwise go to Europe. *The question is,* have these been encouraged? Has congress *been able,* by national laws, to prevent the importation of such foreign commodities as are made from such *raw materials* as

we ourselves raise? It is alleged that the citizens of the United States have contracted debts within the last three years, with the subjects of Great Britain, for the amount of near six millions of dollars, and that consequently our lands are mortgaged for that sum. So Corsica was once mortgaged to the Genoese merchants for articles which her inhabitants did not want, or which they could have made themselves; and she was afterwards sold to a foreign power. If we wish to encourage our own manufactures, to preserve our own commerce, to raise the value of our lands, we must give congress the powers in question."—*Elliot's Debates,* vol. i., page 76.

And again:—

"Our agriculture has not been encouraged by the imposition of material duties on *rival* produce, nor can it be, so long as the several States may make contradictory laws."—Page 74.

And an opponent, Mr. Widgery, was annoyed by so much earnest repetition and enforcement of this very topic in favor of the new government. It is perfectly plain that he felt it to be the effective and decisive consideration by which the masses were moved. "All we hear is," he says, "that the merchant and farmer will flourish, and the mechanic and tradesman make their fortunes directly."

The debates of other States the most interested in this species of industry are imperfectly preserved; but nowhere, as Mr. Madison has well said, do you find a particle of evidence that a doubt on the power was entertained. "The general objects of the Union," said Mr. Davie, in the Convention of North Carolina, "are, 1st, to protect us against foreign invasion; 2d, to defend us against internal commotions and insurrections; 3d, to promote the commerce, agriculture, and manufactures of America."—*Elliot's Debates,* vol. iii. p. 31.

Read the memorials in which the mechanics and manufacturers of the large towns, immediately upon the organization of congress, invoked an exertion of this power; and see how confidently its existence is assumed, and its prompt and beneficial exercise relied on. Familiar as they are to you, familiar to everybody who has examined this question at all, they embody in such vivid and comprehensive expression the grand, popular want and conviction in which the Constitution had its birth, and its instantaneous and universal interpretation, that I venture to call your attention again to passages from three of them. They were all presented during the pending of the first revenue and protecting law of congress, and they contributed, I have no doubt, to determine its policy and to shape its details. Hear the "tradesmen and mechanics of Baltimore."

"Setting forth" (I use the condensed summary of the reporter) "that, since the close of the late war and the completion of the Revolution, they have observed with serious regret the manufacturing and the trading interest of the country rapidly declining, and the attempts of the State legislatures to remedy the evil failing of their object; that, in the present melancholy state of our country, the number of poor increasing for want of employment, foreign debts accumulating, houses and land depreciating in value, and trade and manufactures languishing and expiring, they look up to the supreme legislature of the United States as the guardians of the whole empire, and from their united wisdom and patriotism and ardent love of their country, expect to derive that aid and assistance which alone can dissipate their just apprehensions, and animate them with hopes of success in future, by imposing on all foreign articles which can be made in America, such duties as will give a just and decided preference to their labors, discountenancing that trade which tends so materially to injure them and impoverish their country, measures which, in their consequences, may also contribute to the discharge of the national debt and the due support of government; that they have annexed a list of such articles as are or can be manufactured amongst them, and humbly trust in the wisdom of the legislature to grant them, in common with the other mechanics and manufacturers of the United States, that relief which may appear proper."

This was followed in a week by another, of the "mechanics and manufacturers of the city of New York," which, having recited that their prospects of improving wealth had been blasted after the peace by a system of commercial usurpation; that trade had been loaded with foreign fetters; enterprise and industry discouraged; the development of the vast natural resources of the country restrained; agriculture without stimulus; and manufactures, the sister of commerce, participating in its distresses; that a profusion of foreign articles had deluged the country, presenting a delusive appearance of plenty, and deceiving the people into the mistake that excessive and deleterious importation was a flourishing trade, proceeds:—

"Wearied by their fruitless exertions, your petitioners have long looked forward with anxiety for the establishment of a government

which would have power to check the growing evil, and extend a protecting hand to the interests of commerce and the arts. *Such a government
is now established.* On the promulgation of the Constitution just now
commencing its operations, your petitioners discovered in its principles
the remedy which they had so long and so earnestly desired. To your
honorable body the mechanics and manufacturers of New York look up
with confidence, convinced that, as the united voice of America has furnished you with the means, so your knowledge of our common wants
has given you the spirit, to unbind our fetters and rescue our country
from disgrace and ruin."

Then came in the "tradesmen and manufacturers of the town of Boston,"
who say,—

"That on the revival of their mechanical arts and manufactures, now
ruinously depressed, depend the wealth and prosperity of the Northern
States; and that the citizens of these States conceive the object of their
independence but half obtained, till these national purposes are established on a permanent and extensive basis by the legislation of the federal
government."

And who in that assembly of men—many of whom sat in the convention
which framed the Constitution, all of whom had partaken in the discussions
which preceded its adoption—breathed a doubt on the competence of congress
to receive such petitions as these, and to grant their prayer? "I conceive," (said
the most eloquent of the eloquent, Mr. Ames)—"I conceive, Sir, that the present Constitution was dictated by commercial necessity more than any other
cause. The want of an efficient government to secure the manufacturing interest, and to advance our commerce, was long seen by men of judgment, and
pointed out by patriots solicitous to promote our general welfare." But I have
more to say, before I have done, on the proceedings of that congress, and leave
them for the present; in the mean time I submit to you that the proof is complete, that the people who adopted the Constitution universally, and without a
doubt, believed that it embodied this power. It was for that they received it with
one wide acclaim, with tears of exultation, with ceremonies of auspicious significance, befitting the dawn of our age of pacific and industrial glory. Even those
who feared its imperial character and its other powers, who thought they saw the
States attracted to its centre and absorbed by its rays, did not fear this power.

And now, Sir, I wonder if, after all, the people were deluded into this belief! I wonder if that heroic and energetic generation of our fathers, which had studied the controversies and had gone through the tasks of the Revolution; which had framed the Confederation, proved its weakness, proved its defects; which had been trained by a long and dreary experience of the insufficiency of a nominal independence to build up a diffused and massive and national prosperity, if the trade laws of foreign governments, the combinations of foreign capitalists, the necessities of foreign existence, are allowed to take from the native laborer his meal of meat, and from his children their school, and depress his standard of comfortable life; which had been trained by experience, by the discussions of its ablest minds, in an age of extraordinary mental activity, and yet of great morality, sobriety, and subordination, peculiarly favorable to the task, trained thus to the work of constructing a new government,—I wonder if such a generation were deceived, after all! I wonder if it was not living water, that which they supposed they saw gushing from the rock, and sparkling and swelling at their feet, but only a delusive imitation, struck out by the wand of an accursed enchantment! No, Sir; no man who believes that the people of this country were fit to govern themselves, fit to frame a Constitution, fit to judge on it, fit to administer it,—no such man can say that the belief, the popular belief in 1789, of the existence of this power, under all the circumstances, is not absolutely conclusive proof of its existence.

And then, in addition to this, how do you deal with the fact that all the framers of the Constitution themselves, as well as every public man alive in 1789, and the entire intelligence of the country, supposed they had inserted this power in it?

Did not those who made it know what they had done? Considering their eminent general character; their civil discretion, their preparation of much study, and yet more experience of arduous public affairs, for the task; their thorough acquaintance with the existing systems, State and national, and with the public mind and opinions of the day; the long, patient, and solitary labor which they bestowed on it; the immediate necessity imposed on them of explaining and defending it to the country—in view of this, if you find them unanimously concurring in ascribing this power to the instrument, is it not the transcendentalism of unbelief to doubt? Do we really think we are likely to understand their own work now, better than they did the day they finished it?

Well, Sir, you have satisfactory evidence that the members of the convention went, all of them, to their graves in the belief that the Constitution contained this power. Mr. Madison's opinion I have read. We have it on unquestionable authority that Mr. Gallatin has repeatedly said that, upon his entrance into political life in 1789, he found it to be the universal opinion of those who framed the Constitution and those who resisted its adoption, the opinion of all the statesmen of the day, that congress possessed the power to protect domestic industry by means of commercial regulations. Stronger proof to this point, indeed, you cannot desire than is afforded by the history of the first revenue and protection law of the federal government. Let me recall that history a little in detail. Considering how many members of that congress had sat in the convention; that all the members of the convention were still alive, and still observers of what was passing on the public stage; how anxiously the whole people, now divided into two great and already excited parties, and the several local regions of the country, developing already the antagonism of their policy, were looking on—in this view, the express affirmation by some, and the tacit universal concession by others, of this power, in every stage of the protracted and anxious debate which resulted in that law, ought to be conclusive on the question of its existence with every sound mind. But observe its history.

It was Mr. Madison who, on the ninth of April, introduced the subject of providing a revenue by imposts. And it is very material to remark that his original purpose was to pass a strict and temporary revenue law, and to pass it immediately, in order, as he said, to intercept the importations of the spring. Accordingly he took, as the basis of his measure, the propositions of the congress of the Confederation, of 1783. Those propositions imposed a general and uniform ad valorem duty on the whole mass of imported articles, except spirituous liquors, wines, sugars, teas, molasses, cocoa, and coffee, which were charged with higher and specific duties. This old scheme of imposts Mr. Madison proposed to adopt as the basis of the new law, engrafting on it only a tonnage duty discriminating in favor of American vessels. His purpose, therefore, you perceive, as I have said, was *revenue* purely, and not *a commercial regulation for protection.* Not one of the articles on which the specific and higher duties would have been laid, and were laid, under this old model scheme, were produced in the United States, except rum. The discrimination was for revenue, and the whole measure was for revenue. Indeed, Mr. Madison said, on introducing it, in so many words,—

> "In pursuing this measure, I know that two points occur for our consideration. The first respects the general regulation of commerce, which, in my opinion, ought to be as free as the policy of the nations will admit. The second relates to revenue alone; and this is the point I mean more particularly to bring into the view of the committee. Not being at pres-

ent possessed of sufficient materials for fully elucidating these points, and our situation admitting of no delay, I shall propose such articles of regulations only as are likely to occasion the least difficulty. The propositions made on this subject by congress in 1783, having received, generally, the approbation of the several States of the Union, in some form or other, seem well calculated to become the basis of the temporary system which I wish the committee to adopt I am well aware that the changes which have taken place in many of the States, and in our public circumstances, since that period, will require, in some degree, a deviation from the scale of duties then affixed; nevertheless, for the sake of that expedition which is necessary in order to embrace the spring importations, I should recommend a general adherence to the plan."

And later in the debate he said,—

"It was my view to restrain the first essay on this subject principally to the object of revenue, and make this rather a temporary expedient than anything permanent."—*Gales & Seaton's Debates, old series,* vol. i. pp. 107, 115.

But what followed? The next day, Mr. Fitzsimons, of Pennsylvania, presented a suggestion which resulted in a total departure from Mr. Madison's plan, *and in the substitution for a pure and temporary revenue law of a permanent law,* which was at once and avowedly a *measure of revenue* and a *commercial regulation for the encouragement and protection of American agriculture, navigation, and manufactures;* at once an exercise of the power of taxing imports and the power to regulate trade; at once, in the terms of its own preamble, an act "for the support of government, the debt of the United States, and the encouragement and protection of manufactures." He began by saying,—

"I observe, Mr. Chairman, by what the gentlemen have said, who have spoken on the subject before you, that the proposed plan of revenue is viewed by them as a temporary system, to be continued only till proper materials are brought forward and arranged in more perfect form. I confess, Sir, that I carry my views on this subject much further; that I earnestly wish one which, in its operation, will be some way adequate to our present situation, as *it respects our agriculture, our manufactures, and our commerce;*"—

and concluded with a motion, that there be added to the few articles which Mr. Madison had proposed to subject to specific duties, and duties above the general average, *more than fifty others,* which should be also specifically and more highly taxed. Forty-five of these were of the class of articles produced or manufactured in the United States; they were articles coming in competition with almost the entire circle of American manufacturing and agricultural labor; and they were subsequently so increased as to surround that whole circle with a protecting tariff.

This proposition of Mr. Fitzsimons was made for the purpose of uniting the objects of protection and revenue. He avowed this to be his object. "Among the articles," said he, in introducing his motion, (page 111,) "which I would have specifically taxed, are *some* calculated to encourage the productions of our country, and protect our infant manufactures; besides others tending to operate as sumptuary restrictions upon articles which are often termed those of luxury." So he was understood by everybody. Mr. White, of Virginia, who followed him next in the debate, in opposition to his amendment, suggested that its consideration would consume too much time; "for," said he, (page 112,) "in order to charge specific articles of manufacture, so as to encourage our domestic ones, it will be necessary to examine the present state of each throughout the Union." Mr. Tucker, of South Carolina, following him in opposition, "considered the subject of very great importance, as it related to our agriculture, manufactures, and commerce," but advised a temporary, immediate arrangement. Upon this, Mr. Hartley, of Pennsylvania, submitted a brief, but very clear and very sound argument, directly in favor of the policy of protection. He differed from those who preferred a "limited and partial" measure "relating to revenue alone," and advised to place the whole "on as broad a bottom as at that time was practicable." He thought the argument of Mr. Tucker ought not to "discourage the committee from taking such measures as would tend to protect and promote our domestic manufactures." "The old world," he proceeded, "had long pursued the practice of giving great encouragement to the establishment of manufactures, by such partial duties on foreign imports as to give the home manufactures a considerable advantage in the price in market; and it was both politic and just that the general government should do the same thing. Our manufactures had arrived at that stage of advancement, that, according to the policy of every enlightened nation, they ought to receive the encouragement necessary to perfect them without oppressing the other parts of the community." In this posture of the debate, Mr. Madison again rose, and, in a speech of considerable elaborateness, declared, at length, that he thought Mr. Fitzsimons's proposition ought to be entertained.

"Upon the whole," he said, concluding his observations, "as I think some of the propositions may be productive of revenue, and some may protect our domestic manufactures, though the latter subject ought not to be too confusedly blended with the former, I hope the committee will receive them, and let them lie over, in order that we may have time to consider how far they are consistent with justice and policy."

The motion of Mr. Fitzsimons was thereupon immediately adopted; the bill was transformed into a measure of blended revenue and protection; other articles were subsequently added to the class of articles specifically taxed, or taxed by discrimination above the general ad valorem; the rates of duties were arranged; and, after a discussion of extraordinary interest, ability, excitement, and importance, running through three months, the first congress of the new Constitution—at its first session, its very first measure of general legislation, its first measure of any kind after having declared by law in what manner its members should swear to support the Constitution—passed an act to raise revenue; and also to fulfil to the whole, vast, young, and anxious family of American labor; to the agriculture of the South and West; to the fisheries and the navigation of the East; to the mechanical trades of the cities; to the manufacturing industry of the central, and all the States—to fulfil to all, to the cotton, indigo, and hemp grower; to the grain grower and grazier; to the builder of vessels and the fisherman; to the manufactures of leather, clothing, cordage, iron, glass, paper, wood—to fulfil to all something of the promise of the new government, and to extend to all some portion of the security and the stimulus of a real national independence. And now, pause for a moment, and appreciate the light which the history of that act sheds upon the constitutional opinions of that congress, and what inferences those opinions suggest regarding the true meaning of the Constitution.

Sir, the doctrine of the extreme South, I mean rather the extreme doctrine of the South, confined I hope to few, is, that you can impose duties for revenue only; that, in doing so, you may discriminate to be sure, but only for purposes and on principles of revenue as such, laying a low duty or a high one, a specific or an ad valorem, accordingly as one or the other will yield the most revenue at the least expense and with the most certainty. If such a scheme of duties unintentionally (for if you intended the result it avoids the whole) aids the manufacturer or mechanic, well and good; if not, let him take care of himself. This, they say, is *incidental protection,* and it is all the Constitution authorizes! But was this the doctrine of the first congress? I say, on the contrary, that, in its main structure and its substantial character, the act whose history I have detailed was an act for protection as the principal, and for revenue as the incident; that, although at first designed for revenue only, it was wholly reconstructed with another object as the leading object, not indeed inconsistent with revenue, rather in aid of it, intended to be in aid of it, but obtaining it, so far as *purpose* was concerned, incidentally; that, from the beginning to the end, the power of affording protection *directly, as an end, as a main purpose,* was assumed by everybody; and that it was that power which every member must have considered himself exerting, in more than three quarters of all the legislation which was finally embodied in the law. True undoubtedly it is, that all the revenue which the act in its final form could be made to yield was needed by the young government. True it is, therefore, that, in my judgment, this act is not a precedent for bringing, with a view to protection, more money into the treasury than you require for the wants of government. But for discrimination, with a view to protection; for admitting some things free, as materials of manufacture, some under specific duties and some under ad valorem, some under low duties and some under high, for the purpose of protection; for rejecting a measure, efficient and suitable as a revenue measure, precisely because it did not recognize and did not secure protection, and substituting one which did; for putting forward protection as a great object of national policy, of somewhat more consequence than the idle and childish symmetry of horizontal tariffs; for treating a protecting tariff itself as a commercial regulation, and to be referred to the power of regulating commerce—for *this* it is a precedent, and a precedent belonging to a better age, sanctioned by a higher authority than almost any other in our whole series of national legislation.

Observe, Sir, how the mere pursuit of revenue was made to yield to other considerations. Mr. Madison thought that, *for the purposes of revenue,* more was lost than gained by seeking to unite the other object.

"I presume," said he, "that however much we may be disposed to promote domestic manufactures, we ought to pay some regard to the present policy of obtaining revenue. It may be remarked, also, that, by *fixing on a temporary expedient for this purpose, we may gain more than we shall lose by suspending the consideration of the other subject* until we obtain further information of the state of our manufactures. We have at this time the strongest motives for turning our attention to the point I have mentioned. Every gentleman sees that the prospect of our harvest from the spring importations is daily vanishing; and if the committee delay levying and collecting an impost until a system of protecting duties shall be perfected, there will be no importations of any consequence on which the law is to operate, because by that time all the spring vessels will have arrived. Therefore, from a pursuit of this policy, *we shall suffer a loss* equal to the surplus which might be expected from a system of higher duties."

Yet that congress held the loss of duties on spring importations a trifle, in comparison with permanently and systematically sustaining the great interests of domestic labor. Observe, too, and this is a consideration of great importance, where you are inquiring after the *constitutional opinions* and the *quo animo* of legislators, that, in making the successive additions of protected articles, and in fixing the duties upon them, and throughout the whole attempt to recast the original bill, no man assigns revenue, but every man assigns *protection* as his motive and object. I have read the grounds on which Mr. Fitzsimons and Mr. Hartley pressed and carried the original motion. Subsequently, on motion of others, other articles were successively subjected to the specific and higher duty; and every one of them for the avowed object of protection, not one for the avowed object of revenue. Sir, the arguments for the steel, cordage, molasses, beef, hemp, and tonnage duties, are exactly the arguments of those who, in 1816, 1820, 1824, built up that later and more developed policy which you call the American system, an anticipation in effect of the substance and language of those great debates.

Let me remind you now how pregnant the fact is, that not a doubt was whispered on any side about the constitutional power of Congress to think and do so much for protection. The policy of many of the provisions of the bill was vehemently controverted. The cordage duty, the tonnage duty, the duties on molasses, beer, tallow-candles, steel,—of which Mr. Madison observes, "the object of selecting this must be solely the encouragement of the manufacture, and not revenue," (page 154,)—hemp, nails, coal, were successively, and some of them keenly resisted; they were urged on the sole ground of protection, yet no man whispered a suspicion on the power. I should more nearly express the fact, if I said that everybody committed himself in favor of the power. Virginia asked protection for her coal, and prohibition for her beef; and South Carolina "was willing to make sacrifices to encourage the manufacturing and maritime interests of the sister States," but asked protection *for hemp,* which, Mr. Burk said, "her low, strong, rice lands produced in abundance." To appreciate, to approach at all, the strength, significance, and universality of this fact, you must meditate the entire debate. But read at least Mr. Madison's principal speech, upon Mr. Fitzsimons's first proposition. I would rather look there for his constitutional opinions, undesignedly announced, silently assumed as matter incontrovertible, and conceded by all, running underneath and upholding the whole structure of his thoughts upon the general subject, than even to his letter in 1828, written after a controversy had arisen, and age, and intervening events and cares, might have worn the earlier impression in any degree away. Let me open to you the leading idea of that speech, and leave it to you to see for yourselves how he develops it. The proposition of Mr. Fitzsimons, then, he suggested, made it necessary to consider, not merely temporary expedients of revenue, but the principles of a commercial system. He had intended to regard revenue alone, but the proposition led to, and would result in, "the general regulation of commerce," (pages 107 and 116). Observe, sir, the moment it was suggested to blend protection and revenue, he thought himself engaged in a general *regulation of commerce.*

What, then, he proceeded to inquire, are the true principles of a commercial system? The first and the general rule is, to have it *free,*—as free as possible. He supports this briefly and forcibly. But there are exceptions to the rule, he declares, and he proceeds to enumerate them. And what are they, in his judgment? The first embraces discriminating provisions for the protection and encouragement of American vessels; the second, duties on imports to sustain or to develop manufacturing industry; the third, sumptuary prohibitions which, however, in any form but sumptuary duties, he disapproves; the fourth, embargoes in time of war; the fifth, provisions for encouraging the production within the nation of all its military supplies; the sixth, duties for revenue. These are exceptions, he argues, by which we may wisely restrict the general freedom of commerce. These exceptions we have the constitutional power to engraft upon our general law of free trade. We may restrain it to encourage American ships and other American manufactures, for the uses of peace or war; to check luxury; to withdraw our too adventurous commerce from the grasp of an enemy, and to supply a revenue for the wants of government. I commend to your own reflections this enunciation of the general principle of commercial regulations and of the exceptions to it; the affirmation which it involves of the constitutional power of protection; the separation of the protecting and of the revenue power from one another, and the enumeration of each as substantive and distinct; and his acquiescence in Mr. Fitzsimons's proposition to unite the exercise and the objects of both powers in one law, "although he (Mr. Madison) thought the two objects ought not to be too confusedly blended." I commend all this to you, who would know his opinions on this part of that greatest work of his own hands or of any man's, the federal Constitution.

I have said that no man then denied the power. Mr. Ames, I have reminded you, expressly affirmed it. No newspaper denied it. The usurpations, imaginary or real, of the two first administrations upon the Constitution,—their alleged usurpations,—brought into life the party of State rights and of Democracy; but through all that tremendous contest which ended in the revolution of 1801, no man accused them for having dared to protect the planter, the farmer, the fisherman, the mechanic of America. No one laid that sin to their charge. The system of practical protection—founded by the framers and in the age of the Constitution and of Washington—grew with the growth and strengthened with the strength of the nation. Every president, every congress, almost every public man, approved it. It went on widening its circuit, increasing its energy, and multiplying its beneficial effects, but never changing its nature or its aims for more than thirty years, when a subtle and a sectional metaphysics suddenly discerned that it was all a fraud on the Constitution.

It is one of the bad habits of politics which grow up under written systems and limited systems of government to denounce what we think impolitic and oppressive legislation as unconstitutional legislation. The language is at first rhetorically and metaphorically used; excited feeling, producing inaccurate thought, contributes to give it currency; classes of States and parties weave it into their vocabulary, and it grows into an article of faith. I have not a doubt that such is the origin of this heresy.

Look, then, over the whole field of view which we have traversed. The terms of the Constitution, interpreted by the most indisputable and universal use of language of the time and country, expressly grant the power. For years the whole people—men of business, statesmen, speculatists, the masses, all—had demanded a Constitution which should contain the power under those precise terms; and they adopted it, in the belief, and in a substantial sense *for the reason,* that it satisfied that demand. The master-workmen by whom it was constructed,—the entire contemporary intelligence and statesmanship,—supposed it contained the power. With the very first breath it drew, the new government, in the age of Washington, Madison, Hamilton, Adams, and Jefferson, and with their approbation, entered upon its declared exercise; and for more than thirty years its existence was universally admitted.

I propose no more, Sir, than to suggest the general nature and main points of an argument familiar to the thoughts of senators. To my mind it is conclusive. Exercise the power or not, as you deem best for the good and glory of your country, but do not deny its existence, lest you accuse that energetic and heroic generation which gave us Independence and the Constitution, of delusion, fraud, and folly, such as never disgraced any age or race of men before.

I said, Mr. President, that congress had the power, and that it was their duty also to afford adequate protection in this exigency to the entire labor of the country. Something I could wish to add upon this great duty; but perhaps it may better be reserved until we have, as I earnestly hope we soon shall have, a practical measure before us. I trust even that it may be unnecessary to urge its performance on you at all. The mode, the degree in which it shall be performed, may disclose diversities of opinions. On this we shall stand in need of mutual forbearance and indulgence; but, on the solemn and peremptory character of the duty itself, how can we differ? Take counsel of the "ancient prudence;" survey the subject in the spirit of the congress of 1789; purify your minds of the suggestions of a transient expediency, and of a small and local jealousy, by recalling and meditating anew the grand objects for which you know the Constitution was framed; and we cannot differ.

If our trivial and timid manufacturing and mechanical arts, at the organization of the government, not much further out of ground than this premature green grass of the month of March, were not below the care of such a congress as the first, how much more worthy of yours is this diversified and yet sensitive industry, which sends its roots and branches everywhere, but which a storm or a frost would prostrate and kill in an hour! Is that vast circle of employments, which gives to more than 800,000 operatives the means of a comfortable and respectable life; in which nearly three hundred millions of capital are invested directly; which supplies one tenth of all our exports, more in value than the export of rice and tobacco together; feeds our coasting trade, a nation's best trade, or certainly our best; animates, in a hundred ways, the sister or the parent art of agriculture, by keeping up its prices, by turning away from its cultivation the crowds who would overstock it, and by opening to its great staples of cotton, rice, flour, meats, and wool, a market at home, steady, growing, sure; which policy, or unkindness, or the storms of war, cannot close—is that too inconsiderable in the mass of the national policy to deserve your regard? And yet, is that interest by the side of England anything more than an infant, which her statesmen and capitalists coolly talk of "stifling in the cradle," and which thrives and lives by your care alone? If forty years ago, when we had a continent to plant, and so few to do it, and with a whole ocean unoccupied, occupied only for war, inviting us to go forth and carry on the commerce of the world with scarcely a competitor, sound policy was thought to require the establishment of this industry, how much more now, when we have arrived at the period in the course of national advancement in which it should, in the process of things, begin to take root, and when the condition of all our other occupations so impressively urges us to make the most of this for the benefit of all? If the exhausting importations of foreign goods, the overwhelming accumulation of foreign debt, the drain of specie to pay the foreign creditor, the derangement of American currency, the transportation of American produce in foreign ships, the antagonist regulations of foreign policy, and the consequent depression of all employments, were reasons for making the Constitution, are not the same things a reason to-day for administering it in its whole energy? If so many successive presidents, congresses, administrations, have invited, aye, compelled the investment of so much capital in this industry, and connected the labors, hopes, the daily livelihood, the whole scheme of life of so many thousands, their own, their children's, inextricably with it, does it not impose the duty of steady, just, and parental protecting legislation on you? Did you really mean in 1833, when you framed the Compromise Act, that if, unexpectedly, American industry, or one single branch of it, could not live under its ultimate reduction, to let it perish? We told you then that it would endanger the whole system of domestic labor, and that some portions, and they the most precious, the most popular, the first in favor from the date of the government,—woollens, the production of wool, the manufactures of leather, paper, glass, sugar, iron, hats, wood, cotton printing, the whole cotton manufacture in the hands of moderate capitalists,— would be destroyed by it. You differed from us; but do you not mean to admit us to the proof, that our predictions were true? Your compromise does not prevent your replenishing the treasury of the government; shall it prevent your protecting the labor of the people? Will you suffer the country to lose in a year all that it has slowly gained in twenty? Will you squander away the skill which has been acquired; break up your machinery, or send it to the East Indies; close the door to a hundred useful occupations just as men have learned how to pursue them; put your whole scale of prices,—which the establishment of every manufacture at home has regularly reduced and steadied,—into the hands of the experimental capitalists of England, to lower and raise at their pleasure? No, Sir; no, Sir. You will hear the proofs and the discussion with patience; and you will decide with wisdom.

Let me say, Mr. President, in a spirit of the utmost respect to the opinions of senators, that, if there is any power of the Constitution,—I do not know that there is any,—which it might be prudent to suffer to slumber, and, as I have heard it expressed, *to die out,* it is not this. No, Sir. Desirous always, and determined to administer it moderately, discreetly, justly; throwing no burden of discrimination

on the South which the North does not at least equally feel; keeping the aggregate amount which it shall yield to the treasury in subordination to the wants
of government, efficiently and wisely administered; clothing it, if that is preferred, under the forms, the name, and the reality, of a measure of revenue with
discriminations for protection, giving all up but the practical, sufficient, and sure
protecting energy itself;—that I would never give up. No, Sir; the power which
this whole country with one voice demanded to have inserted in the Constitution, and which they hailed as another Declaration of Independence; the power
by which we are able to protect all our children of labor, on whatsoever fields
they wipe the sweat from their brow; by which, as Washington foretold, we may
hope to bind these States together, to run the race of freedom, power, enjoyment, and glory with the nations, and to afford the example of a people, now
counted by millions, every one of whom has work to do, and good pay for his
work;—this power must not be surrendered, must not sleep, till the Union flag
shall be hauled down from the last masthead! That sight, I trust, neither we nor
our children, to the thousandth generation, are doomed to see.

CHAPTER IV.

SPEECH UPON THE SUBJECT OF PROTECTING AMERICAN LABOR BY DUTIES ON IMPORTS.

DELIVERED IN THE SENATE OF THE UNITED STATES, April 12 and 15, 1844.

This third of Choate's major speeches on the importance of maintaining the protective system adopts a practical and logical approach to the question. That industry and manufactures are a boon to a nation is disputed by no one, he argues. Hence the discussion of the tariff issue must revolve around determining what level of protection is necessary for maintaining the nation's manufacturing base. This, he insists, is the starting point of any serious discussion.

Choate, a man of impeccable conservative credentials, speaks here of the need to protect "the daily labor, and the daily bread of men, women, and children, our countrymen and countrywomen, whom we reckon by millions" against the "low wages, under-fed labor and contingent surpluses of foreign States." Once again he weighs this concern against the complaints of the Southern states that the protective tariff lays undue burdens on their section. Although he discounts the Southern argument, he at least treats these claims of injustice as a factor to be considered in formulating a national policy. What he rejects is the suggestion that matters so vital to the health of a nation can be referred to the abstractions of political economy. They are practical questions to be addressed by practical statesmen.

[The Senator from South Carolina [Mr. McDuffie] had introduced, on leave, the following bill:—

A BILL to revive the act of the second of March, one thousand eight hundred and thirty-three, usually called the "Compromise Act," and to modify the existing duties upon foreign imports in conformity to its provisions.

Be it enacted by the Senate and House of Representatives of the United States of America in Congress assembled, That so much of the existing law imposing duties upon foreign imports as provides that duties ad valorem on certain commodities shall be assessed upon an assumed *minimum* value, be, and the same is hereby, repealed, and that said duties be hereafter assessed on the true value of such commodities.

Sec. 2. *And be it further enacted,* That in all cases in which the existing duty upon any imported commodity exceeds thirty per centum on the value thereof, such duty shall be hereafter reduced to thirty per centum ad valorem.

Sec. 3. *And be it further enacted,* That from and after the thirty-first day of December next, all duties upon foreign imports shall be reduced to twenty-five per centum; and from and after the thirty-first of December, one thousand eight hundred and forty-four, to twenty per centum ad valorem.

And the committee on finance of the senate had reported resolutions recommending its indefinite postponement. The debate arose upon those resolutions.]

MR. PRESIDENT,—

IT IS not my purpose, and never has been, to engage in a general discussion of this subject. In the actual circumstances, no consideration could induce me to do so. Good taste, if nothing else, ought to prevent it. In my hands, such a discussion could retain neither interest nor usefulness. There is literally nothing at all left to be said or to be refuted. Truths, threadbare and worn to tatters, or novelties, empty, false, sounding, and mischievous, are at least all that is left. It has come to be preeminently that case in which "true things are not new things, and new things are not true things."

Besides, Sir, for the maintenance of the doctrines to which I am devoted, and with the steady and constant practice of which the comfort, the prosperity, and the greatness of the American people, are inseparably intertwined, more general discussion is needless. The defence of the system of protection is made. It has been made before and elsewhere, by ten thousand tongues and pens, and by that which is more eloquent and more persuasive than any tongue or pen,—the teachings of experience,—the lapse of time,—the revelations of events,—the past and present of our own country, and of all countries. It has been made, here and now, by the Senators from Maine, Connecticut, Vermont, Rhode Island, and Georgia, and by my friend and colleague. [Messrs. Evans, Huntington, Phelps, Simmons, Berrien, and Bates,] with a fulness and ability that leaves nothing to be desired and nothing to be added. If this Troy of ours can be defended; if these daily and indispensable employments of our people can be preserved to them; if these fields and shops of useful, honest, and respectable labor—labor which at once elevates and blesses the individual operative, by hundreds of thousands, and, in its larger results, contributes to fill the measure of the nation's glory—if these can be defended, their hands will have been sufficient to make the defence. If theirs are not, my feeble efforts can avail nothing.

There is another reason, Mr. President, on which I decline that larger and more elementary discussion that has occupied so much of this debate, on which, without the least disrespect to any one, I desire to say a word: and that is, that, for myself, I cannot consent to regard this matter of protection as at all that open question which it might seem to have been regarded by senators on all sides. Sir, I presume to prescribe no rule of debate to others; nor to criticise, or even to observe upon their course; but I shall not allow myself to treat this question as open to the extent, and for the objects that have been assumed and contended for. No doubt, there is a sense and an extent in which it may, under proper limitations, be said to be always open. Details may be said to be so. Having due regard to the great considerations of stability and constancy; of giving all things, when once adopted, a fair and full trial; and of changing nothing from lightness and caprice and the pursuit of abstractions,—details may be admitted to be always open. When the lights of a full and fair experience prescribe the change of a duty, it is to be changed. It is open to inquiry, whether a given or a proposed duty is needed for protection, or is enough for it. It is an open question whether the rates of 1789 are sufficient to-day, and whether those of 1828 are required to-day. In such a sense as this, this subject, like all law, like all policy, like the steadfast nature of the Constitution itself, is open to the gentle and reforming hand of the great innovator, time.

But whether there ought to be in our industrial code such a thing as a policy of adequate protection of the universal labor of the country; such a thing as a system designed and sufficient to develop and sustain our whole capacity and all our forms of domestic employment,—on the land, on the sea, in the arts, everywhere, and in everything,—by the imposition, among other means, of duties on imports; a system designed and sufficient to guard the American workman, on whatever field, against the irregular irruptions of the redundant capital, low rates of interest money, low wages, under-fed labor and contingent surpluses of foreign States; this is a question which I do not mean, by my example, to acknowledge an open one. To the dispute whether protection shall always be treated as *incidental* to revenue, or may be made a *principal* object itself; to the dispute as to when it is an incident and when a principal object; whether there is such a thing, and what it is, as a revenue *maximum;* to disputes about forms of duties, specific, ad valorem, minimums, and the like, I attach no great importance. I mean by protecting duties, *duties which protect:* and whether these duties should or should not be blended with, and form part of our impost system, I repeat, I do not mean to discuss as an open question.

And why not open? Because, Sir, I find such a system of protection in operation, *de jure* and *de facto,* to-day; because I know perfectly well,—or all our annals are a dream and a lie,—that the American people established the Constitution and the Union, very much to insure the maintenance of such a system;

because it has been slowly maturing for years; because so large a concurrence of patriotism, intelligence, and experience, has helped to build it up; because, whether it was wise or unwise to introduce such a system, by direct legislation, at first, it would be supreme madness now, now when the first stages are passed, when the evil, if any there ever was, is all done, and the compensations of good are just fairly commencing; when capital has taken this direction; when prices are brought down, skill learned, habits formed, machinery accumulated, the whole scheme of things accommodated to it; when its propitious influence is felt palpably upon agriculture, upon the comfort and the standing of labor, upon domestic and foreign trade, upon defence, upon independence—it would be supreme madness, worthy only of a government nodding to its fall, now to overturn it; because, finally, it is the daily labor, and the daily bread of men, women, and children, our countrymen and countrywomen, whom we reckon by millions.

It is for these reasons, Sir, that I cannot regard it as a debatable question, whether it is lawful, under the Constitution, or expedient in point of political economy, that this system should exist.

While, therefore, I appreciate, as highly as any one can do, the ability and energy with which the Senator from South Carolina [Mr. McDuffie] has urged his opinions in this debate, I must, in conformity with these views, consider it as a sufficient notice for me to take of the bill which he has introduced, and still more, of such a bill as should embody the principles of policy and the Constitution which he has so powerfully advocated,—to pronounce it a stupendous novelty, and there to leave it. It is all a novelty, from the beginning to the end. In its principle; in its object; in its details; in the argument which accompanies it, it is not only unlike, but it is adverse to, it is at war with, every law that has been passed under the Constitution; and not so only, but it forgets, it disregards, it disappoints the desires and purposes and wants of that generation of our fathers which called the Constitution into existence, and enriched it with all its vast powers of good. Why, Sir, what is the bill of the honorable Senator; or, rather, what would it be, if it still more exactly expressed his constitutional and economical doctrines? It is a bill which aspires to construct an impost system, from which all purpose of intentional protection shall be carefully weeded out with thumb and finger. It goes for revenue, and nothing else. It does not merely seek to bring into the treasury a certain aggregate of revenue, having regard to the wants of an economical administration of the government—that would be right—but in all its details it looks to revenue alone. Every single duty is to be laid upon the notion of getting, from that one item, the largest possible amount at the lowest possible rate of impost. The bill does not try to protect. It does not inquire whether it protects. It does not care whether it protects. Live or die under it who will, if the aggregate amount of money is obtained, and if each particular duty yields its prescribed quota of supply, its end is answered. Yes, Sir! The capital and labor and experience, which are producing three or four or five hundreds of millions of annual values, may go up or go down; the skill which years have been educating may be dismissed and squandered; fountains of national wealth and civilization may be dried up; machinery and processes and methods, the splendid triumphs of mind over matter, may be cast aside, as an old bow, which none of this generation knows how to bend, or has strength to bend; a million hands may miss their accustomed labor, a million months their accustomed food,—yet the bill has done all that it desires, and is perfectly satisfied with itself! I do not speak of, nor allude to, the wishes and dispositions of the honorable mover himself, of course; they, I doubt not, are just and philanthropic; but I speak of the bill. It goes for revenue; and if it obtains it, it disregards all possible intermediate consequences.

Such a bill, Sir, within the views which I take of this whole subject, I cannot consent to discuss. I pass it by, with entire respect to its friends, as an enormous and pernicious novelty. It is enough for me that no such impost system as this was dreamed of by the people who willed the Constitution into being; or by the minds who framed it and adopted it, or by any president, or congress, or party, who ever administered it; and that no precedent and no warrant for such a thing is to be found in all the series of our legislation. Gratified certainly, I have been, with the able and instructive arguments of my friends in this discussion, showing, with resistless force, that all this is not only novel, but impolitic; that our system is not only settled, but rightly settled. To those reasonings I could add nothing if I would; and I would not if I could. If at this time of day, the labor of the country cannot repose upon the policy of protection as an established policy, then indeed is "the pillared firmament rottenness, and earth's base built on stubble."

While, then, I retire from that general discussion of a boundless and exhausted subject to which we have been invited, I admit that a question more practical, and more properly to be regarded as open, is involved in this deliberation; and that is, not whether adequate protection shall or shall not be given to American labor; not whether mechanical and manufacturing arts and industry are worth preserving for their influence upon all industry, and upon individual prosperity and enjoyment, and national wealth and power; but whether a given or a proposed rate of duty affords that adequate protection, and insures the growth of those useful and those imperial arts? In other words, it is this question,—can you make a proposed great change in the existing rates, and still leave enough for the protection which the government and the country have determined to give?

Sir, this is the question which has been moved by the honorable Senator from Missouri, [Mr. Benton,] not now in his place. That distinguished gentleman comes into this deliberation, not as an enemy, but as a friend of a sufficient protective system. He reminded you that he voted for the act of 1824, and voted "cordially" for it: yet that act, beyond all doubt, permanently laid the foundation of what he calls the "new system;" that he voted for the act of 1828 "reluctantly," but that he voted for it; that he voted for that of 1832 "because it reduced duties on many necessaries," although it still left, as I suppose, for most objects, a pretty energetic protecting tariff, against which both the then senators from South Carolina, and six out of nine of her representatives voted; and, finally, that he voted against the Compromise Act, "because he thought the horizontal line wrong in principle, and for other reasons." Retaining his original friendship, as I understood him, for a sufficient protective system, since he expressly declares himself "willing to give manufactures far more protection than they need," he however counsels a vast change of the existing system,— a change which I am profoundly impressed with the conviction that you cannot make without the ultimate, perhaps quick, but at last inevitable destruction of all the interests which it was created to cherish, and all that multiplied variety of individual and general good which illustrates and recommends it. He counsels an abandonment of the existing system, "the new system," the system which began, as he says, in 1816, and has been embodied successively in the acts of 1816, of 1824, of 1828, and of 1842; the last (against which he voted) being in his judgment "the very worst of all." He counsels an abandonment of this system, and a return to the "good old laws," the good old system, the system of our fathers,—the system "which began in 1789, with the beginning of the government," and continued down to the year 1808. He does not advise you to revive any one law, or any one precise rate of duty, that obtained in the happy and peaceful period to which he turns you back. It is the *system* which he would revive. In his terse, forcible, and clear expression, he sketches rapidly its general features, as he would reproduce them. He indicates certain conditions which must be satisfied, and such protection as can be afforded consistently with the satisfaction of those conditions he means to leave. As well as I remember,—and I speak with the most anxious desire, in his absence this morning from his seat, not to misrepresent him,—among these conditions are these: all minimums are to be abolished; ad valorem duties are, as I infer, although I cannot pronounce positively of his views in this particular, to be computed upon the foreign values; luxuries are to be taxed high; necessaries, although coming in competition with what are woven in your own looms, hammered out on your own anvils, cut and stitched on your own shoemakers' or merchant-tailors' seats, are to be taxed low; and no duty, under whatever denomination, is to ascend above thirty-three and one third per cent. "The average on the whole, he fully believes, will not be equal to the twenty per cent. ad valorem of the Compromise Act." Subject to these conditions, satisfying these conditions to this extent, the distinguished Senator would give you protection. This system he advises you to substitute for the existing one. If it should happen to turn out inadequate, the manufacturer and mechanic have this consolation,—that they have mistaken their calling, and that the system, by which they die, is the good old one of their fathers.

Mr. President, upon this counsel of the honorable Senator let me say a few words. Certainly, in the very form of speech in which it is conceived, there is persuasive argument. He, who advises to return to the good old system of our fathers, has half gained his audience already. He supposes you to have wandered, it is true; but not far, since he encourages you that it is practicable and is easy to come back. He touches your pious and filial memories. He appeals to that powerful prepossession towards the past, which influences the best natures the most. He points to the "old paths," and our feet unconsciously turn to take hold on them.

But we must pause, Sir, somewhat, before we legislate on such sentiments as these. We must distinguish a little in this matter of the imitation of our fathers. It is not what they did, exactly as they did it, in the special and transient circumstances of their time, that we are to reproduce with a timid and literal fidelity of resemblance; but it is what their principles, their spirit, the general character of their permanent aims and substantial objects, as exemplified in their actual policy, would lead them to do *now,* in the altered circumstances of our time,— this is what we are to discern and to imitate, if we are to imitate at all, as becomes them, or as becomes ourselves. Always, Sir, it is good to be emulous of the purity, the simplicity, the patriotism, and all the heroic virtues of a great and wise ancestry. Very often is it wise to meditate their legislation. But before we copy the details of such policy, we must take many an anxious observation; we must heave the lead again and again; we must find out on what new seas, along what unexplored coasts of what new continents, the great current is bearing us; we must sweep the field of midnight sky, to see what stars have risen, and what stars have set; and thus we must learn what change of duty the change of situation prescribes, and what the navigators of a former age would do, were they, not we, piloting the ship to-day. To be true to the *principles* of our fathers, we must sometimes wholly desert or substantially modify their *details.*

What, then, are the arguments by which we are to be persuaded to substitute the system which began in 1789, and endured until 1808, for the system which began in 1816, was matured or nearly so in 1824, and exists now?

Well, in the first place, Sir, we are pointed to an alleged diversity, to an alleged "opposition" between the spirit and principles and objects which presided over the establishment of the former of these systems, and those which presided over the establishment of the latter. The former, it is said, was framed and founded in a loftier spirit, for better objects, under higher influences, with "opposite views," on a sounder principle. It was framed and founded not by "millionary capitalists and ambitious politicians," for "political advancement" and "sectional enrichment," but, as I understand the implication, by statesmen and men of business, fairly, in good faith. In that system revenue was the principal; protection, was the incident; duties were moderate, and values were true values. The latter, the existing system, it is said, on the contrary, was framed by, or under the influence of, "millionary capitalists and aspiring politicians;" for "political advancement and sectional enrichment;" "it makes protection principal, and revenue the incident;" its duties are exorbitant, and its valuations fictitious and delusive.

Now, Mr. President, I find myself quite unable to assent to the historical postulate on which this argument proceeds. I do not agree to this allegation, that a spirit presided over the legislation of 1789 so opposite to that which produced the legislation of 1816 and 1824. I maintain, on the contrary, that both generations of statesmen, those of 1789 and those of 1816 and 1824, had exactly the same object in view. Both intended to do one and the same thing; that is, to foster and protect adequately the existing mechanical and manufacturing industry of the country. They lived in different ages of the world; in different epochs of our national history; and this circumstance prescribed some diversity of instrumental details. The impost duties of 1789, sufficient and designed to protect the domestic labor of 1789, would have been insufficient to protect the labor of 1824, and therefore in part they were enlarged. The impost duties of 1824 would have been unnecessary to the protection of the domestic labor of 1789, and therefore they were not then resorted to. But of both systems the objects were the same; the principle was the same; the policy was the same. I cannot denounce one and applaud the other. I cannot strike a blow at the great men of 1824, that does not pass through and light on the reverend and charmed form of the Father of his Country himself. It is all one policy of protection, one identical policy, *mutatis mutandis*—as of the fathers, so of the children! It is I, then, Sir, who claim the lights and teachers of the first and purest age of our political church for our own in this controversy. It is I who would reconcile the living and the dead, and on their consentaneous authority uphold, if I can, the system of this day.

See then, Mr. President, if this is not so. And in the first place, let us be sure that we comprehend perfectly the objects and the policy, the constitutional and economical doctrines, of the founders of our "first system," as the Senator from Missouri has called it, the system of 1789. This is an indispensable first step. It is not enough to know and to say that they laid what you call moderate duties. The question is, on what principles did they lay them; for what object; with what intent; on what interpretation of the Constitution; on what theory of political economy? Details vary. Principles are the same yesterday, to-day, and through the ages of a nation's life.

To know, then, in this just and adequate sense, the principles which lie at the foundation of our first system, as, after the honorable Senator, I shall continue to call it, we will turn, *first,* to the model law of July 4th, 1789. It is entitled "An act for laying a duty on goods, wares, and merchandises, imported into the United States." It sets off with this preamble: "Whereas it is necessary for the support of government, for the discharge of the debts of the United States, and the encouragement and protection of manufactures, that duties be laid on goods, wares, and merchandises imported." It was the second act passed under the new Constitution; the first having simply "regulated the time and manner of administering certain oaths."

Of this model law, then, Mr. President, I assert: 1. That it was as really and truly, in its principle and intention, a protective tariff, as the act of 1824. 2. That its framers meant so to construct it as adequately to foster the rising but infant manufactures and mechanic arts of America, and thought they had done so. 3. That it was cast and fashioned into the particular form in which we see it, instead of having been left, as at first was contemplated, in a very different form,— it was moulded into this form, expressly and avowedly, for the purpose of protection. 4. That of the whole number of duties which it imposes, more than twenty were made specific duties,—were made and left what they are, instead of being left ad valorem duties, as at first was contemplated; and that this was done, expressly and avowedly, for the purpose of protection. 5. That of the ad valorem duties imposed by it, from fifteen to twenty were enumerated, and placed under a higher rate than the residuary, horizontal, unenumerated level of five per cent. under which it was at first contemplated to leave them; and that this was done, expressly and avowedly, for the purpose of protection. 6. That fifteen or sixteen articles, which on principles of revenue should pay duties, and which it was at first contemplated to subject to duties, are made free, expressly and avowedly for the purpose of encouraging manufactures and the mechanic arts. 7. That the act was under consideration of congress for a period of nearly three months, and was most laboriously debated and constructed; that throughout the whole discussion the constitutional power to impose, vary, increase duties even to the point of prohibition, for the express and declared purpose of protecting, and fostering the agriculture, the tonnage, the navigation, the commerce, and the manufactures of the nation,—the economical expediency, and the social and political justice of doing so, were assumed or asserted by all, and were denied and doubted by no one member of either branch of the legislature. 8. That the choice was, in the progress of business, distinctly presented to that congress, to pass an act in a different form from this, which would produce more revenue in a shorter time than this, but which would not afford so much protection; or to pass this, which would be less immediately productive of revenue, but would afford more protection to general domestic labor; and that this was chosen, expressly and avowedly, because it afforded more adequate protection. 9. That the actual protection afforded by this act proved to be, as its framers designed it to be, entirely adequate.

Sir, if I can maintain these assertions, you may admire, but perhaps not approve, and not imitate that ingenuity of discrimination, which praises the spirit that produced this law, yet denounces the spirit which produced the law of 1824. You will see, and you will respect, and you will cherish, in both, one and the same identical policy of protection, growing with the growth, strengthening with the strength, flexible to the circumstances of one and the same common country. To see, then, if these assertions are true, I must ask you to trace in the debates of that day the history of this law,—its origin, its first form, its changes, its growth, its consummation. Look beyond its preamble, which, however, most exactly and completely unfolds and announces its objects; look beyond that, to its history. This, I am aware, is familiar to many of you. I am afraid it will be tedious to all. Yet to us, to all of us, to all who would know the constitutional doctrines and the economical and political theories and practice of the age of Washington; to all who would know whether the legislation of 1824 was in principle new folly or "ancient prudence"—how far more important is this investigation than the history of many a council of Trent; many a Magna Charta; many a statute of Edward, or Henry, or Charles the First! I will first relate the history of this law, and then prove and illustrate it.

It was on the eighth of April, 1789, that Mr. Madison opened the business of constructing a system of impost duties, by proposing to the house to pass a mere brief and simple revenue bill. He said that there was not time to prepare a more comprehensive and complete measure; that the object of immediate importance was the speediest practicable supply of the federal treasury; that to effect that object it was expedient to pass an act which should intercept the spring importations, by which means more money would be procured, and in shorter time, than by a more elaborate system which would be longer in constructing. In the actual circumstances, despatch, he thought, was everything. He proposed, therefore, "that congress should take, as the basis of the temporary system which he advised to have adopted," the resolution passed by the old congress of 1783. That resolution imposed specific duties on seven enumerated articles, to wit: spirituous liquors, wines, tea, coffee, sugar, cocoa, and pepper, (not one of which, except rum, could be reckoned of the class of protected articles, no other of them coming into competition with anything produced in the United States;) and on all other articles, without enumeration, a horizontal ad valorem of five per cent. This resolution, "with a clause or two respecting tonnage," he proposed to adopt as a temporary measure of revenue, adapted to the actual circumstances of the moment.

You understand, then, Mr. Madison's first plan. If it had been adopted, we should have seen, for the first and last time, that "faultless monster which the world ne'er saw," a pure, sheer, mere revenue tariff. Some unintentional and unhappy *incidental* protection even such a tariff would yield,—with which constitutional and economical purists must have borne as well as they could. But, upon the whole, it would have come as near the notion of an unadulterated "revenue measure" as the lot of humanity will admit. But was it adopted? Nothing like it, Sir.

Upon its being opened, Mr. Fitzsimons, of Pennsylvania, rose and said that he desired to see a more permanent system adopted, and one that should "carry its views much farther;" a system some way adequate to our whole actual situation, "as it respects our agriculture, our manufactures, and our commerce;" a system which "should encourage domestic production, and foster the infant manufactures of America." He proposed, therefore, that instead of adopting the little revenue resolution of the old congress, an extended bill of detail should be framed, proceeding by enumeration of all the subjects of duty, and imposing on each the particular rate which should blend with revenue the requisite amount of protection.

Here, then, you see, two plans, two bills, different in object, different in details, were presented to the choice of congress. And thereupon a short debate arose on the question, which general scheme and frame of impost law should be adopted. In support of Mr. Madison's original proposition, it was urged "that the great object of the moment was revenue; that, for this, despatch was indispensable; and that the brief revenue resolution, adopted at once, would, by intercepting the expected importations of the spring, bring more money into the treasury, in a shorter time, than a law more carefully matured and passed at a later day." To this it was answered, by Mr. Fitzsimons and others, "that it might be admitted, and was probably true, that the plan first proposed would yield a more immediate supply to an exhausted treasury, but that there were objects of even more importance than that,—objects which that plan could not accomplish; that among these were the 'encouragement of domestic productions, and the protection of American manufactures;' and that if time were necessary to frame a bill which should comprehend and accomplish these, time must be taken for it, whether the treasury were immediately filled or remained somewhat longer empty."

After a short debate, Mr. Madison yielded to the suggestion of Mr. Fitzsimons; the basis, which he at first had proposed to proceed on, was abandoned, and the house engaged assiduously in the business of constructing a blended revenue and tariff bill, by enumeration; each member bringing forward such articles as he deemed worthy of being taken out of, and raised above the unenumerated level of five per cent., and moving such duties upon them as he thought proper, whether on considerations of revenue or protection. The bill was matured and became a law on the fourth of July, 1789. Instead of a law of ten lines, laying a half dozen specific duties upon articles not coming in competition with any domestic manufacture, and an ad valorem duty of five per cent. on all other articles, without enumeration; it became a law of six sections; imposing more than twenty specific and more than fifteen ad valorem duties, expressly for protection; admitting sixteen articles free of duty, which a mere revenue tariff should and would tax,—for the sole purpose of encouraging domestic arts; laying tonnage duties for the benefit of American tonnage; distributing, with a comprehensive and parental impartiality, its fostering care over the agriculture of the South and West; the fisheries and navigation of the East; the mechanical trades of the villages and towns; the manufacturing industry of the whole country; over the producer of cotton, indigo, and hemp; the grain grower and grazier; fishermen, and the owners of ships; workmen in leather, clothing, cordage, iron, glass, paper, and wood,—the universal existing labor of the young America,—a law exactly and completely conforming to the announcement of its preamble; laying duties "for the support of government, for the discharge of the debts of the United States, and the encouragement and protection of manufactures."

Such, Sir, is the history of the model tariff, the corner-stone of the Senator's "good old system" of our fathers. I am now to prove this; and I shall do it by a few selections from the speeches of different gentlemen in that debate, reported in the first volume of "Debates and Proceedings in Congress, &c., compiled by Joseph Gales, senior."

I begin with a passage or two indicating Mr. Madison's original plan, and the reasons assigned for adopting it. Upon introducing it, he said,—

> "The deficiency *in our treasury* has been too notorious to make it necessary for me to animadvert upon that subject. *Let us content ourselves with endeavoring to remedy the evil.*"
>
> "The second point to be regarded in adjusting import duties relates to *revenue alone; and this is the point* I mean more particularly to bring into the view of the committee."
>
> "The propositions made on this subject by congress in 1783 having received, generally, the approbation of the several States of the Union, in some form or other, seem well calculated to become the basis of the *temporary system which I wish the committee to adopt.* I am well aware that the changes which have taken place in many of the States, and in our public circumstances, since that period, will require, in some degree, a deviation from the scale of duties then affixed: nevertheless, *for the sake of that expedition which is necessary in order to embrace the spring importations,* I should recommend a *general* adherence to the plan."
>
> "This, with the addition of a clause on tonnage, I will now read, and, with leave, submit it to the committee, hoping it may meet their approbation as an *expedient,* rendered eligible by the *urgent occasion there is for the speedy supplies* of the federal treasury, and a speedy rescue of our trade from its present anarchy."

He then read the resolution of 1783, which was in these words:—

> "*Resolved,* (as the opinion of this committee,) That the following duties ought to be levied on goods, wares, and merchandise, imported into the United States, viz: On rum, per gallon,—of a dollar; on all other spirituous liquors,—; on molasses,—; on Madeira wine,—; on all other wines,—; on common bohea teas, per lb.,—; on all other teas,—; on pepper,—; on brown sugars,—; on loaf sugars,—; on all other sugars,—; on cocoa and coffee,—; on all other articles,— per cent. on their value at the time and place of importation."

And after Mr. Fitzsimons had disclosed his preference for a more comprehensive and protective measure, and Mr. Madison had yielded to the suggestion, he (Mr. Madison) said,—

"From what has been suggested by the gentlemen that have spoken on the subject before us, I am led to apprehend we shall be under the necessity of *travelling further into an investigation of principles than what I supposed would be necessary, or had in contemplation when I offered the propositions before you.*"

"It was my view to restrain the first essay on this subject *principally* to the object of revenue, and make this rather a *temporary expedient* than anything permanent. I see, however, that there are strong exceptions against deciding immediately on a part of the plan, which I had the honor to bring forward, as well as against an application to the resources mentioned in the list of articles just proposed by the gentleman from Pennsylvania."

"I presume that, *however much we may be disposed to promote domestic manufactures,* we ought to pay *some* regard to the *present* policy of obtaining revenue. It may be remarked, also, that by fixing *on a temporary expedient for this purpose, we may gain more than we shall lose by suspending the consideration of the other subject until we obtain fuller information of the state of our manufactures.* We have *at this time* the *strongest* motives for turning our attention to the point I have mentioned; every gentleman sees that the *prospect of our harvest from the spring importations is daily vanishing;* and if the committee delay levying and collecting an impost *until a system of protecting duties shall be perfected,* there will *be no importations* of any consequence on which the law is to operate, *because by that time all the spring vessels will have arrived. Therefore, from a pursuit of this policy, we shall suffer a loss equal to the surplus which might be expected from a system of higher duties.*"

See, too, how others understood Mr. Madison's first proposition. Speaking of it, Mr. Boudinot said,—

"The plan which he has submitted to the committee appears to be simple and sufficiently complete *for the present purpose;* I shall, therefore, for my own part, be content with it."

Mr. Lawrence concurred in this construction of it:—

"If I am not mistaken, the honorable mover of the plan viewed it as a *temporary system,* particularly calculated *to embrace the spring importations;* hence it may be proper to lay a duty at a certain rate per cent. on the value of all articles, without attempting an enumeration of any; because, if we attempt to specify every article, it will expose us to a question which must require *more time* than can be spared, to obtain the object that appears to be in the view of the committee."

"By adopting the plan I have mentioned, *you will embrace the spring importation, and give time for digesting and maturing one upon more perfect principles;* and, as the proposed system is intended to be but a temporary one, *that* I esteem to be best which requires the least time to form it."

And Mr. White, opposing Mr. Fitzsimons's suggestion in favor of substituting a more mature measure in place of Mr. Madison's, observed,—

"I am inclined to think, that entering so minutely into the detail will consume too much of our time, and thereby *lose us a greater sum than the additional impost on the last-mentioned articles will bring in;* because there may be doubts whether many of them are capable of bearing an increased duty."

"This law would continue until mature deliberation, ample discussion, and full information, enabled us to complete a perfect system of revenue; for, in order to charge specified articles of manufacture, so as to encourage our domestic ones, it will be necessary to examine the present state of each throughout the Union. This will certainly be a work of labor and time, and will perhaps require more of each than the committee have now in their power."

I have read more than enough to show you the nature and objects of Mr. Madison's first revenue resolution. Let me now advert to a selection or two which may display the nature and grounds and objects of the plan presented by Mr. Fitzsimons in opposition, and which was approved by congress.

In introducing it, Mr. Fitzsimons said,—

"I observe, Mr. Chairman, by what the gentlemen have said, who have spoken on the subject before you, that the proposed plan of revenue is viewed by them as a temporary system, to be continued only until proper materials are brought forward and arranged in more perfect form. I confess, Sir, that I carry my views on this subject much further; that I earnestly wish such a one which, in its operation, will be some way adequate to our present situation, as it respects our agriculture, our manufactures, and our commerce."

"I have prepared myself with an additional number of enumerated articles, which I wish subjoined to those already mentioned in the motion on your table. Among these are some calculated to encourage the productions of our country, and protect our infant manufactures; besides others tending to operate as sumptuary restrictions upon articles which are often termed those of luxury."

He therefore offered the following resolution:—

"*Resolved,* (as the opinion of this committee,) That the following duties ought to be laid on goods, wares, and merchandise, imported into the United States."

I will not read the entire list of articles enumerated in his resolution, but among them were upwards of thirty coming in competition with those produced or made in the United States, the production and manufacture of which was intended to be encouraged.

He was followed and supported by his colleague, Mr. Hartly, who said,—

"I have observed, Sir, from the conversation of the members, that it is in the contemplation of some to enter on this business in a limited and partial manner, *as it relates to revenue alone;* but, for my own part, I wish to do it on as broad a bottom as is at this time practicable. The observations of the honorable gentleman from South Carolina [Mr. Tucker] may have weight in some future stage of the business, for the article of tonnage will not probably be determined for several days, before which time his colleagues may arrive and be consulted in the manner he wishes; but surely no argument derived from that principle can operate to discourage the committee from taking such measures *as will tend to protect and promote our domestic manufactures.* If we consult the history of the ancient world, we shall see that they have thought proper, for a long time past, to give great encouragement to the establishment of manufactures, by laying such par-

tial duties on the importation of foreign goods as to give the home manufactures *a considerable advantage in the price when brought to market.* It is also
well known to this committee, that there are many articles that will bear
a higher duty than others, which are to remain in the common mass, and
be taxed with a certain impost ad valorem. From this view of the subject,
I think it both politic and just that the *fostering hand of the* general government *should extend* to all those manufactures which will tend to national
utility. I am therefore sorry that gentlemen seem to fix their mind to so
early a period as 1783; for we very well know our circumstances are much
changed since that time: we had then but few manufactures among us, and
the vast quantities of goods that flowed in upon us from Europe, at the
conclusion of the war, rendered those few almost useless; since then we
have been forced by necessity, and various other causes, to increase our
domestic manufactures to such a degree as to be able to furnish some in
sufficient quantity to answer the consumption of the whole Union, while
others are daily growing into importance. Our stock of materials, is, in
many instances, equal to the greatest demand, and our artisans sufficient
to work them up, even for exportation. In these cases, I take it to be the
policy of every enlightened nation to give their manufactures that degree
of encouragement necessary to perfect them, without oppressing the other
parts of the community; and under this encouragement, the industry of
the manufacturer will be employed to add to the wealth of the nation.
Many of the articles in the list proposed by my worthy colleague will have
this tendency; and therefore I wish them to be received and considered by
the committee; if sufficient information cannot be obtained as to the circumstances of any particular manufacture, so as to enable the committee
to determine a proper degree of encouragement, it may be relinquished;
but at present it will, perhaps, be most advisable to receive the whole."

And Mr. Madison, yielding to these and other considerations in favor of a
more extended and comprehensive scheme of imposts than his own first plan,
proceeded to unfold, in a speech of much clearness and frankness, the principles upon which such a scheme should be constructed. Declaring himself then
in favor, as the general rule, of a "very free system of commerce," he said,—

"If my general principle is a good one, that commerce ought to be
free, and labor and industry left at large to find its proper object, the only
thing which remains will be to discover the exceptions that do not come

within the rule I have laid down. I agree with the gentleman from Pennsylvania, that there are exceptions, important in themselves, and which claim the particular attention of the committee. Although the freedom of commerce would be advantageous to the world, yet, in some particulars, one nation might suffer to benefit others, and this ought to be for the general good of society."

"If America were to leave her ports perfectly free, and make no discrimination between vessels owned by her citizens and those owned by foreigners, while other nations make this discrimination, it is obvious that such policy would go to exclude American shipping altogether from foreign ports, and she would be materially affected in one of her most important interests. To this we may add another consideration, that by encouraging the means of transporting our productions with facility, we encourage the raising them: and this object, I apprehend, is likely to be kept in view by the general government."

"Duties laid on imported articles may have an effect which comes within the idea of national prudence. It may happen that materials for manufactures may grow up without any encouragement for this purpose. It has been the case in some of the States; but in others regulations have been provided, and have succeeded in producing some establishments, *which ought not to be allowed to perish, from the alteration which has taken place. It would be cruel to neglect them, and divert their industry to other channels:* for it is not possible for the hand of man to shift from one employment to another, without being injured by the change. There may be some manufactures, which, being once formed, can advance towards perfection, without any *adventitious aid, while others,* for want of the fostering hand of government will be unable *to go on at all.* Legislative attention will therefore be necessary to collect the proper objects for this purpose, *and this will form another exception to my general principle."*

"Upon the whole, as I think, *some of the propositions may be productive of revenue, and some may protect our domestic manufactures,* though the latter subject ought not to be too confusedly blended with the former, I hope the committee will receive them, and let them lie over, in order that we may have time to consider how far they are consistent with justice and policy."

You see, then, that in place of the original mere revenue measure, it was proposed to substitute a law which should reconcile with the purpose and the effect of raising revenue the purpose and effect of an adequate protection of domestic labor. This proposition was adopted, and thereupon the house proceeded to frame a bill of enumerations and of discriminations. After Mr. Madison had intimated his opinion that a more elaborate measure than he at first designed was made necessary, and after Mr. Fitzsimons's motion, and his list of enumerated articles had been received and was pending, Mr. Goodhue said,—

"I think, when the original motion was introduced, it was only intended as a temporary expedient; but, from what has fallen from the gentleman on this subject, *I am led to believe that idea is abandoned, and a permanent system is to be substituted in its place. I do not know that this is the best mode of the two, but perhaps it may take no more time than the other, if we apply ourselves with assiduity to the task.*"

In the same stage of the business,—

"Mr. Clymer submitted it to the consideration of the committee, how far it was best to bring propositions forward in this way. Not that he objected to this mode of *encouraging manufactures and obtaining revenue,* by combining *the two objects in one bill.* He was satisfied that a political necessity existed *for both the one and the other,* and it would not be a amiss to do it in this way, but perhaps the business would be more speedily accomplished by entering upon it systematically."

And Mr. Boudinot said,—

"The subject in debate *was originally brought forward as a temporary expedient to obtain revenue to support the exigencies of the Union. It has been changed* by successive motions for amendment; and the idea of a *permanent system, to embrace every object connected with commerce, manufactures, and revenue, is held up in its stead.*"

"Let us take, then, the resolution of congress, in 1783, as presented by the honorable gentleman from Virginia, (Mr. Madison,) and make it the basis of our system, *adding only such protecting duties as are necessary to support the manufactures established by the legislatures of the manufacturing States.*"

The house then plunged at once into the details of a revenue and protective tariff. Every member presented such articles as he thought deserving of enumeration for encouragement by a particular duty; and his motion was resisted and supported very much as similar motions are supported and resisted in the tariff debates of our day. It would carry me too far to read this part of the history of the law, but a few passages, which might seem gathered from "Niles's Weekly," Register of 1828, (so little is there new under the sun, so immortal is truth, so immortal is error, so narrow is the circle of identical, recurrent ideas in which these discussions go round and round,) a few passages will not be irrelevant to my purpose.

Hear the debate about the proposed duty on *steel:*—

"Mr. Lee moved to strike out this duty; observing that the consumption of steel was very great, and essentially necessary to agricultural improvements. He did not believe any gentleman would contend that enough of this article to answer consumption *could be fabricated* in any part of the Union; hence it would operate as an oppressive, though an indirect tax upon agriculture; and any tax, whether direct or indirect, upon this interest, at this juncture, would be unwise and impolitic."

"Mr. Tucker joined the gentleman in his opinion, observing that it was impossible for some States to get it but by importation from foreign countries. He conceived it more deserving a bounty to increase the quantity, than an impost which would lessen the consumption and make it dearer also."

"Mr. Clymer replied, that the manufacture of steel in America was rather in its infancy; but as all the materials necessary to make it were the produce of almost every State in the Union, and as the manufacture *was already established, and attended with considerable success,* he deemed it prudent to emancipate our country from the manacles in which she was held by foreign manufacturers. A furnace in Philadelphia, with a very small aid from the legislature of Pennsylvania, made three hundred tons in two years, and now makes at the rate of two hundred and thirty tons annually, and with a little further encouragement would supply enough for the consumption of the Union. He hoped, therefore, gentlemen would be disposed, under these considerations, *to extend a degree of patronage to a manufacture which* a moment's reflection would convince them was highly deserving protection."

"Mr. Madison thought the object of selecting this article *to be solely* the encouragement of the manufacture, and not revenue; for on any other consideration, it would be more proper, as observed by the gentleman from Carolina, (Mr. Tucker,) to give a bounty on the importation. It was so materially connected with the improvement of agriculture and other manufactures, that he questioned its propriety *even on that score*. A duty would tend to depress many mechanic arts in the proportion that it protected this; he thought it best to reserve this article to the non-enumerated ones, where it would be subject to a five per cent. ad valorem."

"Mr. Fitzsimons. Some States were, from local circumstances, better situated to carry on the manufacture than others, and would derive some little advantage on this account in the commencement of the business. But, laying aside local distinctions, what operates to the benefit of one part, in establishing useful institutions, will eventually operate to the advantage of the whole."

"Suppose five shillings per hundred weight was imposed, it might be, as stated, a partial duty, *but would not the evil be soon overbalanced by the establishment of such an important manufacture?—a great and principal manufacture for every agricultural country,* but particularly useful in the United States."

On beer, ale, and porter:—

"Mr. Fitzsimons meant to make an alteration in this article, by distinguishing beer, ale, and porter, imported in casks, from what was imported in bottles. He thought this manufacture one highly deserving of encouragement. If the morals of the people were to be improved by what entered into their diet, it would be prudent in the National Legislature *to encourage* the manufacture of malt liquors. The small protecting duties laid in Pennsylvania had a great effect towards *the establishment of breweries;* they no longer imported this article, but, on the contrary, exported considerable quantities, and, in two or three years, with the fostering aid of government, would be able to furnish enough for the whole consumption of the United States. He moved nine cents per gallon."

"Mr. Lawrence seconded the motion. He would have this duty so high as to give a decided preference to American beer; it would tend also to encourage agriculture, because the malt and hops consumed in the manufacture were the produce of our own grounds."

"Mr. Sinnickson declared himself a friend of this manufacture, and thought if the duty was *laid high enough to effect a prohibition, the manufacture would increase, and of consequence, the price be lessened.* He considered it of importance, inasmuch as the materials were produced in the country, and tended to advance the agricultural interest."

"Mr. Madison moved to lay an impost of eight cents on all beer imported. He did not think this sum would give a monopoly, *but hoped it would be such an encouragement as to induce the manufacture to take deep root in every State in the Union;* in this case, it would produce the collateral good hinted at by the gentleman from New Jersey, which, in his opinion, was an object well worthy of being attended to."

On candles:—

"Mr. Fitzsimons moved to lay a duty of two cents on all candles of tallow, per pound."

"Mr. Tucker observed, that some States were under the necessity of importing considerable quantities of this article also, while others had enough, and more than enough, for their own consumption; therefore the burden would be partially borne by such States."

"Mr. Fitzsimons. The manufacture of candles is an important manufacture, and far advanced towards perfection. I have no doubt but, in a few years, we shall be able to furnish sufficient to supply the consumption for every part of the continent. In Pennsylvania we have a duty of two pence per pound; and under the operation of this small encouragement the manufacture has gained considerable strength. We no longer import candles from Ireland or England, of whom, a few years ago, we took considerable quantities; the necessity of continuing those encouragements which the State legislatures have deemed proper, exist in a considerable degree; therefore it will be politic in the government of the United States to continue such duties till their object is accomplished."

"Mr. Boudinot apprehended that most States imported considerable quantities of this article from Russia and Ireland; he expected they would be made cheaper than they could be imported, if a small encouragement was held out by the government, as the materials were to be had in abundance in our country."

"Mr. Lawrence thought that, if candles were an object of considerable importation, they ought to be taxed for the sake of obtaining revenue; and, if they were not imported in considerable quantities, the burden upon the consumer would be small, while it tended to cherish a valuable manufacture."

On coal:—

"Mr. Bland, of Virginia, informed the committee that there were mines opened in Virginia capable of supplying the whole of the United States; and, if some restraint was laid on the importation of foreign coal, those mines might be worked to advantage. He thought it needless to insist upon the advantages resulting from a colliery, as a supply for culinary and mechanical purposes, and as a nursery to train up seamen for a navy. He moved three cents a bushel."

On hemp:—

"Mr. Moore declared the Southern States were well calculated for the cultivation of hemp, and, from certain circumstances, well inclined thereto. He conceived it the duty of the committee to pay as much respect to the encouragement and protection of husbandry (the most important of all interests in the United States) as they did to manufactures."

"Mr. Scott stated a fact or two; being, perhaps, as well acquainted with the Western country as any member of the committee. The lands along the frontiers, he could assure the committee, were well calculated for the cultivation of this plant; it is a production that will bear carriage by land better than any other, tobacco not excepted. He believed an encouragement of the kind now moved for would bring, in a year or two, vast quantities from that country, at little expense, to Philadelphia, even from the waters of the Ohio; the inhabitants expect some encouragement, and will be grateful for it."

"Mr. White. If the legislature take no notice of this article, the people will be led to believe it is not an object worthy of encouragement, and the spirit of cultivation will be damped; whereas, if a small duty only was laid, it might point out to them that it was desirable, and would induce an increase of the quantity."

"Mr. Moore. By the encouragement given to manufactures you raise them in price, while a competition is destroyed, which tended to the advantage of agriculture. He thought the manufacturing interest ought not to stand in the way of the other; but, as the committee had agreed to give it encouragement, he hoped the other would receive its share of legislative support."

"Mr. Burke thought it proper to suggest to the committee what might be the probable effect of the proposed measure in the State he represented, (South Carolina,) and the adjoining one, (Georgia). The staple products of that part of the Union were hardly worth cultivation, on account of their fall in price; the planters are therefore disposed to pursue some other. The lands are certainly well adapted to the growth of hemp, and he had no doubt but its culture would be practised with attention. Cotton is likewise *in contemplation among them;* and, if good seed could be procured, *he hoped it might succeed.* But the low, strong, rice lands would produce hemp in abundance,—many thousand tons even this year, if it was not so late in the season. He liked the idea of laying a low duty now, *and encouraging it* against the time when a supply might be had from our own cultivation."

On glass:—

"Mr. Carroll moved to insert window and other glass. A manufacture of this article was begun in Maryland, and attended with considerable success; if the legislature were to grant a small encouragement, it would be permanently established; the materials were to be found in the country in sufficient quantities to answer the most extensive demands."

On paper:—

"Mr. Clymer informed the house that the manufacture of paper was an important one; and, *having grown up under legislative encouragement,* it *will be wise to continue it.*"

On wool cards:—

"Mr. Ames introduced wool cards, with observing that they were manufactured to the eastward as good and as cheap as the imported ones."
"Mr. Clymer mentioned that, in the State of Pennsylvania, the manufacture was carried to great perfection, and enough could be furnished to supply the demand. A duty of fifty cents per dozen was imposed on wool cards."

Prohibitory duties were moved, without a word of doubt, from any quarter, of the constitutional power, and, in some cases, the economical expediency, of imposing them. Thus,—

"Mr. Bland, of Virginia, thought that very little revenue was likely to be collected on the article of beef, let the duty be more or less; and, as it was to be had in sufficient quantities within the United States, *perhaps a tax amounting to a prohibition would be proper.*"

It was rejected as totally unnecessary, "nothing being to be apprehended from rivalship."

On manufactured tobacco,—

"Mr. Sherman moved six cents, *as he thought the duty ought to amount to a prohibition. This was agreed to.*"

I have detained the senate longer than I could have wished, upon these proofs and illustrations of the constitutional and economical doctrines which compose the foundation of our "old system" of impost duties. They establish conclusively, if I rightly apprehend them, that in every just sense of the language, in principle, aims, and forms, the "model law" was a protective tariff. It was as much so as the law of 1824. It assumed and asserted exactly the same theory of power, of right, of duty, of expediency. It sought to bring such a sum of money into the treasury as the wants of administration exacted; but it sought to effect this by such arrangements of detail, by such discriminations of high and low duties, by prohibition here, by total exemption there, as should secure to the vast and various labor of America, on the land, in the shop, on the sea, a clear and adequate advantage over the labor of the alien nations of the world. The proofs that these opinions and these intentions presided over and controlled the whole law, and every part of it, are everywhere,—in its preamble, in its provisions, in its history, origin, growth, successive changes, and final form. Sir, the very day of its passage, July 4th, 1789, seems to mark the energetic "Americanism" of its nature!

But it has been a hundred times repeated in the debate, that the duties laid by this law are moderate duties. Much arithmetical pains have been wasted in calculating their average percent. I say wasted; for, in the first place, we cannot reduce the numerous specific duties, in which it abounds, to their equivalent ad valorems, because we do not know the prices of 1789; in the next place, an average, ever so exactly calculated, conveys no idea of the degree of protection

secured by a highly discriminating tariff; and, finally, however moderate may
be the duties of this law, it is not the less, in principle, in intent, in its constitutional and economical doctrines, and in its effect, a protective tariff. What is
such a tariff? What makes it such? Where, and how, do you draw the line
between it and a revenue tariff? Of two tariffs, each yielding about the same supply to the treasury, by what standard, by what tests, do you pronounce that one
is a measure of finance, the other a measure of protection? Sir, although these
two things run very much into each other, although they have a good deal in
common, and all definitions are inadequate and are hazardous, yet are they
essentially distinct; and I will venture to submit, that, by universal consent, a
tariff which looks to the protection of domestic labor against foreign labor, as
one important, substantial, influencive object and purpose, either jointly with,
or in exclusion of, the object and purpose of revenue; a tariff which, in numerous instances, selects a certain form and a certain rate of duties, rather than
another and lower, upon the avowed ground that the form and rate chosen are
better for protection than the form and rate rejected, though no better and not
as good for revenue; which lays some duties of prohibition, and asserts the
power to lay others; which lays many duties which, in and by themselves, are
expected and designed to check particular kinds of importations, in order to give
the domestic producer an advantage in the market over the foreign producer,
and thus to diminish the revenue to be drawn from those particular and numerous sources; and which does all this, to a greater degree than an equally or more
effective revenue tariff would do it, in consideration and contemplation of
prospective ultimate advantages to result from the establishment of certain
domestic employments—a tariff which does all this, upon these reasons, is a protecting tariff, or there is no such thing in any legislative code in the world. I do
not care whether the duties are high or low; how they average, or what are the
extremes. Such a tariff asserts the constitutional power, the social and political
right, and the economical expediency of so regulating foreign commerce, of so
gathering in revenue, as to bring to life, and to keep alive, the whole or particular forms of domestic labor, as distinct from foreign labor; and it asserts it practically. This covers the whole ground. Such a tariff, exactly, is this of 1789. Such
a tariff totally rejects the doctrine which has been maintained in the debate, that
of several duties on the same subject, each yielding the same amount of revenue,
the lowest is to be preferred. It adopts and exemplifies the directly opposite doctrine, that, even where the highest will yield less revenue, it may wisely, justly,
constitutionally be preferred, because it will produce a compensation of other
good in another way. It rejects the doctrine asserted in this debate, that under

our system protection is merely an accidental incident to revenue, to be endured, not favored; it declares, on the contrary, that the two purposes of revenue and protection, may be harmoniously blended; may be regarded as of equal importance; that one may predominate in this duty, and another in that; that it is a legitimate and a noble enterprise of statesmanship, to transform the very evil and burden of taxation into a means of individual comfort and enjoyment and national greatness and glory. It teaches the lawgiver, that instead of bewildering himself, and wasting his precious time in trying to find the revenue maximum of duty,—more hopeless and more useless than the search after the quadrature of the circle or the perpetual motion,—he should just, sincerely, honestly, and constantly propose this problem to himself: How can I procure that amount of revenue which an economical administration of government demands, in such manner as most impartially and most completely to develop and foster the universal industrial capacities of the country, of whose vast material interests I am honored with the charge?

Whether its duties are high or low, then, this is a protecting tariff. But who knows whether that portion of them which is specific is high or low? We have no prices current, and no other proof of the prices of that day; and without such proof how can you reduce these duties to their equivalent ad valorem? I read a passage from one of the speeches of Mr. Bland, of Virginia, during the debate, from which it would seem that some of the rates would be called high even now:—

"The enumerated articles in this bill are very numerous; they are taxed from fifty per cent. downwards; the general mass pays five per cent."

We are told in this discussion that thirty per cent. and thirty-three and one third per cent. are the maximum of revenue duty. Here were fifty per cent. duties, and in *the specific form,* and therefore certain of collection; while the ad valorem forms, on foreign values, are as certain to be evaded and defrauded.[pa

But, Mr. President, there is another answer to the suggestion that these duties were moderate. Sir, in the actual circumstances of the time, they were entirely sufficient for the protection of the agricultural, navigating, commercial, manufacturing, and mechanical industry, which they were intended to protect. They effected their object perfectly. And when you consider the circumstances, how plain, coarse, hardy, simple, were the existing mechanical manufacturing employments of the country; how unlike the various, refined, and sensitive forms, which in a later age they put on; that they were, very much, manufactures of wood into cabinet-ware, furniture, carriages, and ships; of leather, in tanneries; of iron in blacksmiths' shops; of cloth, from cotton, wool, and flax, chiefly in private families; that they were many of them very far in the interior; that there was not yet a single cotton mill, and perhaps not a single woollen mill, in the country; that thus they exacted no large accumulations of capital, nor high degrees of skill slowly acquired, nor expensive machinery continually changing; and when you consider, too, that England, that all Europe, was just about to rush into the wars of the French revolution, drawing the sword which was never to be sheathed until night should fall on the hushed and drenched field of Waterloo—in view of these circumstances, you will not wonder that even these duties were sufficient. The statesmen of that time, Sir, meant to protect domestic labor; they knew how to do it, and they did it. In point of fact, from 1789 to 1808, the progress of manufactures was slow but sure. Then began a new era, of which I will speak in its place.

I think, Mr. President, that it is scarcely necessary to look beyond this survey of the history of the law of 1789, to discover the spirit, principles, and aims, which presided in and framed it. Let me give you, however, a little supplementary evidence to prove that I have not misconceived its essential structure and nature. Hear, first, in what terms Washington could speak of it, and of the subsequent and kindred legislation upon the same policy. In his last Address, in December, 1796, he says,—

> "Congress *have repeatedly, and not without success, directed their attention to the encouragement of manufactures.* The object is of too much consequence not to insure a continuance of their efforts in every way that shall appear eligible. Ought our country to remain dependent on foreign supply, precarious, because liable to be interrupted? If the necessary article should in this mode *cost more in time of peace,* will not the security and independence thence arising form an ample compensation?"

That great man thought, you perceive, that even if a protective policy should enhance the prices of a time of peace, security and independence were equivalents with which a nation might be content. Sir, we have won the equivalents, and yet we do not pay the compensation. The "necessary article costs" less, not more; yet is our security more absolute, our independence more real, our greatness more steadfast.

See, too, how Mr. Jefferson, in 1802, describes the policy, which, when he wrote, had been pursued from 1789, for thirteen years:—

"To cultivate peace and maintain commerce and navigation in all their lawful enterprises, and *to protect the manufactures adapted to our circumstances, are* (among others) *the landmarks by which to guide ourselves in all our proceedings.* By *continuing* to make these the rule of our action, we shall endear to our countrymen the true principles of the Constitution, and promote an union of sentiment and of action equally auspicious to their happiness and safety."

And Mr. Dallas, Secretary of the Treasury, in 1816, in his very able report to congress upon the subject of a tariff of duties, remarks,—

"There are few if any governments which do not regard the establishment of domestic manufactures as a chief object of public policy. The United States have always so regarded it. In the earliest acts of congress which were passed after the adoption of the present Constitution, the obligation of providing, by duties on imports, for the discharge of the public debts, is expressly connected with the policy of encouraging and protecting manufactures."

And Mr. Madison, looking back, in 1828, to a scene in which his part had been so conspicuous, says, in his letter to Mr. Cabell: "That the encouragement of manufactures was an object of the power to regulate trade, is proved by the use made of the power for that object, in the first session of the first congress under the Constitution; when among the members present were so many who had been members of the federal convention which framed the Constitution, and of the state conventions which ratified it; each of these classes consisting also of members who had opposed and who had espoused the Constitution in its actual form. It does not appear, from the printed proceedings of congress on that occasion that the power was denied by any of them. And it may be remarked, that members from Virginia, in particular, as well of the Anti-federal as the Federal party, the names then distinguishing those who had opposed and those who had approved the Constitution, did not hesitate to propose duties and to suggest even prohibitions in favor of several articles of her productions. By one, a duty was proposed on mineral coal, in favor of the Virginia coal pits; by another, a duty on hemp was proposed, to encourage the growth of that article; and by a third, a prohibition even of foreign beef was suggested, as a measure of sound policy."

And now, Mr. President, let me say, passing strange it would have been, if that congress had not made just such a law; had not founded just such a system!

Composed as it was, to so large an extent, of members of the convention which had framed the new Constitution, and of the conventions which had adopted it,—fresh, all of them, from the people, and intimately familiar with the evils, the fears, and the hopes, of which the recent government was born: the excessive importations; the exhausting drain of specie to pay for them; the mountain weight of debt not yet paid to the foreign manufacturer and mechanic; the depression of labor, the derangement of currency, the decline of trade; penetrated profoundly with the certain knowledge that a leading, a paramount object, held universally in view throughout the great effort, just crowned with success, to frame a new Constitution, was to insure the capacity and the will to extend governmental protection to domestic labor,—such a congress, thus admonished, thus enlightened, could not help making such a law and founding such a system. They would not have dared to go home without doing so! I once, Mr. President, in this place, on a former occasion, and with a different purpose, attempted to collect and combine, and to exhibit under a single view, the proofs contained in the writings, such as they are, which appeared in this country between the peace of 1783 and the adoption of the Constitution, tending to show that *a policy of protection by means of duties on the productions of foreign labor* was most prominent among the beneficial instrumentalities which the new government was expected to possess and exert, and among the controlling inducements to its establishment. Those proofs are very numerous; they are very widely scattered over many hundred pages of newspapers and larger periodical publications, and over a space of six years and more, during which the public mind was in a state of unexampled agitation, anxiety, and activity; they consist of essays, addresses, the proceedings of public meetings, and the like; and they are contributed in almost an equal proportion by every part of the country, although the largest number perhaps come from the central States. Taken altogether, and making every allowance for the fact that a great deal of the writing and speech, in which the opinions, hopes, fears, and intentions of that age were embodied, perished; and that among the opinions and intentions thus expressed, but of whose existence no contemporary record is left, there may have been some of a different character—taken altogether, they prove as clearly that a leading, main, prominent purpose of that generation of our fathers was to create a government which could and should protect American labor, by regulating the introduction of the products of foreign labor, by prohibiting them, by subjecting them to duties of discrimination, and by such other policy as the accomplishment of the object should prescribe—they prove this as clearly as you can prove out of the Irish newspapers of this day that Catholic Ireland is agitating for repeal. Sir, I shall not trouble the senate with the repetition of all or many of the proofs which I at that time exhibited; but I cannot resist the temptation of reminding you how North Carolina and South Carolina could reason then on the nature and the cure of the evils which bore down the young America to the dust; on the difference between manufacturing abroad and manufacturing at home,—the difference to national wealth, to currency, to true and durable public and private prosperity; on the general policy of the protection of American labor, by a more restrained importation of the productions of foreign labor. I read for that purpose, first, a selection or two from certain letters written in North Carolina in 1787, which I find in the American Museum for August, 1787. The name of the writer is not given, but he sets out by declaring,—

"That his complaints are not occasioned by personal misfortunes; but he finds himself a member of a great family; he interests himself as a brother in the happiness of his fellow-citizens, and he suffers when they are grieved."

The annunciation of his subject marks his fitness to discuss it.

"We are going to consider whether the administration of government, in these infant States, is to be a system of patchwork and a series of expedients—whether a youthful empire is to be supported, like the walls of a tottering ancient palace, by shores and temporary props, or by measures which may prove effectual and lasting—measures which may improve by use and strengthen by age. We are going to consider whether we shall deserve to be a branch of the most poor, dishonest, and contemptible, or of the most flourishing, independent, and happy nation on the face of the earth."

And what do you think is his "measure which is to improve by use, and strengthen by age"? Why, exactly, the encouragement of domestic manufactures, by taxes on foreign manufactures.

"The more I consider the progress of credit and the increase of wealth in foreign nations, the more fully am I convinced that paper money must prove hurtful to this country; that we *cannot be relieved from our debts except by promoting domestic manufactures.*"

Having adverted to the vast accumulation of our foreign debt since the peace, and to the discreditable and startling fact that it had been contracted for numerous articles of necessity which we could better produce, and numerous articles of luxury which we could better dispense with, he proceeds:—

"Let us turn our attention to manufactures, and the staple of our country will soon rise to its proper value, for we have already glutted every foreign market. By this expedient, instead of using fictitious paper, we shall soon obtain hard money sufficient; instead of toiling in the field, and becoming poor, *that we may enrich the manufactures of other countries,* we shall prosper by our labor, *and enrich our own citizens.*"

"Every domestic manufacture is cheaper than a foreign one, for this plain reason: by the first nothing is lost to the country; by the other, the whole value is lost,—it is carried away, never to return. It is perfectly indifferent to this State or to the United States, *what may be the price of domestic manufactures,* because that price remains in the country."

"All wise governments" (such is his argument, page 124) "have thought it their duty, on special occasions, to offer bounties for the encouragement of domestic manufactures; but an excise on foreign goods must operate as a bounty."

"I have said that an excise is more favorable to the poor than a land or poll tax. I will venture an additional sentiment: there never was a government in which an excise could be of so much use as in the United States of America. In all other countries, taxes are considered as grievances. In the United States, an excise on foreign goods would not be a grievance: like medicine to a sick man, it would give us strength; it would close that wasteful drain by which our honor and our wealth are consumed. What though money was not wanted,—though we did not owe a florin to any foreign nation,—though we had no domestic debt,—and though the expenses of civil government could be supported for many years without a tax, still it may be questioned whether an excise would not be desirable. It would certainly be the best expedient *for promoting domestic manufactures;* and the condition in which we now live, our general dependence on a foreign country for arms and clothing, is dishonorable—it is extremely dangerous."

"It is the duty of the statesman either to or to promote the several streams of commerce by taxes or bounties, as to render them profitable to the nation. Thus it happened in Massachusetts. A tax of twenty-five per cent. was lately imposed on nails, and the poor of Tamton were immediately returned to life and vigor."

"*If any man has doubts concerning the effect of large taxes on foreign manufactures, he should turn his eyes to the Eastern States.* The mechanic is generally the first who perceives of a pernicious commerce; for the support of his family depends on his daily labor." "Hence it is that the merchant may be profited by a particular branch of commerce, and may promote it diligently, while his country is sinking into a deadly consumption."

Sir, these opinions had spread, still earlier, still farther south. Let me recall to your recollection a few passages from the book of the wisdom of South Carolina. Here is an essay, in two letters, written in Charleston, in that State, in 1786, by some one whose enlarged and wise nationality of spirit and aims is indicated by his signature,—"American." The position which he asserts is, that the "only method, consistent with humanity, by which nations have raised themselves to opulence and power, is the encouraging agriculture, manufactures, and commerce." In proof of this, he glances at the history of Egypt, "which to tilling the land soon joined the mechanic arts," and whose "pyramids and sepulchres, fine linens and purples, attested the degree to which she advanced them;" of Tyre, which "enriched herself by her *manufactures* and commerce;" of Carthage, "which carried with her the mechanic arts and the spirit of commerce;" of Venice, the greatest *entrepôt* in the world, "which imported the raw materials of other nations, manufactured them, and exported them to an immense amount;" of Spain, which "expelled her manufacturers and merchants from the kingdom,— a loss that she has not recovered to this day, and perhaps will not for centuries to come,"—a loss which all the mines of America have not compensated; for "*with them went the spirit of manufacturing and commerce, which always gives vigor to agriculture*"—Spain, "which, possessing one of the finest climates and soils of Europe, must remain poor, till manufactures and commerce can convince the haughty Spaniard that they alone are the only true permanent source of wealth;" England, which, "in the reign of Queen Elizabeth, made but a small figure in the political or mercantile scale of Europe, which exported chiefly in foreign bottoms her wheat, which is now consumed by her manufacturers, a little lead, tin, and wool, to Flanders, and, in return received foreign manufactures;" Scotland, "a century ago almost as poor as the satire of Churchill painted it, but which had increased in wealth with a rapidity never exceeded, and by these means: manufacturers were invited thither,—these, with the great number of sailors, and victualling their ships, raised the price of provisions, and gave life to agriculture,—land rose in value,—the barren heaths were manured and tilled,—rents rose,—the tenants grew rich,—the numbers increased,—their cities were improved,—their large villages became cities,—and new towns were built in places that, till lately, seemed to defy human art to improve them. This is," he adds, "the effect, and always will be, of manufactures and commerce in every country."

"It is in vain," he concludes, "for any people to attempt to be rich or have a sufficient circulating specie among them, whose imports exceed their exports; the hand of the manufacturer in a distant land seems to act upon gold and silver as the loadstone does upon the needle."

Commenting on the fact that England once raised annually a revenue of three millions and a half by monopolizing our trade, he says,—

"A great part of this may be saved to these States by our becoming our own merchants and carriers; and a great part of the remaining sum may be saved in a few years *by encouraging our* own manufacturers; and even this encouragement will be of service to our revenues. I mean, laying *a duty on our imports,* and giving a small part in bounties to our own tradesmen."

"I do not wish our planters to turn from planting to manufacturing; I only wish to encourage European tradesmen to come to reside here. I wish to see as much as possible exported and as little imported. The planters that buy the manufactures of America stop so much money in this country, which must return again to the planters' hands as long as traders eat."

Of such as this is the whole political literature of that day. There breathes throughout it all a profound and earnest conviction that, without a government which can, and which will, develop and guard the labor of America by protective tariffs and other kindred instrumentality, independence was not yet achieved; the hopes of liberty were a delusive dream; a barren sceptre only had been grasped, unfruitful of joy, unfruitful of glory.

Sir, the congress of 1789 might have known, by another and shorter process, the public sentiment of that day,—the public sentiment of the age of the Constitution. There were members who had witnessed and united in some one of the processions and assemblies which, in so many towns and villages, had just been celebrating the institution of the new government; and they might have learned there what the people expected of them! Very striking exhibitions they were, Sir; and altogether worthy of the contemplation of him who would truly and adequately know for what the Constitution was created. On an appointed day, men came in from the country, and, mingling themselves with those of the town, were arranged in order by thousands. Beneath bright skies,—the moral and national prospect how much brighter than the natural!—with banners and music, gazed on, sympathized with by wives and mothers and daughters and sisters, thronging at windows, in balconies, and up to the house-tops, the long and serried files, not of war, but of peace, the long and serried files of labor, moved from street to street, and at length composed themselves to unite in thanksgiving to God, and in listening to discourses commemorative of the event, and embodying the gratitude and the expectations with which the new government was welcomed in,—embodying a survey of its powers and objects, and a sketch of the transcendent good of which it was full, for that age, and for all time. Sir, in the banners of various device which marked the long course of those processions; in the mottoes upon their flags; in the machines, and models and figures, with which the pacific and more than triumphal march was enriched and enlivened; in the order of its arrangements; in the organizations of tradesmen and artisans, and all the families of labor which swelled it; in the conversation of individuals of those "grave and anxious multitudes" one with another; in the topics and thoughts of the orators of the day; in the applause of the audience; in all this vast, vivid, and various accumulation and exhibition of the general mind, almost as well as in the journals of the convention, the "Madison Papers," the debates of public bodies or the grave discussions of "The Federalist" itself you may read—the congress of 1789 might read—what kind of government the people thought they had constructed. I could almost say that the Constitution is what the general belief of that age held it to be; and in these great and solemn festal scenes is the expression of that general belief.

Take the Philadelphia procession for an instance, of the fourth of July, 1788, and see what the readers of "Poor Richard's Almanac," the pupils and contemporaries of Franklin, expected of the federal Constitution. It was a column of many thousands of persons, of all trades and callings. The more advanced figures and devices of the procession were intended to represent, in a chronological series, the great events which preceded the adoption of the new government. There was one on horseback, representing Independence, and bearing the staff and cap of liberty; next followed one, riding upon a horse, formerly of Count Rochambeau, and carrying a flag with devices of lilies and stars, commemorative of the French alliance, to which we owed so much; then another, with a staff surmounted with laurel and olive, announcing the treaty of peace; after him, another, bearing aloft the name of Washington; then a herald, proclaiming with sound of trumpet the NEW ERA; then a representation of the convention which framed the Constitution; and then others, of the Constitution itself; "a lofty ornamental car, in the form of an eagle;" and a grand federal edifice, the dome supported by thirteen columns, and surmounted by a "figure of plenty." After these, came an appropriate and golden train, the long line of the various labor of America, for whom the new era had risen, with healing in its wings. First, as it ought to have been, was the agricultural society. Then came the manufacturing society, with spinning and carding machines; looms and apparatus for the printing of muslins and calicoes. This bore three flags. The device on one was a bee-hive, with bees issuing from it, standing in the beams of a rising sun; the field of the flag blue, and the motto, "in its rays we shall feel new vigor." The motto on the next was, "may the Union government protect the manufactures of America;" and, on the next, "may government protect us." On the carriage of the manufacturers, drawn by ten horses, were a carding machine, worked by two persons "carding cotton;" a spinning machine, worked by a woman, and drawing cotton suitable for fine jeans; looms on which laces and jeans were being woven; a man designing and cutting prints for shawls; and "Mrs. Hewson and her four daughters," in cotton dresses of their own manufacture, pencilling a piece of chintz of Mr. Hewson's printing. There followed then great numbers; I believe there may have been more than fifty bodies of tradesmen and mechanics, each with its banner, devices, and motto, expressive of the same hopes and the same convictions, evidencing equally the universal popular mind. But I need pursue the matter no further. Sir, what was seen in this procession was seen, on a larger or smaller scale, everywhere. The pageant is passed. The actors have retired from human view. The awful curtain has dropped on them forever. All the world's a stage, and this part is played! Yet the spirit of philosophical history—that spirit to which the half-obliterated figures of a procession upon a wasting architectural fragment reveal intelligibly and instructively some glory or some sorrow of a past age— will not disdain to gather up and ponder these manifestations of the hopes, desires, and purposes, of that mighty heart now hushed. I do not wish or expect to understand the objects for which the Constitution was framed better than the generation which made it; and of their understanding of them I have referred you to very vivid and very authentic proofs. I cannot forbear to read you a sentence or two, before I take leave of the subject, from "Observations on the Philadelphia Procession," written by an eye-witness, very soon after the celebration:—

"The large stage on which the carding and spinning machines displayed the manufacture of cotton was viewed with astonishment and delight by every spectator. On that stage were carried the emblems of the future wealth and independence of our country. Cotton may be cultivated in the Southern and manufactured in the Eastern and Middle States, in such quantities, in a few years, as to clothe every citizen of the United States. *Hence will arise a bond of Union to the States, more powerful than any article of the new Constitution.* Cotton possesses several advantages over wool as an article of dress and commerce. It is not liable to be moth-eaten, and is proper both for winter and summer garments. It may, moreover, be manufactured in America at a less expense than it can be imported from any nation in Europe. From these circumstances, I cannot help hoping that we shall soon see cotton not only the uniform of the citizens of America, but an article of exportation to foreign countries. Several respectable gentlemen exhibited a prelude of these events by appearing in complete suits of jeans, manufactured by the machines that have been mentioned."

Compare this with the judgment of Mr. Calhoun, in his speech in the house of representatives, April, 1816:—

"Capital employed in manufacturing is calculated to bind together more closely our widely spread Republic. It will greatly increase our mutual dependence and intercourse."

I leave, then, the first period of our policy. The law of 1789 was a protective tariff, in principle, intention, and effect. It was made so in execution of the universal will of the age of the Constitution. In the "good old days," protection, whether "principal" or "incident," was held indispensable, and was made sufficient.

And now we are prepared to compare or to contrast with this the second system,—the existing system,—that which began in 1816, and was matured in 1824 and 1828. Sir, it is exactly the system of 1789, accommodated to the altered circumstances of the nation and the world. The statesmen of the last period followed in the very footsteps of their fathers. It is not enough to say their objects were as honest and as useful, their spirit and aims as high, their principles as sound. They were *the same,*—just the same,—*mutatis mutandis.* The law of 1789 was framed to protect the existing manufacturing and mechanical industry of the country. So was that of 1816 and 1824. The times compelled a change of details, and details were changed. Principles, policy, were unchanged. I cannot discern the hand of "millionary capitalists," or "trading politicians" in the framing of the later, more than in that of the earlier system. I see it in neither. Sir, I defend the lawgivers of 1816 and 1824, first, by the example of their fathers, and then by every consideration of enlightened patriotism which may influence American statesmen.

The congress of 1789 found many manufacturing and mechanical arts starting to life, and soliciting to be protected. The congress of 1816, and that of 1824, found families and groups and classes of manufacturing and mechanical arts, far more numerous, far more valuable, far more sensitive also, and with more urgent claim, soliciting protection. In the interval between 1789 and 1816, this whole enterprise had not only immensely enhanced its value, but it had totally changed its nature. It had increased its annual productions to $120,000,000 in 1810, and to $150,000,000 or perhaps $200,000,000 in 1816. But its nature had become different. Instead of a few plain, hardy, coarse, simple, household employments, it had become a various, refined, sensitive industry,—demanding associated capital, skill, long and highly trained, costly and improving machinery,—more precious, but presenting a far broader mark to the slings and arrows of fortune, to hostility, to change, to the hotter foreign competitions which its growth was sure to provoke. Now, you all praise the husbandry of 1789, which so carefully guarded the few blades, just timidly peeping forth into the rain and sunshine, of that April day, hardly worth the treading down; will you depreciate the husbandry of 1824, which with the same solicitude, but at the expense of a higher wall, guarded the grain, then half-grown, and evincing what the harvest was to be?

The statesmen of 1816 and 1824 then might justify themselves by the example of the age of Washington and the Constitution. But I desire to make their defence upon considerations even higher and broader.

In the first place, Sir, their legislation may not only be justified, but it is entitled to praise, honor, and imitation, on the ground of the transcendent value of manufacturing and mechanical industry to a people. Do not fear that I am about to inflict upon you a commonplace upon this topic. I do not understand that there are two different opinions upon it in the civilized world. Certainly there are not two here. Senators who will not lift a finger to introduce or to foster such industry; who think that neither this government nor the State governments have any power to do so, by the only means that are worth a straw, protective duties—this government having none because the Constitution does not give it, and the State governments having none because the Constitution takes it from them to bestow it on nobody—senators who think that, power or no power, you ought to do nothing directly, openly, and avowedly, to exert it—all vie with one another in glowing and lofty estimates of the uses and value of this industry to our nation—to any nation. Doubtless, Sir, to the higher forms of a complete civilization, a various, extensively developed, intellectual manufacturing and mechanical industry, aiming to multiply the comforts and supply the wants of the great body of the people, is wholly indispensable. Its propitious influence upon the wages and enjoyments of labor; the reasonable rewards which it holds out by means of joint stock, in shares, to all capital, whether the one hundred dollars of the widow and orphan, or the one hundred thousand of their wealthier neighbor; its propitious influence upon all the other employments of society; upon agriculture, by relieving it of over-production and over-competition, and securing it a market at home, without shutting up its market abroad; upon commerce, creating or mainly sustaining its best branch, domestic trade, and giving to its foreign trade variety, flexibility, an enlargement of field, and the means of commanding a needful supply of the productions of other nations, without exhausting drains on our own; its influence upon the comforts of the poor, upon refinement, upon security, defence, independence, power, nationality—all this is conceded by everybody. Senators denounce the means, but they glorify the end. Protective duties make a bill of abominations; but an advanced and diversified mechanical industry is excellent. The harvest is delightful to behold; it is the sowing and fencing only that offend the constitutionalist who denies the power, and the economist who denies the expediency, of reaping anything but spontaneous growths of untilled soils. While, therefore, a general defence of this class of employments, and this species of industry would be wholly out of place, there is, however, an illustration or two of their uses, not quite so commonly adverted to; on which I pause to say a word. And one of them is this: that, in connection with the other tasks of an advanced civilization, with which they are always found associated, they offer to every faculty and talent and taste, in the community, the specific work best suited to it; and thus effect a more universal development and a more complete education of the general intellect than otherwise would be practicable. It is not merely that they keep everybody busy, in the evening and before light as well as in the daytime, in winter as well as in summer, in wet weather as well as in fair, women and children as well as men, but it is that everybody is enabled to be busy on the precise thing the best adapted to his capacity and his inclinations. In a country of few occupations, employments go down by an arbitrary, hereditary, coercive designation, without regard to peculiarities of individual character. The son of a priest is a priest; the son of a barber is a barber; a man raises onions and garlic, because a certain other person did so when the Pyramids were building, centuries ago. But a diversified, advanced, and refined mechanical and manufacturing industry, coöperating with these other numerous employments of civilization which always surround it, offers the widest choice, detects the slightest shade of individuality, quickens into existence and trains to perfection the largest conceivable amount and the utmost possible variety of national mind. It goes abroad with its handmaid labors, not like the elegiac poet into the church-yard, but among the bright tribes of living childhood and manhood, and finds there in more than a figurative sense, some mute, inglorious Milton, to whom it gives a tongue and the opportunity of fame; the dauntless breast of some Hampden still at play, yet born to strive with the tyrant of more than a village; infant hands that may one day sway the rod of empire; hearts already pregnant with celestial fire; future Arkwrights and Watts and Whitneys and Fultons, whom it leads forth to a discipline and a career that may work a revolution in the arts and commerce of the world. Here are five sons in a family. In some communities they would all become hedgers and ditchers; in others, shore fishermen; in others, hired men in fields, or porters or servants in noblemen's families. But see what the diversified employments of civilization may make of them. One has a passion for contention and danger and adventure. There are the gigantic game of the sea; the vast fields of the Pacific; the pursuit even "beneath the frozen serpent of the South," for him. Another has a taste for trade: he plays already at bargains and barter. There are Wall Street and Milk Street, and clerkships and agencies at Manilla and Canton and Rio Janeiro, for him. A third early and seriously inclines to the quiet life, the fixed habits, the hereditary opinions and old ways of his fathers; there is the plough for him. Another develops from infancy extraordinary mechanical and inventive talent; extraordinary in degree, of not yet ascertained direction. You see it in his first *whittling*. There may be a Fulton, or an Arkwright; there may be wrapped up the germs of an idea which, realized, shall change the industry of nations, and give a new name to a new era. Well, there are the machine-shops at Lowell and Providence for him; there are cotton mills and woollen mills for him to superintend; there is stationary and locomotive steam-power for him to guide and study; of a hundred departments and forms of useful art, some one will surely reach and feed the ruling intellectual passion. In the flashing eye, beneath the pale and beaming brow of that other one, you detect the solitary first thoughts of genius. There are the seashore of storm or calm, the waning moon, the stripes of summer evening cloud, traditions, and all the food of the soul, for him. And so all the boys are provided for. Every fragment of mind is gathered up. Nothing is lost. The hazel rod, with unfailing potency, points out, separates, and gives to sight every grain of gold in the water and in the sand. Every taste, every faculty, every peculiarity of mental power, finds its task, does it, and is made the better for it.

Let me say, Sir, that there is another influence of manufacturing and mechanical arts and industry, which should commend them to the favor of American statesmen. In all ages and in all nations they have been the parents and handmaids of popular liberty. If I had said of democratical liberty, I should have expressed myself more accurately. This praise, if not theirs alone, or preëminently, they share perhaps with commerce only. I observe, with surprise, that Mr. Calhoun, in his speech in opposition to Mr. Randolph's motion to strike out the minimum valuation on cotton goods, in the house of representatives, April, 1816, a speech in many respects remarkable and instructive, and to which I shall make frequent reference before I have done—in that speech Mr. Calhoun gives some slight countenance to the suggestion that "capital employed in manufacturing produced a greater dependence on the part of the employed, than in commerce, navigation, or agriculture." Sir, I think this is contradicted by the history of the whole world. "Millionary manufacturing capitalists," like all other persons possessed of large accumulations, are essentially conservative, timorous, disinclined to change, on the side of law, order, and permanence. So are millionary commercial capitalists, and millionary cotton-growing and sugar-growing capitalists, and millionary capitalists of all sorts. But the artisans of towns—mechanics, manufacturing operatives, that whole city and village population, wherever concentrated, by whom the useful arts of a civilized society are performed—are among the freest of the free, the world over. They are no man's slaves; they are "no man's men." Brought together in considerable numbers, and forming part of a still larger urban population in immediate contact; reciprocally acting on, and acted on by, numerous other minds; enjoying every day some time of leisure, and driven by the craving for stimulus which the monotony of their employments, their own mental activity, and all the influences about them, are so well calculated to produce—driven to the search of some external objects of interest, they find these in conversation, in discussion, in reading newspapers and books, in all the topics which agitate the crowded community of which they are part; and thus they become curious, flexible, quick, progressive. Something too in their position and relations,—just starting in the world, their fortunes to seek or to make; something in their half antagonistical, half auxiliary connection with their employers,—free associated labor employed by large associated capital; something, with unfailing certainty, determines them to the side of the largest liberty. So always it has been. So it was in the freest of the Greek republics. So too, in the Middle Age, after her sleep of a thousand years from the battle of

Pharsalia, liberty revived and respired among the handicraftsmen and traders of the small commercial and manufacturing towns of Germany, Italy, and England. There, in sight of the open and glorious sea, law, order, self-government, popular liberty, art, taste, and all the fair variety of cultivated things, sprung up together, and set out together on that "radiant round," never to cease but with the close of time. And where do you feel the pulses of democratical England and Scotland beat quickest and hottest to-day? What are the communities that called loudest for parliamentary reform; and call loudest now for those social and political ameliorations, the fear of which perplexes the throne, the church, and the aristocracy? Certainly, the large and small manufacturing towns. "The two great powers," I read from the ablest Tory journal in Great Britain, "operating on human affairs, which are producing this progressive increase of democratical influence, are the extension of manufactures and the influence of the daily press." What British periodical is it, which most zealously advocates the cause, asserts the dignity, appreciates the uses and claims, of manufacturing industry? Precisely the most radical and revolutionary of them all. And whose rhymes are those which convey to the strong, sad heart of English labor "thoughts that wake to perish never," the germs of a culture growing up to everlasting life, the "public and private sense of a man;" the dream, the hope, of social reform; and a better, but not revolutionary liberty? Whose, but Elliot's, the worker in iron, the "artisan poet of the poor"?

The real truth is, Sir, that manufacturing and mechanical, and commercial industry, is "the prolific source of democratic feeling." Of the two great elements, which must be combined in all greatness of national character and national destiny,—permanence and progression,—these employments stimulate the latter; agriculture contributes to the former. They are one of those acting and counteracting, opposing yet not discordant powers, from whose reciprocal struggle is drawn out the harmony of the universe. Agriculture is the other. The country is the home of rest. The town is the theatre of change. Senators are very fond of reminding us that the census shows so large a preponderance of numbers at work on the land. Then, Sir, over and above all the good you do them, by calling off some who would crowd that employment into other business, and providing a better market for those who remain in it, why should you be afraid, on a larger and deeper reason, to temper and attend this by other occupation? You have provided well for permanence. Be not afraid of the agents of intelligent progress. It is the union of social labors which causes the wealth, develops the mind, prolongs the career, and elevates and adorns the history of nations.

But, Mr. President, there was another consideration, which might well have weight to induce the statesmen of 1816 and 1824 to protect the manufacturing and mechanical arts of their country. It was not merely that they were useful, but that they were *a thing actually existing,* not requiring to be made out of the whole cloth, if I may borrow a figure from the subject, but only requiring to be *saved,* preserved, sheltered. It is one thing to force these arts by main strength, by a violent policy, right out of the ground, out of the mine, out of the waterfall; and quite another, after they have so started, after capital has taken that direction, after the evil is done and the good is beginning, after skill is acquired, machinery accumulated, investments made, habits formed—after all this, not to let them die. The first may be unwise; the other cannot be. The statesmen of 1816 and 1824 were not required to choose between the theory of Adam Smith, and the practice of England. They were not required to choose between Scotch and French philosophy, and that immemorial, steady, daring, and perhaps happy disregard of such philosophy, which has domesticated and naturalized the whole circle of civilized arts on that narrow and stormy isle; which has raised on it the throne of the sea; which has given it the wealth that (poured out on the banks of the Neva, of the Danube, and of the Tagus) may have disappointed the dream of a universal French monarchy. They had no such choice to make. Not at all. There were the arts in existence—*non sine diis animosi infantes!* before them. It no more followed, because they might not have forced them into being, that they were to let them perish, than it follows, because you advise a young friend not to marry till he is older, that you mean, if he disregards your counsel, to have him kill his infant child. In such a case, new and precious elements mingle in the deliberation. The existence of interests, spontaneously, undesignedly arisen, may turn the scale. And so Mr. Calhoun, in the speech from which I have once read, reasoned. He said,—

> "Besides, we have already surmounted the greatest difficulty that has ever been found in undertakings of this kind. The cotton and woollen manufactures are not to be *introduced,*—they are *already* introduced to a great extent; freeing us entirely from the hazards, and, in a great measure, the sacrifices experienced in giving the capital of the country a new direction. The restrictive measures and the war, though not intended for that purpose, have, by the necessary operation of things, turned a large amount of capital to this new branch of industry."

"A good patriot and true politician," says Burke, "always considers how he shall make the most of the existing materials of his country." Sir, we are forced

to hear it sometimes said, in these tariff discussions, that the precepts of philosophy, the dictates of common sense, and the teachings of experience, appear to
come in conflict. I do not know how that is; but this I will say, that if in all that
political economy has reasoned or dogmatized or dreamed, in any one page of
any one book on the subject, of high authority, or of little authority, there can
be found one solitary sentence which asserts, that in the actual circumstances of
this country in 1816, 1824, and 1842—after manufacturing industry had
advanced to the state in which then it existed, after so much capital was invested,
and skill learned—that it was, at these periods, wise and expedient to have given
to that industry less than an adequate protection, and to have suffered it to die,
or asserts any principle which fairly applies to and governs such a case, then I
will confess that the dictates of common sense and the revelations of experience
are a far better guide than such madness and foolishness of science. I have heard
no such proposition read, now or formerly.

In this attempt, Mr. President, to show that the statesmen of 1816 and 1824,
the framers of the "second system," acted not under the influence of "millionary
capitalists," not in the spirit of "ambitious politicians," for "sectional enrichment
and political advancement," but upon grounds and considerations worthy of
them, and which should even recommend the system itself, I must not forget
one influence which I doubt not had its effect. Sir, between the year 1807 and
the year 1816, the national character, or at least the national spirit, tone, temper,
underwent a great change. A more intense nationality was developed. Everybody felt taller, stronger, more wholly American, prouder of America than he
did in 1807. Everybody felt that we had passed through one epoch and stage of
our history, and were come to another. We felt that we were emerging from the
class of small States, to the class of large States. We had just gone through a war
with honor; we had contended not ingloriously with the first power in the
world; we had recovered our long lost self-respect. The long wrongs of England
for a quarter of a century had been avenged. Our flag floated again, all unstained
as on the day when freedom

> "Tore the azure robe of night,
> And set the stars of glory there."

Yes, Sir, everybody felt that that age—never to be remembered without a
tear for America—the age of gunboats and torpedoes; of proclamations and philanthropy, falsely so called; when we were knocked down one day by a Berlin or
Milan decree, and the next by an order in council; when we retired from all the

seas, and hid ourselves under embargoes and acts of non-intercourse—everybody felt that that age was gone forever. The baptism of blood and fire was on our brow, and its influence was on our spirit and our legislation. Sir, I believe it was under the influence of this change of national feeling that the public men of 1816, scarcely conscious of it, perhaps, turned with the instinct of a true and happy civil discretion to a policy which was appropriate to the altered temper, the prouder spirit, the more national sentiments, the new age of their country. They turned to find in her various climate, diversified soil, exhaustless mines, ample water-power, in her frugality and industry, the materials of that self-derived and durable greatness to which they now felt that she was destined. They turned to make her independent in reality as in name. Foul shame they deemed it, that the American soldier at least should not sleep under an American blanket; that the very halyards by which we send up the stars and stripes in the hour of naval battle should be made in a Russian ropewalk; that an American frigate should ride at anchor by a British chain cable!

These, Mr. President, I believe, I hope, these, and such as these, and not the influence of avarice or of personal ambition, were among the sentiments and convictions which produced and which justify our legislation of 1816 and 1824. Wise statesmen, true patriots, admonished by the bitter experience of the war, kindling with the sentiments and carrying out the policy of a new era of our history, not "millionary capitalists" or "trading politicians," were its authors. I claim for it as noble an origin as for the elder system. With what degree of truth and justice I have done so, it is for you to judge.

The tariffs, then, of 1816 and 1824, were framed on the same interpretation of the Constitution, and the same doctrines of political economy, as was the tariff of 1789. You need not ascend from the later to the earlier, to find a better spirit, worthier objects, or sounder policy. The statesmen of 1824 did just what the statesmen of 1789 would have done in the same age, by the same lights, on the same facts. Why, then, I shall be asked, were the duties of 1824 so much higher than those of 1789? Sir, I pause to answer the question, because, in doing so, I make an argument, *valeat tantum,* for the duties of 1842. They were so much higher, because the duties of 1789, sufficient for revenue and protection then, were totally insufficient for either in the altered circumstances of 1824, and would be totally insufficient for either now.

Consider, in the first place, that the manufacturing and mechanical arts and industry of the country, as they existed and were to be provided for in 1816, had not *grown* up to the state in which Congress found them, under the influence of the protecting duties of 1789. They were, on the contrary, the stimulated and joint product of certain artificial and temporary causes of great energy, to wit: the commercial embarrassments which preceded the war, and the war itself. Upon this subject I think I have remarked two erroneous views: one attributes too much influence to the war, and supposes that manufacturing employments had not made much progress before the war; the other correctly appreciates their very prosperous condition as early as 1810, but ascribes it to inadequate causes,—to spontaneous growth, to the natural progress and developments of things, or to the gentle influence of the moderate protection of the legislation of 1789. Both are erroneous. That in 1810 manufacturing industry had been very far advanced is certain. It was then that Mr. Gallatin, while Secretary of the Treasury, surveyed and analyzed it, and arrived at the conclusion that its annual product exceeded one hundred and twenty millions of dollars. He says,—

"From this imperfect sketch of American manufactures it may, with certainty, be inferred that their annual product exceeds *one hundred and twenty millions of dollars.* And it is not improbable that the raw materials used, and the provisions and other articles consumed by the manufacturers, create a home market for agricultural products not very inferior to that which arises from foreign demand—a result more favorable than might have been expected from a view of the natural causes which impede the introduction and retard the progress of manufactures in the United States."—*Mr. Gallatin's report, April* 17, 1810.

But what had caused this? Certainly not the duties of 1789; certainly not those duties cooperating with the natural and spontaneous course and progression and changes of national industry. I do not know that the honorable Senator from Missouri intended to express the opinion that these were the cause of the manufacturing prosperity of 1810. But in the effort to show, what is certainly true, that the war did not produce it, he, unintentionally, doubtless, leaves the implication that it was a purely spontaneous growth under the duties of the "old system." Thus he says, "I must again advert to the date. The modern champions of manufactures say it was the war which gave birth to manufactures; and that we must have high duties now, to protect what the war created. But the work of Mr. Coxe shows this to be a grand mistake; that this great interest had taken deep and wide root before the war, and was going on well even before the year 1810." This is certainly true; but the honorable Senator omits to advert to those other causes which before the war had exerted an influence similar and almost equal to war itself. Sir, the exact historical fact is this. Down to the year 1807, the progress of American manufactures was very slow. Our capital was richly rewarded upon the sea, and upon the sea it remained. In, 1807, two new and most powerfully stimulating influences supervened, by which a sudden, new, and vast impulse was communicated to these employments, and which really produced that splendid result which, in 1810, attracted the notice and justified the admiration of Mr. Gallatin. These causes were, first, the violations of our rights of neutrality by the great belligerents, England and France; and, second, our own commercial restrictions. These causes had the double operation of driving our capital from the sea, to seek other investments, and of keeping foreign fabrics out. The instantaneous effect of the two, in conjunction, was, that manufacturing industry started at once, in a hundred new or enlarged forms, to life, and grew, I will not say with a rank and unhealthy, but with a stimulated and hastened luxuriance, down to the war, and through the war. I suppose that nine tenths, perhaps more, of all that Mr. Gallatin surveyed and analyzed and admired, in 1810, had sprung up within the three years before.

The proofs of this are familiar and decisive. Look first at the dates of certain not very agreeable events. The Berlin decree was made in November, 1806; the first order in council, January, 1807; the Milan decree in November, 1807. The embargo was laid in December, 1807; it continued till March, 1809, when it was succeeded by the act of non-intercourse, which continued until the war. Here, therefore, were three years—more than three years—during which one of the causes to which I have adverted was in operation, and more than two years during which they both were so, before Mr. Gallatin made his report. Well, Sir, mark the results. In 1789 there was not a cotton spindle in the United States. In 1805 and 1806 there were only 5,000; in 1810, there were 80,000! an increase of sixteen-fold in four or five years. I gather these facts, in part, from Mr. Gallatin's report itself, and in part from an instructive report upon the subject of cotton, submitted to congress by the Senator from New Hampshire, [Mr. Woodbury,] when Secretary of the Treasury. But let me refer you to the proof a little more largely. I read first a few passages from Mr. Gallatin's report:—

"The first cotton-mill was erected in the State of Rhode Island *in the year* 1791; another in the same State in the year 1795; and two more in the State of Massachusetts in 1803 and 1804. During the three succeeding years, ten more were erected, or commenced, in Rhode Island, and one in Connecticut—making, altogether, *fifteen* mills erected before the

year 1808, working at that time about *eight thousand spindles,* and producing about three hundred thousand pounds of yarn a year.

"Returns have been received of *eighty-seven* mills which were erected
at the end of the year 1809, sixty-two of which (forty-eight water and
fourteen horse mills) were in operation, and worked at that time thirty-
one thousand spindles. The other twenty-five will all be in operation in
the course of this year, and, together with the former ones, (almost all of
which are increasing their machinery,) will, by the estimate received, work
more than *eighty thousand* spindles at the commencement of the year 1811."

"The increase of carding and spinning of cotton by machinery in
establishments for that purpose, and exclusively of that done in private
families, has, therefore been *fourfold,* during the last two years, and will
have been *tenfold* in *three years.*"

"But by far the greater part of the goods made of those materials
(cotton, flax, and wool) are manufactured in private families, mostly for
their own use, and partly for sale. They consist principally of coarse cloth,
flannel, cotton stuffs and stripes of every description, linen and mixtures
of wool with flax or cotton. The information received from every State,
and from more than sixty different places, concurs in establishing the fact
of *an extraordinary increase during* THE LAST TWO YEARS, and rendering it
probable that about two thirds of the clothing, including hosiery, and of
the house and table linen worn and used by the inhabitants of the United
States who do not reside in cities, is the product of family manufactures."

"The *demand of last year was double of that* of 1808, and is still rapidly
increasing."

"The annual importations of foreign hemp amounted to 6,200 tons.
*But the interruption of commerce has greatly promoted the cultivation of that arti-
cle* in Massachusetts, New York, Kentucky, and several other places; and
it is believed that a sufficient quantity will, in a short time, be produced
in the United States. *The injurious violations of the neutral commerce of the
United States, by forcing industry and capital into other channels, have broken
inveterate habits, and given a general impulse,* to which *must be ascribed the
great increase of manufactures during the last two years.*"

So far Mr. Gallatin.
But listen to the not less weighty evidence of Mr. Jefferson, in his message
of 1808:—

"*The suspension of foreign commerce produced by the injustice of the belligerent Powers, and the consequent losses and sacrifices of our citizens, are subjects of
just concern. The situation into which we have thus been forced has impelled us to
apply a portion of our industry and capital to internal manufactures and improvements.* The extent of this conversion is daily increasing, and little doubt
remains that the establishments formed and forming will, under the aus-
pices of cheaper materials and subsistence, the freedom of labor from taxation with us, and of *protecting duties* and *prohibitions,* become *permanent.*"

And of Mr. Madison, in his message of 1810:—

"I feel particular satisfaction in remarking that an interior view of our
country presents us, with grateful proofs of its substantial and increasing
prosperity. To a thriving agriculture, and the improvements relating to
it, is added a highly interesting extension of useful manufactures, the
combined product of professional occupations and of household industry. Such, indeed, is the experience of economy, as well as of policy, in
these substitutes for supplies heretofore obtained by foreign commerce,
that in a *national* view the change is justly regarded as, of itself, more than
a *recompense for those privations and losses resulting from foreign injustice, which
furnished the general impulse required for its accomplishment.* How far it may be
expedient to guard the infancy of this improvement in the distribution of
labor, *by regulations of the commercial tariff,* is a subject which cannot fail to
suggest itself to your patriotic reflections."

And in his message of 1811:—

"Although other subjects will press more immediately on your deliberations, a portion of them cannot but be well bestowed on the *just and
sound* policy of *securing* to our manufactures the success they have attained,
and are still attaining, *under the impulses of causes not permanent, and to our
navigation* the fair extent of which is at present abridged by the unequal
regulations of foreign governments. Besides the reasonableness of saving
our manufactures from sacrifices which a change of circumstances might
bring upon them, the national interest requires that, with respect to such
articles, at least, as belong to our defence and primary wants, we should
not be left in a state of unnecessary dependence on external supplies."

Let me call your attention to a selection from the report of Mr. Dallas, when Secretary of the Treasury, in 1816:—

"It was emphatically during the period of the restrictive system and the war that the importance of domestic manufactures became conspicuous to the nation, and made a lasting impression on the mind of every statesman and every patriot. From 1783 to 1808, the march of domestic manufactures was slow, but steady. It has since been bold, rapid, and firm."

Mr. Newton, of Virginia, chairman of the committee on commerce and manufactures, in a liberal and able report, in February, 1816, expressed the same opinion:—

"Prior to 1806 and 1807, establishments for manufactures of cotton had not been attempted, but in a few instances, and on a limited scale. Their rise and progress are attributable to embarrassments to which commerce was subjected."

The impulse thus given was continued and increased by the war; and thus the manufactures of 1816 were, as I have said, the joint and stimulated product of that event, of the interruptions of commerce which for five years preceded it, and of what I may call the national progress and changes of national industry.

Now, Sir, for the protection of manufactures thus called into existence, and which, instead of the plain, hardy, coarse, and household employments of 1789, had grown a refined, complicated, and sensitive industry, the duties of 1789 had become totally inadequate in 1816. It cannot be too often repeated nor too literally understood, that then a new age had opened on the world. With the battle of Waterloo one era ended, and another begun. The thunders of that day of doom—what were they but the great bell of time sounding out another hour? Then arose a new age on the exhausted nations; an age to which "no monarch shall affix his name; the age of industry; the age of comforts to the poor; the age of the people." Immediately they all turned to the development and culture of their own resources; to the contests of peace, more glorious than the contests of war. England, in a preminent sense and degree, went back, with all her energies, all her capital, and all her numbers, from the Tagus, the Rhine, the Neva, to contend in Birmingham and Manchester and Liverpool for the markets of the United States. On that field, Sir, we were then no match for her. On others, we had won some laurels; there we were not yet her match. It became indispensable that the government should throw its protecting arm around the labor of the country; should guard it against the fierce, new, and hot competition which assailed it; should shelter it from the torrent heat and the sudden blasts of the new world in which it found itself. The duties of 1789 would have been as unavailing as bow and arrow against the bayonet and flying artillery of modern war. Sir, one most striking and decisive proof of this is at hand. The tariff of 1816 was meant to be a protecting tariff. As such, it was assailed and defended. Some things it did protect. Some effects it did produce. It put an end to the importation of cotton fabrics made in the East Indies of East Indian cotton; and to that extent it extended the market of the cotton of America. I have no doubt that, taking it all together, it was a better tariff than this bill of the Senator from South Carolina; better than such a bill as the principles indicated by the Senator from Missouri would construct. But what were its effects? Manufactures were prostrated. From an annual product of two hundred millions in 1816, they had fallen in 1820 to an annual product of thirty-six millions only. This it was which stimulated that great effort in 1820 for a more adequate system. In this, as in 1789, Pennsylvania took the lead. She was powerfully seconded by the eloquence and zeal of Mr. Clay; a better law passed the house, but failed by one vote in this body. We lived along, languishing, until 1824, when government at length recognized the existence and the demands of the new age of the world. We came fairly into line, and entered on that contest of industrial glory with the nations, where the prizes are unstained by tears or blood; where the victory is without guilt, and the triumph without abatement.

I have spoken, Mr. President, of a new age. I hold here a curious and striking proof and product of such an age. It is a pamphlet called "Foreign Tariffs; their injurious effects on British manufactures, especially the woollen manufacture; and it is a collection of the protecting regulations of different governments, adopted since 1815, with "proposed remedies." It is compiled by Mr. Bischoff, a British manufacturer, no doubt; but who at all events "most potently and powerfully believes" that the world was created solely for the sake of consuming British manufactures. You could get no other idea into his head. If he could see the nations, one and all coming back to British cottons, woollens, iron, and glass, and all else which makes up the circle of her arts, he would die happy. Read the motto on his title-page. "Encourage those trades most that vend most of *our* manufactures." He takes it from Sir Josiah Childs's discourses on trade; but it embodies the whole sum and substance of the political economy of England. What effect the consummation which he so devoutly wishes might have on the comforts, the population, the wealth, the aggrandizement of the consuming and nonmanufacturing nations, he very naturally and very properly leaves them to

consider. That is their business. It is his "to vend the manufactures of England."
Well, it is quite plain that he feels that his country is a little wronged by the way
the world is going. Hear how pathetically he ejaculates:—

"The ink with which the treaties of Vienna were signed was scarce
dry, ere Russia, to which an immense trade used to be carried on in woollens, *prohibited the importation of all coarse* cloth by enormous duties, excepting, indeed, what was ordered by her own government for the clothing of
the troops. The King of Sardinia, who had his Italian dominions restored
to him by British valor, and Genoa with its rich territories and fine seaport
added to his kingdom, not only deprived us of the great privileges we formerly enjoyed, but imposed almost prohibitory duties on the importation
of British manufactures, not only into his own dominions, but into those
territories which were added to his kingdom. The Emperor of Austria
prohibited the introduction of our woollens and cottons into his empire,
including also his newly acquired Italian States, Lombardy, the Milanese,
Venice, &c., which formerly took large quantities of our goods. And other
governments acted in a similar manner."

"Such was the policy, *and such has continued to be the policy of the continental powers,* without apparently a single objection, remonstrance, or
protest, from England, or any effort made to *preserve our manufactures;* and
thus has our trade in the near markets of Europe been almost destroyed."

"The continental States have, moreover, by adopting the mode of
imposing duties on *weight instead of, as formerly, on value,* struck an irrepara-
ble blow, unless that system be altered, at the old staple manufactures of
the country—cloths, coatings, and other woollens of low qualities, which
consume British wool, making a pound weight of the coarsest fabrics pay
the same amount of duty as a pound of the very best superfine cloth. That
system is as injurious to the wool grower as it is to the manufacturer."

"With scarce a single exception, all States have had in view what has
been deemed *protection* or stimulus to their own fabrics. This has been the
policy of France, Spain, Portugal, Belgium, Prussia, Denmark, Sweden,
Russia, Austria, Sardinia, Naples, and even the United States of America.
Whether the coarse so adopted be wise or not—whether the term *shackles*
would not be more properly applied to the system than *'protection'*—
whether it be just or not, to tax the many for the supposed advantage of

the few, is not now the question; they had the example of England, which
appears to have been the rule upon which they have acted."

In all Europe, Holland is perhaps the single country which has not adopted
such a policy. And she, Sir, is not quite the Holland she was in the times of
Charles the Second, when the thunders of her cannon "startled that effeminate
tyrant in his own palace, and in the arms of his mistresses;" not what she was in
1688, when she gave a deliverer to England; not what she was when she was the
carrier and banker of all the world. All but her are taking care of themselves,
with the most total and provoking disregard of all the free-trade preaching by
which England would persuade mankind that the methods which have made
her rich and great will make all other nations poor and feeble. Turkey improves
a little on all, "letting everything come freely into her dominions, but letting
nothing go out;" borrowing her policy, it might seem, from her own Mediter-
ranean, into which there ever runs an unreturning flood.

A distinguished friend not long since remarked to me, that the character and
topics of the British parliamentary debates, compared with those of a half century ago, very strikingly indicated the existence of that new world which statesmen have to act in. I have thought I could remark the same thing. What could
such a leader as the elder Pitt do with such a house of commons and such subjects of debate? What would the exaggerated eloquence of the great war minister find to say about "onion seed"? Sir Robert Peel speaks as well on that
important article as he does on Ireland. "The glory of a great minister in the last
century was, that he made this country flourish still more by war than by peace.
The glory of the present era is, that things have returned to their natural course;
and that peace is become, as it ever ought to be, a greater restorer of national
force than war."

Yes, Sir, the times have changed. That is the wisest nation which the most
adequately comprehends the degree, the permanence, the nature of the change,
and first places itself at the head of the great industrial revolution. It is the praise
of the statesmen of 1816 and 1824, that they understood and acted upon this
truth. It was because they did, that they at once held fast by the principles and
deserted the details of the legislation of 1789. If you would restore the dress and
the cradel of infancy, you must bring back again its tiny limbs, and its stature of
a span long. If the statesmen of the age of Washington were alive to-day, they
would not revive the duties of their time, unless you could give back again from
the dim dominion of the past the world of their time.

Another consideration urged by the honorable Senator from Missouri, for returning to the good old legislation, for abandoning protective duties, and substituting duties which I think are not protective, was this,—that certain statistical tables which he produced reveal some very unfavorable practical results of the present system, as contrasted with the results of the former system. And I agree at once, that if the clear and unequivocal teachings of a sufficient experience pronounce against the existing policy, it is to be abandoned. But do these tables make out such a case?

I find, Sir, that I shall not have occasion to detain you upon them as long as I at first designed to do, because I think that one general observation applies to and disposes of the matter. If the premises are true, the conclusions do not appear to follow. If the tables are true, and the whole truth, they prove nothing against the policy of protection. If every figure in every column is right, still the great question of the effect of that policy on agriculture, commerce, and revenue, which has been so instructively debated, is left just where it was before. No new argument is afforded against the views which the Senators from Maine, Connecticut, Vermont, Rhode Island, Georgia, and my colleague, have taken; and no additional force or illustration is given to the views of the Senators from South Carolina and New Hampshire. The tables either do not show what the working of the existing system has been, or they show nothing which has not been asserted and conceded before.

Suppose, for example, in the first place, that the tables indicate that the receipts from customs were more regular before 1808 than since 1816; that they went on advancing with a more regular progression, with less of fluctuation from large in one year to small in the next, and the reverse; how can you possibly refer this to the low duties of one period, or the high duties of the other? I can very well understand that sudden and great changes from one rate to another, too many of which have disfigured and disturbed the latter period, will cause fluctuations in all things, in imports, exports, business, hopes, fears, plans, everything. It is for that very reason that I deprecate the proposed great change. But that a fixed, settled policy of high duties, known, promulgated to the world, promulgated to the foreign manufacturer and shipper, such a system as that of England, for instance, should cause more fluctuations in the receipts from customs, than a policy of low duties no better known and no more firmly fixed—this I have not organs to comprehend. Sir, you must show some connection between high duties as such and the fluctuations you complain of. You must not say *post hoc ergo propter hoc*. This would be to attribute the rise of cotton to icebergs or meteors, if I may employ an illustration of the Senator from South Carolina. I think it is Addison's country gentleman who insisted upon it there had been no good weather in England since the revolution of 1688. I cannot speak for the weather; but, good or bad, nobody but the Tory fox-hunter himself threw the blame on the going out of the Stuarts. Sir, no doubt there are far more causes of irregularity in our imports and in our receipts from customs, wholly disconnected with the absence or presence of a protective policy, now, than when we were poorer, fewer, traded less, and had a market for which foreign producers less desperately contended. If you go back to good old colonial times, to 1650 and 1670, I dare say you might find still less irregularity in these particulars. Probably, too, the Indians of the North-west have received their annual supplies of gunpowder, blankets and the like, from the British colonial government, with a regularity still more severely and beautifully guarded. A thousand causes of this kind of fluctuations there must be, with which the rates of duties have no more to do than the icebergs with the price of cotton, or the revolution with the bad weather. In a country whose numbers have been growing from ten millions to seventeen millions; with a commerce extending as far as winds blow and waters roll; a commerce which trades in everything, with everybody; a country partly supplying its home market, and partly carrying its own productions in its own ships, and yet contending for that market and that navigation with numerous and greedy foreign competitors; passing through more than one great convulsion which has shaken the whole world of trade; agitated by the currents and winds of its own seasons of local speculation; its currency sometimes disordered; its policy too often changing; all things, business, values, wages, the solemn temples of its Constitutions themselves rising and falling on the waters of opinion which know no rest— in such a country I shall neither be surprised nor scared to see, under whatever rates of duty, a great deal of irregularity in imports and in revenue from imports. Whether it be an evil or not, and to whatever extent it be one, I see no connection between it and a known, settled, promulgated, well and widely understood policy of protection.

Perhaps I might not entirely concur with the distinguished Senator from Missouri, in his estimate of the magnitude of the evil. An evil, it no doubt is. Sometimes, in some circumstances, irregularity would be an intolerable one. In the case he puts, of a balloon in the air, now "bursting with distention, now collapsing from depletion," it would be greatly inconvenient. But all greatness is irregular. All irregularity is not defect, is not ruin. Take a different illustration from that of the balloon. Take the New England climate in summer—you would think the world was coming to an end. Certain recent heresies on that subject may have had a natural origin there. Cold to-day, hot to-morrow;

mercury at 80° in the morning, with wind at south-west; and in three hours
more, a sea turn, wind at east, a thick fog from the very bottom of the ocean,
and a fall of 40 degrees of Fahrenheit; now so dry as to kill all the beans in New
Hampshire, then floods carrying off the bridges and dams of the Penobscot and
Connecticut; now in Portsmouth in July, and the next day a man and a yoke of
oxen killed by lightning in Rhode Island—you would think the world was
twenty times coming to an end! But I don't know how it is; we go along; the
early and the latter rain falls each in his season; seed-time and harvest do not fail;
the sixty days of hot corn weather are pretty sure to be measured out to us; the
Indian summer, with its bland southwest and mitigated sunshine brings all up;
and on the twenty-fifth of November, or thereabouts, being Thursday, three
millions of grateful people, in meeting-houses, or around the family board, give
thanks for a year of health, plenty, and happiness. All irregularity, whatever the
cause, is not defect, nor ruin.

Suppose, in the next place, that these tables show a diminished consumption of foreign imports, since 1816, in proportion to our numbers, compared
with the consumption before 1807? The protective policy is not the cause. This
is my first answer. And the evil is over-balanced by the good. This is my next
answer. You may consume less of foreign fabrics, in proportion to your numbers, than before 1808, for the reason that the decline of agricultural prices, the
diminished agricultural exportation, the loss of the profits and freights of the
golden age of commerce and navigation, may really have made you less able
than before to exchange your labor for foreign labor. Is the policy of protection
to blame for this? Is it not, on the other hand, its office, its aim, to counteract
this very evil which it does not produce, by enabling you to exchange that labor
for domestic fabrics, which you cannot pass for foreign fabrics? You may consume less of some imported fabrics than before, for the reason, that while your
general ability is greater, your demand is supplied by the domestic manufacturer.
And is there anything very dreadful in this? Suppose that, by this means, that
useful foreign commerce which binds the nations together may not grow quite
in proportion to our increasing numbers; or rather, that its outward and home-
ward cargoes somewhat change their nature; still enough of it is left, enough for
philanthropy, for civilization, for national wealth, for diversified social employment, while that far more useful domestic commerce which binds together associated States, and kindred hearts and tribes, has expanded till it carries a value of
a thousand millions of dollars in a year.

Suppose, finally, the honorable Senator's tables announce a diminished export
of agricultural productions since the year 1816,—diminished since the time when

Europe forgot agriculture, to pursue war,—how is the tariff of protection responsible for this? Does anybody believe that we should sell one pound or one peck the more, if we imported from England the very shoes which we put upon our horses' feet? No, Sir; you sell all which the necessities of foreigners oblige them to buy at remunerating prices; so you would, tariff or no tariff; and you would do no more. Sir, to hold our protective legislation responsible for this falling off of these exports, is to hold it responsible for the very evils whose existence compelled you to resort to it, in order to break their force; evils which, but for this, you could not bear at all. You lay the fault, not on the ferocious assailant, but on the defensive armor, and the manly resistance, without which the attack would have been fatal. Yes, Sir, it is far nearer the truth to say this: that it was because foreign tariffs, discriminating for colonial agriculture and against yours; the increased agricultural production of Europe; the great bulk of that class of commodities compared with the value—it was because these and other causes had deprived your farmers of their foreign market, that your statesmen turned to find them one at home, and have already to an encouraging extent succeeded; it was because the wings of our ancient golden foreign commerce had been clipped, that they turned to find a substitute in domestic commerce; it was because the old world had unexpectedly developed new and extraordinary resources and powers and productiveness, that they sought, in another sense than Mr. Canning used the lofty boast, "to restore the balance," by bringing a new world into existence *in the new world.* This is far nearer the truth than to describe the protective policy as the author of the evils which it seeks to mitigate.

I have done, then, Sir, with the argument drawn from the tables. As I said, I do not think they affect at all the great question which we have had so long and ably discussed, of the operation of protective duties on commerce, agriculture, and revenue. They leave that where they find it. I do not mean to repeat a word of that discussion. Neither these tables, nor any quantity of tables, nor any amount of reasoning, nor any public opinion of one region, or of all regions of the country, nor all the polemical political economy of manufacturing England, will bring me to doubt that I do good service to agriculture by lessening the numbers that pursue it, and giving them a nearer and better market; that even the foreign trade of a nation, which manufactures as well as tills the earth, will be richer, wider, steadier, better prepared to spread its sails to every breeze, than the foreign trade of a nation which only tills the earth; and, finally, that domestic commerce among such States as ours is better than an exclusive foreign commerce. These truths, at last, are above all cavil. I will not confess that they require vindication, by attempting to vindicate them.

It has been urged, Sir, as another consideration to induce or to reconcile us to a return to the old system, that manufacturing and mechanical industry is in a highly prosperous general condition. Its products are said to be vast. Its profits are said to be great.

I admit, undoubtedly, that an immense amount of capital is invested in it. I admit that it employs and feeds millions—men, women, and children—of our own household. I admit that it has spread over the whole country; that it is inseparably intertwined with the labor and the prosperity of the whole; that it benefits all; that it harms none. I admit that, with the general business of the nation, it is just now prosperous.

But what then? Does the Senator from Missouri say, that because these employments are so numerous, so widespread, so interwoven with all the nerves of business, and so flourishing, that therefore he would destroy or lessen or impoverish them? The direct reverse. He desires to see them prosper. He is willing to leave them more protection than they need. So I understood his speech; and so I understood him to say in reply to my friend from Rhode Island, [Mr. Simmons,] whom he supposed to have suspected him of unfriendliness to protection. I mean to treat, then, this argument from the prosperous condition of this industry, as the argument of a friend of adequate protection, who will maintain the existing degree and mode of protection, if it is necessary; who would, however, be desirous to reduce that degree, and depart from that mode, if manufacturing employments can bear the reduction and the change, and who infers from their present prosperity that they can bear it.

To him, then, Sir, who, being a friend of sufficient protection, and of a diffused, multiform, advanced manufacturing and mechanical industry, tells us, that a reduction of one half or one third of the existing protection will leave enough, I answer by asking, how do you know this? How do you make me, how do you make the senate, know it? How do you prove it? Where is your evidence? I respect your opinions highly. But I must see the grounds of this opinion.

The burden is on you. The presumption in the first instance is, that the existing rates of duty cause, and are necessary to, the existing prosperity. *Prima fronte* it is so. Here is the apparent cause. There is the apparent effect. Here is the law of 1842. Side by side, contemporaneous, coexistent, is the acknowledged prosperity. Here are the fruits: figs and grapes; they *seem* to grow, not on that thorn, or that thistle, but on the kindred tree and vine.

Well, this presumption is heightened by looking back a little. Duties ran down, in 1841, into the neighborhood of those which you say will give ample protection now. Manufacturing labor ran down too, and *pari passu*. You raised the duties, by the present law, to their present height. These employments sprung up, too, with an instantaneous and marvellous sympathy. The revival followed so close upon the passage of the law of 1842, it followed so naturally, it was so exactly what was predicted, so exactly what was expected, it was so entirely conformable to all our experience and to all analogy, that we can hardly in the first instance resist the conviction that the law was cause, the revival effect.

Then, I repeat it, the burden is heavy on you, who say that half or any other proportion of the duties of 1842 will give adequate protection, to prove it. This law of 1842 is no *new* law; it has no new, inflamed, untried rates of protection in it. It is for substance the law of 1828—the law of 1824. It has been twenty years in maturing. It has been constructed with great care; with much labor and much thought; by the aid of much investigation and much evidence. The system which it embodies has been long and thoroughly tried. You have tried it as in 1825, 1829, 1843, by keeping it in force; and you have tried it as in 1820 and 1841, by suffering it to fall. If now you say it is a great blunder, and that it lays duties in any proportion larger than its own objects require, you must prove it.

Well, what are the proofs? Have you any evidence of experienced persons, collected by a committee? Have any witnesses been examined, any opinions taken, any parliamentary inquisition holden? Nothing at all of the sort.

You say, manufactures flourished on the low duties of 1789 and 1807. Why, we might as well be told that antediluvians lived a thousand years. Where is the period from 1789 to 1807? With the days beyond the flood. Why reason from the experience of a world, which neither you nor I shall ever see again? Why not consult the experience of the actual world for which you legislate? You tried low duties in 1816, since the present age began, and you failed. You tried them in 1841, and you failed again. Is not this experience, decisive and stern, to dispel the delusive dreams, whispered by the irrevocable and inapplicable past? To go back to the protection of 1789, for the prosperity of 1789, is to go back in old age to the place of our birth, to seek for the singing-birds of childhood which now sing no more.

You say some branches of manufactures are earning enormous profits. Well, what then? What does the bill of the Senator from South Carolina thereupon propose? What do the principles of the Senator from Missouri provide for such a case? Do you institute an investigation into the appalling phenomenon, to ascertain whether the fact is so; how long it has been so; what are the temporary and accidental causes; whether the laws of business hydrostatics are not already bringing such profits down to the general level of all employments? Not at all. Do you proceed to reduce the duties on these unreasonably prosperous branches? No such thing. You seize the scythe, and just swing it at large over the whole field of labor, prosperous or unprosperous. Worse than Procrustes, who only pared down the too tall one, you, because one man is longer than the standard, cut the whole regiment in two in the middle. Cottons thrive, say the free-trade newspapers,—and down go the duties on hats! Fustians are lively,— and off comes the shoemaker's protection! Great stories are credibly and anony- mously told of large salaries at Lowell; dividends which they are afraid to divide; and calico printing which is making all their fortunes; whereupon, in our zeal, we propose to take off about one third, more or less, of the duties on ready- made clothing! I do not understand the logic of the operation. Here is a build- ing, some seven or ten stories high, with a thousand tenants. You propose to put your hands on the top of it, and press it down, bodily, into the ground about one half way. I humbly suggest the question, whether it is altogether safe for the persons in it? Perfectly so, say you, perfectly so; why do these people want to live seven, eight, ten stories in the air? Well, for them it may be safe, but what becomes of those who inhabit the basement and the ground rooms? They will be stifled to death!

Sir, let me respectfully recommend cautious and delicate handling of these interests. Vast, various, prosperous, as they are, a breath can unmake them, as a breath has made. This bill strikes a blow, the extent, degree, and nature of whose injurious effect no man can foresee or limit or cure. That which you certainly mean to do, involves consequences which you certainly do not mean. You begin by saying profits are too high. Then you propose to reduce profits. You begin by saying more foreign manufactures must be imported, because you propose to increase revenue by reducing duties. This demands, of course, enlarged importations. To that extent, to a new and undefined extent, you displace, disturb, diminish the domestic market of your own man- ufacturers. But can you really strike down the general profits and break up the actual market of American labor, and yet leave it prosperous, rewarded, and contented?

I intended, Sir, to have said something on the fallacy of the argument, that when manufactures are so firmly established as to have reduced prices, and made them reasonable, stable, and proportional to other prices, that then you may abolish protecting duties. But this topic has been so well handled by others, and particularly by my colleague, and I have already detained you so long, that I for- bear. Let me read a single passage from the same speech of Mr. Calhoun, to which I have referred so much:—

"But it will no doubt be said, if they are so far established, and if the situation of the country is so favorable to their growth, where is the necessity of affording them protection? It is to put them beyond the reach of contingency."

I may say, however, in a more general way, that, in the universal judgment of the world, stability, steadiness, the lapse of considerable periods of time, years, years of adequate protection, are required to build up manufacturing and mechanical arts to a consummated and durable prosperity. The policy of caprice will not do it; the policy of high duties to-day and low ones to-morrow; of inflation and collapse, jumping back fifty years, to rock grown men in the cradles of infants—this never will do it. Let me call to your notice a few extracts from the "Monthly Review," London, March, 1844, which convey, I think, a certain and important truth:—

"It is to be hoped free trade sophistry will not go so far as to exclaim: England having once brought her manufactures—no matter by what means—to the utmost degrees of perfection, free trade can only prove her advantage, since foreign competition in her market is out of question in most articles, while her own will be brought to foreign markets free of duty."

"They (the continental statesmen) well know that, as soon as the system of free trade is adopted, all idea must be abandoned of ever establishing manufactories in the present agricultural countries, even for home consumption alone; since it lies in the nature of a manufacturing country to have at command a mass of knowledge, expertness, practice, implements, and machinery, wholesome public institutions and regulations, vast connections and wealth, in all of which agricultural countries are deficient, as they can only be acquired slowly and gradually, *through an uninterrupted series of ages,* and the possession of which is manifest in the comparative *cheapness of the manufactures.* It is the principle of stability, continuation, and perseverance, that constitutes the basis of all the great works and institutions realized by the hands of men."

"The history of dynasties, nations, countries, and towns, as well as of the arts and sciences, corroborate the power of that principle. The latter (arts and sciences) have arrived at their present state of develop-

ment, as the former did at power, riches, and authority, only through
the exertions of a series of generations, striving and working to one and
the same end, the succeeding generation always taking up the thread
where the preceding had left off. By this principle alone was it possible
to erect monuments, the stupendousness of which we now admire, even
in their decay. To bring their principle more home, inquire of every
master mechanic or manufacturer, and he will tell you to how many difficulties and expenses the outset of a contrivance is subject, and how comparatively easy and profitable the more advanced progress is. In looking
more attentively into the history of the useful arts, and the various departments of industry, which are now brought to so flourishing a condition,
we find that one branch has sprung out of the other, and that the success
of one depended on that of the others; in short, that they all mutually
influence each other, and that the elements hostile to the principle of stability and continuation—such as civil disturbances, critical periods in
trade, and *fluctuations in prices*—have destroyed in a very short time the
labor of ages."

Germany is attempting, as we are, to develop her industrial capacities, and
is annoyed, as we are, by the selfish and senseless prattle of free trade. I like the
good sense and the firmness with which a writer in the "Augsburg Journal"
remarks on the honeyed and gilded plausibilities of Dr. Bowring:—

"Dr. Bowring deceives himself very much, if it be his belief that Germany desires no better fortune than to be allowed exportation of her corn
and wood to England, receiving in return English manufactures. Some
few landholders on the Lower Elbe, and some few possessors of forests
on the Baltic, may cherish the same hopes, and have expressed the same
wishes, as the Doctor."

"*Manufactures are plants of slow growth; and in a few years is easily destroyed
that which took ages to build. Now or never is the time to found durably German
industrial independence and the greatness of Germany.* To this end, it is before
all things necessary that the Germans themselves should feel full confidence *in the solidity of German industry.*"

"The more Germany advances on the path of industry which she has
adopted, the more decidedly appears the necessity of *a determined and
changeless duty* system, having for its aim *the regular advancement of German
industry.*"

Let me say, Mr. President, that it would seem to me no matter of rejoicing or pride to see the absolutism of the European continent attracting and retaining about its steadfast thrones these useful and manly arts, denied to us, yet so much more appropriately and more naturally forming the ornament, strength, and enrichment of popular liberty. Other arts I could give those governments up. I could resign, without a sigh, all the beauty and all the grace that live on canvas. They may have the breathing and speaking marble, for me. I could give them up all the poetry and all the music that ever consoled a nation for the loss of freedom. But I cannot so far divest myself of the prejudices, if they are such, instilled by the study of the history of the Constitution and of its earlier administration; I cannot so far forget the counsels of so many presidents and great men, the living and the dead; I cannot so far overlook the mighty causes of the wealth and power of nations, as not to feel a profound anxiety that these nobler and manlier arts, these arts which, as Washington thought, guard our independence, insure our security, and clothe and feed our masses; these arts, whose only regulator, whose only patron, whose only reward, is the wants of the people—that these arts should be all our own. Whether they shall be or not, depends on the stability and energy of our policy. It depends on you. It depends on the deliberations of this day.

You see, then, Mr. President, that I concur with the distinguished Senator from Missouri in the importance of stability and of harmony,—harmony in the country; stability in the law. They are worth something. They are worth a great deal. But, Sir, without an adequate protection to these forms of labor, you can have no harmony and no stability; and they would not be worth having, if you could. Our seasons of inadequate protection have not been seasons of harmony, because they have not been seasons of prosperity. Such was the period from 1783 to 1789. Such that from 1816 to 1824. Bad legislation; bad systems; systems inadequate to the demands, the hopes, the glory, of a free, busy, and aspiring people, will not be stable. They ought not to be. They will not be so till the pulses of liberty are dead, and the cold, bitter, unfruitful, and calm sea of despotism shall cover us over. Stable protecting legislation, not an unprotecting stability, and not a fluctuating protection, is the one grand desideratum for American harmony and prosperity.

I have done, Sir, with the discussion of the general subject, and will soon resume my seat. The honorable Senator from Missouri thinks that the present is an unpropitious moment for the adjustment of the tariff; referring, as I understand him, to the approaching presidential election. The Senator from Georgia [Mr. Berrien] concurs in this opinion. I go further, Sir, than either, and for reasons somewhat different. I should be quite willing, for my part, if for the six months preceding such an election, such a subject as this should be *tabooed* ground. It should be interdicted. The time should be *dies non juridicus*—the time of stump speaking, if you please, not of congressional legislation. I distrust my own ability to come with the requisite care and calmness to such a deliberation. I distrust myself; almost I distrust you. We are within a few months of an election which is to determine who is to wield the vast executive powers of this government for the next four years; who are to administer the executive departments; who to represent you at all the courts of the world, who to fill all the national offices; what will, what spirit, what dispositions, are to preside in the administration, for all good or evil which administration can accomplish. We are surrounded by many millions of people, whose hearts are throbbing, as the heart of one man, with anxiety for the result. Among these all, are we sure that we are quite cool ourselves? Are we sure that we are quite in a condition to adjust this vast system, to settle these infinite and delicate details? Is there no danger that disturbing elements may enter into the deliberation? Is there no danger that we shall be thinking how this rate of duty or how that may *affect votes,* instead of inquiring exclusively how it will affect labor, prices, revenue? Do you think the master of a steamboat is quite so good a judge how much his boilers will bear while he is running a race with a new rival on a ten thousand dollar wager?

I declare, Sir, that it has more than once crossed my mind, barely crossed it, that this circumstance of our legislating under the pernicious heat of this dog-star may help to explain the extraordinary attention that has been paid to Massachusetts in the debate. It is her profits for which newspapers have been ransacked. It is her advocacy of the tariff to which senators have supposed themselves replying. If a sneer could be insinuated against her opinions about the last war, or, better still, about abolition, it seems to have passed for some sort of argument against a protecting policy. The silence which has been observed towards Pennsylvania has been quite as remarkable as the eloquence which has been expended on Massachusetts. I deceive myself, if there has been the slightest allusion to her, or her iron duties, in the whole winter's debate. I perceive that, in the report of the committee of ways and means of the house, very affectionate and patriotic things are even said about iron. Now, Sir, when you consider that Massachusetts never made a protecting tariff; that she took no leading or influencive part in 1816; that she opposed that of 1824 with almost her entire vote, and with great zeal and ability; that she voted against that of 1828; that she has done nothing but just to stay where you placed her; that Pennsylvania, on the other hand, has been the founder, the steadfast support and stay of the whole system; that she made the protecting parts of the act of 1789; that in 1816, 1820, 1824, 1828, always, always her numerous vote, and her powerful and cultivated talents, have been prominent and controlling in maintaining and giving energy and completeness to the policy; and when you consider, too, what are the interests which it protects for her—considering all this, is it strange that the question has passed through my mind, whether the extraordinary notice of Massachusetts, and the extraordinary reserve towards Pennsylvania, may not possibly be attributable to her having a large electoral vote which is thought to be somewhat doubtful; while ours is a small one, *not at all* doubtful? Whatever the cause, the fact is certain. I amused myself the other evening with imagining what sort of history of the tariff a writer two thousand years hence might make up, from materials derived exclusively from one side of this debate. The Senator from New Hampshire once wrote a very good discourse on the uncertainties of history; he will not wonder, therefore, to find this sketch pretty full of blunders. It might run nearly thus: "In the year 1824, the State of Massachusetts somewhat abruptly ejaculated, Go to, now! let us make a protecting tariff. And thereupon that State, having, as it would appear, by some means not clearly explained, acquired a large majority of votes in both houses of congress, did actually proceed to force such a thing down the throats of the other astounded and reluctant States. What renders this the more remarkable is, that the Constitution evidently contemplated no such thing, that celebrated compact having been a mere great free-trade league, entered into mainly with a view to promoting the culture of a certain beautiful vegetable wool, called cotton. However, she made a tariff. And thenceforward the domestic history of the States seems to have consisted very much of a series of the most desperate and most chivalrous struggles, on the part of all the others, to get rid of a system which at once debauched their understandings and picked their pockets. In this contest, though all did well, South Carolina and New Hampshire particularly distinguished themselves; one being the great cotton-growing, and the other the great navigating State of the Union. Well might they take the lead; they were most ably represented, (there the historian is right;) and it appears to have been an indisputable and melancholy fact, that the tariff had killed all the cotton in the fields of South Carolina, and had rotted down the ten thousand masts of the merchant navy of New Hampshire, piecemeal,—so that in 1842 the whole number of human beings who sailed from her ports, in her vessels, were only fifty-six men and three boys!" Here the manuscript terminates; and it is about as true as the first five books of Livy, nine tenths of Plutarch, and a considerable part of Hume's history of the Puritans and the Stuarts!

Certainly, Sir, we are very much in these employments. You may thank your-selves for that. And is it not an excellent thing for you that we are? Are we not a very much more useful member of the partnership, more useful to the other part-ners, than we could be without? Is it not a good, honest, genial, social, "live and let live" sort of business you have driven us into? Suppose, Sir, you could drive us out of it again, as you may; suppose you should send us back to ice and gran-ite, to sawing boards, raising beans and corn, drying nets and making fish on the rocks of our iron-bound and stern coast, or to roaming the ocean for freights, in competition with the black-bread sailors of Bremen and Hamburg; suppose that thus you could drive three quarters of our people away, to return no more,— what good would it do you? Now, if we had a Chinese wall around Massachu-setts; if our work was done two thousand feet under ground; if it was the digging of gold or quicksilver, to be sent abroad in our vessels or foreign vessels; if all that you saw of us was when, once a year, we came here with the soot of the furnace on our faces, to beg for bounties and prohibitory duties,—why, that would be one thing. But is it nothing that we take and consume within that single State an annual amount of more than forty millions of dollars of your productions; an amount out of all manner of proportion to any other State, except Rhode Island; an amount equal to about one half of the whole exports of the whole Union, exclusive of manufactures? Is it nothing that we take these productions, not only from all the great regions, East, Central, South, and West, but from every State something,—cotton, grain, rice, sugar from the South, and South-west; naval stores from North Carolina; grain and meats from the Central regions; lead and corn from Missouri; buffalo robes from the Rocky Mountains? I hold here the enumeration of these productions, in an excellent speech of Mr. Hudson, of Massachusetts, delivered at the session of 1842, in the other house, to which sen-ators may have access.—[See Note, p. 245.] And is this nothing? Is it not a truly national business which we pursue; national in the surface it spreads over; national in the good it does; national in the affections it generates? Well said Mr. Calhoun, in 1816,—

"It produces an interest strictly American, as much so as agricul-ture, in which it had the decided advantage of commerce or naviga-tion. The country will from this derive much advantage. Again: it is calculated to bind together more closely our widely spread Republic. It will greatly increase our mutual dependence and intercourse; and will, as a necessary consequence, excite an increased attention to inter-nal improvements—a subject every way so intimately connected with the ultimate attainment of national strength and the perfection of our political institutions."

Yes, Sir, manufacturers and mechanics are Unionists by profession; Unionists by necessity; Unionists always. Learn to know your friends. The time may come you will need them!

I have been pained inexpressibly, Sir, by some things which have been insinuated, not very distinctly said, in this debate. In a discussion of the tariff, I have heard allusions to the course of Massachusetts in 1812, and to the abolition sentiments which she cherishes to-day. How am I to understand them? Does any one dare to propose, or dare to intimate, that speculative opinions on one subject are to be punished by unkind, deleterious, practical legislation on other subjects? For our opinions on the last war, or on the institution of slavery, do you propose to drive our artisans and mechanics from their livings and their homes? God forbid. Do not think of such a thing. Banish it. Disdain it. Despise it. Despise, I am sure you do, a retaliation so absurd, so mean, so unjust, so profligate. Permit me to say, that you must take the States of America as you find them. All of them have their peculiarities. All have their traits. All have their history; traditions; characters. They had them before they came into the Union. They will have them after.

—"Rome in Tiber melts, and the wide arch
   Of the ranged empire falls."

South Carolina has hers—Massachusetts has hers. She will continue to think, speak, print, just what she pleases, on every subject that may interest the patriot, the moralist, the Christian. But she will be true to the Constitution. She sat among the most affectionate at its cradle; she will follow, the saddest of the procession of sorrow, its hearse! She sometimes has stood for twenty years together in opposition to the general government. She cannot promise the implicit politics of some of her neighbors. I trust, however, that she will not be found in opposition to the next administration. I have heard that once her senate refused to vote thanks for a victory for which her people had shed their blood. Sir, you must take the States as you find them! You must take her as you find her! Be just to her, and she will be a blessing to you. She will sell to you at fair prices, and on liberal credits; she will buy of you when England and Canada and the West Indies and Ireland will not; she will buy your staples, and mould them into shapes of beauty and use, and send them abroad, to represent your taste and your genius in the great fairs of civilization. Something thus she may do, to set upon your brow that crown of industrial glory, to which "the laurels that a Cæsar reaps are weeds." More, Sir, more. Although she loves not war, nor any of its works; although her interests, her morals, her intelligence, are all against it; although she is with South Carolina, with all the South, on that ground; yet, Sir, at the call of honor, at the call of liberty, if I have read her annals true, she will be found standing, where once she stood, side by side with you, on the darkened and perilous ridges of battle.

Be just to her, coldly, severely, Constitutionally just, and she will be a blessing to you.

Chapter V.

THE POWER OF A STATE DEVELOPED BY MENTAL CULTURE.
A Lecture Delivered before the Mercantile Library Association,
November 13, 1844.

The true foundation of a state, Choate believes, lay less in its material accomplish-
ments than in its cultivation of the mind. Mere technological advance is necessarily incom-
plete, for a dull mind equipped with a machine is still a dull mind. (It hardly needs
pointing out that Choate's insight retains its value and relevance today.)

His ambitions for New England in the life of the nation bring to mind the enthusi-
asm of an Alcuin living through the heady excitement of the Carolingian Renaissance.
Choate wants New England to supply the Union with more than the occasional presi-
dent or congressional majority. He looks to his native section to have "such an influence
as Athens exerted on the taste and opinion first of Greece, then of Rome, then of the uni-
versal modern world."

"Doubtless the Pilgrim race—the Puritan race—shall go everywhere, and possess largely
of everything," Choate writes. It has surely done so, but emancipated from the conservative
Calvinism that had once defined its existence. Historian Eldon Eisenach has pointed out
that the leading lights of the Progressive Era were overwhelmingly of New England stock,
whether in fact located in the six New England states themselves or "wherever the children
of the Puritans are found." Thus Choate identifies the missionary role that his section
would once again assume, but could not have known that the form it would take would be
radically different from what he expected.

THE TRANSITION from the scenes which have been passing before us for the
last few months, to such a spectacle as this, is so sudden, so delightful, that I can
scarcely refrain, as I cast my eyes over this composed and cultivated assembly,
from exclaiming, "Hail, holy light!" The clamor, tumult, and stimulations
which attend that great trial and great task of liberty through which we have
just gone,—a nation's choice of its ruler,—those vast gatherings of the people,—
not quite in their original and ultimate sovereignty above or without the law,

but in mass and bodily numbers without number; processions without end,—
by daylight and torchlight—under the law; the stormy wave of the multitude rising and falling to the eloquence of liberty,—if it were eloquence at all; the hope,
the fear, the anxious care, the good news waited for and not coming, the bad
news riding somewhere about a couple of hundred miles in advance of the
express of either side; the cheers of your co-workers; the hissings and groan-
ings, not to be uttered, of your opponents,—all are passed away as dreams. We
find ourselves collected without distinction of party, without memory of party,
in the security and confidence of reconciliation, or at least of truce, in the still
air,—upon the green and neutral ground of thoughts and studies common and
grateful to us all. To look backward brings to mind what Lenox says to Mac-
beth in the morning, before he had heard of the murder of the king.

> "The night has been unruly; where we lay
> Our chimneys were blown down, and as they say
> Lamentings heard in the air,
> And prophesyings, with accents terrible,
> Of dire combustion and confused events
> New-hatched to the woful time!"

The night has passed, and the morning of an eventful day is risen. So much we
know; and it is all we know.

Delightful, in some sense, as I feel this change of scene, of society, and of
influences to be, I have found myself unable and unwilling, in the selection of
a topic for the hour of this meeting, altogether to forget the occasion to which
I have referred. I have rather desired to see if we might not all, without distinction of party, (for of the existence of party we know nothing here,)—if we
might not all, the winner and the loser—contrive to learn some useful lesson
from the occasion. All that happens in the world of Nature or Man,—every war;
every peace; every hour of prosperity; every hour of adversity; every election;
every death; every life; every success and every failure,—all change,—all permanence,—the perished leaf; the unutterable glory of stars,—all things speak
truth to the thoughtful spirit.

> "List ever, then, to the words of Wisdom, whether she speaketh to
> the soul in the full chords of revelation, in the teaching of earth or air or
> sky, or in the still melodies of thought!"

I wonder, then, if during the labors and excitations of the late election, and in
the contemplation of possible results near and far forward, the inquiry has not

occurred to you, as to me it has a thousand times, is there no way, are there no expedients by which such a State as Massachusetts, for example, may remain in the Union, performing the duties, partaking as far as may be of the good of Union, and yet be in some greater degree than now she is, independent of and unaffected by the administrative and legislative policy of Union? Is there no way to secure to ourselves a more steady, sure, progressive prosperity,—such a prosperity in larger measure than we are apt to imagine,—whatever national politics come uppermost? Is there no way to sink the springs of our growth and greatness so deep, that the want of a little rain or a little dew, a little too much sunshine or too much shade from Washington, shall not necessarily cut off "the herd from the stalls" and cause the "fields to yield no meat"? Must it be, that because the great central regions, the valley of the Mississippi, the undefined and expanding South-west, have attracted to themselves the numerical supremacy—that our day is done? Is our voice, once

> —"Their liveliest pledge
> Of hope in fears and dangers, heard so oft
> In worst extremes, and on the perilous edge
> Of battle when it raged in all assaults
> Their surest signal,"—

is that voice to be heard no more? Have we declined, must we decline, into the condition of a province—doomed to await passively the edict of a distant palace, which shall cause it to thrive to-day and pine to-morrow; now raise it to a gaudy and false prosperity, and then press "its beaming forehead to the dust"? Or is there a way by which we yet may be, and forever may be, the arbiters of our own fortunes; may yet be felt in the counsels of America; may yet help to command a national policy which we approve, or at least to bear unharmed a national policy which we condemn? Must we pale and fade and be dissolved in the superior rays of the great constellation, or yet "flame in the forehead of the morning sky" with something of the brightness of our rising?

I take it for granted in all such speculations, in all such moods as this, that we are to remain in the Federal Union. With our sisters of the Republic we would live—we would die—

> "One hope, one lot, one life, one glory."

I agree, too, that whatever we may do for Massachusetts, the influence of national politics upon our local prosperity must always be inappreciably great for evil or for good.

It is of individuals, not States, that Goldsmith exclaims,

"How small, of all that human hearts endure,
That part which kings or laws can cause or cure!"

The joy and sorrow, the greatness and decline, of nations, are to a vast extent the precise work of kings or laws; and although in our system every State has its own government and its own civil polity, to which important functions are assigned, yet when you consider that it is to the great central power that war, peace, diplomacy, finance, our whole intercourse with the world, trade, as far as winds blow or waters roll, the trust of our glory, the protection of our labor, are confided,—nobody can indulge the dream that a State may remain in the Union at all, and yet be insensible of the good and evil, the wisdom or the folly, the honor and the shame, of its successive administrations.

And yet I think that the statesmen of Massachusetts may well ask themselves, whether there are no expedients of empire or imperial arts worthy her,—worthy them,—by which they may enable her either to retain consideration and lead in the general government, to be conspicuous and influence an American opinion, by which they may enable her either to extort what she calls good policy,— or else to break the force of what she calls occasional bad policy, which she cannot hinder and to which she must submit.

Passing over all other expedients as unsuitable to the character and relations of this assembly, is it not worth while to consider this matter, for example,— whether a higher degree of general mental culture, a more thorough exercising and accomplishing of the whole mass of our popular and higher mind, more knowledge, a wider diffusion of knowledge, loftier attainments in useful and in graceful knowledge than we have ever reached, or that any State has reached, might not help us to meet the enlarging demand of time, and the successive crises of the commonwealth? Is it certain that in our speculations on the causes of the grandeur and decay, of the wealth and the poverty, the importance and the insignificance, of States, we have given quite as high a place as it deserves to the intellect of the State? Have we not thought too much of capacious harbors or teeming inland, navigable rivers, fleets of merchant ships and men-of-war, fields of wheat, plantations of cotton and rice and sugar, too much of tariffs and drawbacks and banks, and too little, too little, of that soul, by which only, the nation shall be great and free? In our speculations on knowledge and the bettering of the mind, is it right or is it wise to treat them as useful or as ornamental individual accomplishments alone, and not sometimes also to think of them as mines of national riches wealthier than Ormus or Ind, as perennial and salient springs of national power, as foundations, laid far below earthquake or frost, of a towering and durable public greatness? After all, this is the thought I would present to you,—is there a surer way of achieving the boast of Themistocles, that he knew how to make a small State a great one, than by making it wise, bright, knowing, apprehensive, quick-witted, ingenious, thoughtful; by communicating to the whole mass of its people the highest degree of the most improved kind of education in its largest sense, which is compatible with the system of practical things; by beginning at the cradle, by touching the infant lip with fire from heaven; by perfecting the methods of the free schools, and of all schools, so that the universal understanding shall be opened, kindled, guided at its very birth, and set forward, without the loss of a day, on the true path of intellectual life; by taking care that all the food of which the soul of the people eats shall be wholesome and nutritious,—that the books and papers which they read, the sermons and speeches which they hear, shall possess at least a predominance of truth, fact, honesty, of right and high thought, just and graceful feeling; by providing institutions to guide the mature mind to the heights of knowledge; by collections of art and taste that shall unfold and instruct the love of beauty; by planting betimes the gardens of a divine philosophy, and spreading out the pavilion of the Muses?

Let us think a little of mental culture as the true local policy of Massachusetts.

I do not propose to repeat anything quite so general and elementary, as that easy commonplace which my Lord Bacon has illustrated so fondly and so gorgeously, that learned States have been usually prosperous States, that the eras of lettered glory have been eras of martial and civil glory too, that an instructed people has been for the most part a rich, laborious, energetic, and powerful people. The historical fact is undoubtedly as he records it; and it is as encouraging as it is true. I wish to unfold the operations and uses of learning and culture in a little more detail, and with a more confined and local reference to the case before us. Mental culture, as the true local policy of Massachusetts, I have said, is the topic to which I am restricted.

Let me say, however, in the first place, generally, that mental culture should contribute to our power and our consideration, by communicating or by developing those traits of character that lie at the foundation of all splendid and remarkable national distinction. All the greatness which is recorded in the histories or the epics of all the great States of the earth, all the long series of their virtues, all their compass of policy, all their successful contention with nature or with man, all their great works well performed, all their great dangers bravely met, all the great perils which harass them resisted and scattered, all their industrial renown, their agriculture, their trade, their art, their science, their libraries, their architecture, all their contributions to thought, to humanity, to progress, all the charm that attaches to their living name and that lingers on the capacious tomb into which at last they go down,—all this you trace at length to a few energetic qualities of mind and character. It does not spring from any fortuitous concurrence of any quantity of mere material atoms; it is not the growth of any number of hundred years of rain and sunshine falling upon the surface of the earth; it is not a spontaneous or necessary development and manifestation according to some mechanical and organic laws;—it is a production of the human mind; it is a creation of the human will; it is just the nobler and larger parts of man, in their most appropriate and grandest exemplifications. All of it rests at last on enterprise, energy, curiosity, perseverance, fancy, talent,—loftily directed, heroically directed. A few simple, commanding traits, a dignified aim, a high conception of the true glory of a State,—with a little land and water to work with,—and you have a great nation. I approve, therefore, of these expressions: the Roman mind, the Grecian mind, the Oriental mind, the European mind. There is true philosophy and an accurate history in them. They penetrate to the true criteria which distinguish races,—the mental criteria. It is not her "plumed and jewelled turban," her tea-plant and her cinnamon-plant, her caves, temples, and groves of palms, her exhaustless fertility of soils, her accumulations of imperial treasures,—"barbaric pearl and gold," as in a dream of the Arabian Nights,—by which I recognize the primeval East; it is that universal childhood of reason,—not a day older than in the age of Sardanapalus or of Ninus,—that subjugated popular character bowed to the earth beneath the superincumbent despotism of ages, that levity and vanity and effeminacy of the privileged few, the elaborate luxury in which their lives are steeped, their poetry of the fancy, their long contemplations on nature and divinity, on which the whole intellect of the East might brood for six thousand years and not bring away as much truth as is taught in six months to the oldest boys and girls in our high schools—these are the true characteristics of Asia; these it is which solve all the facts of her history; these it is which, put into action, are her history itself. And then passing westward to Athens,—to Attica,—is it her area, not quite so large, not half as fertile, as our own Rhode Island, her mountain steeps sprinkled with dwarf oaks and fir trees, her sun-burnt valleys covered with meagre herbage, her wintry torrents dried up in summer, her olive trees with their pale leaf and pliable branches—is it these things which seem to you to have made up the grace of Greece, or was it that flexible, brave, and energetic character, so prompt and full of resource, that curiosity and perseverance and fire, that love of Athens and of glory, that subtilty of practical understanding, that unrivalled elegance of taste, that teeming and beautiful fancy,—were not these the traits, and these the gifts which created the Athens of the world and of all ages,—the one and only Athens; which are embodied for us in the Iliad and in the Odipus and in the Parthenon, in the treatises of Aristotle, the dialogues of Plato, the orations of Demosthenes,— that eloquence of an expiring nation; which stand out on the sculptured page of Plutarch in the port of a hundred demi-gods; which created her to be a teacher of patriotism and a light to liberty; which won for her in her own time the place of the first power of the world, and seated her with a more rare felicity on an intellectual throne, from which no progress of the species may cast her down?

Now, if the nations differ by their minds, the right kind and the right degree of mental culture goes to the very springs of the national nature. It applies itself directly to the *causa causans*. It imparts and it shapes that basis of qualities, good or bad, large or little, stone or wood, or hay or stubble,—on which the State ascends to its duration of a day, or its duration of ages.

I do not say that mental culture alone can completely educate a nation,—far from it. There must be action. There must be labor. There must be difficulty. There must be the baptism of blood and of fire. If there is a not very fertile soil under foot, a not very spicy air around, a not very luxurious heaven overhead,— it is all the better.

Nor is it every kind and every degree of mental culture that will do this work. It must be such culture as may be given to an employed, a grave, an earnest, a moral, and a free people. It must be a culture of the reason and of the heart. It must not be a culture like that which consoled the Paris of Louis XIV., which consoles the Rome, the Florence, and the Venice of our time for the loss, for the want, of liberty. It must not be a culture which supplies trifles to the eye, stimulations to the senses, shows to the fancy, the music of a holiday to the ear. It must not be a culture which turns mortal life, that solemn and that grand reality and waking, into a fine dream,—and presents death, not as an interruption of profound attachments, earnest labors, and serious aims,—but as a drooping of the garlands of a feast from which the guests have departed. It must be a very different kind of mental culture from this. It must be one which shall be so directed as to give force, power, depth, effectiveness, to the intellect of the whole people. It must be one which, beginning with the youngest child, shall seek to improve the heart of the people, shall propose to the infant and to the adolescent will and sensibilities, great examples, as well as wholesome counsel,—the careers of nations and of men—pure, rapid, and majestic, as rivers—grand, swelling sentiments of liberty, patriotism, duty, and honor,—triumphant, awful, splendid deaths,—the Puritan at the stake, the patriot on the scaffold, those who fell at Thermopyæ in obedience to the law, those who were buried at Plymouth in the first, awful winter. Such a culture as this it is, which, blending with the other discipline of public and private life, may prove the mother and nurse of a great, thoughtful, and free people. "Remember that the learning of the few is despotism; the learning of the multitude is liberty;—and that intelligent and principled liberty is fame, wisdom, and power."

In the next place, to come down to a little more detail, mental culture may contribute to our security, our independence, our local aggrandizement, by informing and directing our labor.

I need not tell you that labor is the condition—I will not say, of our greatness, but—of our being. What were Massachusetts without it? Lying away up under the North star,—our winters long and cold, our springs backward and capricious, our sky ungenial, our coast iron-bound,—our soil not overproductive, barren almost altogether of the great staples of commerce which adorn and enrich the wheat fields of the central regions, the ocean prairies of the West, the rice grounds and sugar and cotton plantations of the South,—our area small,—our numbers few,—our earlier occupations of navigation and fishing divided with us by a whole world at peace,—what is there for us but labor,— *labor improbus, labor omnia vincens?* And what kind of labor is it which is to vanquish the antagonist powers of nature, and build the palace of a commodious and conspicuous national life over against these granite mountains and this unfruitful sea? Is it one kind, or two; or is it the whole vast and various labor of intellectual civilization,—not agriculture only and trade and fishing, but the whole family of robust and manly arts, which furnish occupation to everybody every moment of working time,—occupation, to every taste and talent and faculty, that which it likes best, that which improves it most, that which it can do easiest,—occupation for the strong and the weak, the bright and the dull, the young and the old, and both the sexes,—occupation for winter and summer, daylight and lamplight, cold weather and warm, wet and dry,—occupation that shall, with more than magnetic touch, seize on, develop, discipline, and perfect every capacity, the whole mass of ability, gathering up all fragments of mind and of time, so that nothing be lost—is not this the labor by which we are to grow great? Is not this the labor which is to be to us in the place of mines, of pearls, of vineyards, of cinnamon gardens, of enamelled prairies, of wheat-fields, of rice-grounds and cotton-fields and sugar-plantations tilled by the hands of slaves? This is that transmuting power without which we are poor, give what they will—with it rich, take what they will away! This it is, labor, ever labor, which, on the land, on the sea, in the fields, in all its applications, with all its helps, from the straw bonnet braided or plaited by the fingers, up to those vast processes in which, evoking to its aid the powers of nature and the contrivances of ages of skill, it takes the shapeless or from its bed, the fleece from the felt, the cotton from the pod, and moulds them into shapes of beauty and use and taste,—the clothing, the armor, the furniture of civilization, sought for in all the markets of the world—this it is which is to enrich and decorate this unlovely nature where our lot is cast, and fit it for the home of cultivated man!

Now, if the highest practicable degree of mental culture and useful knowledge is really the best instrumentality for instructing, guiding, vivifying, helping this rough power of labor,—if it will supply the chemistry which teaches it how to enrich barren soils, reclaim and spare exhausted soils, irrigate parched soils, make two blades of grass grow where one grew before,—if it will teach it how to build tunnels through mountains or beneath beds of rivers and under populous towns, how to fill or bridge the valley, how to stretch out and fasten in their places those long lines of iron roads which, as mighty rivers, pour the whole vast inland into a market of exchange for what trade has gathered from every quarter of the globe,—if it will teach it better how to plan its voyages and make its purchases, so as most seasonably to meet the various and sudden and changing demands of men by the adequate supply,—if it can teach it how to construct its tools, how to improve old ones and invent new, how to use them, by what shortest and simplest and cheapest process it can arrive at the largest results of production,—if it can thus instruct and thus aid that labor, which is our only source of wealth, and of all material greatness,—if, above all, when rightly guided by the morality and religion which I assume everywhere to preside over our education, it communicates that moral and prudential character which is as needful and as available for thrift as for virtue, thoughtfulness, economy, self-estimation, sobriety, respect for others' rights,—is it not an obvious local and industrial policy to promote, diffuse, and perfect it?

Well, I must not spend a moment in the proof of a proposition so palpable as this. I say there is not an occupation of civilized life, from the making of laws and poems and histories, down to the opening of New Jersey oysters with a broken jack-knife, that is not better done by a bright than a dull man, by a quick than a slow mind, by an instructed man than a gross or simple man, by a prudent, thoughtful, and careful man, than by a light and foolish one. Every one of these occupations—in other words, the universal labor of civilization—involves, demands, *is,* a mental effort, putting forth a physical effort; and you do but only go to the fountain-head, as you ought to do, when you seek, by an improved culture and a better knowledge, to give force and power to the imperial capacity behind, and to set a thoughtful and prudent spirit to urge and to guide it. You say that you bestow a new power on man, when you give him an improved machine. Do you not bestow a more available gift, when you bestow on him an improvement of that mental and moral nature which makes, improves, and uses, profitably or unprofitably, all machines? In one case you give him a limited and definite amount of coined money, in the other a mine of gold or silver. Nay, what avails the improved machine to the untaught mind? Put a forty-feet telescope, with its mirrors of four feet diameter, into the hands of a savage, whether in civilized or Indian life, and he sees about as much as our children see through a glass prism,— gaudy outlines, purple and orange and green crossing and blending on everything. Let the exercised mind of Herschel lift that same tube from the Cape of Hope toward the southern sky, and the architecture of the heavens—not made with hands—ascends before him,—

> "Glory beyond all glory ever seen
> By waking sense, or by the dreaming soul!"

firmaments of fixed stars,—of which all the stars in our heaven, all our eye takes in, form but one firmament, one constellation only of a universe of constellations, separated by unsounded abysses, yet holden together by invisible bands,— moving together, perhaps, about some centre, to which the emancipated soul may in some stage of being ascend, but which earthly science shall vanish away without seeing!

Such in kind, not of course in degree, is the additional power you give to labor by improving the intellectual and prudential character which informs and guides it.

It is within the knowledge of you all that Mr. Mann, in one of those reports to the Board of Education to which the community is so much indebted, I believe the fifth, has developed this thought with that keenness of analysis and clearness and force of expression for which he is remarkable. You will be particularly struck with the proofs which he has there collected from several most intelligent and respectable superintendents or proprietors of manufacturing establishments, showing by precise statistical details, derived from a long course of personal observation, that throughout the whole range of mechanical industry the well educated operative does more work, does it better, wastes less, uses his allotted portion of machinery to more advantage and more profit, earns more money, commands more confidence, rises faster, rises higher, from the lower to the more advanced positions of his employments, than the uneducated operative. And now, how interestingly and directly this fact connects itself with my subject, I need not pause to show. You speak of tariffs to protect your industry from the redundant capital, the pauper labor, the matured skill, the aggressive and fitful policy, of other nations. You cannot lay a tariff under the Constitution, and you cannot compel Congress to do so; but you can try to rear a class of working-men who may help you to do something without one. You speak of specific duties, and discriminating duties, and what not! Are you sure that if everybody,—*every mind,* I should say,—which turns a wheel or makes a pin in this great workshop of ours, all full from basement to attic with the various hum of free labor, was educated up to the utmost degree compatible with his place in life,—that this alone would not be equal to at least a uniform duty of about twenty-eight per cent. ad valorem, all on the home value? You must have more skill you say, more skill than now, or you must have governmental protection. Very well; go to work to make it, then. You manufacture almost everything. Suppose you go into the manufacture of skill. Try your hand at the skill business. Skill in the arts is mental power exercised in arts, that is all. Begin by making mental power. You can do that as easily as you can make satinets or fustian or chain-cable. You have a great deal of money. The world never saw such a provision for popular and higher education as you could make in a year in Massachusetts, and not feel it. Consider how true and fine in this application would be the words of the charitable man's epitaph be: "What I spent I had. What I kept I lost. What I gave away remains with me!"

By what precise course of instruction, elementary and advanced, by what happier methods, by what easier access to the mind and heart, by "what drugs, what charms, what conjuration, and what mighty magic," this heightened mental ability and accomplishment may be achieved, which I know is practicable, and which I know is power,—it is not within my plan, if I could, to suggest. I may be permitted to remember, that the first time I ever ventured to open my lips in a deliberative body, I had the honor to support a bill in the House of Representatives, in Massachusetts, providing for educating teachers of common schools. I should be perfectly willing to open them for the last time, in the same place in support of the same proposition exactly. I can conceive of a body of teachers,—I know individuals now,—who would do this great work for Massachusetts, as patriotism and religion would wish it done,—who would take the infant capacity of the people, as it came to life, into their arms, and breathe into it the quickening breath,—who receiving it, bathed and blessed by a mother's love, would apply to it, instead of stripes, the gentle, irresistible magnet of scientific instruction, opening it as a flower to light and rain,—who, when the intellectual appetite was begun to be developed, would feed it with the angels' food of the best mental and moral culture which years of reflection and experience and interchange of thought could suggest,—would carry forward the heart, and the reason together,—would fit the whole bright tribe of childhood as completely, in so far as intellect and acquisition are concerned, for beginning to wrestle with the practical realities of life at fourteen, as now at one-and-twenty.

To such teachers I leave details, with one suggestion only,—that I would not take the Bible from the schools so long as a particle of Plymouth Rock was left, large enough to make a gun-flint of, or as long as its dust floated in the air. I would have it read not only for its authoritative revelations, and its commands and exactions, obligatory yesterday, to-day, and forever, but for its English, for its literature, for its pathos, for its dim imagery, its sayings of consolation and wisdom and universal truth,—achieving how much more than the effect which Milton ascribes to music:

"Nor wanting power to mitigate and swage,
With solemn touches, troubled thoughts, and chase
Anguish and doubt and fear and sorrow and pain
From mortal, or immortal minds."

Perhaps as striking an illustration on a large scale as could be desired, of the connection between the best directed and most skillful labor and the most cultivated and most powerful intellect, is afforded by the case of England. British industry, as a whole, is among the most splendid and extraordinary things in the history of man. When you consider how small a work-bench it has to occupy altogether,—a little stormy island bathed in almost perpetual fogs, without silk, or cotton, or vineyards, or sunshine; and then look at that agriculture so scientific and so rewarded, that vast net-work of internal intercommunication, the docks, merchant-ships, men-of-war, the trade encompassing the globe, the flag on which the sun never sets,—when you look above all at that vast body of useful and manly art,—not directed like the industry of France—the industry of vanity—to making pier-glasses and air-balloons and gobelin tapestry and mirrors, to arranging processions and chiselling silver and twisting gold into filagrees,— but to clothing the people, to the manufacture of woollen, cotton, and linen cloth, of railroads and chain-cables and canals and anchors and achromatic telescopes, and chronometers to keep the time at sea,—when you think of the vast aggregate mass of their manufacturing and mechanical production, which no statistics can express, and to find a market for which she is planting colonies under every constellation, and by intimidation, by diplomacy, is knocking at the door of every market-house upon the earth,—it is really difficult to restrain our admiration of such a display of energy, labor, and genius, winning bloodless and innocent triumphs everywhere, giving to the age we live in the name of the age of the industry of the people. Now, the striking and the instructive fact is, that exactly in that island workshop, by this very race of artisans, of coal-heavers and woollen manufacturers, of machinists and blacksmiths and ship-carpenters, there has been produced and embodied forever, in words that will outlast the mountains as well as the Pyramids, a literature which, take it for all in all, is the richest, most profound, most instructive, combining more spirituality with more common sense, springing from more capacious souls, conveying a better wisdom, more conformable to the truth in man, in nature, and in human life, than the literature of any nation that ever existed. That same race, side by side with the unparalleled growth of its industry, produces Shakspeare, Milton, Bacon, and Newton, all four at the summit of human thought,—and then, just below these unapproachable fixed lights, a whole firmament of glories, lesser than they, as all created intelligence must be, yet in whose superior rays the age of Augustus, of Leo X., of Louis XIV., all but the age of Pericles, the culture of Greece, pale and fade. And yet the literature of England is not the only, scarcely the most splendid, fruit or form of the mental power and the energetic character of England. That same race, along with their industry, along with their literature, has built up a jurisprudence which is for substance our law to-day,—has constructed the largest mercantile and war navy, and the largest commercial empire with its pillars encircling the globe, that men ever saw,—has gained greater victories on sea and land than any power in the world,—has erected the smallest spot to the most imperial ascendancy recorded in history. The administrative triumphs of her intellect are as conspicuous as her imaginative and her speculative triumphs.

Such is mental power. Mark its union with labor and with all greatness; deduce the law; learn the lesson; see how you, too, may grow great. Such an industry as that of England demanded such an intellect as that of England. *Sic vobis etiam itur ad astra!* That way to you, also, glory lies!

I have now been speaking of a way in which mental culture may help your labor to grow independent of governmental policy, and thus to disregard and endure what you cannot control. But may not the same great agent do more than this? May it not, not merely enable you to bear an administrative policy which you cannot prevent, but enable you to return the more grateful power of influencing national councils and national policy, long after the numerical control has gone to dwell in the imperial valley of the West?

I will not pause to say so obvious a thing, as that those you call public men, those whom you send to urge your claims and consult your interests in the national assembly, are better fitted for their task by profound and liberal studies. This were too obvious a thought; and yet, I cannot help holding up to your notice a very splendid exemplification of this, in that "old man eloquent," who counts himself to have risen from the Presidency to represent the people in the House of Representatives. See there what the most universal acquisitions will do for the most powerful talents. How those vast accumulations of learning are fused, moulded, and projected, by the fiery tide of mind! How that capacious memory, realizing half the marvels of Pascal and of Cicero, yields up in a moment the hived wisdom of a life of study and a life of action,—the happiest word, the aptest literary illustration, the exact detail, the precise rhetorical instrument the case demands,—how it yields all up instantly to the stimulated, fervid, unquenchable faculties! How little of dilettanteism and parade, and vagueness of phrase and mysticism of idea; how clear, available, practical, direct,—one immense torrent, rushing as an arrow, all the way from the perennial source to the hundred mouths!

If mental culture did nothing for you but send such men to consult on your welfare in the councils of the nation, it would do much to preserve your political ascendancy. But look at this matter a little more largely. Suppose that by succession of effort, by study, by time, you could really carry up the literary character of Massachusetts to as high a degree of superiority to the general literary character of these States, as that of Attica compared with the other States of Greece in the age after the Persian war; suppose the school-boy boast could be achieved, and you were the Athens of America; suppose the libraries, the schools, the teachers, the scholars, were here, the galleries of art, the subtle thinkers, the weavers of systems, the laurelled brow, "the vision and the faculty divine;" suppose the whole body of our written productions, from newspapers upwards or downwards, had obtained a recognized superiority over those of any other region, were purer, better expressed, more artist-like, of wider compass; suppose that the general taste of the world and the nation should authenticate and settle all this,—would it or would it not profit you as an instrument of political ascendancy? It would be soothing to our pride, certainly. Perhaps that would not be all. Knowledge is power as well as fame. You could not, perhaps, hold the lettered and moral relation to America which I have sketched—it is,

alas! a sketch—without holding a political relation in some degree of correspondence with it. Think of that subtle, all-embracing, plastic, mysterious, irresistible thing called public opinion, the god of this lower world, and consider
what a State, or a cluster of States, of marked and acknowledged literary and
intellectual lead might do to color and shape that opinion to their will. Consider how winged are words, how electrical, light-like the speed of thought,
how awful human sympathy. Consider how soon a wise, a beautiful thought
uttered here,—a sentiment of liberty perhaps, or word of succor to the oppressed,
of exhortations to duty, to patriotism, to glory, the refutation of a sophism, the
unfolding of a truth for which the nation may be better,—how soon a word
fitly or wisely spoken here is read on the Upper Mississippi and beneath the
orange-groves of Florida, all through the unequalled valley; how vast an audience it gains, into how many bosoms it has access, on how much good soil the
seed may rest and spring to life, how easily and fast the fine spirit of truth and
beauty goes all abroad upon the face of the world. Consider that the meditations of a single closet, the pamphlet of a single writer, have inflamed or composed nations and armies, shaken thrones, determined the policy of governments
for years of war or peace. Consider that the Drapier's Letters of Swift set Ireland
on fire, cancelled the patent of King William, inspired or kept breathing the
spirit which in a later day the eloquence of Grattan evoked to national life.
Burke's Reflections on the French Revolution began that great contention of
nations that lasted a quarter of a century, till the sun went down on the drenched
field of Waterloo. The sarcasms of Voltaire had torn away its grandeur from the
throne, and its sacredness from the kindred church, or popular violence might
not have blown them both into the air. He who guides public opinion moves
the hand that moves the world!

There is an influence which I would rather see Massachusetts exert on her
sisters of this Union, than see her furnish a President every twelve years or command a majority on any division in Congress; and that is such an influence as
Athens exerted on the taste and opinion first of Greece, then of Rome, then of
the universal modern world; such as she will exert while the race of man exists.
This, of all the kinds of empire, was most grateful and innocent and glorious
and immortal. This was won by no bargain, by no fraud, by no war of the Pelo-
ponnesus, by the shedding of no human blood. It would rest on admiration of
the beautiful, the good, the true in art, in poetry, in thought; and it would last
while the emotions, its object, were left in a human soul. It would turn the eye
of America hitherwards with love, gratitude, and tears, such as those with which
we turn to the walk of Socrates beneath the plane-tree, now sere, the summer

hour of Cicero, the prison into which philosophy descended to console the spirit of Boethius, that room through whose opened window came into the ear of Scott, as he died, the murmur of the gentle Tweed,—love, gratitude, and tears, such as we all yield to those whose immortal wisdom, whose divine verse, whose eloquence of heaven, whose scenes of many-colored life, have held up the show of things to the insatiate desires of the mind, have taught us how to live and how to die! Herein were power, herein were influence, herein were security. Even in the madness of civil war it might survive for refuge and defence!

> "Lift not thy spear against the Muse's bower.
> The great Emathian conqueror bid spare
> The house of Pindarus, when temple and tower
> Went to the ground. And the repeated air
> Of sad Electra's poet had the power
> To save the Athenian walls from ruin bare."

And now if any one, any child of Massachusetts, looking round him and forward, trying to cast the horoscope of his local fortunes, feels a sentiment of despondency upon his spirit, and thinks all this exhortation to mental culture as a means of retaining endangered or receding power to be but the dream of pedantry, and begins to think that if he would belong to a great State, an historical State, an ascendant State, he must be setting out toward the tranquil sea,—to him I say, turn back to her origin, and be of thy unfilial fears ashamed! Thou, a descendant of that ancestry of heroes, and already only in the two hundredth year, afraid that the State is dying out! Do you forget that it took two hundred years of training in England, in Scotland, in Geneva, in the Netherlands,—two hundred years of persecution, of life passed in exile and in chains, of death triumphing over fires,—to form out of the general mind of England these one hundred men and women, our fathers and mothers, who landed on the Rock, and do you think a plant so long in rearing has begun already to decay?

It took a hundred and fifty years more,—one long war, one long labor, one long trial, one long sorrow, as we count sorrow, years of want and disease, of bereavements, of battle, of thought, of every heroical faculty tasked by every heroical labor, one long, varied, searching, tremendous educational process, just the process to evolve and mature these traits on which a commonwealth might repose for a thousand years of glory,—it took all this more to train them for the loftier sphere, the grander duties, the more imperial and historical renown, of independence and union; and do you think that the energies of such a nature, so tempered and refined, are become exhausted in half a century? Who believes in such an idle expenditure of preparation? Why, that would be to hew out a throne of granite on the side of everlasting hills by the labor of generations, for one old king, the last of his line, to die on! No; be true to your origin and to yourselves, and dynasties shall fill by successive accessions the prepared and steadfast seat.

Doubtless the Pilgrim race,—the Puritan race,—shall go everywhere, and possess largely of everything. The free North-west, especially, will be theirs; the skies of Ontario and Erie and Michigan, the prairies of Illinois, the banks of the river of beauty, the mines of Wisconsin and Iowa, shall be theirs. But the old homestead, and the custody of the Rock, are in the family also. Nearest of all the children to the scenes of the fathers' earthly life, be it ours the longest and the most fondly to bear their names, and hold fast their virtues. Be it ours, especially, to purify, enrich, adorn this State,—our own, our native land,—our fathers' monument,—our fathers' praise!

Chapter VI.

THE POSITION AND FUNCTIONS OF THE AMERICAN BAR, AS AN ELEMENT OF CONSERVATISM IN THE STATE.
An Address Delivered before the Law School in Cambridge, July 3, 1845.

Choate was a lawyer first and foremost, and he was acutely aware of the role that legal thinkers played in upholding the American constitutional order. His writings reveal him to be, like all his contemporaries, a partisan of the revolutionary cause of the 1770s and 1780s. At the same time, he is conservative enough to insist that the law is a thing at once so indispensable and so sublime that it ought under normal circumstances to be properly respected and venerated by the citizenry. It is this address by Choate that according to Jean V. Matthews, a modern biographer, contains "perhaps the most complete statement of his conservatism."

Indeed, Choate here describes conservatism as "the one grand and comprehensive duty of a thoughtful patriotism." It does not fall to every generation to perform the monumental task of reconstituting the framework under which it will be governed. Having established an outstanding Constitution, more or less satisfactory to all, it is enough for the United States simply to guard and preserve this great patrimony, and to explain its virtues to those unschooled in political philosophy. This is the task of the man of the law.

It is, finally, the man of the law whose meditation on his subject acquaints him most intimately with its transcendence, with the realization that the law, properly understood, is no mere product of human contrivance but the reflection of a divine wisdom animating the world. "We come to think of it," he says, "not so much as a set of provisions and rules which we can unmake, amend, and annul, as of a guide whom it is wiser to follow, an authority whom it is better to obey, a wisdom which it is not unbecoming to revere, a power—a superior—whose service is perfect freedom."

THE SPEAKER, on one of the anniversaries observed by a literary association in this ancient university, congratulated himself, as he cast his eye over an audience of taste and learning, that in such company he could have no temptation to stray beyond the walls of the academy, or within the noise of the city and the forum. I have supposed that our way, on the contrary, lies directly into the city and the forum. I have assumed that in calling me to this duty you expected and designed that I should consider some topic of a strictly professional interest. All the objects and proprieties of the hour require me to do so. It is a seminary of the law, to which the day is set apart. It is to students of the law, assembled in the presence of teachers of the law,—your masters and my own,—and composing with them a school worthy to begin a new era of the enriched and various jurisprudence of America,—it is to the members of a profession, that I address myself,—all of you immersed in its intricate studies, and fired by what Milton has called its "prudent and heavenly contemplations." Some of you just going forth to attempt its practice, to do its hard work, to kindle with its excitations, to be agitated by its responsibilities, to sound its depths and shoals of honor,—and it is therefore of things professional that I seem to be commanded to speak. Doubtless, there is somewhat in the spirit of the place that might suggest the wish at least for matter more "airy and delicious." I will not deny that I never visit these scenes, so dear to learning, without a very vehement impulse to be disengaged for the day from all the idle business of the law and of life,— from litigious terms, fast contentions, and the dream of "flowing fees,"—from facts sometimes without interest, and rules sometimes without sense,—to be disengaged from all this, and to abandon myself evermore to the vernal fancies and sensations of your time of life, to the various banquet of general knowledge on which so many spirits have been fed, to all those fair ideals which once had power to touch and fill the heart. The sentiment is not very professional; and yet it is not wholly uncountenanced by authority. You remember that it was the great Chancellor d'Aguesseau, who, full of fame as of years, at the very summit of the jurisprudence of France, the most learned of her orators, the most eloquent of her lawyers,—in the confidence of a letter to his son, could confess that literature had always been to him a sort of mental debauch into which he perpetually and secretly relapsed. "I was born," he said, "in the republic of elegant letters; there I grew to be a man; there I passed the happiest years of my life; and to it I come back as a wanderer on sea revisits his native land." But these were the confessions of an illustrious reputation, which could afford to make them. Win his fame, attain his years, emulate his polished eloquence, do as much for the law of a free country as he did for that of the despotism of Louis XIV. and the regency, and you may make the same confession too. Meantime, even here and to-day our theme, our aim, is the law. The literary influences and solicitations of the scene and hour we resist and expel. We put them, one and all, out of court. *Academiam istam exoremus ut sileat!*

There are reasons without number why we should love and honor our noble profession, and should be grateful for the necessity or felicity or accident which called us to its service.

But of these there is one, I think, which, rightly apprehended, ought to be uppermost in every lawyer's mind, on which he cannot dwell too thoughtfully and too anxiously; to which he should resort always to expand and erect his spirit and to keep himself up, if I may say so, to the height of his calling; from which he has a right to derive, in every moment of weariness or distaste or despondency,—not an occasion of pride, but,—ceaseless admonitions to duty and incentives to hope. And that reason is, that better than any other, or as well as any other position or business in the whole subordination of life, his profession enables him to *serve the State*. As well as any other, better than any other profession or business or sphere, more directly, more palpably, it enables and commands him to perform certain grand and difficult and indispensable duties of patriotism,—certain grand, difficult and indispensable duties to our endeared and common native land.

Turning for the present then, from other aspects of the profession, survey it under this. Certainly it presents no nobler aspect. It presents none so well adapted—I do not say, to make us vain of it, but—to make us fit for it, to make us equal to it, to put us on turning it to its utmost account, and working out its whole vast and various and highest utilities. It raises it from a mere calling by which bread, fame, and social place may be earned, to a function by which the republic may be served. It raises it from a dexterous art and a subtle and flexible science,—from a cunning logic, a gilded rhetoric, and an ambitious learning, wearing the purple robe of the sophists, and letting itself to hire,—to the dignity of almost a department of government,—an instrumentality of the State for the well-being and conservation of the State. Consider then the position and functions of the American Bar in the Commonwealth.

I make haste to say that it is not at all because the legal profession may be thought to be peculiarly adapted to fit a man for what is technically called "public life," and to afford him a ready, too ready an introduction to it,—it is not on any such reason as this that I shall attempt to maintain the sentiment which I have advanced. It is not by enabling its members to leave it and become the members of a distinct profession,—it is not thus that in the view which I could wish to exhibit, it serves the State. It is not the jurist turned statesman whom I mean to hold up to you as useful to the republic,—although jurists turned statesmen have illustrated every page, every year of our annals, and have taught how admirably the school of the law can train the mind and heart for the service of constitutional liberty and the achievement of civil honor. It is not the jurist turned statesman; it is the jurist as jurist; it is the jurist remaining jurist; it is the bench, the magistracy, the bar,—the profession as a profession, and in its professional character,—a class, a body, of which I mean exclusively to speak; and my position is, that as such it holds, or may aspire to hold, a place, and performs a function of peculiar and vast usefulness in the American Commonwealth.

Let me premise, too, that instead of diffusing myself in a display of all the motles by which the profession of the law may claim to serve the State, I shall consider but a single one, and that is its agency as an element of conservation. The position and functions of the American Bar, then, as an element of conservation in the State,—this precisely and singly is the topic to which I invite your attention.

And is not the profession such an element of conservation? Is not this its characteristical office and its appropriate praise? Is it not so that in its nature, in its functions, in the intellectual and practical habits which it forms, in the opinions to which it conducts, in all its tendencies and influences of speculation and action, it is and ought to be professionally and peculiarly such an element and such an agent,—that it contributes, or ought to be held to contribute, more than all things else, or as much as anything else, to preserve our organic forms, our civil and social order, our public and private justice, our constitutions of government,—even the Union itself? In these crises through which our liberty is to pass, may not, must not, this function of conservatism become more and more developed, and more and more operative? May it not one day be written, for the praise of the American Bar, that it helped to keep the true idea of the State alive and germinant in the American mind; that it helped to keep alive the sacred sentiments of obedience and reverence and justice, of the supremacy of the calm and grand reason of the law over the fitful will of the individual and the crowd; that it helped to withstand the pernicious sophism that the successive generations, as they come to life, are but as so many successive flights of summer flies, without relations to the past or duties to the future, and taught instead that all—all the dead, the living, the unborn—were one moral person,—one for action, one for suffering, one for responsibility,—that the engagements of one age may bind the conscience of another; the glory or the shame of a day may brighten or stain the current of a thousand years of continuous national being? Consider the profession of the law, then, as an element of conservation in the American State. I think it is naturally such, so to speak; but I am sure it is our duty to make and to keep it such.

It may be said, I think with some truth, of the profession of the Bar, that in all political systems and in all times it has seemed to possess a twofold nature; that it has seemed to be fired by the spirit of liberty, and yet to hold fast the sentiments of order and reverence, and the duty of subordination; that it has resisted despotism and yet taught obedience; that it has recognized and vindicated the rights of man, and yet has reckoned it always among the most sacred and most precious of those rights, to be shielded and led by the divine nature and immortal reason of law; that it appreciates social progression and contributes to it, and ranks in the classes and with the agents of progression, yet evermore counsels and courts permanence and conservatism and rest; that it loves light better than darkness, and yet like the eccentric or wise man in the old historian, has a habit of looking away as the night wanes to the western sky, to detect there the first streaks of returning dawn.

I know that this is high praise of the professional character; and it is true. See if there is not some truth in it. See at least whether we may not deserve it, by a careful culture of the intrinsical tendencies of our habitual studies and employments, and all that is peculiar to our professional life.

It is certain, on the one hand, that the sympathies of the lawyer in our system are with the people and with liberty. They are with the greatest number of the people; they are with what you call the masses; he springs from them; they are his patrons; their favor gives him bread; it gives him consideration; it raises him, as Curran so gracefully said of himself, "the child of a peasant to the table of his prince." The prosperity of the people employs and enriches him.

It does not fall within my immediate object to dwell longer on this aspect of the twofold nature of the profession of the Bar,—its tendencies and leanings to the people and to liberty. It might not be uninstructive to sustain and qualify the view by a glance at a few remarkable periods of its history, under a few widely discriminated political systems of ancient States and times,—the Roman Bar, for example, before and under the earliest times of the Empire; the French Bar at the Revolution; the American Bar from the planting of the colonies. But I must hasten to my principal purpose in this address,—an exhibition of the other aspect of the profession, its function of conservatism.

In proceeding to this, I think I may take for granted that conservatism is, in the actual circumstances of this country, the one grand and comprehensive duty of a thoughtful patriotism. I speak in the general, of course, not pausing upon little or inevitable qualifications here and there,—not meaning anything so absurd as to say that this law, or that usage, or that judgment, or that custom or condition, might not be corrected or expunged,—not meaning still less to invade the domains of moral and philanthropic reform, true or false. I speak of our general political system; our organic forms; our written constitutions; the great body and the general administration of our jurisprudence; the general way in which liberty is blended with order, and the principle of progression with the securities of permanence; the relation of the States and the functions of the Union,—and I say of it in a mass, that conservation is the chief end, the largest duty, and the truest glory of American statesmanship.

There are nations, I make no question, whose history, condition, and dangers, call them to a different work. There are those whom everything in their history, condition, and dangers admonishes to reform fundamentally, if they would be saved. With them the whole political and social order is to be rearranged. The stern claim of labor is to be provided for. Its long antagonism with capital is to be reconciled. Property is all to be parcelled out in some nearer conformity to a parental law of nature. Conventional discriminations of precedence and right are to be swept away. Old forms from which the life is gone are to drop as leaves in autumn. Frowning towers nodding to their fall are to be taken down. Small freeholds must dot over and cut up imperial parks. A large infusion of liberty must be poured along these emptied veins and throb in that great heart. With those, the past must be resigned; the present must be convulsed, that "an immeasurable future," as Carlyle has said, "may be filled with fruitfulness and a verdant shade."

But with us the age of this mode and this degree of reform is over; its work is done. The passage of the sea, the occupation and culture of a new world, the conquest of independence,—these were our eras, these our agency, of reform. In our jurisprudence of liberty, which guards our person from violence and our goods from plunder, and which forbids the whole power of the State itself to take the ewe lamb, or to trample on a blade of the grass of the humblest citizen without adequate remuneration; which makes every dwelling large enough to shelter a human life its owner's castle which winds and rain may enter but which the government cannot,—in our written constitutions, whereby the people, exercising an act of sublime self-restraint, have intended to put it out of their own power forever, to be passionate, tumultuous, unwise, unjust; whereby they have intended, by means of a system of representation; by means of the distribution of government into departments, independent, coördinate for checks and balances; by a double chamber of legislation; by the establishment of a fundamental and paramount organic law; by the organization of a judiciary whose function, whose loftiest function it is to test the legislation of the day by this standard for all time,—constitutions, whereby by all these means they have intended to secure a government of laws, not of men; of reason, not of will; of justice, not of fraud,—in that grand dogma of equality,—equality of right, of burthens, of duty, of privileges, and of chances, which is the very mystery of our social being—to the Jews, a stumbling block; to the Greeks, foolishness—

our strength, our glory,—in that liberty which we value not solely because it is a natural right of man; not solely because it is a principle of individual energy and a guaranty of national renown; not at all because it attracts a procession and lights a bonfire, but because when blended with order, attended by law, tempered by virtue, graced by culture, it is a great practical good; because in her right hand are riches, and honor, and peace; because she has come down from her golden and purple cloud to walk in brightness by the weary ploughman's side, and whisper in his ear as he casts the seed with tears, that the harvest which frost and mildew and canker-worm shall spare, the government shall spare also; in our distribution into separate and kindred States, not wholly independent, not quite identical, in "the wide arch of the ranged empire" above,—these are they in which the fruits of our age and our agency of reform are embodied; and these are they by which, if we are wise,—if we understand the things that belong to our peace,—they may be perpetuated. It is for this that I say the fields of reform, the aims of reform, the uses of reform here, therefore, are wholly unlike the fields, uses, and aims of reform elsewhere. Foreign examples, foreign counsel,—well or ill meant,—the advice of the first foreign understandings, the example of the wisest foreign nations, are worse than useless for us. Even the teachings of history are to be cautiously consulted, or the guide of human life will lead us astray. We need reform enough, Heaven knows; but it is the reformation of our individual selves, the bettering of our personal natures; it is a more intellectual industry; it is a more diffused, profound, and graceful, popular, and higher culture; it is a wider development of the love and discernment of the beautiful in form, in color, in speech, and in the soul of man,—this is what we need,—personal, moral, mental reform—not civil—not political! No, no! Government, substantially as it is; jurisprudence, substantially as it is; the general arrangements of liberty, substantially as they are; the Constitution and the Union, exactly as they are,—this is to be wise, according to the wisdom of America.

To the conservation, then, of this general order of things, I think the profession of the Bar may be said to be assigned, for this reason, among others—the only one which I shall seek to develop—that its studies and employments tend to form in it and fit it to diffuse and impress on the popular mind a class of opinions—one class of opinions—which are indispensable to conservation. Its studies and offices train and arm it to counteract exactly that specific system of opinions by which our liberty must die, and to diffuse and impress those by which it may be kept alive.

By what means a State with just that quantity of liberty in its constitution which belongs to the States of America, with just those organizations into which our polity is moulded, with just those proportions of the elements of law and order and restraint on the one hand, and the passionate love of freedom, and quick and high sense of personal independence on the other,—by what means such a State may be preserved through a full life-time of enjoyment and glory, what kind of death it shall die, by what diagnostics the approach of that death may be known, by what conjuration it is for a space to be charmed away, through what succession of decay and decadence it shall at length go down to the tomb of the nations,—these questions are the largest, pertaining to the things of this world, that can be pondered by the mind of man. More than all others, too, they confound the wisdom of man. But some things we know. A nation, a national existence, a national history, is nothing but a production, nothing but an exponent, of a national mind. At the foundation of all splendid and remarkable national distinction there lie at last a few simple and energetic traits: a proud heart, a resolute will, sagacious thoughts, reverence, veneration, the ancient prudence, sound maxims, true wisdom; and so the dying of a nation begins in the heart. There are sentiments concerning the true idea of the State, concerning law, concerning liberty, concerning justice, so active, so mortal, that if they pervade and taint the general mind, and transpire in practical politics, the commonwealth is lost already. It was of these that the democracies of Greece, one after another, miserably died. It was not so much the spear of the great Emanthian conqueror which bore the beaming forehead of Athens to the dust, as it was that diseased, universal opinion, those tumultuous and fraudulent practical politics, which came at last to supersede the constitution of Solon, and the equivalents of Pericles, which dethroned the reason of the State, shattered and dissolved its checks, balances, and securities against haste and wrong, annulled its laws, repudiated its obligations, shamed away its justice, and set up instead, for rule, the passion, ferocity, and caprice, and cupidity, and fraud of a flushed majority, cheated and guided by sycophants and demagogues,—it was this diseased public opinion and these politics, its fruits, more deadly than the gold or the phalanx of Philip, that cast her down untimely from her throne on high.

And now, what are these sentiments and opinions from which the public mind of America is in danger, and which the studies and offices of our profession have fitted us and impose on us the duty to encounter and correct?

In the first place, it has been supposed that there might be detected, not yet in the general mind, but in what may grow to be the general mind, a singularly inadequate idea of the State as an unchangeable, indestructible, and, speaking after the manner of men, an immortal thing. I do not refer at this moment exclusively to the temper in which the Federal Union is regarded, though that is a startling illustration of the more general and deeper sentiment, but I refer in a larger view to what some have thought the popular or common idea of the civil State itself, its sacredness, its permanence, its ends,—in the lofty phrase of Cicero, its eternity. The tendency appears to be, to regard the whole concern as an association altogether at will, and at the will of everybody. Its boundary lines, its constituent numbers, its physical, social, and constitutional identity, its polity, its law, its continuance for ages, its dissolution,—all these seem to be held in the nature of so many open questions. Whether *our country*—words so simple, so expressive, so sacred; which, like father, child, wife, should present an image familiar, endeared, definite to the heart—whether our country shall, in the course of the next six months extend to the Pacific Ocean and the Gulf, or be confined to the parochial limits of the State where we live, or have no existence at all for us; where its centre of power shall be; whose statues shall be borne in its processions; whose names, what days, what incidents of glory commemorated in its anniversaries, and what symbols blaze on its flag,—in all this there is getting to be a rather growing habit of politic non-committalism. Having learned from Rousseau and Locke, and our own revolutionary age, its theories and its acts, that the State is nothing but a contract, rests in contract, springs from contract; that government is a contrivance of human wisdom for human wants; that the civil life, like the Sabbath, is made for man, not man for either; having only about seventy years ago laid hold of an arbitrary fragment of the British empire, and appropriated it to ourselves, which is all the country we ever had; having gone on enlarging, doubling, trebling, changing all this since, as a garment or a house; accustomed to encounter every day, at the polls, in the market, at the miscellaneous banquet of our Liberty everywhere, crowds of persons whom we never saw before, strangers in the country, yet just as good citizens as ourselves; with a whole continent before us, or half a one, to choose a home in; teased and made peevish by all manner of small, local jealousies; tormented by the stimulations of a revolutionary philanthropy; enterprising, speculative, itinerant, improving, "studious of change, and pleased with novelty" beyond the general habit of desultory man;—it might almost seem to be growing to be our national humor to hold ourselves free at every instant, to be and do just what we please, go where we please, stay as long as we please and no longer; and that the State itself were held to be no more than an encampment of tents on the great prairie, pitched at sun-down, and struck to the sharp crack of the rifle next morning, instead of a structure, stately and eternal, in which the generations may come, one after another, to the great gift of this social life.

On such sentiments as these, how can a towering and durable fabric be set up? To use the metaphor of Bacon, on such soil how can "greatness be sown"? How unlike the lessons of the masters, at whose feet you are bred! The studies of our profession have taught us that the State is framed for a duration without end,—without end—till the earth and the heavens be no more. *Sic constituta civitas ut eterna!* In the eye and contemplation of law, its masses may die; its own corporate being can never die. If we inspect the language of its fundamental ordinance, every word expects, assumes, foretells a perpetuity, lasting as "the great globe itself, and all which it inherit." If we go out of that record and inquire for the designs and the hopes of its founders *ab extra,* we know that they constructed it, and bequeathed it, for the latest posterity. If we reverently rise to a conjecture of the purposes for which the Ruler of the world permitted and decreed it to be instituted, in order to discern how soon it will have performed its office and may be laid aside, we see that they reach down to the last hour of the life of the last man that shall live upon the earth; that it was designed by the Infinite Wisdom, to enable the generation who framed it, and all the generations, to perfect their social, moral, and religious nature; to do and to be good; to pursue happiness; to be fitted, by the various discipline of the social life, by obedience, by worship, for the life to come. When these ends are all answered, the State shall die! When these are answered, *intereat et concidat omnis hic mundus!* Until they are answered, *esto, eritque perpetua!*

In the next place, it has been thought that there was developing itself in the general sentiment, and in the practical politics of the time, a tendency towards one of those great changes by which free States have oftenest perished,—a tendency to push to excess the distinctive and characteristic principles of our system, whereby, as Aristotle has said, governments usually perish,—a tendency towards transition from the republican to the democratical era, of the history and epochs of liberty.

Essentially and generally, it would be pronounced by those who discern it, a tendency to erect the actual majority of the day into the *de jure* and actual government of the day. It is a tendency to regard the actual will of that majority as the law of the State. It is a tendency to regard the shortest and simplest way of collecting that will, and the promptest and most irresistible execution of it, as the true polity of liberty. It is a tendency which, pressed to its last development, would, if considerations of mere convenience or inconvenience did not hinder, do exactly this: it would assemble the whole people in a vast mass, as once they used to assemble beneath the sun of Athens; and there, when the eloquent had spoken, and the wise and the foolish had counselled, would commit the transcendent questions of war, peace, taxation, and treaties; the disposition of the fortunes and honor of the citizen and statesman; death, banishment, or the crown of gold; the making, interpreting, and administration of the law; and all the warm, precious, and multifarious interests of the social life, to the madness or the jest of the hour.

I have not time to present what have been thought to be the proofs of the existence of this tendency; and it is needless to do so. It would be presumptuous, too, to speculate, if it has existence, on its causes and its issues. I desire to advert to certain particulars in which it may be analyzed, and through which it displays itself, for the purpose of showing that the studies, employments, and, so to say, professional politics, of the bar are essentially, perhaps availably, antagonistical to it, or moderative of it.

It is said, then, that you may remark this tendency, first, in an inclination to depreciate the uses and usurp the functions of those organic forms in which the regular, definite, and legally recognized powers of the State are embodied,—to depreciate the uses and usurp the function of written constitutions, limitations on the legislature, the distribution of government into departments, the independence of the judiciary, the forms of orderly proceeding, and all the elaborate and costly apparatus of checks and balances, by which, as I have said, we seek to secure a government of laws and not of men.

"The first condition"—it is the remark of a man of great genius, who saw very far by glances into the social system, Coleridge,—"the first condition in order to a sound constitution of the body politic, is a due proportion between the free and permeative life and energy of the State and its organized powers." For want of that proportion the government of Athens was shattered and dissolved. For want of that proportion the old constitutions of Solon, the reforms of Clisthenes, the sanctity of the Areopagus, the temperaments of Pericles, were burnt up in the torrent blaze of an unmitigated democracy. Every power of the State—executive, legal, judicial—was grasped by the hundred-handed assembly of the people. The result is in her history. She became a byword of dissension and *injustice;* and that was her ruin.

I wonder how long that incomprehensible democracy would have hesitated, after the spirit of permeative liberty had got the better of the organized forms, upon our Spot Pond, and Long Pond, and Charles River water-questions. This intolerable hardship and circumlocution of applying to a legislature of three independent and coördinate departments, sitting under a written constitution, with an independent judiciary to hold it up to the fundamental law,—the hardship of applying to such a legislature for power to bring water into the city; this operose machinery of orders of notice, hearings before committees, adverse reports, favorable reports rejected, disagreements of the two Houses, veto of Governor, a charter saving vested rights of other people, meetings of citizens in wards to vote unawed, unwatched, every man according to his sober second thought,— how long do you think such conventionalities as these would have kept that beautiful, passionate, and self-willed Athens, standing, like the Tantalus of her own poetry, plunged in crystal lakes and gentle historical rivers up to the chin, perishing with thirst? Why, some fine, sunshiny forenoon, you would have heard the crier calling the people, one and all, to an extraordinary assembly, perhaps in the Piræus, as a pretty full expression of public opinion was desirable and no other place would hold everybody; you would have seen a stupendous mass-meeting roll itself together as clouds before all the winds; standing on the outer edges of which you could just discern a speaker or two gesticulating, catch a murmur as of waves on the pebbly beach, applause, a loud laugh at a happy hit, observe some six thousand hands lifted to vote or swear, and then the vast congregation would separate and subside, to be seen no more. And the whole record of the transaction would be made up in some half-dozen lines to this effect,—it might be in Æschines,—that in the month of____, under the archonate of____, the tribe of____, exercising the office of prytanes____, an extraordinary assembly was called to consult on the supply of water; and it appearing that some six persons of great wealth and consideration had opposed its introduction for some time past, and were moreover vehemently suspected of being no better than they should be, it was ordained that they should be fined in round sums, computed to be enough to bring in such a supply as would give every man equal to twenty-eight gallons a day; and a certain obnoxious orator having inquired what possible need there was for so much a head, Demades, the son of the Mariner, replied, that that person was the very last man in all Athens who should put that question, since the assembly must see that he at least could use it to great advantage by washing his face, hands, and robes; and thereupon the people laughed and separated.

And now am I misled by the influence of vocation, when I venture to suppose that the profession of the Bar may do somewhat—should be required to do somewhat—to preserve the true proportion of liberty to organization,—to moderate and to disarm that eternal antagonism?

These "organic forms" of our system—are they not in some just sense committed to your professional charge and care? In this sense, and to this extent, does not your profession approach to, and blend itself with, one, and that not the least in dignity and usefulness, of the departments of statesmanship? Are you not thus statesmen while you are lawyers, and because you are lawyers? These constitutions of government by which a free people have had the virtue and the sense to restrain themselves,—these devices of profound wisdom and a deep study of man, and of the past, by which they have meant to secure the ascendency of the just, lofty, and wise, over the fraudulent, low, and insane, in the long run of our practical politics,—these temperaments by which justice is promoted, and by which liberty is made possible and may be made immortal,—and this *jus publicum,* this great written code of public law,—are they not a part, in the strictest and narrowest sense, of the appropriate science of your profession? More than for any other class or calling in the community, is it not for you to study their sense, comprehend their great uses, and explore their historical origin and illustrations,—to so hold them up as shields, that no act of legislature, no judgment of court, no executive proclamation, no order of any functionary of any description, shall transcend or misconceive them—to so hold them up before your clients and the public, as to keep them at all times living, intelligible, and appreciated in the universal mind?

Something such has, in all the past periods of our history, been one of the functions of the American Bar. To vindicate the true interpretation of the charters of the colonies, to advise what forms of polity, what systems of jurisprudence, what degree and what mode of liberty these charters permitted,—to detect and expose that long succession of infringement which grew at last to the Stamp Act and Tea Tax, and compelled us to turn from broken charters to national independence,—to conduct the transcendent controversy which preceded the Revolution, that grand appeal to the reason of civilization,—this was the work of our first generation of lawyers. To construct the American constitutions,—the higher praise of the second generation. I claim it in part for the sobriety and learning of the American Bar; for the professional instinct towards the past; for the professional appreciation of order, forms, obedience, restraints; for the more than professional, the profound and wide intimacy with the history of all liberty, classical, mediæval, and above all, of English liberty,—I claim it in part for the American Bar that, springing into existence by revolution,— revolution, which more than anything and all things lacerates and discomposes the popular mind,—justifying that revolution only on a strong principle of natural right, with not one single element or agent of monarchy or aristocracy on our soil or in our blood,—I claim it for the Bar that the constitutions of America so nobly closed the series of our victories! These constitutions owe to the Bar more than their terse and exact expression and systematic arrangements; they owe to it, in part, too, their elements of permanence; their felicitous reconciliation of universal and intense liberty with forms to enshrine and regulations to restrain it; their Anglo-Saxon sobriety and gravity conveyed in the genuine idiom, suggestive of the grandest civil achievements of that unequalled race. To interpret these constitutions, to administer and maintain them, this is the office of our age of the profession. Herein have we somewhat wherein to glory; hereby we come into the class and share in the dignity of founders of States, of restorers of States, of preservers of States.

I said and I repeat that, while lawyers, and because we are lawyers, we are statesmen. We are by profession statesmen. And who may measure the value of this department of public duty? Doubtless in statesmanship there are many mansions, and large variety of conspicuous service. Doubtless to have wisely decided the question of war or peace,—to have adjusted by a skilful negotiation a thousand miles of unsettled boundary-line,—to have laid the corner-stone of some vast policy whereby the currency is corrected, the finances enriched, the measure of industrial fame filled,—are large achievements. And yet I do not know that I can point to one achievement of this department of American statesmanship, which can take rank for its consequences of good above that single decision of the Supreme Court, which adjudged that an act of legislature contrary to the Constitution is void, and that the judicial department is clothed with the power to ascertain the repugnancy and to pronounce the legal conclusion. That the framers of the Constitution intended this should be so, is certain; but to have asserted it against the Congress and the Executive,—to have vindicated it by that easy yet adamantine demonstration than which the reasonings of the mathematics show nothing surer,—to have inscribed this vast truth of conservatism on the public mind, so that no demagogue, not in the last stage of intoxication, denies it,—this is an achievement of statesmanship of which a thousand years may not exhaust or reveal all the good.

It has been thought, in the next place, that you may remark this unfavorable tendency in a certain false and pernicious *idea of law,* which to some extent possesses the popular mind,—law, its source, its nature, its titles to reverence. Consider it a moment, and contrast it with our idea of law.

It is one of the distemperatures to which an unreasoning liberty may grow, no doubt, to regard *law* as no more nor less than just the will—the actual and present will—of the actual majority of the nation. The majority govern. What the majority pleases, it may ordain. What it ordains is law. So much for the source of law, and so much for the nature of law. But, then, as law is nothing but the will of a major number, as that will differs from the will of yesterday, and will differ from that of to-morrow, and as all law is a restraint on natural right and personal independence, how can it gain a moment's hold on the reverential sentiments of the heart, and the profounder convictions of the judgment? How can it impress a filial awe; how can it conciliate a filial love; how can it sustain a sentiment of veneration; how can it command a rational and animated defence? Such sentiments are not the stuff from which the immortality of a nation is to be woven. Oppose now to this, the loftier philosophy which we have learned. In the language of our system, the law is not the transient and arbitrary creation of the major will, nor of any will. It is not the offspring of will at all. It is the absolute justice of the State, enlightened by the perfect reason of the State. That is law. Enlightened justice assisting the social nature to perfect itself by the social life. It is ordained, doubtless, that is, it is chosen, and is ascertained by the wisdom of man. But, then, it is the master-work of man. Quæ est enim istorum oratio tam exquisita, quæ sit anteponenda bene constitutæ civitati publico jure, et moribus?[1]

By the costly and elaborate contrivances of our constitutions we have sought to attain the transcendent result of extracting and excluding haste, injustice, revenge, and folly from the place and function of giving the law, and of introducing alone the reason and justice of the wisest and the best. By the aid of time,—time which changes and tries all things; tries them, and works them pure,—we subject the law, after it is given, to the tests of old experience, to the reason and justice of successive ages and generations, to the best thoughts of the wisest and safest of reformers. And then and thus we pronounce it good. Then and thus we cannot choose but reverence, obey, and enforce it. We would grave it deep into the heart of the undying State. We would strengthen it by opinion, by manners, by private virtue, by habit, by the awful hoar of innumerable ages. All that attracts us to life, all that is charming in the perfected and adorned social nature, we wisely think or we wisely dream, we owe to the all-encircling presence of the law. Not even extravagant do we think it to hold, that the Divine approval may sanction it as not unworthy of the reason which we derive from His own nature. Not extravagant do we hold it to say, that there is thus a voice of the people which is the voice of God.

Doubtless the known historical origin of the law contributes to this opinion of it. Consider for a moment—what that law really is, what the vast body of that law is, to the study and administration of which the lawyer gives his whole life, by which he has trained his mind, established his fortune, won his fame, the theatre of all his triumphs, the means of all his usefulness, the theme of a thousand

---

1. Cicero, *de Republica*, I., 2

earnest panegyrics,—what is that law? Mainly, a body of digested rules and processes and forms, bequeathed by what is for us the old and past time, not of one age, but all the ages of the past,—a vast and multifarious aggregate, some of which you trace above the pyramids, above the flood, the inspired wisdom of the primeval East; some to the scarcely yet historical era of Pythagoras, and to Solon and Socrates; more of it to the robust, practical sense and justice of Rome, the lawgiver of the nations; more still to the teeming birthtime of the modern mind and life; all of it to some epoch; some of it to every epoch of the past of which history keeps the date. In the way in which it comes down to us, it seems one mighty and continuous stream of experience and reason, accumulated, ancestral, widening and deepening and washing itself clearer as it runs on, the grand agent of civilization, the builder of a thousand cities, the guardian angel of a hundred generations, our own hereditary laws. To revere such a system, would be natural and professional, if it were no more. But it is reasonable, too. There is a deep presumption in favor of that which has endured so long. To say of anything, that it is old, and to leave the matter there,—an opinion, a polity, a code, a possession, a book,—is to say nothing of praise or blame. But to have lived for ages; to be alive to-day,—in a real sense alive,—alive in the hearts, in the reason of to-day; to have lived through ages, not swathed in gums and spices and enshrined in chambers of pyramids, but through ages of unceasing contact and sharp trial with the passions, interests, and affairs of the great world; to have lived through the drums and tramplings of conquests, through revolution, reform, through cycles of opinion running their round; to have lived under many diverse systems of policy, and have survived the many transmigrations from one to another; to have attended the general progress of the race, and shared in its successive ameliorations,—thus to have gathered upon itself the approbation or the sentiments and reason of all civilization and all humanity,— that is, *per se,* a *prima-facie* title to intelligent regard. There is a virtue, there is truth, in that effacing touch of time. It bereaves us of our beauty; it calls our friends from our side, and we are alone; it changes us, and sends us away. But spare what it spares. Spare till you have proved it. Where that touch has passed and left no wrinkle nor spot of decay, what it has passed and left ameliorated and beautified, whatever it be, stars, sea, the fame of the great dead, the State, the law, which is the soul of the State, be sure that therein is some spark of an immortal life.

It is certain that in the American theory, the free theory of government, it is the right of the people, at any moment of its representation in the legislature, to make all the law, and by its representatives in conventions, to make the Constitution anew. It is their right to do so peaceably and according to existing forms, and to do it by revolution against all forms. This is the theory. But I do not know that any wise man would desire to have this theory every day, or ever, acted upon up to its whole extent, or to have it eternally pressed, promulgated, panegyrized as the grand peculiarity and chief privilege of our condition. Acting upon this theory, we have made our constitutions, founded our policy, written the great body of our law, set our whole government going. It worked well. It works to a charm. I do not know that any man displays wisdom or common sense, by all the while haranguing and stimulating the people to change it. I do not appreciate the sense or humanity of all the while bawling: true, your systems are all good; life, character, property, all safe,—but you have the undoubted right to rub all out and begin again. If I see a man quietly eating his dinner, I do not know why I should tell him that there is a first-rate, extreme medicine, prussic acid, aquafortis, or what not, which he has a perfectly good right to use in any quantity he pleases! If a man is living happily with his wife, I don't know why I should go and say: yes, I see; beautiful and virtuous; I congratulate you,— but let me say, you can get a perfectly legal divorce by going to Vermont, New Jersey, or Pennsylvania. True wisdom would seem to advise the culture of dispositions of rest, contentment, conservation. True wisdom would advise to lock up the extreme medicine till the attack of the alarming malady. True wisdom would advise to place the power of revolution, overturning all to begin anew, rather in the background, to throw over it a politic, well-wrought veil, to reserve it for crises, exigencies, the rare and distant days of great historical epochs. These great, transcendental rights should be preserved, must be, will be. But perhaps you would place them away, reverentially, in the profoundest recesses of the chambers of the dead, down in deep vaults of black marble, lighted by a single silver lamp,—as in that vision of the Gothic king,—to which wise and brave men may go down, in the hour of extremity, to evoke the tremendous divinities of change from their sleep of ages.

> "Ni faciat, maria, ac terras, columque profundum,
> Quippe ferant rapidi secum, verrantque per auras."[2]

To appreciate the conservative agency and functions of the legal profession, however, it is time to pass from an analysis of the sentiments and opinions which distinguish it, to the operation by which it is employed. The single labor of our

2. Æn. I., 58, 59.

lives is the administration of the law; and the topic on which I wish to say a word
in conclusion is, the influence of the actual administration of law in this country on the duration of our free systems themselves. The topic is large and high,
and well deserves what I may not now attempt, a profound and exact discussion.

I do not know that in all the elaborate policy by which free States have
sought to preserve themselves, there is one device so sure, so simple, so indispensable, as justice,—justice to all; justice to foreign nations of whatever class
of greatness or weakness; justice to public creditors, alien or native; justice to
every individual citizen, down to the feeblest and the least beloved; justice in
the assignment of political and civil right, and place, and opportunity; justice
between man and man, every man and every other,—to observe and to administer this virtue steadily, uniformly, and at whatever cost,—this, the best policy
and the final course of all governments, is preeminently the policy of free governments. Much the most specious objection to free systems is, that they have
been observed in the long run to develop a tendency to some mode of injustice. Resting on a truer theory of natural right in their constitutional construction than any other polity, founded in the absolute and universal equality of
man, and permeated and tinged and all astir with this principle through all their
frame, and, so far, more nobly just than any other, the doubt which history is
supposed to suggest is, whether they do not reveal a tendency towards injustice
in other ways. Whether they have been as uniformly true to their engagements.
Whether property and good name and life have been quite as safe. Whether the
great body of the *jus privatum* has been as skilfully composed and rigorously
administered as under the less reasonable and attractive systems of absolute rule.
You remember that Aristotle, looking back on a historical experience of all sorts
of governments extending over many years—Aristotle who went to the court
of Philip a republican, and came back a republican—records, in his Politics,
injustice as the grand and comprehensive cause of the downfall of democracies.
The historian of the Italian democracies extends the remark to them. That all
States should be stable in proportion as they are just, and in proportion as they
administer justly, is what might be asserted.

If this end is answered; if every man has his own exactly and uniformly, absolutism itself is found tolerable. If it is not, liberty—slavery, are but dreary and
transient things. *Placida quies sub libertate,* in the words of Algernon Sydney and
of the seal of Massachusetts,—that is the union of felicities which should make
the State immortal. Whether Republics have usually perished from injustice,
need not be debated. One there was, the most renowned of all, that certainly
did so. The injustice practised by the Athens of the age of Demosthenes upon

its citizens, and suffered to be practised by one another, was as marvellous as the capacities of its dialect, as the eloquence by which its masses were regaled, and swayed this way and that as clouds, as waves,—marvellous as the long banquet of beauty in which they revelled,—as their love of Athens, and their passion of glory. There was not one day in the whole public life of Demosthenes when the fortune, the good name, the civil existence of any considerable man was safer there than it would have been at Constantinople or Cairo under the very worst forms of Turkish rule. There was a sycophant to accuse, a demagogue to prosecute, a fickle, selfish, necessitous court—no court at all, only a commission of some hundreds or thousands from the public assembly sitting in the sunshine, directly interested in the cause—to pronounce judgment. And he who rose rich and honored, might be flying at night for his life to some Persian or Macedonian outpost, to die by poison on his way in the temple of Neptune.

Is there not somewhat in sharing in that administration, observing and enjoying it, which tends to substitute in the professional and in the popular mind, in place of the wild consciousness of possessing summary power, ultimate power, the wild desire to exert it, and to grasp and subject all things to its rule,— to substitute for this the more conservative sentiments of reverence for a law independent of, and distinct from, and antagonistical to, the humor of the hour? Is there not something in the study and administrative enjoyment of an elaborate, rational, and ancient jurisprudence, which tends to raise the law itself, in the professional and in the general idea, almost up to the nature of an independent, superior reason, in one sense out of the people, in one sense above them,—out of and above, and independent of, and collateral to, the people of any given day? In all its vast volumes of provisions, very little of it is seen to be produced by the actual will of the existing generation. The first thing we know about it is, that we are actually being governed by it. The next thing we know is, we are rightfully and beneficially governed by it. We did not help to make it. No man now living helped to make much of it. The judge does not make it. Like the structure of the State itself, we found it around us at the earliest dawn of reason, it guarded the helplessness of our infancy, it restrained the passions of our youth, it protects the acquisitions of our manhood, it shields the sanctity of the grave, it executes the will of the departed. Invisible, omnipresent, a real yet impalpable existence, it seems more a spirit, an abstraction,—the whispered yet authoritative voice of all the past and all the good,—than like the transient contrivance of altogether such as ourselves. We come to think of it, not so much as a set of provisions and rules which we can unmake, amend, and annul, as of a guide whom it is wiser to follow, an authority whom it is better to obey, a wisdom which it is not unbecoming to revere, a power—a superior—whose service is perfect freedom. Thus at last the spirit of the law descends into the great heart of the people for healing and for conservation. Hear the striking platonisms of Coleridge: "Strength may be met with strength: the power of inflicting pain may be baffled by the pride of endurance: the eye of rage may be answered by the stare of defiance, or the downcast look of dark and revengeful resolve: and with all this there is an outward and determined object to which the mind can attach its passions and purposes, and bury its own disquietudes in the full occupation of the senses. But who dares struggle with an *invisible* combatant, with an enemy which exists and makes us know its existence, but *where* it is we ask in vain? No space contains it, time promises no control over it, it has no ear for my threats, it has no substance that my hands can grasp or my weapons find vulnerable; it commands and cannot be commanded, it acts and is insusceptible of my reaction, the more I strive to subdue it, the more am I compelled to think of it, and the more I think of it, the more do I find it to possess a reality out of myself, and not to be a phantom of my own imagination;— that all but the most abandoned men acknowledge its authority, and that the whole strength and majesty of my country are pledged to support it; and yet that *for me* its power is the same with that of my own permanent self, and that all the choice which is permitted to me consists in having it for my guardian angel or my avenging fiend. This is the spirit of LAW,—the lute of Amphion,— the harp of Orpheus. This is the true necessity which compels man into the social state, now and always, by a still beginning, never ceasing, force of moral cohesion."[3]

In supposing that conservation is the grand and prominent public function of the American Bar in the State, I have not felt that I assigned to a profession, to which I count it so high a privilege to belong, a part and a duty at all beneath its loftiest claims. I shall not deny that to found a State which grows to be a nation, on the ruins of an older, or on a waste of earth where was none before, is, intrinsically and in the judgment of the world, of the largest order of human achievements. Of the chief of men are the *conditores imperiorum*. But to keep the city is only not less difficult and glorious than to build it. Both rise, in the estimate of the most eloquent and most wise of Romans, to the rank of divine achievement. I appreciate the uses and the glory of a great and timely reform. Thrice happy and honored who leaves the Constitution better than he found it. But to find it good and keep it so, this, too, is virtue and praise.

3. *The Friend.*

It was the boast of Augustus,—as Lord Brougham remembers in the close of his speech on the improvement of the law,—that he found Rome of brick and left it of marble. Ay. But he found Rome free, and left her a slave. He found her a republic, and left her an empire! He found the large soul of Cicero unfolding the nature, speaking the high praise, and recording the maxims of regulated liberty, with that eloquence which so many millions of hearts have owned,— and he left poets and artists! We find our city of marble, and we will leave it marble. Yes, all, all, up to the grand, central, and eternal dome; we will leave it marble, as we find it. To that office, to that praise, let even the claims of your profession be subordinated. *Pro clientibus sæpe; pro lege, pro republica semper.*

CHAPTER VII.

SPEECH DELIVERED AT THE CONSTITUTIONAL MEETING IN
FANEUIL HALL.
November 26, 1850.

So passionate was Choate's attachment to the Union that he usually perceived threats and dangers to its existence more acutely than did his contemporaries. The year 1850 had been marked by a dissension and ill will that recalled the worst days of the nullification crisis, and some claimed that the Union had been saved from dissolution only by the legislative legerdemain of Stephen Douglas. Choate, indeed, was gravely concerned for his country's future. The year, he remarks below, had witnessed such peril for the continued existence of the United States that "the future historian of America will pause with astonishment and terror when he comes to record it."

The Union, he reminds his audience, is not something that can be preserved without effort, without a deliberate exercise of the will. It is necessarily more abstract and distant than the state and local governments with which people are more intimately acquainted, and hence attachment to the Union must be deliberately cultivated in order for it to take root. Instead of engaging in the enterprise of mutual charity necessary to keep the Union in existence, however, bitter invective—on the part of Northern partisans in particular— threatens to rend asunder that political accomplishment which in Choate's mind belongs in the annals of the great achievements of man.

["The Citizens of Boston and its vicinity, who reverence the Constitution of the United States; who wish to discountenance a spirit of disobedience to the laws of the land, and refer all questions arising under those laws to the proper tribunals; who would regard with disfavor all further popular agitation of subjects which endanger the peace and harmony of the Union, and who deem the preservation of the Union the paramount duty of every citizen, are requested to meet and express their sentiments on the present posture of public affairs, in Faneuil Hall, Nov. 26, 1850, at 4 o'clock, P.M."

The above call having been published in the newspapers, and posted up in the "Merchants' Reading Room" for some days, received the signatures of about five thousand citizens of Massachusetts, and the meeting was convened agreeably to the request therein expressed.

At a few minutes before four o'clock, the Committee of Arrangements came in, and were received with loud cheers. At four o'clock, precisely, Thomas B. Curtis, Esq. mounted the rostrum, and nominated for President John C. Warren.

A series of resolutions having been read, the meeting was addressed by B. R. Curtis, B. F. Hallett, and S. D. Bradford; after which Mr. Choate spoke as follows:]

I FEEL it, fellow-citizens, to be quite needless, for any purpose of affecting your votes now, or your judgment and acts for the future, that I should add a word to the resolutions before you, and to the very able addresses by which they have been explained and enforced. All that I would have said has been better said. In all that I would have suggested, this great assembly, so true and ample a representation of the sobriety, and principle, and business, and patriotism of this city and its vicinity,—if I may judge from the manner in which you have responded to the sentiments of preceding speakers,—has far outrun me. In all that I had felt and reflected on the supreme importance of this deliberation, on the reality and urgency of the peril, on the indispensable necessity which exists, that an effort be made, and made at once, combining the best counsels, and the wisest and most decisive action of the community—an effort to turn away men's thoughts from those things which concern this part or that part, to those which concern the whole of our America—to turn away men's solicitude about the small politics that shall give a State administration this year to one set, and the next year to another set, and fix it on the grander politics by which a nation is to be held together—to turn away men's hearts from loving one brother of the national household, and hating and reviling another, to that larger, juster and wiser affection which folds the whole household to its bosom—to turn away men's conscience and sense of moral obligation from the morbid and mad pursuit of a single duty, and indulgence of a single sentiment, to the practical ethics in which all duties are recognized, by which all duties are reconciled, and adjusted, and subordinated, according to their rank, by which the sacredness of compacts is holden to be as real as the virtue of compassion, and the supremacy of the law declared as absolute as the luxury of a tear is felt to be sweet—to turn away men's eyes from the glare of the lights of a philanthropy—they call it philanthropy—some of whose ends may be specious, but whose means are bad faith, abusive speech, ferocity of temper, and resistance to law; and whose fruit, if it ripens to fruit, will be woes unnumbered to bond and free,—to turn all eyes from the glitter of such light to the steady and unalterable glory of that wisdom, that justice, and that best philanthropy under which the States of America have been enabled and may still be enabled to live together in peace, and grow together into the nature of one people,—in all that I had felt and reflected on these things, you have outrun my warmest feelings and my best thoughts. What remains, then, but that I congratulate you on at least this auspicious indication, and take my leave? One or two suggestions, however, you will pardon to the peculiarity of the times.

I concur then, *first,* Fellow-citizens, with one of the resolutions, in express-ing my sincerest conviction that the Union is in extreme peril this day. Some good and wise men, I know, do not see this; and some not quite so good or wise, deny that they see it. I know very well that to sound a false alarm is a shallow and contemptible thing. But I know, also, that too much precaution is safer than too little, and I believe that less than the utmost is too little now. Better, it is said, to be ridiculed for too much care, than to be ruined by too confident a security. I have then a profound conviction, that the Union is yet in danger. It is true that it has passed through one peril within the last few months,—such a peril, that the future historian of America will pause with astonishment and terror when he comes to record it. The sobriety of the historic style will rise to eloquence,— to pious ejaculation,—to thanksgivings to Almighty God,—as he sketches that scene and the virtues that triumphed in it. "Honor and praise," will he exclaim, "to the eminent men of all parties—to Clay, to Cass, to Foote, to Dickinson, to Webster—who rose that day to the measure of a true greatness,—who remem-bered that they had a country to preserve as well as a local constituency to grat-ify,—who laid all the wealth, and all the hopes of illustrious lives on the altar of a hazardous patriotism,—who reckoned all the sweets of a present popularity for nothing in comparison of that more exceeding weight of glory which follows him who seeks to compose an agitated and save a sinking land."

That night is passed, and that peril; and yet it is still night, and there is peril still. And what do I mean by this? I believe, and rejoice to believe, that the gen-eral judgment of the people is yet sound on this transcendent subject. But I will tell you where I think the danger lies. It is, that while the people sleep, politi-cians and philanthropists of the legislative hall—the stump, and the press—will talk and write us out of our Union. Yes—while you sleep, while the merchant is loading his ships, and the farmer is gathering his harvests, and the music of the hammer and shuttle wake around, and we are all steeped in the enjoyment of that vast and various good which a common government places within our

reach—there are influences that never sleep, and which are creating and diffusing a PUBLIC OPINION, in whose hot and poisoned breath, before we yet perceive
our evil plight, this Union may melt as frost-work in the sun. Do we sufficiently
appreciate how omnipotent is opinion in the matter of all government? Do we
consider especially in how true a sense it is the creator, must be the upholder,
and may be the destroyer of our united government? Do we often enough advert
to the distinction, that while our State governments *must* exist almost of necessity, and with no effort from within or without, the UNION of the States is a
totally different creation—more delicate, more artificial, more recent, far more
truly a mere production of the reason and the will—standing in far more need
of an ever-surrounding care, to preserve and repair it, and urge it along its highway? Do we reflect that while the people of Massachusetts, for example, are in
all senses one—not *E Pluribus Unum*—but one single and uncompounded substance, so to speak—and while every influence that can possibly help to hold a
social existence together—identity of interest; closeness of kindred; contiguity of
place; old habit; the ten thousand opportunities of daily intercourse; everything—
is operating to hold such a State together, so that it must exist whether we will
or not, and "cannot, but by annihilating, die"—the people of America compose
a totally different community—a community miscellaneous and widely scattered;
that they are many States, not one State, or if one, made up of many which still
coexist; that numerous influences of vast energy, influences of situation, of political creeds, of employments, of supposed or real diversities of material interest,
tend evermore to draw them asunder; and that is not, as in a single State, that
instinct, custom, a long antiquity, closeness of kindred, immediate contiguity,
the personal intercourse of daily life and the like, come in to make and consoli-
date the grand incorporation, whether we will or not; but that is to be accomplished by carefully cultivated and acquired habits and states of feeling; by an
enlightened discernment of great interests, embracing a continent and a future age;
by a voluntary determination to love, honor, and cherish, by mutual tolerance,
by mutual indulgence of one another's peculiarities, by the most politic and careful withdrawal of our attention from the offensive particulars in which we differ,
and by the most assiduous development and appreciation, and contemplation
of those things wherein we are alike—do we reflect as we ought, that it is only
thus—by varieties of expedients, by a prolonged and voluntary educational
process, that the fine and strong spirit of NATIONALITY may be made to penetrate
and animate the scarcely congruous mass—and the full tide of American feeling
to fill the mighty heart?

I have sometimes thought that the States in our system may be compared to
the primordial particles of matter, indivisible, indestructible, impenetrable,

whose natural condition is to repel each other, or, at least, to exist, in their own independent identity,—while the Union is an artificial aggregation of such particles; a sort of *forced state,* as some have said, of life; a complex structure made with hands, which gravity, attrition, time, rain, dew, frost, not less than tempest and earthquake, coîperate to waste away, and which the anger of a fool— or the laughter of a fool—may bring down in an hour; a system of bodies advancing slowly through a *resisting medium,* operating at all times to retard, and at any moment liable to arrest its motion; a beautiful, yet fragile creation, which a breath can unmake, as a breath has made it.

And now, charged with the trust of holding together such a nation as this, what have we seen? What do we see to-day? Exactly this. It has been, for many months,—years, I may say; but, assuredly for a long season,—the peculiar infelicity, say, rather, terrible misfortune of this country, that the attention of the people has been fixed without the respite of a moment, exclusively on one of those subjects—the only one—on which we disagree precisely according to geographical lines. And not so only, but this subject has been one—unlike tariff, or internal improvements, or the disbursement of the public money, on which the dispute cannot be maintained, for an hour, without heat of blood, mutual loss of respect, alienation of regard—menacing to end in hate, strong and cruel as the grave.

I call this only a terrible misfortune. I blame here and now, no man, and no policy for it. Circumstances have forced it upon us all; and down to the hour that the series of compromise measures was completed and presented to the country, or certainly to congress, I will not here and now say, that it was the fault of one man, or one region of country, or one party more than another.

"But the pity of it, Iago—the pity of it."

How appalling have been its effects; and how deep and damning will be his guilt who rejects the opportunity of reconcilement, and continues this accursed agitation, without necessity, for another hour!

Why, is there any man so bold or blind as to say he believes that the scenes through which we have been passing, for a year, have left the American heart where they found it? Does any man believe that those affectionate and respectful regards, that attachment and that trust, those "cords of love and bands of a man"— which knit this people together as one, in an earlier and better time,—are as strong to-day as they were a year ago? Do you believe that there can have been so tremendous an apparatus of influences at work so long, some designed, some undesigned, but all at work in one way, that is, to make the two great divisions of the national family hate each other, and yet have no effect? Recall what we have seen in that time, and weigh it well! Consider how many hundreds of speeches were made in congress—all to show how extreme and intrepid an advocate the speaker could be of the extreme Northern sentiment, or the extreme Southern sentiment. Consider how many scores of thousands of every one of those speeches were printed and circulated among the honorable member's constituents,—not much elsewhere,—the great mass of whom agreed with him perfectly, and was only made the more angry and more unreasonable by them. Consider what caballings and conspirings were going forward during that session in committee rooms and members' chambers, and think of their private correspondence with enterprising waiters on events. Turn to the American newspaper press, secular and religious—every editor—or how vast a proportion! transformed into a manufacturer of mere local opinion—local opinion—local opinion— working away at his battery—big or little—as if it were the most beautiful operation in the world to persuade one half of the people how unreasonable and how odious were the other half. Think of conventions sitting for secession and dismemberment, by the very tomb of Jackson—the "buried majesty" not rising to scatter and blast them. Call to mind how many elections have been holden— stirring the wave of the people to its profoundest depths—all turning on this topic. Remember how few of all who help to give direction to general sentiment, how few in either house of congress, what a handful only of editors and preachers and talkers have ventured anywhere to breathe a word above a whisper to hush or divert the pelting of this pitiless storm; and then consider how delicate and sensitive a thing is public opinion,—how easy it is to mould and color and kindle it, and yet that when moulded and colored and fired, not all the bayonets and artillery of Borodino can maintain the government which it decrees to perish; and say if you have not been encompassed, and are not now, by a peril, awful indeed! Say if you believe it possible that a whole people can go on—a reading and excitable people—hearing nothing, reading nothing, talking of nothing, thinking of nothing, sleeping and waking on nothing, for a year, but one incessant and vehement appeal to the strongest of their passions,—to the pride, anger, and fear of the South, to the philanthropy, humanity, and conscience of the North,—one half of it aimed to persuade you that they were cruel, ambitious, indolent, and licentious, and therefore hateful; and the other half of it to persuade them that you were desperately and hypocritically fanatical and aggressive, and therefore hateful—say, if an excitable people can go through all this, and not be the worse for it! I tell you nay. Such a year has sowed the seed of a harvest, which, if not nipped in the bud, will grow to armed men, hating with the hate of the brothers of Thebes.

It seems to me as if our hearts were changing. Ties the strongest, influences the sweetest, seem falling asunder as smoking flax. I took up, the day before yesterday, a religious newspaper, published in this city, a leading Orthodox paper, I may describe it, to avoid misapprehension. The first thing which met my eye was what purported to be an extract from a Southern religious newspaper, denouncing the Boston editor, or one of his contributors, as an infidel—in just so many words— on the ground that one of his anti-slavery arguments implied a doctrine inconsistent with a certain text of the New Testament. Surely, I said to myself, the Christian thus denounced will be deeply wounded by such misconstruction; and as he lives a thousand miles away from slavery, as it really does not seem to be his business, as it neither picks his pocket nor breaks his leg, and he may, therefore, afford to be cool, while his Southern brother lives in the very heart of it, and may, naturally enough, be a little more sensitive, he will try to soothe him, and win him, if he can, to reconsider and retract so grievous an objurgation. No such thing! To be called an infidel, says he, by this Southern Presbyterian, I count a real honor! He thereupon proceeds to denounce the slaveholding South as a downright Sodom,—leaves a pretty violent implication that his Presbyterian antagonist is not one of its few righteous, whoever else is—and without more ado sends him adrift. Yes, Fellow-citizens, more than the Methodist Episcopal Church is rent in twain. But if these things are done in the green tree, what shall be done in the dry? If the spirit of Christianity is not of power sufficient to enable its avowed professors to conduct this disputation of hatred with temper and decorum,—to say nothing of charity,—what may we expect from the hot blood of men who own not, nor comprehend the law of love?

I have spoken what I think of the danger that threatens the Union. I have done so more at length than I could have wished, because I know that upon the depth of our convictions and the sincerity of our apprehensions upon this subject, the views we shall take of our duties and responsibilities, must all depend.

If you concur with me that there is danger, you will concur with me in the *second place,* that thoughtful men have something to do to avert it; and what is that? It is not, in my judgment, Fellow-citizens, by stereotyped declamation on the utilities of the Union to South or North that we can avert the danger. It is not by shutting our eyes and ears to it that we can avert it. It is not by the foolish prattle of "Oh, those people off there need the Union more than we, and will not dare to quit." It is not by putting arms a-kimbo here or there and swearing that we will stand no more bullying; and if any body has a mind to dissolve the Union, let him go ahead. Not thus, not thus, felt and acted that generation of our fathers, who, out of distracted counsels, the keen jealousies of States, and a decaying nationality, by patience and temper as admirable as their wisdom, constructed the noble and proportioned fabric of our federal system. "Oh, rise some other such!"

No, Fellow-citizens—there is something more and other for us to do. And what is that? Among other things, chiefly this: to accept that whole body of measures of compromise, as they are called, by which the government has sought to compose the country, in the spirit of 1787,—and then, that henceforward every man, according to his measure, and in his place, in his party, in his social, or his literary, or his religious circle, in whatever may be his sphere of influence, set himself to suppress the further political agitation of this whole subject.

Of these measures of compromise I may say, in general, that they give the whole victory to neither of the great divisions of the country, and are therefore the fitter to form the basis of a permanent adjustment. I think that under their operation and by the concurrence of other agencies it will assuredly come to pass, that on all that vast accession of territory beyond and above Texas, no slave will ever breathe the air, and I rejoice at that. They abolish the slave-trade in the District of Columbia, and I rejoice at that. They restore the fugitive to the master,—and while I mourn that there is a slave who needs to run, or a master who desires to pursue, I should be unworthy of the privilege of addressing this assembly, if I did not declare that I have not a shadow of doubt that congress has the constitutional power to pass this law just as it is, and had no doubt, before I listened to the clear and powerful argument of Mr. Curtis to-night, that it was out of all question their duty to pass some effectual law on the subject, and that it is incumbent on every man who recognizes a single obligation of citizenship, to assist, in his spheres, in its execution.

Accepting, then, these measures of constitutional compromise, in the spirit of Union, let us set ourselves to suppress or mitigate the political agitation of slavery.

And in the first place, I submit that the two great political parties of the North are called upon by every consideration of patriotism and duty to strike this whole subject from their respective issues. I go for no amalgamation of parties, and for the forming of no new party. But I admit the deepest solicitude that those which now exist, preserving their actual organization and general principles and aims,— if so it must be,—should to this extent coalesce. Neither can act in this behalf effectually alone. Honorable concert is indispensable, and they owe it to the country. Have not the eminent men of both these great organizations united on this adjustment? Are they not both primarily national parties? Is it not one of their most important and beautiful uses that they extend the whole length and breadth of our land, and that they help or ought to help to hold the extreme North to the extreme South by a tie stronger almost than that of mere patriotism, by that surest cement of friendship,—common opinions on the great concerns of the Republic? You are a Democrat; and have you not for thirty-two years in fifty united with the universal Democratic party in the choice of Southern presidents? Has it not been your function for even a larger part of the last half century to rally with the South for the support of the general administration? Has it not ever been your boast, your merit as a party, that you are in an intense, and even character-istic degree, national and Unionist in your spirit and politics, although you had your origin in the assertion of State rights; that you have contributed in a thou-sand ways to the extension of our territory and the establishment of our martial fame; and that you follow the flag on whatever field or deck it waves?—and will you for the sake of a temporary victory in a State, or for any other cause, insert an article in your creed and give a direction to your tactics which shall detach you from such companionship and unfit you for such service in all time to come?

You are a Whig—I give you my hand on that—and is not your party national too? Do you not find your fastest allies at the South? Do you not need the vote of Louisiana, of North Carolina, of Tennessee, of Kentucky, to defend you from the redundant capital, matured skill, and pauper labor of Europe? Did you not just now, with a wise contempt of sectional issues and sectional noises, unite to call that brave, firm and good OLD MAN from his plantation, and seat him with all the honors in the place of Washington? Circumstances have forced both of these parties—the Northern and the Southern divisions of both—to suspend for a space the legitimate objects of their institution. For a space, laying them aside, and resolving ourselves into our individual capacities, we have thought and felt on nothing but slavery. Those circumstances exist no longer,—and shall we not instantly revive the old creeds, renew the old ties, and by manly and honorable concert, resolve to spare America that last calamity,—the formation of parties according to geographical lines?

I maintain, in the *second place,* that the CONSCIENCE of this community has a duty to do, not yet adequately performed; and that is, on grounds of moral obli-gation, not merely to call up men to the obedience of law, but on the same grounds to discourage and modify the further agitation of this topic of slavery, *in the spirit in which, thus far, that agitation has been conducted.* I mean to say, that our moral duties, not at all less than our political interests, demand that we accept this compromise, and that we promote the peace it is designed to restore.

Fellow-citizens, was there ever a development of sheer fanaticism more un-instructed, or more dangerous than that which teaches that conscience prescribes the continued political, or other exasperating agitation of this subject? That it will help, in the least degree, to ameliorate the condition of one slave, or to hasten the day of his emancipation, I do not believe, and no man can be certain that he knows. But the philanthropist, so he qualifies himself, will say that slavery is a relation of wrong, and whatever becomes of the effort, conscience impels him to keep up the agitation till the wrong, somehow, is ended. Is he, I answer, quite sure that a conscience enlightened to a comprehension and comparison of all its duties impels him to do any such thing? Is he quite sure that that which an English or French or German philanthropist might in conscience counsel or do, touching this matter of Southern slavery, that that also he, the American philanthropist, may, in conscience, counsel or do? Does it go for nothing in his ethics, that he stands, that the whole morality of the North stands, in a totally different relation to the community of the South from that of the foreign propagandist, and that this relation may possibly somewhat—aye, to a vast extent—modify all our duties? Instead of hastily inferring that, because those States are *sister States,* you are bound to meddle and agitate, and drive pitch-pine knots into their flesh and set them on fire, may not the fact that they are *sister States,* be the very reason why, though others may do so, you may not? In whomsoever else these enterprises of an offensive and aggressive morality are graceful or safe or right, are you quite sure that in you they are either graceful or safe or right?

I have heard that a great statesman, living in the North, but living and thinking for the country, has been complained of for saying that we have no more to do with slavery in the South, than with slavery in Cuba. Are you quite sure that the sentiment went far enough? Have we quite as much to do—I mean can we wisely or morally assume to do quite as much—with Southern as with Cuban slavery? To all the rest of the world we are united only by the tie of philanthropy, or universal benevolence, and our duties to that extent flow from that tie. All that such philanthropy prompts us to print or say or do, touching slavery in Cuba, we may print, say, or do, for what I know or care, subject, I would recommend, to the restraints of common sense, and taking reasonable thought for our personal security. But to America—*to our America,* we are united by another tie, and may not a principled patriotism, on the clearest grounds of moral obligation, limit the sphere and control the aspirations and prescribe the flights of philanthropy itself?

In the first place, remember, I entreat you, that on considerations of policy and wisdom—truest policy, profoundest wisdom, for the greater good and the higher glory of America—for the good of the master and slave, now and for all generations—you have entered with the Southern States into the most sacred and awful and tender of all the relations,—the relation of country; and there-fore, that you have, expressly and by implication, laid yourselves under certain restraints; you have pledged yourselves to a certain measure, and a certain spirit of forbearance; you have shut yourselves out from certain fields and highways of philanthropic enterprise—open to you before, open to the rest of the world now;—but from which, *in order to bestow larger and mightier blessings on man, in another way,* you have agreed to retire.

Yes, we have entered with them into the most sacred, salutary, and perma-nent of the relations of social man. We have united with them in that great mas-ter performance of human beings, that one work on which the moralists whom I love concur in supposing that the Supreme Governor looks down with pecu-liar complacency, the building of a Commonwealth. Finding themselves side by side with those States some sixty years ago in this new world, thirteen States of us then in all! thirty-one to-day,—touching one another on a thousand points,—discerning perfectly that unless the doom of man was to be reversed for them, there was no alternative but to become dearest friends or bitterest ene-mies,—so much Thucydides and the historians of the beautiful and miserable Italian republics of the Middle Age had taught them,—drawn together, also felicitously, by a common speech and blood, and the memory of their recent labor of glory,— our fathers adopted the conclusion that the best interests of humanity, in all her forms, demanded that we should enter into the grand, sacred, and tender relations of country. All things demanded it,—the love of man, the hopes of liberty,—all things. Hereby, only, can America bless herself, and bless the world.

Consider, in the *next place,* that to secure that largest good, to create and pre-serve a country, and thus to contribute to the happiness of man as far as that grand and vast instrumentality may be made to contribute to happiness, it became indis-pensable to take upon themselves, for themselves, and for all the generations who should follow, certain engagements with those to whom we became united. Some of these engagements were express. Such is that for the restoration of per-sons owing service according to the law of a State, and flying from it. That is express. It is written in this Constitution in terms. It was inserted in it, by what passed, sixty years ago, for the morality and religion of Massachusetts and New England. Yes; it was written there by men who knew their Bible, Old Testament and New, as thoroughly, and reverenced it and its Divine Author and his Son, the Saviour and Redeemer, as profoundly as we. Others of those engagements, and those how vast and sacred, were implied. It is not enough to say that the Con-stitution did not give to the new nation a particle of power to intermeddle by law with slavery within its States, and therefore it has no such power. This is true, but not all the truth. No man pretends we have power to intermeddle by law. But how much more than this is implied in the sacred relation of country. It is a marriage of more than two, for more than a fleeting natural life. "It is to be looked on with other reverence." It is an engagement, as between the real parties to it, an engagement the most solemn, to love, honor, cherish, and keep through all the ages of a nation. It is an engagement the most solemn, to cultivate those affections that shall lighten and perpetuate a tie which ought to last so long. It is an engagement then, which limits the sphere, and controls the enterprises of philanthropy itself. If you discern that by violating the express pledge of the Constitution, and refusing to permit the fugitive to be restored; by violating the implied pledges; by denying the Christianity of the holder of slaves; by proclaiming him impure, cruel, undeserving of affection, trust, and regard; that by this passionate and vehement aggression upon the prejudices, institutions, and investments of a whole region—that by all this you are dissolving the ties of country; endangering its disruption; frustrating the policy on which our fathers created it; and bringing into jeopardy the multiform and incalculable good which it was designed to secure, and would secure,—then, whatever foreign philanthropy might do, in such a prospect,—*your* philanthropy is arrested and rebuked by a "higher law." In this competition of affections, Country,— *"omnes omnium charitates complectens,"* the expression, the sum total of all things most dearly loved, surely holds the first place.

Will anybody say, that these engagements thus taken, for these ends, are but "covenants with hell," which there is no morality and no dignity in keeping? From such desperate and shameless fanaticism—if such there is—I turn to the moral sentiments of this assembly. It is not here—it is not in this hall—the blood of Warren in the chair—the form of Washington before you—that I will defend the Constitution from the charge of being a compact of guilt. I will not here defend the Convention which framed it, and the Conventions and people which adopted it, from the charge of having bought this great blessing of country, by immoral promises, more honored in the breach than the observance. Thank God, we yet hold that that transaction was honest, that work beautiful and pure; and those engagements, in all their length and breadth and height and depth, sacred.

Yet, I will say that, if to the formation of such a Union, it was indispensable, as we know it was, to contract these engagements expressed and implied, no covenant made by man ever rested on the basis of a sounder morality. They tell us that although you have the strict right, according to the writers on public law, to whom Mr. Curtis has referred, to restore the fugitive slave to his master, yet that the virtue of compassion commands you not to do so. But in order to enable ourselves to do all that good, and avert all that evil—boundless and inappreciable both—which we do and avert by the instrumentality of a Union under a common government, may we not, on the clearest moral principles, agree not to exercise compassion in that particular way? The mere virtue of compassion would command you to rescue any prisoner. But the citizen, to the end that he may be enabled, and others be enabled, to indulge a more various and useful compassion in other modes, agrees not to indulge it practically in that mode. Is such a stipulation immoral? No more so is this of the Constitution.

They tell us that slavery is so wicked a thing, that they must pursue it, by agitation, to its home in the States; and that if there is an implied engagement to abstain from doing so, it is an engagement to neglect an opportunity of doing good, and void in the forum of conscience. But was it ever heard of, that one may not morally bind himself to abstain from what he thinks a particular opportunity of doing good? A contract in general restraint of philanthropy, or any other useful calling, is void; but a contract to abstain from a specific sphere of exertion, is not void, and may be wise and right. To entitle himself to instruct heathen children on week days, might not a pious missionary engage not to attempt to preach to their parents on Sunday? To win the opportunity of achieving the mighty good summed up in the pregnant language of the preamble to the Constitution, such good as man has not on this earth been many times permitted to do or dream of, we might well surrender the privilege of reviling the masters of slaves with whom we must "either live or bear no life."

Will the philanthropist tell you that there is nothing conspicuous enough, and glorious enough for him, in thus refraining from this agitation, just because our relations to the South, under the Constitution, seem to forbid it? Aye, indeed! Is it even so? Is his morality of so ambitious and mounting a type that an effort, by the exercise of love or kindness or tolerance, to knit still closer the hearts of a great people, and thus to insure ages of peace—of progress, of enjoyment—to so vast a mass of the family of man, seems too trivial a feat? Oh, how stupendous a mistake! What achievement of philanthropy bears any proportion to the pure and permanent glory of that achievement whereby clusters of contiguous States, perfectly organized governments in themselves every one, full of energy, conscious of strength, full of valor, fond of war,—instead of growing first jealous, then hostile,—like the tribes of Greece after the Persian had retired,—like the cities of Italy at the dawn of the modern world,—are melted into one, so that for centuries of internal peace, the grand agencies of amelioration and advancement shall operate unimpeded; the rain and dew of Heaven descending on ground better and still better prepared to admit them; the course of time—the Providence of God—leading on that noiseless progress whose wheels shall turn not back, whose consummation shall be in the brightness of the latter day. What achievement of man may be compared with this achievement? For the slave, alone, what promises half so much? And this is not glorious enough for the ambition of philanthropy!

No, Fellow-citizens—first of men are the builders of empires! Here it is, my friends, here—right here—in doing something in our day and generation towards "forming a more perfect Union"—in doing something by literature, by public speech, by sound industrial policy, by the careful culture of fraternal love and regard, by the intercourse of business and friendship, by all the means within our command—in doing something to leave the Union, when we die, stronger than we found it,—here—here is the field of our grandest duties and highest rewards. Let the grandeur of such duties, let the splendor of such rewards, suffice us. Let them reconcile and constrain us to turn from that equivocal philanthropy which violates contracts, which tramples on law, which confounds the whole subordination of virtues, which counts it a light thing that a nation is rent asunder, and the swords of brothers sheathed in the bosoms of brothers, if thus the chains of one slave may be violently and prematurely broken.

Chapter VIII.

MR. CHOATE'S ADDRESS
ON KOSSUTH AND NON-INTERVENTION.

Correspondence of the New-York Daily Times

University of Vermont.

Commencement Celebration.

Burlington, Vt., Tuesday, Aug. 3, 1852.★

The Commencement exercises of the University of Vermont, at this place, have been attended with an unusual degree of interest. They were distinguished especially by the attendance of Hon. Rufus Choate, who delivered an Address before the Phi Beta Kappa Society, on Tuesday afternoon, remarkable not less for the interest and importance of its subject and sentiments than for its eloquence and literary beauty. It was preceded by the Exercises of two other literary societies, before which addresses of marked ability and interest were delivered, with a highly meritorious and striking Poem by Hon. C. G. Eastman, Editor of the *Patriot,* the leading Democratic paper in the State, published at Montpelier. As I propose to sketch for your readers, as fully as I may find convenient, the Address of Mr. Choate, I shall defer what I desire to say concerning the other exercises of the occasion to a future letter.

Mr. Choate's Address, by a very ill-considered and unfortunate arrangement, was delivered late in the afternoon, after the audience had listened to three other extended and elaborate literary performances during the day; and he was therefore unable to present the entire Address which he had prepared. But he spoke for about an hour-and-a-half,—in a continuous and sustained stream of eloquence such as it seldom falls to the lot of man to hear. It is needless to say that he was listened to with the most profound attention, by one of the largest and most intelligent audiences ever gathered out of our large and crowded cities.

You know Mr. Choate well enough to appreciate the difficulty of presenting any intelligible sketch of his discourses, and the impossibility of preserving, in

★ Taken from a report in the *New-York Daily Times* [Ed.].

such an attempted sketch, any of that gorgeous and tropical luxuriance of beauty which so distinguishes his eloquence from that of any other living man. Still I cannot forbear the endeavor to give you some notion, however inadequate, of this transcendently eloquent and splendid *Oration*.

Mr. CHOATE began his address by saying that he had, more than once, when standing as then before an assembly of Scholars, recalled the words of another, who congratulated himself, in the opening of a discourse on such an occasion, and before such an audience as this, that in such company he could feel no temptation to stray beyond the limits of the Academy, or within the noise of the City and the Forum. He meant, of course, simply that all things around him prescribed the treatment of a topic strictly literary. Mr. CHOATE said he had inferred, from their choice of a speaker, that his audience might have expected the selection of a subject somewhat different, and less rigidly scholastic,—demanding only and always, that what is said shall be said to the spirit of a scholar, and with manly freedom. He had imagined they might prescribe to him, if the choice were theirs, that he should find his topics in some of the warm interests,—some of the dazzling moral scenery,—some of the thoughts and teachings of the passing time.

Happy—said he—certainly, I should have been, and proud, to have partaken at this banquet of learning as a guest who felt himself in his place and at his ease; to have dared to give way to the impulses of the tune, to have diffused myself in some discussion of the charmed and changeless past;—to have recalled the days when life was young, and promised to be happy,—when I shared the friendship, and took some small part in the studies of some of those ripe and pure minds of the living and the dead, with whom the renown and the usefulness of this University are associated imperishably,—to have dreamed my dream of the ideal, too,—to have hung with you on the praise of some cherished character,—some "guide, philosopher, and friend,"—renewing our youth, if that might be, in the stream of his thoughts and images, as it flows, transparent and deep, over sands of gold,—to have evoked, for our instruction, for our worship, some great character, some heroic moment, some word of ancient virtue, on which Death, Time, and the gathering homage of the generations, have set the seal of immortality!

But all this, said he, I resign with a sigh. Turning now, quite another way, indulge for a moment a different train of feeling and reflection.

To his eye—who observes the present of our own country, and of the age, heedfully—looking before and after, every day offers some incident which first awakens a vivid emotion, and then teaches some great duty. Contemplate, then, a single one of such a class of incidents; give room to the emotions it stirs; gather up the lessons of which it is full.

On the fifth day of the last December, there came to this land a man of alien blood, of foreign and unfamiliar habit, costume and accent; yet the most eloquent of speech, according to his mode; the most eloquent of history and circumstance; the most eloquent of his mission and topics whom the world has, for many ages, seen; and began, among us a brief sojourn, began, say, rather, a brief and strange, eventful pilgrimage, which is just now concluded. Imperfect in his mastery of our tongue, he took his first lessons in it in the little room over the barrack gate of Buda, a few months before, his only practice in it had been a few speeches to quite uncritical audiences in Southampton, in Birmingham, Manchester and Guildhall, bred in a school of taste and general culture with which our Anglo-Saxon training had little affinity, little sympathy, the representative and impersonation, though not, I believe, the native child of a race from the East, planted some centuries ago in Europe, but Oriental still as ever, in all but its Christianity, the pleader of a cause in which we might seem to be as little concerned as in the story of the Ion Pelops or that of Troy divine, coming before us *even such*—that silver voice, that sad abstracted eye, before which one image seemed alone to hover, one procession to be passing, the fallen Hungary—the "unnamed demi gods," her thousand deathless sons; that earnest, full soul, laboring with one emotion; have held thousands and thousands of all degrees of susceptibility, the coldness and self-control of the East; the more spontaneous sympathies of the West; the masses in numbers without number; Women; Scholars, our greatest names in highest places; by the seashore, in banquet halls; in halls of legislation, among the memories of Bunker Hill; everywhere, he has held all, with a charm as absolute as that with which the Ancient Mariner kept back the bridal guest after the music of the marriage feast had begun.

The tribute of tears and applaudings; the tribute of sympathy and of thoughts too deep for applaudings—too deep for tears, have attested his sway. For the first time since the transcendent genius of DEMOSTHENES strove with the downward age of Greece; or since the Prophets of Israel announced—each tone of the hymn grander, sadder than before—the successive foot-falls of the approaching Assyrian beneath whose spears the Law should cease and the vision be seen no more; our ears, our hearts, have drank the sweetest, most mournful, most awful of the tones which man may ever utter, or may ever hear—the eloquence of an Expiring Nation.

For of all this tide of speech, flowing without ebb, there was one source only. To one note only was this harp of enchantment strung. It was an appeal not to the interests, not to the reason, not to the prudence, not to the justice, not to the instructed conscience of America and England; but to the mere emotion of sympathy for a single family of man oppressed by another—contending to be free—cloven down on the field, yet again erect; his body dead, his spirit incapable to die; the victim of treachery; the victim of power; the victim of intervention; yet breathing, sighing, lingering, dying, hoping through all the pain, the bliss of an *agony of glory!* For this perishing nation—not one inhabitant of which we ever saw; on whose territory we had never set a foot; whose books we had never read; to whose ports we never traded; not belonging in an exact sense to the circle of independent States; a Province rather of an Empire which alone is known to international law and to our own diplomacy; for this nation he sought Pity—the intervention, the armed intervention, the material aid of Pity; and if his audiences could have had their will, he would have obtained it, without mistrust or measure, to his heart's content.

When shall we be quite certain again, that the lyre of Orpheus did not kindle savage natures to a transient discourse of reason;—did not suspend the labors and charm the pains of the damned, did not lay the guardian of the grave asleep, and bring back Eurydice from the region beyond the river, to the warm, upper air.

And now that this pilgrimage of romance is ended, the harp hushed, the minstrel gone, let us pause a moment, attend the lessons and gather up the uses of the unaccustomed performance.

Mr. CHOATE proceeded to say it would not, he hoped, be supposed that he was about to treat or touch the question of the specific mission on which LOUIS KOSSUTH came to this country,—or to inquire whether he could rightly ask, or we could rightly grant, material aid, or any aid, in this struggle of Hungary. He should forbear from that discussion altogether, as it had become too directly connected with the politics of the day for proper introduction here. But abstracting all these considerations from the case, he proposed to inquire whether the New World does not owe some sort of benevolence to the Old;—to inquire how, in what form, through what ministrations, and in what degree and measure, this debt of good will shall be paid. We may not, he agreed, thunder on the Theiss, or the Danube, nor seek to gather the glories of Chippewa, of Cherubusco, of Palo Alto, on the heights of Kapolna, or to carry up the Stars and Stripes side by side, or in advance of the crimson flag of Hungary, or the eagle banner of the risen Poland, through the breaches of Buda, or in the defiles of Bramienka, that other Thermopyla. This we may not do, though the cry of a race, ready to perish on the ridges of adverse battle, rise in our ears. But we may nevertheless exert upon Europe an influence, working not by proclamation, by no violation of treaties, but like light, attraction,—as the Sun and the noiseless influence of the Pleiades,—an intervention which acts by whispering to them of an asylum beyond the sea,—where the hungry may find bread, the enslaved liberty, the weary rest, the stricken and heavy of spirit the oil of joy and the garments of praise,—which acts by setting up on one of the high places of the world an example of self-government,—religious freedom; light taxes; no standing army; going out in our daily life, sounded forth in our eloquence and poetry,—radiant in our acts, gleaming across the waters like the evening star.

Proceeding then to consider the *right kind of intervention* of the New World for the Old—the *duty,* the *limitations,* and the *modes.* Mr. CHOATE said it was certain that when this interesting exile, late our guest, submitted his appeal in such variety of pathos and beauty to the sentiment of Benevolence—the sentiment which loves man as man, which seeks to do him good—he appealed to a sentiment which every nation is morally bound to feel, and with right limitations to display towards every other. In this, religion, ethics, literature, the universal reason, all concur. God has divided into many nations the races of men; but they all remain the children of one Father, and have one common interest. Such is the language, such the spirit of our religion. Such is the theory of Public Law, resting on MONTESQUIEU and on GROTIUS; such is the teaching of moral philosophy in SENECA, in HALL, in MACKINTOSH, in WHEWELL, and in FOSTER. Such is the myriad-voiced, spontaneous testimony of a literature, of all art, of all the schools, in all ages. First of the moral sentiments, constant, supreme—the fulfilment of the whole law, is the love of universal man. We recognize, of course, the claims of patriotism and its uses. Yet, let us own it, the glories of Marathon, of Saragossa, of Bennington, of Buda, pale and fade in the serene and golden light of a benevolence encompassing the world—as the glimmering of stars on the plains of Bethlehem, in that effulgence, breaking on midnight, through which the ears of Shepherds caught the song: "Peace on Earth—good will to men."

Mr. CHOATE next urged that this same sentiment commands us to bestow our sympathies upon the oppressed, and not upon the oppressor; that we may wish them to be in the possession of the highest good—that of liberty. It was a sound and a healthy moral emotion with which the heart of this whole country throbbed towards the Magyar race, when their story was told. We may have been wrong as to the facts of their history; but with the view of them that we had, we must have renounced our sentient, our moral nature, if we had not applauded—if we had not been awestruck when we were told how, when in the Parliament of Hungary it was anounced that 200,000 men and 80 millions of florins were needed to defend her independence, that whole assembly—100 Representatives—rose as one man, and lifting their right arms towards God, solemnly said: "*We grant it*—freedom or death!" And if we had not mourned as it was told us that all that sublimity of emotion had been inspired in vain, could we sit unmoved in the boxes of the theatre when such a drama was unrolling on such a stage? We who give to Odipus at Colonos, to Iphigenia at Aulis, to Medea, to Lear, to Cordelia, to the Bride of Lammermoor, the choking tears of a spontaneous nature, could we withhold them from a nation struck down, with youth and beauty crimson on its lip and on its cheek—the beaming forehead just now lifted to the stars, pressed, soiled, profaned to earth?

And, in the next place, Mr. CHOATE agreed that the same warm sympathy which is thus due to Hungary, may rightfully be extended to the down-trodden and oppressed upon the whole Continent of Europe. We may be wrongly informed as to the facts in special cases; we may err; but in such a case he thought it safest to err upon the right side—to go too far in sympathizing with and seeking to aid the oppressed, rather than in giving countenance and support to their oppressors.

He then proceeded to indicate, in a general way, the *limitations* under which this sentiment must be exercised. And he urged, first, that the same sentiment which prescribes this form of love to man, prescribes with an equal authority that a nation shall exercise it towards another only in strict subordination to its own interests, estimated by a wise statesmanship and a well instructed public conscience. And this point he developed and demonstrated at considerable length—citing and condemning the practice growing quite too common of taking the virtues out of their place, destroying their interdependence, and exalting some one of them to an unphilosophical and mischievous supremacy,—the habit, particularly, of taking some one impulse or sensibility, that, for example, of benevolence waking through compassion, and giving to it a supremacy of rank to which it has no right. He vindicated, also, as one of the primary and essential virtues, prudence, by which all affairs must be governed, to be governed well, and which enjoins a primary regard to our own interests. Even individual benevolence is to be controlled by reason, by respect to times, opportunities and circumstances; and must be proportioned among its objects, according to remoteness or proximity—waking warmest, bearing richest life in the nearer circles of the heart, the family, the vicinage, the country. Even individual benevolence, too, must not cause more pain than it cures, for that would be to defeat the single aim for which compassion is implanted in man. But when we consider how totally unlike is a nation to an individual—how vast the aggregate of its interests, and of those to be affected by whatever it may do—we will see that the same Sovereign Disposer who has distributed the race into nations, wills also that the happiness of each nation shall form to itself the chief aim of its being, the sole or chief end of its policy. After thus showing, with great variety of argument and illustration, that every nation must be guided by its own interests, in determining its policy towards others, Mr. CHOATE proceeded to show that the decision, as to what constitutes the true interest of a nation, must be given by a wise statesmanship. The Science of Practical Politics must decide it,—that noble science whose office it is to order and direct the practical life of a great people—resting upon morality as its basis, subdued, instructed by the examples, warnings of all the past; yet gathering from the study and comparison of all the eras, that there is a silent progress of the race, without pause, without haste, without return,—that is the statesmanship to decide the question.

Dwelling at length upon this general position, and following it into many of its incidental relations, Mr. CHOATE said that there were still many offices which the promptings of our benevolence will incline us to perform towards other nations of the earth. He would pass over all others,—the service we have done to humanity by admitting so many millions from abroad to these prepared and adorned mansions of liberty and a better social life;—our charities hastening to carry succor to the sufferers from severe physical catastrophe: or our despatch of armies of religion to carry the Word of Life to the remotest corners of the earth. He would not dwell upon our wide manufactures, our contributions to human comfort and the promotion of human happiness. But there was one manufactured production we may send abroad, to which all the workshops and marts of the world can offer nothing worthy of comparison—one for which we might take our letters patent and claim a monopoly in all courts of the world, if its nature were not so expansive, its utility so transcendent, its relation to the primal wants and rights of man so close and peremptory as to forbid the attempt and rebuke the wish—and that is, *the largest measure of liberty* which the civil life of man admits, combined with the least alloy of constraint and force with which civil life can consist, embodied in law and order,—announcing itself to the recognition of the world in the form of a rising State, already in the first class of eminence and consideration.

Behold here,—not in COLT's revolvers, nor in reaping machines, nor in eagle skimmers of the seas,—one contribution to the treasures of that Crystal Palace! I am told that while the curious gazers wandered through that lofty pile, and admired the gew gaw imitations of other works in the mountain green of Russia,—the Bavarian or Bohemian stained or painted glass,—Berlin wine coolers in terra cotta,—heraldic chairs,—statuettes of Hindoo girls setting their lamps in the Ganges,—the gaudy and ponderous architecture of Austrian bookcases, (I wonder what *books* they contained,)—the frolic graceful art of France, disporting in Sevres porcelain, Gobelin tapestry, perfumes and embroidery, tripping, as it were, on the light, fantastic toe,—they turned away from the American section,—with well-bred jests, not altogether repressed by that matchless figure of your POWERS, in which the beauty, the soul, the genius of Greece shine forth, as ever, chainless though in chains!

And yet, if there had been upon those shelves old JOHN ADAMS' defence of the American Constitution,—a stray copy of the *Federalist,*—the Life of Washington,—the last census, with its stupendous statistics, carefully digested into easy reading for Bureaucratic comprehension,—they would have found in them a more splendid contribution to the World's Industry,—a surer guarantee of human happiness,—the assurance of a brighter future of moral, industrial and civil glory, that had ever been dreamed of in their philosophy!

Speaking further of the high importance of our continuing thus to hold up to the admiration of the world the example of a Free Republic,—and estimating highly the gradual, steady, and irresistible effect of such an exhibition upon the future of Europe, Mr. CHOATE said that the best of all possible kinds of intervention by which we can and the Freedom of Europe, is the account we continue to give of ourselves. It is not what a stray traveler, flying across the country in a steamboat or a rail-car, as if running a race with the treaty of extradition and somewhat expecting and deserving to be beaten,—it is not what such a one may say of us, by which we shall stand or fall among nations. It shall be your own Historians,—your own Philosophers,—your own Poets,—your own workers in marble, in iron or in brass,—through whom ye shall teach,—by whom ye shall attract the nations,—recommending, exemplifying to them the beauty and the whiteness of LIBERTY! Be ours, then, the fit task and the rare praise to show forth the mind and the life of this great, free Country. Yes, if you and such as you, will have it so, this shall be the mode in which the New World shall shape and control the destiny of the Old. There shall be HISTORY,—not as in all the past, the echo of a few great names and sounding deeds,—teacher of ambition, the hollow voice however swollen-toned, of the praise that comes from earth; but History, for the first time recording in the spirit of love, the annals of the People,—setting in one glorious view one era of the Progress of the race,—unfolding the manifold achievements of Liberty. Reason and Order, not neglectful of the Mighty and Peerless,—of the living and the dead,—yet careful rather, with motherly sympathy, to gather and teach those more universal lessons of philanthropy, humanity, peace, commerce, plain living, high thinking, and beautiful feeling, whereof all may profit,—treasuring carefully the series of influences which have moulded all into one stupendous whole, —leading the reader with safe and firm guidance upward and upward, through the long succession of years, to the *genti incunabula,* the May-Flower and the Rock,—evermore setting on the head of Virtue the crown of gold, and pausing ever to tremble in fear of human judgment to come. There shall be PHILOSOPHY, not unmindful certainly of material nature, of number, of quantity, of mechanical force and the Preadamite Earth; but conversant more with man, with human life;—such philosophy as your MARSH loved, adorned and honored;—seeking to discern and fix the nature and the ground of justice; the office and education of conscience; the grounds of government; the conditions and dangers and blessings of liberty, with all holy, beautiful and useful speculations and institutions whereof the fruit is the highest style of man. There shall be ELOQUENCE, not of the shade and of the holiday, not the rhetoric of phrases and images,— but the eloquence of truth, of reason, of passion and of thought. There shall be POETRY, which ever, as BACON has said, was thought to have some participation of divineness, which ever serveth and conferreth to magnanimity and morality, as well as to delectation. The ARTS shall be there,—the builder with all his seven lamps, all lighted to the glory of God,—to the glory of his chosen land;— and the Pantheon gallery of enchantment shall be full.

But if thus it be, that thus our example is to do anything to change the world to our likeness, think what manner of persons ought ye to be—ye who breathe this air, and on whom rests this responsibility. It is not the public opinion of this day or this land alone you are to shape; it is no local current or eddy of the air; it is the atmosphere that enfolds the globe. Consider how quickly thoughts and words are carried to the utmost ends of the earth; how what is spoken here— how a lofty thought, a watchword of liberty or duty spoken here, may be conned and studied upon the sides of the vine hills of the Rhine, by the swift Danube, in the hollow Appenines; how vast an audience it may have; how many bosoms it may thrill; on how much good soil the seed may spring to life. Do we not live in the age of the Empire of Ideas? Do not the flying leaves of a single pamphleteer— the syren music of the eloquence of a single tongue, to-day, inflame or compose armies or people—shake thrones, change dynasties, drive the Head of the Church from Rome and the Grand Lama of Absolutism from Vienna—determine the policy of Governments, and shape the fate of man? And how much more, think ye, if the united voice of the united intellect and genius of a nation practically, wholly free, should sound across the hand-breadth of ocean one grand, consenting, perpetual hymn to the source of all its enjoyments, of all its power, of all its hopes, of all its glory—one reasoned and heart-breathed exhortation to all the lands to walk also in that light, to worship in that temple—how much more quickly, because more safely, more innocently for you than by all the power of material aid, than all the bayonets and artillery of Borodino, will you work that work which shall bless the lands!

The sketch I have thus given will at least indicate the general outline of this Discourse. The language, gorgeous with imagery and with epithets, each one at once an image of an argument; the elaborately complicated, yet exceedingly powerful and effective sentences; and all, indeed, which makes his eloquence thoroughly original and peculiar, to which in English literature there is nothing *aut simile aut secundum,* cannot be preserved or even fairly indicated in such a sketch.

Mr. CHOATE was present on the evening of the same day, and took an active interest at the Dinner of the Alumni of the University, of which, together with other matters connected with the University and its Commencement exercises, I shall give you some further account hereafter. Mr. CHOATE was quite ill on Wednesday, so much so as to be confined to his room and his bed, at the house of his old friend, Rev. Dr. WHEELER, for the greater part of the day. He has however recovered and left this afternoon, with Prof. BROWN, of Dartmouth College, for Quebec. I regret to learn that J. G. SAXE, Esq., who was to deliver a Poem on the occasion, was prevented by serious illness, from which he has seriously suffered of late.

Yours,   R.

CHAPTER IX.

REMARKS BEFORE THE CIRCUIT COURT ON THE DEATH OF MR. WEBSTER.

As a Massachusetts Whig, Choate was of course a profound admirer of Daniel Webster, one of the most illustrious orators ever to represent his state in Congress. We see in the three addresses on Webster that we reproduce in this volume Choate's affection for a man he considered the ideal statesman: a gifted speaker, a man of principled moderation, and a true patriot.

His "Remarks Before the Circuit Court on the Death of Mr. Webster" was delivered four days after Webster's death. In the words of one commentator, "He spoke with entire quietness of manner, and with the deepest feeling, and his words seem to contain the germs of almost all the eulogies afterwards pronounced upon the great New England statesman."

[Mr. Webster died on Sunday morning, October 24, 1852. The members of the Suffolk Bar met on Monday morning, and appointed a committee to report a series of resolutions. These were read and adopted at an adjourned meeting, Thursday, October 28th, and immediately presented to the Circuit Court of the United States for the District of Massachusetts, CURTIS and SPRAGUE, Justices, on the Bench. They were read by the Hon. George S. Hillard, after which Mr. Choate made the following remarks.]

MAY IT PLEASE YOUR HONORS:——

I HAVE been requested by the members of the Bar of this Court to add a few words to the resolutions just read, in which they have embodied, as they were able, their sorrow for the death of their beloved and illustrious member and countryman, Mr. Webster; their estimation of his character, life, and genius; their sense of the bereavement,—to the country as to his friends,—incapable of repair; the pride, the fondness,—the filial and the patriotic pride and fondness,—with which they cherish, and would consign to history to cherish, the memory of a great and good man.

And yet, I could earnestly have desired to be excused from this duty. He must have known Mr. Webster less, and loved him less, than your honors or than I have known and loved him, who can quite yet,—quite yet,—before we can comprehend that we have lost him forever,—before the first paleness with which the news of his death overspread our cheeks has passed away,—before we have been down to lay him in the Pilgrim soil he loved so well, till the heavens be no more,—he must have known and loved him less than we have done, who can come here quite yet, to recount the series of his service, to display with psychological exactness the traits of his nature and mind, to ponder and speculate on the secrets—on the marvellous secrets—and source of that vast power, which we shall see no more in action, nor aught in any degree resembling it, among men. These first moments should be given to grief. It may employ, it may promote a calmer mood, to construct a more elaborate and less unworthy memorial.

For the purposes of this moment and place, indeed, no more is needed. What is there for this Court or for this Bar to learn from me, here and now, of him? The year and the day of his birth; that birthplace on the frontier, yet bleak and waste; the well, of which his childhood drank, dug by that father of whom he has said, "that through the fire and blood of seven years of revolutionary war he shrank from no danger, no toil, no sacrifice, to serve his country, and to raise his children to a condition better than his own;" the elm-tree that father planted, fallen now, as father and son have fallen; that training of the giant infancy on catechism and Bible, and Watts's version of the Psalms, and the traditions of Plymouth, and Fort William Henry, and the Revolution, and the age of Washington and Franklin, on the banks of the Merrimack, flowing sometimes in flood and anger, from his secret springs in the crystal hills; the two district schoolmasters, Chase and Tappan; the village library; the dawning of the love and ambition of letters; the few months at Exeter and Boscawen; the life of college; the probationary season of school-teaching; the clerkship in the Fryeburg Registry of Deeds; his admission to the bar, presided over by judges like Smith, illustrated by practisers such as Mason, where, by the studies, in the contentions of nine years, he laid the foundation of the professional mind; his irresistible attraction to public life; the oration on commerce; the Rockingham resolutions; his first term of four years' service in Congress, when, by one bound, he sprang to his place by the side of the foremost of the rising American statesmen; his removal to this State; and then the double and parallel current in which his life, studies, thoughts, cares, have since flowed, bearing him to the leadership of the Bar by universal acclaim, bearing him to the leadership of public life,—last of that surpassing triumvirate, shall we say the greatest, the most widely known and admired?—all these things, to their minutest details, are known and rehearsed familiarly. Happier than the younger Pliny, happier than Cicero, he has found his historian, unsolicited, in his lifetime, and his countrymen have him all by heart!

There is, then, nothing to tell you,—nothing to bring to mind. And then, if I may borrow the language of one of his historians and friends,—one of those through whose beautiful pathos the common sorrow uttered itself yesterday, in Faneuil Hall,—"I dare not come here and dismiss in a few summary paragraphs the character of one who has filled such a space in the history, one who holds such a place in the heart, of his country. It would be a disrespectful familiarity to a man of his lofty spirit, his great soul, his rich endowments, his long and honorable life, to endeavor thus to weigh and estimate them,"—a half-hour of words, a handful of earth, for fifty years of great deeds, on high places!

But, although the time does not require anything elaborated and adequate,—forbids it, rather,—some broken sentences of veneration and love may be indulged to the sorrow which oppresses us.

There presents itself, on the first and to any observation of Mr. Webster's life and character, a twofold eminence,—eminence of the very highest rank,—in a twofold field of intellectual and public display,—the profession of the law and the profession of statesmanship,—of which it would not be easy to recall any parallel in the biography of illustrious men.

Without seeking for parallels, and without asserting that they do not exist, consider that he was, by universal designation, the leader of the general American Bar; and that he was, also, by an equally universal designation, foremost of her statesmen living at his death; inferior to not one who has lived and acted since the opening of his own public life. Look at these aspects of his greatness separately, and from opposite sides of the surpassing elevation. Consider that his single career at the bar may seem to have been enough to employ the largest faculties, without repose, for a lifetime; and that, if then and thus the *"infinitus forensium rerum labor"* should have conducted him to a mere professional reward,—a bench of chancery or law, the crown of the first of advocates, *jurisperitorum eloquentissimus,*—to the pure and mere honors of a great magistrate,—that that would be as much as is allotted to the ablest in the distribution of fame. Even that half, if I may say so, of his illustrious reputation—how long the labor to win it, how worthy of all that labor! He was bred first in the severest school of the common law, in which its doctrines were expounded by Smith, and its administration shaped and directed by Mason, and its foundation principles, its historical sources and illustrations, its connection with the parallel series of statutory enactments, its modes of reasoning, and the evidence of its truths, he grasped easily and completely; and I have myself heard him say, that for many years while still at that bar, he tried more causes, and argued more questions of fact to the jury than perhaps any other member of the profession anywhere. I have heard from others how, even then, he exemplified the same direct, clear, and forcible exhibition of proofs, and the reasonings appropriate to proofs, as well as the same marvellous power of discerning instantly what we call the decisive points of the cause in law and fact, by which he was later more widely celebrated. This was the first epoch in his professional training.

With the commencement of his public life, or with his later removal to this State, began the second epoch of his professional training, conducting him through the gradation of the national tribunals to the study and practice of the more flexible, elegant, and scientific jurisprudence of commerce and of chancery, and to the grander and less fettered investigations of international, prize, and constitutional law, and giving him to breathe the air of a more famous forum, in a more public presence, with more variety of competition, although he never met abler men, as I have heard him say, than some of those who initiated him in the rugged discipline of the Courts of New Hampshire; and thus, at length, by these studies, these labors, this contention, continued without repose, he came, now many years ago, to stand *omnium assensu* at the summit of the American Bar.

It is common and it is easy, in the case of all in such position, to point out other lawyers, here and there, as possessing some special qualification or attainment more remarkably, perhaps, because more exclusively,—to say of one that he has more cases in his recollection at any given moment, or that he was earlier grounded in equity, has gathered more black letter or civil law, or knowledge of Spanish or of Western titles,—and these comparisons were sometimes made with him. But when you sought a counsel of the first rate for the great cause, who would most surely discern and most powerfully expound the exact law, required by the controversy, in season for use; who could most skilfully encounter the opposing law; under whose powers of analysis, persuasion and display, the asserted right would assume the most probable aspect before the intelligence of the judge; who, if the inquiry became blended with or resolved into facts, could most completely develop and most irresistibly expose them; one "the law's whole thunder born to wield,"—when you sought such a counsel, and could have the choice, I think the universal profession would have turned to him. And this would be so in nearly every description of cause, in any department. Some able men wield civil inquiries with a peculiar ability; some criminal. How lucidly and how deeply he elucidated a question of property, you all know. But then, with what address, feeling, pathos, and prudence he defended, with what dignity and crushing power, *accusatorio spiritu,* he prosecuted the accused of crime, whom he believed to have been guilty, few have seen; but none who have seen can ever forget it.

Some scenes there are, some Alpine eminences rising above the high table-land of such a professional life, to which, in the briefest tribute, we should love to follow him. We recall that day, for an instance, when he first announced, with decisive display, what manner of man he was, to the Supreme Court of the Nation. It was in 1818, and it was in the argument of the case of Dartmouth College. William Pinkney was recruiting his great faculties, and replenishing that reservoir of professional and elegant acquisition, in Europe. Samuel Dexter, "the honorable man, and the counsellor, and the eloquent orator," was in his grave. The boundless old-school learning of Luther Martin; the silver voice and infinite analytical ingenuity and resources of Jones; the fervid genius of Emmett pouring itself along *immenso ore;* the ripe and beautiful culture of Wirt and Hopkinson—the steel point, unseen, not unfelt, beneath the foliage; Harper himself, statesman as well as lawyer,—these, and such as these, were left of that noble bar. That day Mr. Webster opened the cause of Dartmouth College to a tribunal unsurpassed on earth in all that gives illustration to a bench of law, not one of whom any longer survives.

One would love to linger on the scene, when, after a masterly argument of the law, carrying, as we may now know, conviction to the general mind of the court, and vindicating and settling for his lifetime his place in that forum, he paused to enter, with an altered feeling, tone, and manner, with these words, on his peroration: "I have brought my *Alma Mater* to this presence, that, if she must fall, she may fall in her robes and with dignity;" and then broke forth in that strain of sublime and pathetic eloquence, of which we know not much more than that, in its progress, Marshall,—the intellectual, the self-controlled, the unemotional,— announced, visibly, the presence of the unaccustomed enchantment.

Other forensic triumphs crowd on us, in other competition, with other issues. But I must commit them to the historian of constitutional jurisprudence.

And now, if this transcendent professional reputation were all of Mr. Webster, it might be practicable, though not easy, to find its parallel elsewhere, in our own, or in European or classical biography.

But, when you consider that, side by side with this, there was growing up that other reputation,—that of the first American statesman; that, for thirty-three years, and those embracing his most Herculean works at the bar, he was engaged as a member of either House, or in the highest of the executive departments, in the conduct of the largest national affairs, in the treatment of the largest national questions, in debate with the highest abilities of American public life, conducting diplomatic intercourse in delicate relations with all manner of foreign powers, investigating whole classes of truths, totally unlike the truths of the law, and resting on principles totally distinct,—and that here, too, he was wise, safe, controlling, trusted, the foremost man; that Europe had come to see in his life a guaranty for justice, for peace, for the best hopes of civilization, and America to feel surer of her glory and her safety as his great arm enfolded her,— you see how rare, how solitary, almost, was the actual greatness! Who, anywhere, has won, as he had, the double fame, and worn the double wreath of Murray and Chatham, of Dunning and Fox, of Erskine and Pitt, of William Pinkney and Rufus King, in one blended and transcendent superiority?

I cannot attempt to grasp and sum up the aggregate of the service of his public life at such a moment as this; and it is needless. That life comprised a term of more than thirty-three years. It produced a body of performance, of which I may say, generally, it was all which the first abilities of the country and time, employed with unexampled toil, stimulated by the noblest patriotism, in the highest places of the State, in the fear of God, in the presence of nations, could possibly compass.

He came into Congress after the war of 1812 had begun, and though probably deeming it unnecessary, according to the highest standards of public necessity, in his private character, and objecting, in his public character, to some of the details of the policy by which it was prosecuted, and standing by party ties in general opposition to the administration, he never breathed a sentiment calculated to depress the tone of the public mind, to aid or comfort the enemy, to check or chill the stirrings of that new, passionate, unquenchable spirit of nationality, which then was revealed, or kindled to burn till we go down to the tombs of States.

With the peace of 1815 his more cherished public labors began; and thenceforward he devoted himself,—the ardor of his civil youth, the energies of his maturest manhood, the autumnal wisdom of the ripened year,—to the offices of legislation and diplomacy; of preserving the peace, keeping the honor, establishing the boundaries, and vindicating the neutral rights of his country; restoring a sound currency, and laying its foundation sure and deep; in upholding public credit; in promoting foreign commerce and domestic industry; in developing our uncounted material resources,—giving the lake and the river to trade,—and vindicating and interpreting the constitution and the law. On all these subjects,—on all measures practically in any degree affecting them,—he has inscribed his opinions and left the traces of his hand. Everywhere the philosophical and patriot statesman and thinker will find that he has been before him, lighting the way, sounding the abyss. His weighty language, his sagacious warnings, his great maxims of empire, will be raised to view, and live to be deciphered when the final catastrophe shall lift the granite foundation in fragments from its bed.

In this connection I cannot but remark to how extraordinary an extent had Mr. Webster, by his acts, words, thoughts, or the events of his life, associated himself forever in the memory of all of us with every historical incident, or, at least, with every historical epoch, with every policy, with every glory, with every great name and fundamental institution, and grand or beautiful image, which are peculiarly and properly American. Look backwards to the planting of Plymouth and Jamestown; to the various scenes of colonial life in peace and war; to the opening and march and close of the revolutionary drama; to the age of the constitution; to Washington and Franklin and Adams and Jefferson; to the whole train of causes, from the reformation downwards, which prepared us to be republicans; to that other train of causes which led us to be unionists,—look round on field, workshop, and deck, and hear the music of labor rewarded, fed, and protected; look on the bright sisterhood of the States, each singing as a seraph in her motion, yet blending in a common harmony,—and there is nothing which does not bring him by some tie to the memory of America. We seem to see his form and hear his deep, grave speech everywhere. By some felicity of his personal life; by some wise, deep, or beautiful word, spoken or written; by some service of his own, or some commemoration of the services of others, it has come to pass that "our granite hills, our inland seas, and prairies, and fresh, unbounded, magnificent wilderness," our encircling ocean, the Rock of the Pilgrims, our new-born sister of the Pacific, our popular assemblies, our free schools, all our cherished doctrines of education, and of the influence of religion, and material policy, and the law, and the constitution, give us back his name. What American landscape will you look on, what subject of American interest will you study, what source of hope or of anxiety, as an American, will you acknowledge, that does not recall him!

I shall not venture, in this rapid and general recollection of Mr. Webster, to attempt to analyze that intellectual power which all admit to have been so extraordinary, or to compare or contrast it with the mental greatness of others, in variety or degree, of the living or the dead; or even to attempt to appreciate, exactly, and in reference to canons of art, his single attribute of eloquence. Consider, however, the remarkable phenomenon of excellence in three unkindred, one might have thought, incompatible forms of public speech,—that of the forum, with its double audience of bench and jury, of the halls of legislation, and of the most thronged and tumultuous assemblies of the people.

Consider, further, that this multiform eloquence, exactly as his words fell, became at once so much accession to permanent literature, in the strictest sense, solid, attractive, and rich, and ask how often in the history of public life such a thing has been exemplified. Recall what pervaded all these forms of display, and every effort in every form,—that union of naked intellect, in its largest measure, which penetrates to the exact truth of the matter in hand, by intuition or by inference, and discerns everything which may make it intelligible, probable, or credible to another, with an emotional and moral nature profound, passionate, and ready to kindle, and with an imagination enough to supply a hundred-fold more of illustration and aggrandizement than his taste suffered him to accept; that union of greatness of soul with depth of heart, which made his speaking almost more an exhibition of character than of mere genius; the style, not merely pure, clear Saxon, but so constructed, so numerous as far as becomes prose, so forcible, so abounding in unlabored felicities; the words so choice; the epithet so pictured; the matter absolute truth, or the most exact and specious resemblance the human wit can devise; the treatment of the subject, if you have regard to the kind of truth he had to handle,—political, ethical, legal,—as deep, as complete as Paley's, or Locke's, or Butler's, or Alexander Hamilton's, of their subjects; yet that depth and that completeness of sense, made transparent as through crystal waters, all embodied in harmonious or well-composed periods, raised on winged language, vivified, fused, and poured along in a tide of emotion, fervid, and incapable to be withstood; recall the form, the eye, the brow, the tone of voice, the presence of the intellectual king of men,—recall him thus, and, in the language of Mr. Justice Story, commemorating Samuel Dexter, we may well "rejoice that we have lived in the same age, that we have listened to his eloquence, and been instructed by his wisdom."

I cannot leave the subject of his eloquence without returning to a thought I have advanced already. All that he has left, or the larger portion of all, is the record of spoken words. His works, as already collected, extend to many volumes,—a library of reason and eloquence, as Gibbon has said of Cicero's,—but they are volumes of speeches only, or mainly; and yet, who does not rank him as a great American author? an author as truly expounding, and as characteristically exemplifying, in a pure, genuine, and harmonious English style, the mind, thought, point of view of objects, and essential nationality of his country as any other of our authors, professedly so denominated? Against the maxim of Mr. Fox, his speeches read well, and yet were good speeches,—great speeches,—in the delivery. For so grave were they, so thoughtful and true, so much the eloquence of reason at last, so strikingly always they contrived to link the immediate topic with other and broader principles, ascending easily to widest generalizations, so happy was the reconciliation of the qualities which engage the attention of hearers, yet reward the perusal of students, so critically did they keep the right side of the line which parts eloquence from rhetoric, and so far do they rise above the penury of mere debate, that the general reason of the country has enshrined them at once, and forever, among our classics.

It is a common belief that Mr. Webster was a various reader; and I think it is true, even to a greater degree than has been believed. In his profession of politics, nothing, I think, worthy of attention had escaped him; nothing of the ancient or modern prudence; nothing which Greek or Roman or European speculation in that walk had explored, or Greek or Roman or European or universal history, or public biography exemplified. I shall not soon forget with what admiration he spake, at an interview to which he admitted me, while in the Law School at Cambridge, of the politics and ethics of Aristotle, and of the mighty mind which, as he said, seemed to have "thought through" so many of the great problems which form the discipline of social man. American history and American political literature he had by heart,—the long series of influences which trained us for representative and free government; that other series of influences which moulded us into a united government; the colonial era; the age of controversy before the revolution; every scene and every person in that great tragic action; every question which has successively engaged our politics, and every name which has figured in them,—the whole stream of our time was open, clear, and present ever to his eye.

Beyond his profession of politics, so to call it, he had been a diligent and choice reader, as his extraordinary style in part reveals; and I think the love of reading would have gone with him to a later and riper age, if to such an age it had been the will of God to preserve him. This is no place or time to appreciate this branch of his acquisitions; but there is an interest inexpressible in knowing who were any of the chosen from among the great dead in the library of such a man. Others may correct me, but I should say of that interior and narrower circle were Cicero, Virgil, Shakespeare,—whom he knew familiarly as the constitution,—Bacon, Milton, Burke, Johnson,—to whom I hope it is not pedantic nor fanciful to say, I often thought his nature presented some resemblance; the same abundance of the general propositions required for explaining a difficulty and refuting a sophism copiously and promptly occurring to him; the same kindness of heart and wealth of sensibility, under a manner, of course, more courteous and gracious, yet more sovereign; the same sufficient, yet not predominant, imagination, stooping ever to truth, and giving affluence, vivacity, and attraction to a powerful, correct, and weighty style of prose.

I cannot leave this life and character without selecting and dwelling a moment on one or two of his traits, or virtues, or felicities, a little longer. There is a collective impression made by the whole of an eminent person's life, beyond and other than, and apart from, that which the mere general biographer would afford the means of explaining. There is an influence of a great man derived from things indescribable, almost, or incapable of enumeration, or singly insufficient to account for it, but through which his spirit transpires, and his individuality goes forth on the contemporary generation. And thus, I should say, one grand tendency of his life and character was to elevate the whole tone of the public mind. He did this, indeed, not merely by example. He did it by dealing, as he thought, truly and in manly fashion with that public mind. He evinced his love of the people, not so much by honeyed phrases as by good counsels and useful service, *vera pro gratis*. He showed how he appreciated them by submitting sound arguments to their understandings, and right motives to their free will. He came before them, less with flattery than with instruction; less with a vocabulary larded with the words humanity and philanthropy, and progress and brotherhood, than with a scheme of politics, an educational, social, and governmental system, which would have made them prosperous, happy, and great.

What the greatest of the Greek historians said of Pericles, we all feel might be said of him: "He did not so much follow as lead the people, because he framed not his words to please them, like one who is gaining power by unworthy means, but was able and dared, on the strength of his high character, even to brave their anger by contradicting their will."

I should indicate it as another influence of his life, acts, and opinions, that it was, in an extraordinary degree, uniformly and liberally conservative. He saw with vision as of a prophet, that if our system of united government can be maintained till a nationality shall be generated, of due intensity and due comprehension, a glory indeed millennial, a progress without end, a triumph of humanity hitherto unseen, were ours; and, therefore, he addressed himself to maintain that united government.

Standing on the Rock of Plymouth, he bade distant generations hail, and saw them rising, "demanding life, impatient for the skies," from what then were "fresh, unbounded, magnificent wildernesses;" from the shore of the great, tranquil sea, not yet become ours. But, observe to what he welcomes them; by what he would bless them. "It is to good government." It is to "treasures of science and delights of learning." It is to the "sweets of domestic life, the immeasurable good of rational existence, the immortal hopes of Christianity, the light of everlasting truth."

It will be happy, if the wisdom and temper of his administration of our foreign affairs shall preside in the time which is at hand. Sobered, instructed by the examples and warnings of all the past, he yet gathered from the study and comparison of all the eras, that there is a silent progress of the race,—without pause, without haste, without return,—to which the counsellings of history are to be accommodated by a wise philosophy. More than, or as much as that of any of our public characters, his statesmanship was one which recognized a Europe, an old world, but yet grasped the capital idea of the American position, and deduced from it the whole fashion and color of its policy; which discerned that we are to play a high part in human affairs, but discerned, also, what part it is,—peculiar, distant, distinct, and grand as our hemisphere; an influence, not a contact,—the stage, the drama, the catastrophe, all but the audience, all our own,—and if ever he felt himself at a loss, he consulted, reverently, the genius of Washington.

In bringing these memories to a conclusion,—for I omit many things because I dare not trust myself to speak of them,—I shall not be misunderstood, or give offence, if I hope that one other trait in his public character, one doctrine, rather, of his political creed, may be remembered and be appreciated. It is one of the two fundamental precepts in which Plato, as expounded by the great master of Latin eloquence and reason and morals, comprehends the duty of those who share in the conduct of the state,—"*ut, quæcunque agunt*, TOTUM *corpus reipublicæ curent, nedum partem aliquam tuentur, reliquas deserant;*" that they comprise in their care the whole body of the Republic, nor keep one part and desert another. He gives the reason,—one reason,—of the precept, "*qui autem parti civium consulunt, partem negligunt, rem perniciosissimam in civitatem inducunt, seditionem atque discordiam.*" The patriotism which embraces less than the whole, induces sedition and discord, the last evil of the State.

How profoundly he had comprehended this truth; with what persistency, with what passion, from the first hour he became a public man to the last beat of the great heart, he cherished it; how little he accounted the good, the praise, the blame of this locality or that, in comparison of the larger good and the general and thoughtful approval of his own, and our, whole America,—she this day feels and announces. Wheresoever a drop of her blood flows in the veins of

men, this trait is felt and appreciated. The hunter beyond Superior; the fisherman on the deck of the nigh night-foundered skiff; the sailor on the uttermost
sea,—will feel, as he hears these tidings, that the protection of a sleepless, all-
embracing, parental care is withdrawn from him for a space, and that his pathway henceforward is more solitary and less safe than before.

But I cannot pursue these thoughts. Among the eulogists who have just
uttered the eloquent sorrow of England at the death of the great Duke, one has
employed an image and an idea which I venture to modify and appropriate.

"The Northmen's image of death is finer than that of other climes; no skele-
ton, but a gigantic figure that envelops men within the massive folds of its dark
garment. Webster seems so enshrouded from us, as the last of the mighty three,
themselves following a mighty series,—the greatest closing the procession. The
robe draws round him, and the era is past."

Yet, how much there is which that all-ample fold shall not hide,—the
recorded wisdom, the great example, the assured immortality.

They speak of monuments!

> "Nothing can cover his high fame but heaven;
> No pyramids set off his memories
> But the eternal substance of his greatness;
> To which I leave him."

Chapter X.

A DISCOURSE COMMEMORATIVE OF DANIEL WEBSTER.
Delivered before the Faculty, Students, and Alumni of Dartmouth College, July 27, 1853.

Choate was unsatisfied with the eulogy for Daniel Webster he delivered at Dartmouth College. His future son-in-law recalls: "I went to Mr. Choate's house about 9 o'clock that evening, and found him in his chamber reclining in bed in a half-sitting posture. On his knees rested an atlas, lying obliquely; in his left hand he held a lamp, while another was balanced on a book; in his right hand was his pen. He playfully excused himself for not shaking hands with me, saying that he feared the sharp reproaches of Mrs. C. if he should by any mischance spill the oil. On my asking him what, at that time of night, and in that singular position, he was doing, he said he was trying to get a few things together to say at Dartmouth College in relation to Mr. Webster. He had put it off so long, he said, was so hampered with work at his office, and had to give so much time to the Constitutional Convention, then in session, that he had almost made up his mind to write to the officers of the college asking to be let off. 'If I deliver it,' he added, 'it will be wholly inadequate to the theme.' He did deliver it, however, but he said to me the day before he went to Dartmouth that any friend of his would stay away, for, although so much time was given to write it in, it was one of the most hurried things he had ever done." That Choate's self-reproach over the speech was too harsh is reflected in the remark of Samuel Gilman Brown that "one would be at a loss to know where, in all the records of such eloquence, for fullness, suggestiveness, and discrimination, for richness and vitality, for beauty of language and felicity of allusion, for compactness and for amplification, to find another to equal it."

IT WOULD be a strange neglect of a beautiful and approved custom of the schools of learning, and of one of the most pious and appropriate of the offices of literature, if the college in which the intellectual life of Daniel Webster began, and to which his name imparts charm and illustration, should give no formal expression to her grief in the common sorrow; if she should not draw near, of the most sad, in the procession of the bereaved, to the tomb at the sea, nor find, in all her classic shades, one affectionate and grateful leaf to set in the garland with which they have bound the brow of her child, the mightiest departed. Others mourn and praise him by his more distant and more general titles to fame and remembrance; his supremacy of intellect, his statesmanship of so many years, his eloquence of reason and of the heart, his love of country, incorruptible, conscientious, and ruling every hour and act; that greatness combined of genius, of character, of manner, of place, of achievement, which was just now among us, and is not, and yet lives still and evermore. You come, his cherishing mother, to own a closer tie, to indulge an emotion more personal and more fond,—grief and exultation contending for mastery, as in the bosom of the desolated parent, whose tears could not hinder him from exclaiming, "I would not exchange my dead son for any living one of Christendom."

Many places in our American world have spoken his eulogy. To all places the service was befitting, for "his renown, is it not of the treasures of the whole country?" To some it belonged, with a strong local propriety, to discharge it. In the halls of Congress, where the majestic form seems ever to stand, and the deep tones to linger, the decorated scene of his larger labors and most diffusive glory; in the courts of law, to whose gladsome light he loved to return,—putting on again the robes of that profession ancient as magistracy, noble as virtue, necessary as justice,—in which he found the beginning of his honors; in Faneuil Hall, whose air breathes and burns of him; in the commercial cities, to whose pursuits his diplomacy secured a peaceful sea; in the cities of the inland, around which his capacious public affections, and wise discernment, aimed ever to develop the uncounted resources of that other, and that larger, and that newer America; in the pulpit, whose place among the higher influences which exalt a State, our guide in life, our consolation in death, he appreciated profoundly, and vindicated by weightiest argument and testimony, of whose offices it is among the fittest to mark and point the moral of the great things of the world, the excellency of dignity, and the excellency of power passing away as the pride of the wave,—passing from our eye to take on immortality,—in these places, and such as these, there seemed a reason beyond, and other, than the universal calamity, for such honors of the grave. But if so, how fit a place is this for such a service! We are among the scenes where the youth of Webster awoke first and fully to the life of the mind. We stand, as it were, at the sources—physical, social, moral, intellectual—of that exceeding greatness. Some now here saw that youth; almost it was yours, *Nilum parvum videre*. Some, one of his instructors certainly, some possibly of his classmates, or nearest college friends, some of the books he read, some of the apartments in which he studied, are here. We can almost call up from their habitation in the past, or in the fancy, the whole spiritual circle which environed that time of his life; the opinions he had embraced; the theories of mind, of religion, of morals, of philosophy, to which he had surrendered himself; the canons of taste and criticism which he had accepted; the great authors whom he loved best; the trophies which began to disturb his sleep; the facts of history which he had learned, believed, and begun to interpret; the shapes of hope and fear in which imagination began to bring before him the good and evil of the future. Still the same outward world is around you, and above you. The sweet and solemn flow of the river, gleaming through interval here and there; margins and samples of the same old woods, but thinned and retiring; the same range of green hills yonder, tolerant of culture to the top, but shaded then by primeval forests, on whose crest the last rays of sunset lingered; the summit of Ascutney; the great northern light that never sets; the constellations that walk around, and watch the pole; the same nature, undecayed, unchanging, is here. Almost, the idolatries of the old paganism grow intelligible. "*Magnorum fluminum capita veneramur*," exclaims Seneca. "*Subita et ex abrupto vasti amnis eruptio aras habet!*" We stand at the fountain of a stream; we stand, rather, at the place where a stream, sudden, and from hidden springs, bursts to light; and whence we can follow it along and down, as we might our own Connecticut, and trace its resplendent pathway to the sea; and we venerate, and would almost build altars here. If I may adopt the lofty language of one of the admirers of William Pitt, we come naturally to this place, as if we could thus recall every circumstance of splendid preparation which contributed to fit the great man for the scene of his glory. We come, as if better here than elsewhere "we could watch, fold by fold, the bracing on of his Vulcanian panoply, and observe with pleased anxiety the leading forth of that chariot which, borne on irresistible wheels, and drawn by steeds of immortal race, is to crush the necks of the mighty, and sweep away the serried strength of armies."

And, therefore, it were fitter that I should ask of you, than speak to you, concerning him. Little, indeed, anywhere can be added now to that wealth of eulogy that has been heaped upon his tomb. Before he died, even, renowned in two hemispheres, in ours he seemed to be known with a universal nearness of knowledge. He walked so long and so conspicuously before the general eye; his actions, his opinions, on all things which had been large enough to agitate the public mind for the last thirty years and more, had had importance and consequences so remarkable,—anxiously waited for, passionately canvassed, not adopted always into the particular measure, or deciding the particular vote of government or the country, yet sinking deep into the reason of the people,—a stream of influence whose fruits it is yet too soon for political philosophy to appreciate completely; an impression of his extraordinary intellectual endowments, and of their peculiar superiority in that most imposing and intelligible of all forms of manifestation, the moving of others' minds by speech,—this impression had grown so universal and fixed, and it had kindled curiosity to hear him and read him so wide and so largely indulged; his individuality altogether was so absolute and so pronounced, the force of will no less than the power of genius; the exact type and fashion of his mind, not less than its general magnitude, were so distinctly shown through his musical and transparent style; the exterior of the man, the grand mystery of brow and eye, the deep tones, the solemnity, the sovereignty, as of those who would build States, where every power and every grace did seem to set its seal, had been made, by personal observation, by description, by the exaggeration, even, of those who had felt the spell, by art, the daguerrotype and picture and statue, so familiar to the American eye, graven on the memory like the Washington of Stuart; the narrative of the mere incidents of his life had been so often told,—by some so authentically and with such skill,—and had been so literally committed to heart, that when he died there seemed to be little left but to say when and how his change came; with what dignity, with what possession of himself, with what loving thought for others, with what gratitude to God, uttered with unfaltering voice, that it was appointed to him there to die; to say how thus, leaning on the rod and staff of the promise, he took his way into the great darkness undismayed, till death should be swallowed up of life; and then to relate how they laid him in that simple grave, and turning and pausing, and joining their voices to the voices of the sea, bade him hail and farewell.

And yet, I hardly know what there is in public biography, what there is in literature, to be compared, in its kind, with the variety and beauty and adequacy of the series of discourses through which the love and grief, and deliberate and reasoning admiration of America for this great man, have been uttered. Little, indeed, there would be for me to say, if I were capable of the light ambition of proposing to omit all which others have said on this theme before,—little to add, if I sought to say anything wholly new.

I have thought,—perhaps the place where I was to speak suggested the topic,— that before we approach the ultimate and historical greatness of Mr. Webster in its two chief departments, and attempt to appreciate by what qualities of genius and character and what succession of action he attained it, there might be an interest in going back of all this, so to say, and pausing a few moments upon his youth. I include in that designation the period from his birth, on the eighteenth day of January, 1782, until 1805, when, twenty-three years of age, he declined the clerkship of his father's court, and dedicated himself irrevocably to the profession of the law and the chances of a summons to less or more of public life. These twenty-three years we shall call the youth of Webster. Its incidents are few and well known, and need not long detain us.

Until May, 1796, beyond the close of his fourteenth year, he lived at home, attending the schools of Masters Chase and Tappan, successively; at work sometimes, and sometimes at play like any boy; but finding already, as few beside him did, the stimulations and the food of intellectual life in the social library; drinking in, unawares, from the moral and physical aspects about him, the lesson and the power of contention and self-trust; and learning how much grander than the forest bending to the long storm; or the silver and cherishing Merrimack swollen to inundation, and turning, as love become madness, to ravage the subject interval; or old woods sullenly retiring before axe and fire—learning to feel how much grander than these was the coming in of civilization as there he saw it, courage, labor, patience, plain living, heroical acting, high thinking, beautiful feeling, the fear of God, love of country and neighborhood and family, and all that form of human life of which his father and mother and sisters and brother were the endeared exemplification. In the arms of that circle, on parent knees, or later, in intervals of work or play, the future American Statesman acquired the idea of country, and became conscious of a national tie and a national life. There and then, something, glimpses, a little of the romance, the sweet and bitter memories of a soldier and borderer of the old colonial time and war, opened to the large dark eyes of the child; memories of French and Indians stealing up to the very place where the story was telling; of men shot down at the plough, within sight of the old log house; of the massacre at Fort William Henry; of Stark, of Howe, of Wolfe falling in the arms of victory; and then of the next age, its grander scenes and higher names,—of the father's part at Bennington and White Plains; of Lafayette and Washington; and then of the Constitution, just adopted, and the first President, just inaugurated, with services of public thanksgiving to Almighty God, and the Union just sprung into life, all radiant as morning, harbinger and promise of a brighter day. You have heard how in that season he bought and first read the Constitution on the cotton handkerchief. A small cannon, I think his biographers say, was the ominous plaything of Napoleon's childhood. But this incident reminds us rather of the youthful Luther, astonished and kindling over the first Latin Bible he ever saw,—or the still younger Pascal, permitted to look into the Euclid, to whose sublimities an irresistible nature had secretly attracted him. Long before his fourteenth year, the mother first, and then the father, and the teachers and the schools and the little neighborhood, had discovered an extraordinary hope in the boy; a purpose, a dream, not yet confessed, of giving him an education began to be cherished; and in May, 1796, at the age of a little more than fourteen, he was sent to Exeter. I have myself heard a gentleman, long a leader of the Essex bar and eminent in public life, now no more, who was then a pupil at the school, describe his large frame, superb face, immature manners, and rustic dress, surmounted with a student's gown, when first he came; and say, too, how soon and universally his capacity was owned. Who does not wish that the glorious Buckminster could have foreseen and witnessed the whole greatness, but certainly the renown of eloquence, which was to come to the young stranger, whom, choking, speechless, the great fountain of feelings sealed as yet, he tried in vain to encourage to declaim before the unconscious, bright tribes of the school? The influences of Exeter on him were excellent, but his stay was brief. In the winter of 1796 he was at home again; and in February, 1797, he was placed under the private tuition, and in the family of Rev. Mr. Wood, of Boscawen. It was on the way with his father, to the house of Mr. Wood, that he first heard, with astonishment, that the parental love and good sense had resolved on the sacrifice of giving him an education at college. "I remember," he writes, "the very hill we were ascending, through deep snows, in a New England sleigh, when my father made his purpose known to me. I could not speak. How could he, I thought, with so large a family, and in such narrow circumstances, think of incurring so great an expense for me? A warm glow ran all over me, and I laid my head on my father's shoulder and wept." That speechlessness, that glow, those tears reveal to us what his memory and consciousness could hardly do to him, that already, somewhere, at some hour of day or evening or night, as he read some page, or heard some narrative, or saw some happier schoolfellow set off from Exeter to begin his college life, the love of intellectual enjoyment, the ambition of intellectual supremacy, had taken hold of him; that, when or how he knew not, but before he was aware of it, the hope of obtaining a liberal education and leading a professional life had come to be his last thought before he slept, his first when he awoke, and to shape his dreams. Behold in them, too, his whole future. That day, that hour, that very moment, from the deep snows of that slow hill he set out on the long ascent that bore him—"no step backward"—to the high places of the world! He remained under the tuition of Mr. Wood until August, 1796, and then entered this college, where he was, at the end of the full term of four years, graduated in 1801. Of that college life you can tell me more than I can tell you. It is the universal evidence that it was distinguished by exemplary demeanor, by reverence for religion, respect for instructors, and obser-

vance of law. We hear from all sources, too, that it was distinguished by assiduous and various studies. With the exception of one or two branches, for which
his imperfect preparation had failed to excite a taste, he is reported to have
addressed himself to the prescribed tasks, and to have availed himself of the
whole body of means of liberal culture appointed by the government, with
decorum and conscientiousness and zeal. We hear more than this. The whole
course of traditions concerning his college life is full to prove two facts. The first
is, that his reading—general and various far beyond the requirements of the Faculty, or the average capacity of that stage of the literary life—was not solid and
useful merely—which is vague commendation—but it was such as predicted
and educated the future statesman. In English literature,—its finer parts, its
poetry and tasteful reading, I mean,—he had read much rather than many
things; but he had read somewhat. That a young man of his emotional nature,—
full of eloquent feeling, the germs of a fine taste, the ear for the music of words,
the eye for all beauty and all sublimity, already in extraordinary measure his,—
already practising the art of composition, speech, and criticism,—should have
recreated himself—as we know he did—with Shakspeare and Pope and Addison; with the great romance of Defoe; with the more recent biographies of
Johnson, and his grand imitations of Juvenal; with the sweet and refined simplicity and abstracted observation of Goldsmith, mingled with sketches of
homefelt delight; with the "Elegy" of Gray, whose solemn touches soothed the
thoughts or tested the consciousness of the last hour; with the vigorous originality of the then recent Cowper, whom he quoted when he came home, as it
proved, to die,—this we should have expected. But I have heard, and believe,
that it was to another institution more austere and characteristic, that his own
mind was irresistibly and instinctively even then attracted. The conduct of what
Locke calls the human understanding; the limits of human knowledge; the
means of coming to the knowledge of the different classes of truth; the laws of
thought; the science of proofs which is logic; the science of morals; the facts of
history; the spirit of laws; the conduct and aims of reasonings in politics,—these
were the strong meat that announced and began to train the great political
thinker and reasoner of a later day.

I have heard that he might oftener be found in some solitary seat or walk, with
a volume of Gordon's or Ramsay's Revolution, or of the "Federalist," or of
Hume's "History of England," or of his "Essays," or of Grotius, or Puffendorf, or
Cicero, or Montesquieu, or Locke, or Burke, than with Virgil, or Shakspeare,
or the "Spectator." Of the history of opinions, in the department of philosophy, he was already a curious student. The oration he delivered before the

United Fraternity, when he was graduated, treated that topic of opinion, under some aspects,—as I recollect from once reading the manuscript,—with copiousness, judgment, and enthusiasm; and some of his ridicule of the Berkleian theory of the non-existence of matter, I well remember, anticipated the sarcasm of a later day on a currency all metallic, and on nullification as a strictly constitutional remedy.

The other fact, as well established by all we can gather of his life in college is, that the faculty, so transcendent afterwards, of moving the minds of men by speech, was already developed and effective in a remarkable degree. Always there is a best writer or speaker or two in college; but this stereotyped designation seems wholly inadequate to convey the impression he made in his time. Many, now alive, have said that some of his performances, having regard to his youth, his objects, his topics, his audience—one on the celebration of Independence, one a eulogy on a student much beloved—produced an instant effect, and left a recollection to which nothing else could be compared; which could be felt and admitted only, not explained; but which now they know were the first sweet tones of inexplicable but delightful influence of that voice, unconfirmed as yet, and unassured, whose more consummate expression charmed and suspended the soul of a nation. To read these essays now, disappoints you somewhat. As Quintilian says of Hortensius, *Apparet placuisse aliquid eo dicente quod legentes non invenimus.* Some spell there was in the spoken word which the reader misses. To find the secret of that spell, you must recall the youth of Webster. Beloved fondly, and appreciated by that circle as much as by any audience, larger, more exacting, more various, and more fit, which afterwards he found anywhere; known to be manly, just, pure, generous, affectionate; known and felt by his strong will, his high aims, his commanding character, his uncommon and difficult studies; he had every heart's warmest good wish with him when he rose; and then, when, unchecked by any very severe theory of taste, unoppressed by any dread of saying something incompatible with his place and fame, or unequal to himself, he just unlocked the deep spring of that eloquent feeling, which, in connection with his power of mere intellect, was such a stupendous psychological mystery, and gave heart and soul, not to the conduct of an argument, or the investigation and display of a truth of the reason, but to a fervid, beautiful, and prolonged emotion, to grief, to eulogy, to the patriotism of scholars—why need we doubt or wonder, as they looked on that presiding brow, the eye large, sad, unworldly, incapable to be fathomed, the lip and chin, whose firmness as of chiselled, perfect marble, profoundest sensibility alone caused ever to tremble, why wonder at the traditions of the charm which they owned, and the fame which they even then predicted?

His college life closed in 1801. For the statement that he had thought of selecting the profession of theology, the surviving members of his family, his son and his brother-in- law, assure me that there is no foundation. Certainly, he began at once the study of the law, and interrupted only by the necessity of teaching an academy a few months, with which he united the recreation of recording deeds, he prosecuted it at Salisbury in the office of Mr. Thompson, and at Boston in the office of Mr. Gore, until March, 1805, when, resisting the sharp temptation of a clerkship, and an annual salary of fifteen hundred dollars, he was admitted to the bar.

And so he has put on the robe of manhood, and has come to do the work of life. Of his youth there is no need to say more. It had been pure, happy, strenuous; in many things privileged. The influence of home, of his father, and the excellent mother, and that noble brother, whom he loved so dearly, and mourned with such sorrow—these influences on his heart, principles, will, aims, were elevated and strong. At an early age, comparatively, the then great distinction of liberal education was his. His college life was brilliant and without a stain; and in moving his admission to the bar, Mr. Gore presented him as one of extraordinary promise.

> "With prospects bright, upon the world he came,—
> Pure love of virtue, strong desire of fame;
> Men watched the way his lofty mind would take,
> And all foretold the progress he would make."

And yet, if on some day, as that season was drawing to its close, it had been foretold to him, that before his life, prolonged to little more than threescore years and ten, should end, he should see that country, in which he was coming to act his part, expanded across a continent; the thirteen States of 1801 multiplied to thirty-one; the territory of the North- west and the great valley below sown full of those stars of empire; the Mississippi forded, and the Sabine and Rio Grande, and the Neuces; the ponderous gates of the Rocky Mountains opened to shut no more; the great tranquil sea become our sea; her area seven times larger, her people five times more in number; that through all experiences of trial, the madness of party, the injustice of foreign powers, the vast enlargement of her borders, the antagonisms of interior interest and feeling,—the spirit of nationality would grow stronger still and more plastic; that the tide of American feeling would run ever fuller; that her agriculture would grow more scientific; her arts more various and instructed, and better rewarded; her commerce winged to a wider and still wider flight; that the part she would play in human affairs would grow nobler ever, and more recognized; that in this vast growth of national greatness time would be found for the higher necessities of the soul; that her popular and her higher education would go on advancing; that her charities and all her enterprises of philanthropy would go on enlarging; that her age of lettered glory should find its auspicious dawn—and then it had been also foretold him that even so, with her growth and strength, should his fame grow and be established and cherished, there where she should garner up her heart; that by long gradations of service and labor he should rise to be, before he should taste of death, of the peerless among her great ones; that he should win the double honor, and wear the double wreath of professional and public supremacy; that he should become her wisest to counsel and her most eloquent to persuade; that he should come to be called the Defender of the Constitution and the preserver of honorable peace; that the "austere glory of suffering" to save the Union should be his; that his death, at the summit of greatness, on the verge of a ripe and venerable age, should be distinguished, less by the flags at half- mast on ocean and lake, less by the minute-gun, less by the public procession and the appointed eulogy, than by sudden paleness overspreading all faces, by gushing tears, by sorrow, thoughtful, boding, silent, the sense of desolateness, as if renown and grace were dead,—as if the hunter's path, and the sailor's, in the great solitude of wilderness or sea, henceforward were more lonely and less safe than before—had this prediction been whispered, how calmly had that perfect sobriety of mind put it all aside as a pernicious or idle dream! Yet, in the fulfilment of that prediction is told the remaining story of his life.

It does not come within the plan which I have marked out for this discourse to repeat the incidents of that subsequent history. The more conspicuous are known to you and the whole American world. Minuter details the time does not permit, nor the occasion require. Some quite general views of what he became and achieved; some attempt to appreciate that intellectual power, and force of will, and elaborate culture, and that power of eloquence, so splendid and remarkable, by which he wrought his work; some tribute to the endearing and noble parts of his character; and some attempt to vindicate the political morality by which his public life was guided, even to its last great act, are all that I propose, and much more than I can hope worthily to accomplish.

In coming, then, to consider what he became and achieved, I have always thought it was not easy to lay too much stress, in the first place, on that realization of what might have been regarded incompatible forms of superiority, and that exemplification of what might have been regarded incompatible gifts or acquirements—"rare in their separate excellence, wonderful in their special combination"—which meet us in him everywhere. Remark, first, that eminence—rare, if not unprecedented—of the first rate, in the two substantially distinct and unkindred professions,—that of the law, and that of public life. In surveying that ultimate and finished greatness in which he stands before you in his full stature and at his best, this double and blended eminence is the first thing that fixes the eye, and the last. When he died he was first of American lawyers, and first of American statesmen. In both characters he continued—discharging the foremost part in each—down to the falling of the awful curtain. Both characters he kept distinct,—the habits of mind, the forms of reasoning, the nature of the proofs, the style of eloquence. Neither hurt nor changed the other. How much his understanding was "quickened and invigorated" by the law, I have often heard him acknowledge and explain. But how, in spite of the law, was that mind, by other felicity, and other culture, "opened and liberalized" also! How few of what are called the bad intellectual habits of the bar he carried into the duties of statesmanship! His interpretations of the constitution and of treaties; his expositions of public law—how little do you find in them, where, if anywhere, you would expect it, of the mere ingenuity, the moving of "vermiculate questions," the word-catching, the scholastic subtlety which, in the phrase of his memorable quotation,

> "Can sever and divide
> A hair 'twixt north and north-west side,"—

ascribed by satire to the profession; and how much of its truer function, and nobler power of calling, history, language, the moral sentiments, reason, common sense, the high spirit of magnanimous nationality, to the search of truth! How little do we find in his politics of another bad habit of the profession, the worst "idol of the cave," a morbid, unreasoning, and regretful passion for the past, that bends and weeps over the stream, running irreversibly, because it will not return, and will not pause, and gives back to vanity every hour a changed and less beautiful face! We ascribe to him certainly a sober and conservative habit of mind, and such he had. Such a habit the study and practice of the law doubtless does not impair. But his was my Lord Bacon's conservatism. He held with him, "that antiquity deserveth this reverence, that men should make a stand thereupon, and discover what is the best way; but when the discovery is well taken, then to make progression." He would keep the Union according to the Constitution, not as a relic, a memorial, a tradition,—not for what it has done, though that kindled his gratitude and excited his admiration, but for what it is now and hereafter to do, when adapted by a wise practical philosophy to a wider and higher area, to larger numbers, to severer and more glorious probation. Who better than he has grasped and displayed the advancing tendencies and enlarging duties of America? Who has caught—whose eloquence, whose genius, whose counsels, have caught more adequately the genuine inspiration of our destiny? Who has better expounded by what moral and prudential policy, by what improved culture of heart and reason, by what true worship of God, by what good faith to all other nations, the dangers of that destiny may be disarmed, and its large promise laid hold on?

And while the lawyer did not hurt the statesman, the statesman did not hurt the lawyer. More; the statesman did not modify, did not unrobe, did not tinge, the lawyer. It would not be to him that the epigram could have application, where the old Latin satirist makes the client complain that his lawsuit is concerning *tres capellæ*—three kids; and that his advocate with large disdain of them is haranguing with loud voice and both hands, about the slaughters of Cannæ, the war of Mithridates, the perjuries of Hannibal. I could never detect that in his discussions of law he did not just as much recognize authority, just as anxiously seek for adjudications old and new in his favor, just as closely sift them and collate them, that he might bring them to his side if he could, or leave them ambiguous and harmless if he could not; that he did not just as rigorously observe the peculiar mode which that science employs in passing from the known to the unknown, the peculiar logic of the law, as if he had never investigated any other than legal truth by any other organon than legal logic in his life. Peculiarities of legal reasoning he certainly had, belonging to the peculiar structure and vast power of his mind; more original thought, more discourse of principles, less of that mere subtlety of analysis which is not restrained by good sense, and the higher power of duly tempering and combining one truth in a practical science with other truths, from absurdity or mischief; but still it was all strict and exact legal reasoning. The long habit of employing the more popular methods, the probable and plausible conjectures, the approximations, the compromises of deliberative discussion, did not seem to have left the least trace on his vocabulary, or his reasonings, or his demeanor. No doubt, as a part of his whole culture, it helped to give enlargement and general power and elevation of mind; but the sweet stream passed under the bitter sea, the bitter sea pressed on the sweet stream, and each flowed unmingled, unchanged in taste or color.

I have said that this double eminence is rare, if not unprecedented. We do no justice to Mr. Webster, if we do not keep this ever in mind. How many exemplifications of it do you find in British public life? The Earl of Chatham, Burke, Fox, Sheridan, Windham, Pitt, Grattan, Canning, Peel—were they also, or any one, the acknowledged leader in Westminster Hall or on the circuit? And, on the other hand, would you say that the mere parliamentary career of Mansfield, or Thurlow, or Dunning, or Erskine, or Camden, or Curran, would compare in duration, constancy, variety of effort, the range of topics discussed, the fulness, extent, and affluence of the discussion, the influence exerted, the space filled, the senatorial character completely realized—with his? In our own public life it is easier to find a parallel. Great names crowd on us in each department; greater, or more loved, or more venerable, no annals can show. But how few even here have gathered the double wreath and the blended fame!

And now, having observed the fact of this combination of quality and excellence scarcely compatible, inspect for a moment each by itself.

The professional life of Mr. Webster began in the spring of 1805. It may not be said to have ended until he died; but I do not know that it happened to him to appear in court, for the trial of a cause, after his argument of the Goodyear patent for improvements in the preparation of India-rubber, in Trenton, in March, 1852.

There I saw, and last heard him. The thirty-four years which had elapsed since, a member of this College, at home for health, I first saw and heard him in the Supreme Court of Massachusetts, in the county of Essex, defending Jackman, accused of the robbery of Goodrich, had in almost all things changed him. The raven hair, the vigorous, full frame and firm tread, the eminent but severe beauty of the countenance, not yet sealed with the middle age of man, the exuberant demonstration of all sorts of power, which so marked him at first—for these, as once they were, I explored in vain. Yet how far higher was the interest that attended him now: his sixty-nine years robed, as it were, with honor and with love, with associations of great service done to the state, and of great fame gathered and safe; and then the perfect mastery of the cause in its legal and scientific principles, and in all its facts; the admirable clearness and order in which his propositions were advanced successively; the power, the occasional high ethical tone, the appropriate eloquence, by which they were made probable and persuasive to the judicial reason—these announced the leader of the American bar, with every faculty and every accomplishment, by which he had won that proud title, wholly unimpaired; the eye not dim nor the natural force abated.

I cannot here and now trace, with any minuteness, the course of Mr. Webster at the bar during these forty-eight years from the opening of his office in Boscawen; nor convey any impression whatever of the aggregate of labor which that course imposed; or of the intellectual power which it exacted; nor indicate the stages of his rise; nor define the time when his position at the summit of the profession may be said to have become completely vindicated. You know, in general, that he began the practice of the law in New Hampshire in the spring of 1805; that he prosecuted it, here, in its severest school, with great diligence, and brilliant success, among competitors of larger experience and of consummate ability, until 1816: that he then removed to Massachusetts, and that there, in the courts of that State, and of other States, and in those of the general government, and especially in the Supreme Court sitting at Washington, he pursued it as the calling by which he was to earn his daily bread, until he died. You know, indeed, that he did not pursue it exactly as one pursues it who confines himself to an office; and seeks to do the current and miscellaneous business of a single bar. His professional employment, as I have often heard him say, was very much the preparation of opinions on important questions, presented from every part of the country; and the trial of causes. This kind of professional life allowed him seasonable vacations; and it accommodated itself somewhat to the exactions of his other and public life. But it was all one long and continued practice of the law; the professional character was never put off; nor the professional robe long unworn to the last.

You know, too, his character as a jurist. This topic has been recently and separately treated, with great ability, by one in a high degree competent to the task,—the late learned Chief Justice of New Hampshire, now Professor of Law at Cambridge; and it needs no additional illustration from me. Yet, let me say, that herein, also, the first thing which strikes you is the union of diverse, and, as I have said, what might have been regarded incompatible excellences. I shall submit it to the judgment of the universal American bar, if a carefully prepared opinion of Mr. Webster, on any question of law whatever in the whole range of our jurisprudence, would not be accepted everywhere as of the most commanding authority, and as the highest evidence of legal truth? I submit it to that same judgment, if for many years before his death, they would not have rather chosen to intrust the maintenance and enforcement of any important proposition of law whatever, before any legal tribunal of character whatever, to his best exertion of his faculties, than to any other ability which the whole wealth of the profession could supply?

And this alone completes the description of a lawyer and a forensic orator of the first rate; but it does not complete the description of his professional character. By the side of all this, so to speak, there was that whole class of qualities which made him for any description of trial by jury whatever, criminal or civil, by even a more universal assent, foremost. For that form of trial no faculty was unused or needless; but you were most struck there to see the unrivalled legal reason put off, as it were, and reappear in the form of a robust common sense and eloquent feeling, applying itself to an exciting subject of business; to see the knowledge of men and life by which the falsehood and veracity of witnesses, the probabilities and improbabilities of transactions as sworn to, were discerned in a moment; the direct, plain, forcible speech; the consummate narrative, a department which he had particularly cultivated, and in which no man ever excelled him; the easy and perfect analysis by which he conveyed his side of the cause to the mind of the jury; the occasional gush of strong feeling, indignation, or pity; the masterly, yet natural way, in which all the moral emotions of which his cause was susceptible were called to use, the occasional sovereignty of dictation to which his convictions seemed spontaneously to rise. His efforts in trials by jury compose a more traditional and evanescent part of his professional reputation than his arguments on questions of law; but I almost think they were his mightiest professional displays, or displays of any kind, after all.

One such I stood in a relation to witness with a comparatively easy curiosity, and yet with intimate and professional knowledge of all the embarrassments of the case. It was the trial of John Francis Knapp, charged with being present, aiding, and abetting in the murder of Joseph White, in which Mr. Webster conducted the prosecution for the Commonwealth,—in the same year with his reply to Mr. Hayne, in the Senate and a few months later,—and when I bring to mind the incidents of that trial; the necessity of proving that the prisoner was near enough to the chamber in which the murder was being committed by another hand to aid in the act, and was there with the intention to do so, and thus in point of law did aid in it—because mere accessorial guilt was not enough to convict him; the difficulty of proving this—because the nearest point to which the evidence could trace him was still so distant as to warrant a pretty formidable doubt whether mere curiosity had not carried him thither; and whether he could in any useful or even conceivable manner have coöperated with the actual murderer, if he had intended to do so; and because the only mode of rendering it probable that he was there with a purpose of guilt was by showing that he was one of the parties to a conspiracy of murder, whose very existence, actors, and objects, had to be made out by the collation of the widest possible range of circumstances—some of them pretty loose; and even if he was a conspirator, it did not quite necessarily follow that any active participation was assigned to him for his part, any more than to his brother, who, confessedly took no such part—the great number of witnesses to be examined and cross-examined, a duty devolving wholly on him; the quick and sound judgment demanded and supplied to determine what to use and what to reject of a mass of rather unmanageable materials; the points in the law of evidence to be argued—in the course of which he made an appeal to the Bench on the complete impunity which the rejection of the prisoner's confession would give to the murder, in a style of dignity and energy, I should rather say of grandeur, which I never heard him equal before or after; the high ability and fidelity with which every part of the defence was conducted; and the great final summing up to which he brought, and in which he needed, the utmost exertion of every faculty he possessed to persuade the jury that the obligation of that duty the sense of which, he said, "pursued us ever: it is omnipresent like the Deity: if we take the wings of the morning and dwell in the uttermost parts of the sea, duty performed or duty violated is still with us for our happiness or misery"—to persuade them that this obligation demanded that on his proofs they should convict the prisoner: to which he brought first the profound belief of his guilt, without which he could not have prosecuted him; then skill consummate in inspiring them with a desire or a willingness to be instrumental in detecting that guilt; and to lean on him in the effort to detect it; then every resource of professional ability to break the force of the propositions of the defence, and to establish the truth of his own: inferring a conspiracy to which the prisoner was a party, from circumstances acutely ridiculed by the able counsel opposing him as "Stuff"—but woven by him into strong and uniform tissue; and then bridging over from the conspiracy to the not very necessary inference that the particular conspirator on trial was at his post, in execution of it, to aid and abet—the picture of the murder with which he begun—not for rhetorical display, but to inspire solemnity and horror, and a desire to detect and punish for justice and for security; the sublime exhortation to duty with which he closed—resting on the universality, and authoritativeness, and eternity of its obligation—which left in every juror's mind the impression that it was the duty of convicting in this particular case the sense of which would be with him in the hour of death, and in the judgment, and forever—with these recollections of that trial I cannot help thinking it a more difficult and higher effort of mind than that more famous "Oration for the Crown."

It would be not unpleasing nor inappropriate to pause, and recall the names of some of that succession of competitors by whose rivalry the several stages of his professional life were honored and exercised; and of some of the eminent judicial persons who presided over that various and high contention. Time scarcely permits this; but in the briefest notice I must take occasion to say that perhaps the most important influence—certainly the most important early influence—on his professional traits and fortunes was that exerted by the great general abilities, impressive character, and legal genius of Mr. Mason. Who he was you all know. How much the jurisprudence of New Hampshire owes to him; what deep traces he left on it; how much he did to promote the culture, and to preserve the integrity, of the old common law; to adapt it to your wants, and your institutions; and to construct a system of practice by which it was administered with extraordinary energy and effectiveness for the discovery of truth, and the enforcement of right; you of the legal profession of this State will ever be proud to acknowledge. Another forum in a neighboring commonwealth, witnessed and profited by the last labors, and enlarged studies of the consummate lawyer and practiser; and at an earlier day the Senate, the country, had recognized his vast practical wisdom and sagacity, the fruit of the highest intellectual endowments, matured thought, and profound observation; his fidelity to the obligations of that party connection to which he was attached; his fidelity through all his life, still more conspicuous and still more admirable, to the higher obligations of a considerate and enlarged patriotism. He had been more than fourteen years at the bar, when Mr. Webster came to it; he discerned instantly what manner of man his youthful competitor was; he admitted him to his intimate friendship; and paid him the unequivocal compliment, and did him the real kindness, of compelling him to the utmost exertion of his diligence and capacity by calling out against him all his own. "The proprieties of this occasion"—these are Mr. Webster's words in presenting the resolutions of the Suffolk Bar upon Mr. Mason's death—"compel me, with whatever reluctance, to refrain from the indulgence of the personal feelings which arise in my heart upon the death of one with whom I have cultivated a sincere, affectionate, and unbroken friendship, from the day when I commenced my own professional career to the closing hour of his life. I will not say of the advantages which I have derived from his intercourse and conversation all that Mr. Fox said of Edmund Burke; but I am bound to say, that of my own professional discipline and attainments, whatever they may be, I owe much to that close attention to the discharge of my duties which I was compelled to pay for nine successive years, from day to day, by Mr. Mason's efforts and arguments at the same bar. I must have been unintelligent indeed, not to have learned something from the constant displays of that power which I had so much occasion to see and feel."

I reckon next to his, for the earlier time of his life, the influence of the learned and accomplished Smith; and next to these—some may believe greater—is that of Mr. Justice Story. That extraordinary person had been admitted to the bar in Essex in Massachusetts in 1801; and he was engaged in many trials in the county of Rockingham in this State before Mr. Webster had assumed his own established position. Their political opinions differed; but such was his affluence of knowledge already; such his stimulant enthusiasm; he was burning with so incredible a passion for learning and fame, that the influence on the still young Webster was instant; and it was great and permanent. It was reciprocal too; and an intimacy began that attended the whole course of honor through which each, in his several sphere, ascended. Parsons he saw, also, but rarely; and Dexter oftener, and with more nearness of observation, while yet laying the foundation of his own mind and character; and he shared largely in the universal admiration of that time, and of this, of their attainments and genius and diverse greatness.

As he came to the grander practice of the national bar, other competition was to be encountered. Other names begin to solicit us; other contention; higher prizes. It would be quite within the proprieties of this discourse to remember the parties, at least, to some of the higher causes, by which his ultimate professional fame was built up; even if I could not hope to convey any impression of the novelty and difficulty of the questions which they involved, or of the positive addition which the argument, and judgment, made to the treasures of our constitutional and general jurisprudence. But there is only one of which I have time to say anything, and that is the case which established the inviolability of the charter of Dartmouth College by the Legislature of the State of New Hampshire. Acts of the Legislature, passed in the year 1816, had invaded its charter. A suit was brought to test their validity. It was tried in the Supreme Court of the State; a judgment was given against the College, and this was appealed to the Supreme Federal Court by writ of error. Upon solemn argument the charter was decided to be a contract whose obligation a State may not impair; the acts were decided to be invalid as an attempt to impair it, and you hold your charter under that decision to-day. How much Mr. Webster contributed to that result, how much the effort advanced his own distinction at the bar, you all know. Well, as if of yesterday, I remember how it was written home from Washington, that "Mr. Webster closed a legal argument of great power by a peroration which charmed and melted his audience." Often since, I have heard vague accounts, not much more satisfactory, of the speech and the scene. I was aware that the report of his argument, as it was published, did not contain the actual peroration, and I supposed it lost forever. By the great kindness of a learned and excellent person, Dr. Chauncy A. Goodrich, a professor in Yale College, with whom I had not the honor of acquaintance, although his virtues, accomplishments, and most useful life, were well known to me, I can read to you the words whose power, when those lips spoke them, so many owned, although they could not repeat them. As those lips spoke them, we shall hear them nevermore, but no utterance can extinguish their simple, sweet, and perfect beauty. Let me first bring the general scene before you, and then you will hear the rest in Mr. Goodrich's description. It was in 1813, in the thirty-seventh year of Mr. Webster's age. It was addressed to a tribunal presided over by Marshall, assisted by Washington, Livingston, Johnson, Story, Todd, and Duvall,—a tribunal unsurpassed on earth in all that gives illustration to a bench of law, and sustained and venerated by a noble bar. He had called to his aid the ripe and beautiful culture of Hopkinson; and of his opponents was William Wirt, then and ever of the leaders of the bar, who, with faculties and accomplishments fitting him to adorn and guide public life, abounding in deep professional learning, and in the most various and elegant acquisitions,—a ripe and splendid orator, made so by genius and the most assiduous culture,—consecrated all to the service of the law. It was before that tribunal, and in presence of an audience select and critical, among whom, it is to be borne in mind, were some graduates of the college, who were attending to assist against her, that he opened the cause. I gladly proceed in the words of Mr. Goodrich.

"Before going to Washington, which I did chiefly for the sake of hearing Mr. Webster, I was told that, in arguing the case at Exeter, New Hampshire, he had left the whole courtroom in tears at the conclusion of his speech. This, I confess, struck me unpleasantly,—any attempt at pathos on a purely legal question like this seemed hardly in good taste. On my way to Washington, I made the acquaintance of Mr. Webster. We were together for several days in Philadelphia, at the house of a common friend; and as the College question was one of deep interest to literary men, we conversed often and largely on the subject. As he dwelt upon the leading points of the case, in terms so calm, simple, and precise, I said to myself more than once, in reference to the story I had heard, 'Whatever may have seemed appropriate in defending the College at *home,* and on her own ground, there will be no appeal to the feelings of Judge Marshall and his associates at Washington.' The Supreme Court of the United States held its session, that winter, in a mean apartment of moderate size—the Capitol not having been built after its destruction in 1814. The audience, when the case came on, was therefore small, consisting chiefly of legal men, the *élite* of the profession throughout the country. Mr. Webster entered upon his argument in the calm tone of easy and dignified conversation. His matter was so completely at his command that he scarcely looked at his brief, but went on for more than four hours with a statement so luminous, and a chain of reasoning so easy to be understood, and yet approaching so nearly to absolute demonstration, that he seemed to carry with him every man of his audience without the slightest effort or weariness on either side. It was hardly *eloquence,* in the strict sense of the term; it was pure reason. Now and then, for a sentence or two, his eye flashed and his voice swelled into a bolder note, as he uttered some emphatic thought; but he instantly fell back into the tone of earnest conversation, which ran throughout the great body of his speech. A single circumstance will show you the clearness and absorbing power of his argument."

"I observed that Judge Story, at the opening of the case, had prepared himself, pen in hand, as if to take copious minutes. Hour after hour I saw him fixed in the same attitude, but, so far as I could perceive, with not a note on his paper. The argument closed, and *I could not discover that he had taken a single note.* Others around me remarked the same thing; and it was among the *on dits* of Washington, that a friend spoke to him of the fact with surprise, when the Judge remarked, 'Everything was so clear, and so easy to remember, that not a note seemed necessary, and, in fact, I thought little or nothing about my notes.' "

"The argument ended. Mr. Webster stood for some moments silent before the Court, while every eye was fixed intently upon him. At length, addressing the Chief Justice, Marshall, he proceeded thus:—

" '*This, Sir, is my case!* It is the case, not merely of that humble institution, it is the case of every College in our land. It is more. It is the case of every Eleemosynary Institution throughout our country,—of all those great charities founded by the piety of our ancestors to alleviate human misery, and scatter blessings along the pathway of life. It is more! It is, in some sense, the case of every man among us who has property of which he may be stripped; for the question is simply this: Shall our State Legislatures be allowed to take that which is not their own, to turn it from its original use, and apply it to such ends or purposes as they, in their discretion, shall see fit!' "

" 'Sir, you may destroy this little Institution; it is weak; it is in your hands! I know it is one of the lesser lights in the literary horizon of our country. You may put it out. But if you do so, you must carry through your work! You must extinguish, one after another, all those great lights of science which, for more than a century, have thrown their radiance over our land!' "

" 'It is, Sir, as I have said, a small College. And yet, *there are those who love it*—.' "

"Here the feelings which he had thus far succeeded in keeping down, broke forth. His lips quivered; his firm cheeks trembled with emotion; his eyes were filled with tears, his voice choked, and he seemed struggling to the utmost simply to gain that mastery over himself which might save him from an unmanly burst of feeling. I will not attempt to give you the few broken words of tenderness in which he went on to speak of his attachment to the College. The whole seemed to be mingled throughout with the recollections of father, mother, brother, and all the trials and privations through which he had made his way into life. Every one saw that it was wholly unpremeditated, a pressure on his heart, which sought relief in words and tears."

"The court-room during these two or three minutes presented an extraordinary spectacle. Chief Justice Marshall, with his tall and gaunt figure bent over as if to catch the slightest whisper, the deep furrows of his cheek expanded with emotion, and eyes suffused with tears; Mr. Justice Washington at his side,— with his small and emaciated frame, and countenance more like marble than I ever saw on any other human being,—leaning forward with an eager, troubled look; and the remainder of the Court, at the two extremities, pressing, as it were, toward a single point, while the audience below were wrapping themselves round in closer folds beneath the bench to catch each look, and every movement of the speaker's face. If a painter could give us the scene on canvas,— those forms and countenances, and Daniel Webster as he then stood in the midst, it would be one of the most touching pictures in the history of eloquence. One thing it taught me, that the *pathetic* depends not merely on the words uttered, but still more on the estimate we put upon him who utters them. There was not one among the strong-minded men of that assembly who could think it unmanly to weep, when he saw standing before him the man who had made such an argument, melted into the tenderness of a child."

"Mr. Webster had now recovered his composure, and fixing his keen eye on the Chief Justice, said, in that deep tone with which he sometimes thrilled the heart of an audience,—

" 'Sir, I know not how others may feel,' (glancing at the opponents of the College before him,) 'but, for myself, when I see my Alma Mater surrounded, like Cæsar in the senate-house, by those who are reiterating stab upon stab, I would not, for this right hand, have her turn to me, and say, *Et tu quoque mi fili! And thou too, my son!*' "

"He sat down. There was a deathlike stillness throughout the room for some moments; every one seemed to be slowly recovering himself, and coming gradually back to his ordinary range of thought and feeling."

It was while Mr. Webster was ascending through the long gradations of the legal profession to its highest rank, that by a parallel series of display on a stage, and in parts totally distinct, by other studies, thoughts, and actions, he rose also to be at his death the first of American statesmen. The last of the mighty rivals was dead before, and he stood alone. Give this aspect also of his greatness a passing glance. His public life began in May 1813, in the House of Representatives in Congress, to which this State had elected him. It ended when he died. If you except the interval between his removal from New Hampshire and his election in Massachusetts, it was a public life of forty years. By what political morality, and by what enlarged patriotism, embracing the whole country, that life was guided, I shall consider hereafter. Let me now fix your attention rather on the magnitude and variety and actual value of the service. Consider that from the day he went upon the Committee of Foreign Relations, in 1818, in time of war, and more and more, the longer he lived and the higher he rose, he was a man whose great talents and devotion to public duty placed and kept him in a position of associated or sole command; command in the political connection to which he belonged, command in opposition, command in power; and appreciate the responsibilities which that implies, what care, what prudence, what mastery of the whole ground,—exacting for the conduct of a party, as Gibbon says of Fox, abilities and civil discretion equal to the conduct of an empire. Consider the work he did in that life of forty years—the range of subjects investigated and discussed: composing the whole theory and practice of our organic and administrative politics, foreign and domestic: the vast body of instructive thought he produced and put in possession of the country; how much he achieved in congress as well as at the bar, to fix the true interpretation, as well as to impress the transcendent value of the Constitution itself, as much altogether as any jurist or statesman since its adoption; how much to establish in the general mind the great doctrine that the government of the United States is a government proper, established by the people of the States, not a compact between sovereign communities,—that within its limits it is supreme, and that whether it is within its limits or not, in any given exertion of itself, is to be determined by the Supreme Court of the United States—the ultimate arbiter in the last resort—from which there is no appeal but to revolution; how much he did in the course of the discussions which grew out of the proposed mission to Panama, and, at a later day, out of the removal of the deposits, to place the executive department of the government on its true basis, and under its true limitations; to secure to that department all its just powers on the one hand, and on the other hand to vindicate to the legislative department, and especially to the senate, all that belong to them; to arrest the tendencies which he thought at one time threatened to substitute the government of a single will, of a single person of great force of character and boundless popularity, and of a numerical majority of the people, told by the head, without intermediate institutions of any kind, judicial or senatorial, in place of the elaborate system of checks and bal-

ances, by which the Constitution aimed at a government of laws, and not of
men; how much, attracting less popular attention, but scarcely less important,
to complete the great work which experience had shown to be left unfinished
by the judiciary act of 1789, by providing for the punishment of all crimes
against the United States; how much for securing a safe currency and a true
financial system, not only by the promulgation of sound opinions, but by good
specific measures adopted, or bad ones defeated; how much to develop the vast
material resources of the country, and to push forward the planting of the
West—not troubled by any fear of exhausting old States—by a liberal policy of
public lands, by vindicating the constitutional power of Congress to make or
aid in making large classes of internal improvements, and by acting on that doctrine uniformly from 1813, whenever a road was to be built, or a rapid sup-
pressed, or a canal to be opened, or a breakwater or a lighthouse set up above
or below the flow of the tide, if so far beyond the ability of a single State, or of
so wide utility to commerce and labor as to rise to the rank of a work general
in its influences—another tie of union because another proof of the beneficence
of union; how much to protect the vast mechanical and manufacturing interests of the country, a value of many hundreds of millions—after having been
lured into existence against his counsels, against his science of political economy, by a policy of artificial encouragement—from being sacrificed, and the
pursuits and plans of large regions and communities broken up, and the acquired
skill of the country squandered by a sudden and capricious withdrawal of the
promise of the government; how much for the right performance of the most
delicate and difficult of all tasks, the ordering of the foreign affairs of a nation,
free, sensitive, self-conscious, recognizing, it is true, public law and a morality
of the State, binding on the conscience of the State, yet aspiring to power, eminence, and command, its whole frame filled full and all on fire with American
feeling, sympathetic with liberty everywhere—how much for the right ordering of the foreign affairs of such a State—aiming in all his policy, from his speech
on the Greek question in 1823, to his letters to M. Hulsemann in 1850, to
occupy the high, plain, yet dizzy ground which separates influence from intervention, to avow and promulgate warm good-will to humanity, wherever striving to be free, to inquire authentically into the history of its struggles, to take
official and avowed pains to ascertain the moment when its success may be recognized, consistently, ever, with the great code that keeps the peace of the world,
abstaining from every thing which shall give any nation a right under the law of
nations to utter one word of complaint, still less to retaliate by war—the sympathy, but also the neutrality, of Washington—how much to compose with honor

a concurrence of difficulties with the first power in the world, which any thing less than the highest degree of discretion, firmness, ability, and means of commanding respect and confidence at home and abroad would inevitably have conducted to the last calamity—a disputed boundary line of many hundred miles, from the St. Croix to the Rocky Mountains, which divided an exasperated and impracticable border population, enlisted the pride and affected the interests and controlled the politics of particular States, as well as pressed on the peace and honor of the nation, which the most popular administrations of the era of the quietest and best public feelings, the times of Monroe and of Jackson, could not adjust; which had grown so complicated with other topics of excitement that one false step, right or left, would have been a step down a precipice—this line settled forever—the claim of England to search our ships for the suppression of the slave-trade silenced forever, and a new engagement entered into by treaty, binding the national faith to contribute a specific naval force for putting an end to the great crime of man—the long practice of England to enter an American ship and impress from its crew, terminated forever; the deck henceforth guarded sacredly and completely by the flag—how much by profound discernment, by eloquent speech, by devoted life to strengthen the ties of Union, and breathe the fine and strong spirit of nationality through all our numbers—how much, most of all, last of all, after the war with Mexico, needless if his councils had governed, had ended in so vast an acquisition of territory, in presenting to the two great antagonistic sections of our country so vast an area to enter on, so imperial a prize to contend for, and the accursed fraternal strife had begun— how much then, when rising to the measure of a true and difficult and rare greatness, remembering that he had a country to save as well as a local constituency to gratify, laying all the wealth, all the hopes, of an illustrious life on the altar of a hazardous patriotism, he sought and won the more exceeding glory which now attends—which in the next age shall more conspicuously attend— his name who composes an agitated and saves a sinking land—recall this series of conduct and influences, study them carefully in their facts and results— the reading of years—and you attain to a true appreciation of this aspect of his greatness—his public character and life.

For such a review the eulogy of an hour has no room. Such a task demands research, details, proofs, illustrations, a long labor,—a volume of history, composed according to her severest laws,—setting down nothing, depreciating nothing, in malignity to the dead; suppressing nothing, and falsifying nothing, in adulation of the dead; professing fidelity incorrupt, unswerved by hatred or by love, yet able to measure, able to glow in the contemplation of a true greatness, and a vast and varied and useful public life; such a history as the genius and judgment and delicate private and public morality of Everett, assisted by his perfect knowledge of the facts,—not disqualified by his long friendship, unchilled to the last hour,—such a history as he might construct.

Two or three suggestions, occurring on the most general observation of this aspect of his eminence, you will tolerate as I leave the topic.

Remark how very large a proportion of all this class of his acts are wholly beyond and outside of the profession of the law; demanding studies, experience, a turn of mind, a cast of qualities and character, such as that profession neither gives nor exacts. Some single speeches in Congress, of consummate ability, have been made by great lawyers, drawing for the purpose only on the learning, accomplishments, logic, and eloquence of the forum. Such was Chief Justice, then Mr., Marshall's argument in the case of Jonathan Robbins,—turning on the interpretation of a treaty, and the constitutional power of the executive; a demonstration, if there is any in Euclid, anticipating the masterly judgments in the cause of Dartmouth College, or of Gibbons and Ogden, or of Maculloch and the State of Maryland; but such an one as a lawyer like him—if another there was—could have made, in his professional capacity, at the bar of the House, although he had never reflected on practical politics an hour in his life. Such, somewhat, was William Pinkney's speech in the House of Representatives, on the treaty-making power, in 1815, and his two more splendid displays in the Senate, on the Missouri question, in 1820,—the last of which I heard Mr. Clay pronounce the greatest he ever heard. They were pieces of legal reasoning on questions of constitutional law, decorated, of course, by a rhetoric which Hortensius might have envied, and Cicero would not have despised; but they were professional at last. To some extent this is true of some of Mr. Webster's ablest speeches in Congress; or, more accurately, of some of the more important portions of some of his ablest. I should say so of a part of that on the Panama Mission; of the reply to Mr. Hayne, even; and of almost the whole of that reply to Mr. Calhoun on the thesis, "the Constitution not a compact between sovereign States;" the whole series of discussion of the constitutional power of the executive, and the constitutional power of the senate, growing out of the removal of the deposits and the supposed tendencies of our system towards a centralization of government in a President, and a majority of the people,—marked, all of them, by amazing ability. To these the lawyer who could demonstrate that the charter of this College is a contract within the Constitution, or that the steamboat monopoly usurped upon the executed power of Congress to regulate commerce, was already equal; but to have been the leader, or of the leaders, of his political connection for thirty years; to have been able to instruct and guide on every question of policy, as well as law, which interested the nation in all that time; every question of finance, of currency, of the lands, of the development and care of our resources and labor; to have been of strength to help to lead his country by the hand up to a position of influence and attraction on the highest places of earth, yet to keep her peace and to keep her honor; to have been able to emulate the prescriptive and awful renown of the founders of States, by doing something which will be admitted, when some generations have passed, even more than now, to have contributed to preserve the State,—for all this another man was needed, and he stands forth another and the same.

I am hereafter to speak separately of the political morality which guided him ever; but I would say a word now on two portions of his public life, one of which has been the subject of accusatory, the other of disparaging, criticism,— unsound, unkind, in both instances.

The first comprises his course in regard to a protective policy. He opposed a tariff of protection, it is said, in 1816 and 1820 and 1824; and he opposed, in 1828, a sudden and fatal repeal of such a tariff; and thereupon I have seen it written that "this proved him a man with no great, comprehensive ideas of political economy; who took the fleeting interests and transient opinions of the hour for his norms of conduct;" "who had no sober and serious convictions of his own." I have seen it more decorously written, "that his opinions on this subject were not determined by general principles, but by a consideration of immediate sectional interests."

I will not answer this by what Scaliger says of Lipsius, the arrogant pedant, who dogmatized on the deeper politics as he did on the text of Tacitus and Seneca. *Neque est politicus; nec potest quicquam in politia; nihil possunt pedantes in ipsis rebus: nec ego, nec alius doctus possumus scribere in politicis.* I say only that the case totally fails to give color to the charge. The reasonings of Mr. Webster in 1816, 1820, and 1824, express that, on mature reflection and due and appropriate study, he had embraced the opinion that it was needless and unwise to force American manufactures, by regulation, prematurely to life. Bred in a commercial community; taught from his earliest hours of thought to regard the care of commerce as, in point of fact, a leading object and cause of the Union; to observe around him no other forms of material industry than those of commerce, navigation, fisheries, agriculture, and a few plain and robust mechanical arts, he would come to the study of the political economy of the subject with a certain preoccupation of mind, perhaps; so coming, he did study it at its well-heads, and he adopted his conclusions sincerely, and announced them strongly.

His opinions were overruled by Congress; and a national policy was adopted, holding out all conceivable promises of permanence, under which vast and sensitive investments of capital were made; the expectations, the employments, the habits, of whole ranges of States were recast; and industry, new to us, springing, immature, had been advanced just so far that, if deserted at that moment, there must follow a squandering of skill, a squandering of property, an aggregate of destruction, senseless, needless, and unconscientious,—such as marks the worst form of revolution. On these facts, at a later day, he thought that that industry, the child of government, should not thus capriciously be deserted. "The duty of the government," he said, "at the present moment would seem to be to preserve, not to destroy; to maintain the position which it has assumed; and, for one, I shall feel it an indispensable obligation to hold it steady, as far as in my power, to that degree of protection which it has undertaken to bestow."

And does this prove that these original opinions were hasty, shallow, insincere, unstudied? Consistently with every one of them; consistently with the true spirit and all the aims of the science of political economy itself; consistently with every duty of sober, high, earnest, and moral statesmanship, might not he who resisted the making of a tariff in 1816 deprecate its abandonment in 1828? Does not Adam Smith himself admit that it is "*matter fit for deliberation* how far, or in what manner, it may be proper to restore that free importation after it has been for some time interrupted"? implying that a general principle of national wealth may be displaced or modified by special circumstances; but would these censors, therefore, cry out that he had no "great and comprehensive ideas of political economy," and was willing to be "determined, not by general principles, but by immediate interests"? Because a father advises his son against an early and injudicious marriage, does it logically follow, or is it ethically right, that, after his advice has been disregarded, he is to recommend desertion of the young wife and the young child? I do not appreciate the beauty and "comprehensiveness" of those scientific ideas which forget that the actual and vast "interests" of the community are exactly what the legislator has to protect; that the concrete of things must limit the foolish wantonness of *à priori* theory; that that department of politics which has for its object the promotion and distribution of the wealth of nations, may very consistently and very scientifically preserve what it would not have created. He who accuses Mr. Webster in this behalf of "having no sober and serious convictions of his own," must afford some other proof than

his opposition to the introduction of a policy, and then his willingness to protect it after it had been introduced, and five hundred millions of property, or,
however, a countless sum, had been invested under it, or become dependent
on its continuance.

I should not think that I consulted his true fame, if I did not add that as he
came to observe the practical workings of the protective policy more closely
than at first he had done; as he came to observe the working and influences of
a various manufacturing and mechanical labor; to see how it employs and develops every faculty; finds occupation for every hour; creates or diffuses and disci-
plines ingenuity, gathering up every fragment of mind and time so that nothing
be lost; how a steady and ample home market assists agriculture; how all the
great employments of man are connected by a kindred tie, so that the tilling of
the land, navigation, foreign, coastwise, and interior commerce, all grow with
the growth, and strengthen with the strength of the industry of the arts,—
he came to appreciate, more adequately than at first, how this form of labor contributes to wealth, power, enjoyment, a great civilization; he came more justly
to grasp the conception of how consummate a destruction it would cause—how
senseless, how unphilosophical, how immoral—to arrest it suddenly and capriciously—after it had been lured into life; how wiser, how far truer to the principles of the science which seeks to augment the wealth of the State, to refuse
to destroy so immense an accumulation of that wealth! In this sense, and in this
way, I believe his opinions were matured and modified; but it does not quite
follow that they were not, in every period, conscientiously formed and held, or
that they were not in the actual circumstances of each period philosophically
just, and practically wise.

The other act of his public life to which I alluded is his negotiation of the
Treaty of Washington, in 1842, with Great Britain. This act, the country, the
world, has judged, and has applauded. Of his administrative ability, his discretion, temper, civil courage, his power of exacting respect and confidence
from those with whom he communicated, and of influencing their reason; his
knowledge of the true interests and true grandeur of the two great parties to the
negotiation; of the States of the Union more immediately concerned, and of the
world whose chief concern is peace; and of the intrepidity with which he encountered the disappointed feelings, and disparaging criticisms of the hour, in the
consciousness that he had done a good and large deed, and earned a permanent
and honest renown—of these it is the truest and most fortunate single exemplification which remains of him. Concerning its difficulty, importance, and
merits of all sorts, there were at the time few dissenting opinions among those

most conversant with the subject, although there were some; to-day there are fewer still. They are so few—a single sneer by the side of his grave, expressing that "a man who makes such a bargain is not entitled to any great glory among diplomatists," is all that I can call to mind—that I will not arrest the course of your feelings here and now by attempting to refute that "sneer" out of the history of the hour and scene. "Standing here," he said in April, 1846, in the senate of the United States to which he had returned—"standing here to- day, in this senate, and speaking in behalf of the administration of which I formed a part, and in behalf of the two houses of congress who sustained that administration, cordially and effectively, in everything relating to this treaty, I am willing to appeal to the public men of the age, whether in 1842, and in the city of Washington, something was not done for the suppression of crime; for the true exposition of the principles of public law; for the freedom and security of commerce on the ocean, and for the peace of the world!" In that forum the appeal has been heard, and the praise of a diplomatic achievement of true and permanent glory, has been irreversibly awarded to him. Beyond that forum of the mere "public men of the age," by the larger jurisdiction, the general public, the same praise has been awarded. *Sunt hic etiam sua præmia laudi.* That which I had the honor to say in the senate, in the session of 1843, in a discussion concerning this treaty, is true and applicable, now as then. "Why should I, or why should any one, assume the defence of a treaty here in this body, which but just now, on the amplest consideration, in the confidence and calmness of executive session, was approved by a vote so decisive? Sir, the country by a vote far more decisive, in a proportion very far beyond thirty-nine to nine, has approved your approval. Some there are, some few—I speak not now of any member of this senate—restless, selfish, reckless, "the cankers of a calm world and a long peace," pining with thirst of notoriety, slaves to their hatred of England, to whom the treaty is distasteful; to whom any treaty, and all things but the glare and clamor, the vain pomp and hollow circumstance of war—all but these would be distasteful and dreary. But the country is with you in this act of wisdom and glory; its intelligence; its morality; its labor; its good men; the thoughtful; the philanthropic; the discreet; the masses, are with you." "It confirms the purpose of the wise and good of both nations to be forever at peace with one another, and to put away forever all war from the kindred races: war the most ridiculous of blunders; the most tremendous of crimes; the most comprehensive of evils."

And now to him who in the solitude of his library depreciates this act, first, because there was no danger of a war with England, I answer that according to the overwhelming weight of that kind of evidence by which that kind of ques-

tion must be tried, that is by the judgment of the great body of well-informed
public men at that moment in congress; in the government; in diplomatic
situation—our relations to that power had become so delicate, and so urgent,
that unless soon adjusted by negotiation, there was real danger of war. Against
such evidence what is the value of the speculation of a private person, ten years
afterwards, in the shade of his general studies, whatever his sagacity? The temper of the border population; the tendencies to disorder in Canada, stimulated
by sympathizers on our side of the line; the entrance on our territory of a British
armed force in 1837; cutting the Caroline out of her harbor, and sending her
down the falls; the arrest of McLeod in 1841, a British subject, composing part
of that force, by the government of New York, and the threat to hang him,
which a person high in office in England declared, in a letter which was shown
to me, would raise a cry for war from "whig, radical, and tory" which no ministry could resist; growing irritation caused by the search of our vessels under
color of suppressing the slave-trade; the long controversy, almost as old as the
government, about the boundary line—so conducted as to have at last convinced
each disputant that the other was fraudulent and insincere; as to have enlisted
the pride of States; as to have exasperated and agitated a large line of border; as
to have entered finally into the tactics of political parties, and the schemes of
ambitious men, out-bidding, out-racing one another in a competition of clamor
and vehemence; a controversy on which England, a European monarchy, a
first-class power, near to the great sources of the opinion of the world, by her
press, her diplomacy, her universal intercourse, had taken great pains to persuade
Europe that our claim was groundless and unconscientious—all these things
announced to near observers in public life a crisis at hand which demanded something more than "any sensible and honest man" to encounter; assuring some
glory to him who should triumph over it. One such observer said, "Men stood
facing each other with guns on their shoulders, upon opposite sides of fordable
rivers, thirty yards wide. The discharge of a single musket would have brought
on a war whose fires would have encircled the globe."

Is this act disparaged next because what each party had for sixty years claimed
as the true line of the old treaty was waived, a line of agreement substituted, and
equivalents given and taken for gain or loss? But herein you will see only, what
the nation has seen, the boldness as well as sagacity of Mr. Webster. When the
award of the king of the Netherlands, proposing a line of agreement, was offered
to President Jackson, that strong will dared not accept it in face of the party politics of Maine—although he advised to offer her the value of a million of dollars to procure her assent to an adjustment which his own mind approved. What

he dared not do, inferred some peril I suppose. Yet the experience of twenty years—of sixty years—should have taught all men—had taught many who shrank from acting on it, that the Gordian knot must be cut, not unloosed; that all further attempt to find the true line must be abandoned as an idle and a perilous diplomacy; and that a boundary must be made by a bargain worthy of nations, or must be traced by the point of the bayonet. The merit of Mr. Webster is first that he dared to open the negotiation on this basis. I say the boldness. For, appreciate the domestic difficulties which attended it. In its nature it proposed to give up something which we had thought our own for half a century; to cede of the territory of more than one State; it demanded, therefore, the assent of those States by formal act, committing the State parties in power unequivocally; it was to be undertaken not in the administration of Monroe—elected by the whole people—not in the administration of Jackson, whose vast popularity could carry anything, and withstand anything; but just when the death of President Harrison had scattered his party; had alienated hearts; had severed ties and dissolved connections indispensable to the strength of administration, creating a loud call on Mr. Webster to leave the Cabinet—creating almost the appearance of an unwillingness that he should contribute to its glory even by largest service to the State.

Yet consider finally how he surmounted every difficulty. I will not say with Lord Palmerston, in parliament, that there was "nobody in England who did not admit it a very bad treaty for England." But I may repeat what I said on it in the senate in 1843. "And now, what does the world see? An adjustment concluded by a special minister at Washington, by which four fifths of the value of the whole subject in controversy, is left to you as your own; and by which, for that one fifth which England desires to possess, she pays you over and over, in national equivalents, imperial equivalents, such as a nation may give, such as a nation may accept, satisfactory to your interests, soothing to your honor,—the navigation of the St. John,—a concession the value of which nobody disputes,—a concession not to Maine alone, but to the whole country,—to commerce, to navigation, as far as winds blow or waters roll,—an *equivalent* of inappreciable value, opening an ample path to the sea,—an equivalent in part for what she receives of the territory in dispute,—a hundred thousand acres in New Hampshire; fifty thousand acres in Vermont and New York; the point of land commanding the great military way to and from Canada by Lake Champlain; the fair and fertile island of St. George; the surrender of a pertinacious pretension to four millions of acres westward of Lake Superior. Sir, I will not say that this adjustment admits, or was designed to admit, that our title to the whole territory in controversy was perfect and indisputable. I will not do so much injus-

tice to the accomplished and excellent person who represented the moderation
and the good sense of the English Government and people in this negotiation.
I cannot adopt, even for the defence of a treaty which I so much approve, the
language of a writer in the 'London Morning Chronicle' of September last,—
who has been said to be Lord Palmerston,—which over and over asserts, substantially as his lordship certainly did in parliament, that the adjustment 'virtually
acknowledges the American claim to the whole of the disputed territory,' and
that 'it gives England no share at all,—absolutely none; for the capitulation virtually and practically yields up the whole territory to the United States, and then
brings back a small part of it in exchange for the right of navigating the St. John.'
I will not say this. But I say first, that by concession of everybody it is a better
treaty than the administration of President Jackson would have most eagerly
concluded, if by the offer of a million and a quarter acres of land they could have
procured the assent of Maine to it. That treaty she rejected; this she accepts; and
I disparage nobody when I maintain that on all parts and all aspects of this
question,—national or state, military or industrial,—her opinion is worth that
of the whole country beside. I say next that the treaty admits the substantial justice of your general claim. It admits that in its utmost extent it was plausible,
formidable, and made in pure good faith. It admits before the nations that we
have not been rapacious; have not made false clamor; that we have asserted our
own, and obtained our own. Adjudging to you the possession of four fifths
indisputably, she gives you for the one fifth which you concede, equivalents,—
given *as equivalents—co nomine,—*on purpose to soothe and save the point of
honor; whose intrinsical and comparative value is such that you may accept
them as equivalents without reproach to your judgment, or your firmness, or
your good faith,—whose intrinsical and comparative value, tried by the maxims, weighed in the scales of imperial traffic, make them a compensation over
and over again for all we concede."

But I linger too long upon his public life, and upon this one of its great acts.
With what profound conviction of all the difficulties which beset it; with what
anxieties for the issue, hope and fear alternately preponderating, he entered on
that extreme trial of capacity and good fortune, and carried it through, I shall
not soon forget. As if it were last night, I recall the time when, after the senate
had ratified it in an evening executive session—by a vote of thirty-nine to nine—
I personally carried to him the result, at his own house, and in presence of his
wife. Then, indeed, the measure of his glory and happiness seemed full. In the
exuberant language of Burke, "I stood near him; and his face, to use the expression of the Scripture of the first martyr, was as if it had been the face of an angel.

'Hope elevated, and joy brightened his crest.' I do not know how others feel; but if I had stood in that situation, I would not have exchanged it for all that kings or people could bestow."

Such eminence and such hold on the public mind as he attained demands extraordinary general intellectual power, adequate mental culture, an impressive, attractive, energetic, and great character, and extraordinary specific power also of influencing the convictions and actions of others by speech. These all he had.

That in the quality of pure and sheer power of intellect he was of the first class of men, is, I think, the universal judgment of all who have personally witnessed many of his higher displays, and of all who without that opportunity have studied his life in its actions and influences, and studied his mind in its recorded thoughts. Sometimes it has seemed to me that to enable one to appreciate with accuracy, as a psychological speculation, the intrinsic and absolute volume and texture of that brain,—the real rate and measure of those abilities,—it was better not to see or hear him, unless you could see or hear him frequently, and in various modes of exhibition; for undoubtedly there was something in his countenance and bearing so expressive of command,—something even in his conversational language when saying, *parva summisse et modica temperate,* so exquisitely plausible, embodying the likeness at least of a rich truth, the forms at least of a large generalization, in an epithet,—an antithesis,—a pointed phrase,—a broad and peremptory thesis,—and something in his grander forth-putting, when roused by a great subject or occasion exciting his reason and touching his moral sentiments and his heart, so difficult to be resisted, approaching so near, going so far beyond, the higher style of man; that although it left you a very good witness of his power of influencing others, you were not in the best condition immediately to pronounce on the quality or the source of the influence. You saw the flash and heard the peal, and felt the admiration and fear; but from what region it was launched, and by what divinity, and from what Olympian seat, you could not certainly yet tell. To do that you must, if you saw him at all, see him many times; compare him with himself, and with others; follow his dazzling career from his father's house; observe from what competitors he won those laurels; study his discourses,—study them by the side of those of other great men of this country and time, and of other countries and times, conspicuous in the same fields of mental achievement,—look through the crystal water of the style down to the golden sands of the thought; analyze and contrast intellectual power somewhat; consider what kind and what quantity of it has been held by students of mind needful in order to great eminence in the higher mathematics, or metaphysics, or reason of the law; what capacity to analyze, through and through, to the primordial elements of the truths of that science, yet what wisdom and sobriety, in order to control the wantonness and shun the absurdities of a mere scholastic logic, by systematizing ideas, and combining them, and repressing one by another, thus producing—not a collection of intense and conflicting paradoxes, but—*a code*—scientifically coherent and practically useful,—consider what description and what quantity of mind have been held needful by students of mind in order to conspicuous eminence—long maintained—in statesmanship; that great practical science, that great philosophical art, whose ends are the existence, happiness, and honor of a nation; whose truths are to be drawn from the widest survey of man,—of social man,—of the particular race and particular community for which a government is to be made or kept, or a policy to be provided; "philosophy in action," demanding at once or affording place for the highest speculative genius and the most skilful conduct of men and of affairs; and finally consider what degree and kind of mental power has been found to be required in order to influence the reason of an audience and a nation by speech,—not magnetizing the mere nervous or emotional nature by an effort of that nature,—but operating on reason by reason—a great reputation in forensic and deliberative eloquence, maintained and advancing for a lifetime,—it is thus that we come to be sure that his intellectual power was as real and as uniform as its very happiest particular display had been imposing and remarkable.

It was not quite so easy to analyze that power, to compare or contrast it with that of other mental celebrities, and show how it differed or resembled, as it was to discern its existence.

Whether he would have excelled as much in other fields of exertion—in speculative philosophy, for example, in any of its departments—is a problem impossible to determine and needless to move. To me it seems quite clear that the whole wealth of his powers, his whole emotional nature, his eloquent feeling, his matchless capacity to affect others' conduct by affecting their practical judgments, could not have been known, could not have been poured forth in a stream so rich and strong and full, could not have so reacted on and aided and winged the mighty intelligence, in any other walk of mind, or life, than that he chose; that in any other there must have been some disjoining of qualities which God had united,—some divorce of pure intellect from the helps or hindrances or companionship of common sense and beautiful genius; and that in any field of speculative ideas but half of him, or part of him, could have found its sphere. What that part might have been or done, it is vain to inquire.

I have been told that the assertion has been hazarded that he "was great in understanding; deficient in the large reason;" and to prove this distinction he is compared disadvantageously, with "Socrates; Aristotle; Plato; Leibnitz; Newton; and Descartes." If this means that he did not devote his mind, such as it was, to their speculations, it is true; but that would not prove that he had not as much "higher reason." Where was Bacon's *higher reason* when he was composing his reading on the Statute of Uses? Had he lost it? or was he only not employing it? or was he employing it on an investigation of law? If it means that he had not as much absolute intellectual power as they, or could not, in their departments, have done what they did, it may be dismissed as a dogma incapable of proof, and incapable of refutation; ineffectual as a disparagement; unphilosophical as a comparison.

It is too common with those who come from the reveries of a cloistered speculation to judge a practical life, to say of him, and such as he, that they "do not enlarge universal law, and first principles; and philosophical ideas;" that "they add no new maxim formed by induction out of human history and old thought." In this there is some truth; and yet it totally fails to prove that they do not possess all the intellectual power, and all the specific form of intellectual power, required for such a description of achievement; and it totally fails, too, to prove that they do not use it quite as truly to "the glory of God, and the bettering of man's estate." Whether they possess such power or not, the evidence does not disprove; and it is a pedantic dogmatism, if it is not a malignant dogmatism, which, *from such evidence,* pronounces that they do not; but it is doubtless so, that by an original bias; by accidental circumstances or deliberate choice, he determined early to devote himself to a practical and great duty, and that was to uphold a recent, delicate, and complex political system, which his studies, his sagacity, taught him, as Solon learned, was the best the people could bear; to uphold it; to adapt its essential principles and its actual organism to the great changes of his time; the enlarging territory; enlarging numbers; sharper antagonisms; mightier passions; a new nationality; and under it, and by means of it, and by a steady government, a wise policy of business, a temperate conduct of foreign relations, to enable a people to develop their resources, and fulfil their mission. This he selected as his work on earth; this his task; this, if well done, his consolation, his joy, his triumph! To this, call it, in comparison with the meditations of philosophy, humble or high, he brought all the vast gifts of intellect, whatever they were, wherewith God had enriched him. And now, do they infer that, because he selected such a work to do he could not have possessed the higher form of intellectual power; or do they say that, because, having selected it, he performed it with a masterly and uniform sagacity and prudence and good sense, using ever the appropriate means to the selected end; that therefore he could not have possessed the higher form of intellectual power? Because all his life long he recognized that his vocation was that of a statesman and a jurist, not that of a thinker and dreamer in the shade, still less of a general agitator; that his duties connected themselves mainly with an existing stupendous political order of things, to be kept—to be adapted with all possible civil discretion and temper to the growth of the nation—but by no means to be exchanged for any quantity of amorphous matter in the form of "universal law" or new maxims and great ideas born since the last change of the moon—because he quite habitually spoke the language of the Constitution and the law, not the phraseology of a new philosophy; confining himself very much to inculcating historical, traditional, and indispensable maxims,—neutrality; justice; good faith; observance of fundamental compacts of Union and the like—because it was America—our America—he sought to preserve, and to set forward to her glory—not so much an abstract conception of humanity—because he could combine many ideas; many elements; many antagonisms; in a harmonious, and noble practical politics, instead of fastening on one only, and—that sure sign of small or perverted ability—aggravating it to disease and falsehood—is it therefore inferred that he had not the larger form of intellectual power?

And this power was not oppressed, but aided and accomplished by exercise the most constant, the most severe, the most stimulant, and by a force of will as remarkable as his genius, and by adequate mental and tasteful culture. How much the eminent greatness it reached is due to the various and lofty competition to which he brought, if he could, the most careful preparation—competition with adversaries *cum quibus certare erat gloriosius, quam omnino adversarios non habere, cum præsertim non modo, nunquam sit aut illorum ab ipso cursus impeditus, aut ab ipsis suus, sed contra semper alter ab altero adjutus, et communicando, et monendo, et favendo,* you may well appreciate.

I claim much, too, under the name of mere mental culture. Remark his style. I allow its full weight to the Horatian maxim, *scribendi rectè sapere est et principium et fons,* and I admit that he had deep and exquisite judgment, largely of the gift of God. But such a style as his is due also to art, to practice,—in the matter of style, incessant,—to great examples of fine writing, turned by the nightly and the daily hand; to Cicero, through whose pellucid, deep seas the pearl shows distinct and large and near, as if within the arm's reach; to Virgil, whose magic of words, whose exquisite structure and "rich economy of expression," no other writer ever equalled; to our English Bible, and especially to the prophetical writings, and of these especially to Ezekiel, of some of whose peculiarities, and among them that of the repetition of single words or phrases, for emphasis and impression, a friend has called my attention to some very striking illustrations; to Shakspeare, of the style of whose comic dialogue we may, in the language of the great critic, assert "that it is that which in the English nation is never to become obsolete, a certain mode of phraseology so consonant and congenial to analogy, to principles of the language, as to remain settled and unaltered,—a style above grossness, below modish and pedantic forms of speech, where pro priety resides;" to Addison, whom Johnson, Mackintosh, and Macaulay concur to put at the head of all fine writers, for the amenity, delicacy, and unostentatious elegance of his English; to Pope, polished, condensed, sententious; to Johnson and Burke, in whom all the affluence and all the energy of our tongue, in both its great elements of Saxon and Latin, might be exemplified; to the study and comparison, but not the copying, of authors such as these; to habits of writing and speaking and conversing on the capital theory of always doing his best,—thus, somewhat, I think, was acquired that remarkable production, "the last work of combined study and genius," his rich, clear, correct, harmonious, and weighty style of prose.

Beyond these studies and exercises of taste, he had read variously and judiciously. If any public man, or any man, had more thoroughly mastered British constitutional and general history, or the history of British legislation, or could deduce the progress, eras, causes, and hindrances of British liberty in more prompt, exact, and copious detail, or had in his memory, at any given moment, a more ample political biography, or political literature, I do not know him. His library of English history, and of all history, was always rich, select, and catholic; and I well recollect hearing him, in 1819, while attending a commencement of this College, at an evening party, sketch, with great emphasis and interest of manner, the merits of George Buchanan, the historian of Scotland,—his Latinity and eloquence almost equal to Livy's, his love of liberty and his genius greater, and his title to credit not much worse. American history and American political literature he had by heart. The long series of influences that trained us for representative and free government; that other series of influences which moulded us into a united government,—the colonial era, the age of controversy before the Revolution; every scene and every person in that great tragic action, the age of controversy following the Revolution and preceding the Constitution, unlike the earlier, in which we divided among ourselves on the greatest questions which can engage the mind of America,—the questions of the existence of a national government, of the continued existence of the State governments, on the partition of powers, on the umpirage of disputes between them,—a controversy on which the destiny of the New World was staked;

every problem which has successively engaged our politics, and every name which has figured in them,—the whole stream of our time was open, clear, and present ever to his eye.

I think, too, that, though not a frequent and ambitious citer of authorities, he had read, in the course of the study of his profession or politics, and had meditated all the great writers and thinkers by whom the principles of republican government, and all free governments, are most authoritatively expounded. Aristotle, Cicero, Machiavel,—one of whose discourses on Livy maintains, in so masterly an argument, how much wiser and more constant are the people than the prince, a doctrine of liberty consolatory and full of joy,—Harrington, Milton, Sidney, Locke, I know he had read and weighed.

Other classes of information there were,—partly obtained from books, partly from observation, to some extent referable to his two main employments of politics and law,—by which he was distinguished remarkably. Thus, nobody but was struck with his knowledge of civil and physical geography, and, to a less extent, of geology and races; of all the great routes and marts of our foreign, coastwise, and interior commerce, the subjects which it exchanges, the whole circle of industry it comprehends and passes around; the kinds of our mechanical and manufacturing productions, and their relations to all labor and life; the history, theories, and practice of agriculture,—our own and that of other countries,—and its relations to government, liberty, happiness, and the character of nations. This kind of information enriched and assisted all his public efforts; but to appreciate the variety and accuracy of his knowledge, and even the true compass of his mind, you must have had some familiarity with his friendly written correspondence, and you must have conversed with him with some degree of freedom. There, more than in senatorial or forensic debate, gleamed the true riches of his genius, as well as the goodness of his large heart, and the kindness of his noble nature. There, with no longer a great part to discharge, no longer compelled to weigh and measure propositions, to tread the dizzy heights which part the antagonisms of the Constitution, to put aside allusions and illustrations which crowded on his mind in action, but which the dignity of a public appearance had to reject, in the confidence of hospitality, which ever he dispensed as a prince who also was a friend, his memory,—one of his most extraordinary faculties, quite in proportion to all the rest,—swept free over the readings and labors of more than half a century; and then, allusions, direct and ready quotations, a passing, mature criticism, sometimes only a recollection of the mere emotions which a glorious passage or interesting event had once excited, darkening for a moment the face and filling the eye, often an instructive exposition of a current maxim of philosophy or politics, the history of an invention, the recital of some incident casting a new light on some transaction or some institution,—this flow of unstudied conversation, quite as remarkable as any other exhibition of his mind, better than any other, perhaps, at once opened an unexpected glimpse of his various acquirements, and gave you to experience, delightedly, that the "mild sentiments have their eloquence as well as the stormy passions."

There must be added, next, the element of an impressive character, inspiring regard, trust, and admiration, not unmingled with love. It had, I think, intrinsically a charm such as belongs only to a good, noble, and beautiful nature. In its combination with so much fame, so much force of will, and so much intellect, it filled and fascinated the imagination and heart. It was affectionate in childhood and youth, and it was more than ever so in the few last months of his long life. It is the universal testimony that he gave to his parents, in largest measure, honor, love, obedience; that he eagerly appropriated the first means which he could command to relieve the father from the debts contracted to educate his brother and himself; that he selected his first place of professional practice that he might soothe the coming on of his old age; that all through life he neglected no occasion,—sometimes when leaning on the arm of a friend, alone, with faltering voice, sometimes in the presence of great assemblies, where the tide of general emotion made it graceful,—to express his "affectionate veneration of him who reared and defended the log cabin in which his elder brothers and sisters were born, against savage violence and destruction, cherished all the domestic virtues beneath its roof, and, through the fire and blood of some years of revolutionary war, shrank from no danger, no toil, no sacrifice, to serve his country, and to raise his children to a condition better than his own."

Equally beautiful was his love of all his kindred and of all his friends. When I hear him accused of selfishness, and a cold, bad nature, I recall him lying sleepless all night, not without tears of boyhood, conferring with Ezekiel how the darling desire of both hearts should be compassed, and he, too, admitted to the precious privileges of education; courageously pleading the cause of both brothers in the morning; prevailing by the wise and discerning affection of the mother; suspending his studies of the law, and registering deeds and teaching school to earn the means, for both, of availing themselves of the opportunity which the parental self-sacrifice had placed within their reach; loving him through life, mourning him when dead, with a love and a sorrow very wonderful, passing the sorrow of woman; I recall the husband, the father of the living and of the early departed, the friend, the counsellor of many years, and my heart grows too full and liquid for the refutation of words.

His affectionate nature, craving ever friendship, as well as the presence of kindred blood, diffused itself through all his private life, gave sincerity to all his hospitalities, kindness to his eye, warmth to the pressure of his hand; made his
greatness and genius unbend themselves to the playfulness of childhood, flowed
out in graceful memories indulged of the past or the dead, of incidents when life
was young and promised to be happy,—gave generous sketches of his rivals,—
the high contention now hidden by the handful of earth,—hours passed fifty years
ago with great authors, recalled for the vernal emotions which then they made to
live and revel in the soul. And from these conversations of friendship, no man,—
no man, old or young,—went away to remember one word of profaneness, one
allusion of indelicacy, one impure thought, one unbelieving suggestion, one
doubt cast on the reality of virtue, of patriotism, of enthusiasm, of the progress of
man,—one doubt cast on righteousness, or temperance, or judgment to come.

Every one of his tastes and recreations announced the same type of character. His love of agriculture, of sports in the open air, of the outward world in
starlight and storms, and sea and boundless wilderness,—partly a result of the
influences of the first fourteen years of his life, perpetuated like its other affections and its other lessons of a mother's love—the Psalms, the Bible, the stories
of the wars,—partly the return of an unsophisticated and healthful nature, tiring,
for a space, of the idle business of political life, its distinctions, its artificialities, to
employments, to sensations which interest without agitating the universal race
alike, as God has framed it, in which one feels himself only a man, fashioned from
the earth, set to till it, appointed to return to it, yet made in the image of his
Maker, and with a spirit that shall not die,—all displayed a man whom the most
various intercourse with the world, the longest career of strife and honors, the
consciousness of intellectual supremacy, the coming in of a wide fame, constantly
enlarging, left, as he was at first, natural, simple, manly, genial, kind.

You will all concur, I think, with a learned friend who thus calls my attention to the resemblance of his character, in some of these particulars, to that of
Walter Scott.

"Nature endowed both with athletic frames, and a noble presence; both passionately loved rural life, its labors and sports; possessed a manly simplicity, free
from all affectation, genial and social tastes, full minds, and happy elocution; both
stamped themselves with indelible marks upon the age in which they lived; both
were laborious, and always with high and virtuous aims, ardent in patriotism,
overflowing with love of 'kindred blood,' and, above all, frank and unostentatious Christians."

I have learned by evidence the most direct and satisfactory, that in the last months of his life, the whole affectionateness of his nature; his consideration of others; his gentleness; his desire to make them happy and to see them happy, seemed to come out in more and more beautiful and habitual expression than ever before. The long day's public tasks were felt to be done; the cares, the uncertainties, the mental conflicts of high place, were ended, and he came home to recover himself for the few years which he might still expect would be his before he should go hence to be here no more. And there, I am assured and fully believe, no unbecoming regrets pursued him; no discontent, as for injustice suffered or expectations unfulfilled; no self-reproach for anything done or anything omitted by himself; no irritation, no peevishness unworthy of his noble nature; but instead, love and hope for his country, when she became the subject of conversation; and for all around him, the dearest and most indifferent, for all breathing things about him, the overflow of the kindest heart growing in gentleness and benevolence; paternal, patriarchal affections, seeming to become more natural, warm, and communicative every hour. Softer and yet brighter grew the tints on the sky of parting day; and the last lingering rays, more even than the glories of noon, announced how divine was the source from which they proceeded; how incapable to be quenched; how certain to rise on a morning which no night should follow.

Such a character was made to be loved. It was loved. Those who knew and saw it in its hour of calm—those who could repose on that soft green, loved him. His plain neighbors loved him; and one said, when he was laid in his grave, "How lonesome the world seems!" Educated young men loved him. The ministers of the gospel, the general intelligence of the country, the masses afar off, loved him. True, they had not found in his speeches, read by millions, so much adulation of the people; so much of the music which robs the public reason of itself; so many phrases of humanity and philanthropy; and some had told them he was lofty and cold,—solitary in his greatness; but every year they came nearer and nearer to him, and as they came nearer, they loved him better; they heard how tender the son had been, the husband, the brother, the father, the friend, and neighbor; that he was plain, simple, natural, generous, hospitable,—the heart larger than the brain; that he loved little children and reverenced God, the Scriptures, the Sabbath- day, the Constitution, and the law,—and their hearts clave unto him. More truly of him than even of the great naval darling of England might it be said, that "his presence would set the church-bells ringing, and give school-boys a holiday,—would bring children from school and old men from the chimney-corner, to gaze on him ere he died." The great and unavailing lamentation first revealed the deep place he had in the hearts of his countrymen.

You are now to add to this his extraordinary power of influencing the convictions of others by speech, and you have completed the survey of the means of his greatness. And here, again, I begin, by admiring an aggregate, made up of excellences and triumphs, ordinarily deemed incompatible. He spoke with consummate ability to the bench, and yet exactly as, according to every sound canon of taste and ethics, the bench ought to be addressed. He spoke with consummate ability to the jury, and yet exactly as, according to every sound canon, that totally different tribunal ought to be addressed. In the halls of congress, before the people assembled for political discussion in masses, before audiences smaller and more select, assembled for some solemn commemoration of the past or of the dead,—in each of these, again, his speech, of the first form of ability, was exactly adapted, also, to the critical proprieties of the place; each achieved, when delivered, the most instant and specific success of eloquence,—some of them in a splendid and remarkable degree; and yet, stranger still, when reduced to writing, as they fell from his lips, they compose a body of reading,—in many volumes,—solid, clear, rich, and full of harmony,—a classical and permanent political literature.

And yet, all these modes of his eloquence, exactly adapted each to its stage and its end, were stamped with his image and superscription, identified by characteristics incapable to be counterfeited, and impossible to be mistaken. The same high power of reason, intent in every one to explore and display some truth; some truth of judicial, or historical, or biographical fact; some truth of law, deduced by construction, perhaps, or by illation; some truth of policy, for want whereof a nation, generations, may be the worse,—reason seeking and unfolding truth; the same tone, in all, of deep earnestness, expressive of strong desire that that which he felt to be important should be accepted as true, and spring up to action; the same transparent, plain, forcible, and direct speech, conveying his exact thought to the mind,—not something less or more; the same sovereignty of form, of brow, and eye, and tone, and manner,—everywhere the intellectual king of men, standing before you,—that same marvellousness of qualities and results, residing, I know not where, in words, in pictures, in the ordering of ideas, in felicities indescribable, by means whereof, coming from his tongue, all things seemed mended,—truth seemed more true, probability more plausible, greatness more grand, goodness more awful, every affection more tender, than when coming from other tongues,—these are, in all, his eloquence. But sometimes it became individualized, and discriminated even from itself; sometimes place and circumstances, great interests at stake, a stage, an audience fitted for the highest historic action, a crisis, personal or national, upon him, stirred the depths of that emotional nature, as the anger of the goddess stirs the sea on which the great epic is beginning; strong passions, themselves kindled to intensity, quickened every faculty to a new life; the stimulated associations of ideas brought all treasures of thought and knowledge within command, the spell, which often held his imagination fast, dissolved, and she arose and gave him to choose of her urn of gold; earnestness became vehemence, the simple, perspicuous, measured, and direct language became a headlong, full, and burning tide of speech; the discourse of reason, wisdom, gravity, and beauty, changed to that Δεινότης, that rarest consummate eloquence,—grand, rapid, pathetic, terrible; the *aliquid immensum infinitumque* that Cicero might have recognized; the master triumph of man in the rarest opportunity of his noblest power.

Such elevation above himself, in congressional debate, was most uncommon. Some such there were in the great discussions of executive power following the removal of the deposits, which they who heard them will never forget, and some which rest in the tradition of hearers only. But there were other fields of oratory on which, under the influence of more uncommon springs of inspiration, he exemplified, in still other forms, an eloquence in which I do not know that he has had a superior among men. Addressing masses by tens of thousands in the open air, on the urgent political questions of the day, or designated to lead the meditations of an hour devoted to the remembrance of some national era, or of some incident marking the progress of the nation, and lifting him up to a view of what is, and what is past, and some indistinct revelation of the glory that lies in the future, or of some great historical name, just borne by the nation to his tomb,—we have learned that then and there, at the base of Bunker Hill, before the corner-stone was laid, and again when from the finished column the centuries looked on him; in Faneuil Hall, mourning for those with whose spoken or written eloquence of freedom its arches had so often resounded; on the rock of Plymouth; before the capitol, of which there shall not be one stone left on another, before his memory shall have ceased to live,—in such scenes, unfettered by the laws of forensic or parliamentary debate; multitudes uncounted lifting up their eyes to him; some great historical scenes of America around; all symbols of her glory and art and power and fortune there; voices of the past, not unheard; shapes beckoning from the future, not unseen,—sometimes that mighty intellect, borne upwards to a height and kindled to an illumination which we shall see no more, wrought out, as it were, in an instant, a picture of vision, warning, prediction; the progress of the nation; the contrasts of its eras; the heroic deaths; the motives to patriotism; the maxims and arts imperial by which the glory has been gathered and may be heightened,—wrought out, in an instant, a picture to fade only when all record of our mind shall die.

In looking over the public remains of his oratory, it is striking to remark how, even in that most sober and massive understanding and nature, you see gathered and expressed the characteristic sentiments and the passing time of our America. It is the strong old oak which ascends before you; yet our soil, our heaven, are attested in it as perfectly as if it were a flower that could grow in no other climate and in no other hour of the year or day. Let me instance in one thing only. It is a peculiarity of some schools of eloquence that they embody and utter, not merely the individual genius and character of the speaker, but a national consciousness,—a national era, a mood, a hope, a dread, a despair,—in which you listen to the spoken history of the time. There is an eloquence of an expiring nation, such as seems to sadden the glorious speech of Demosthenes; such as breathes grand and gloomy from the visions of the prophets of the last days of Israel and Judah; such as gave a spell to the expression of Grattan and of Kossuth,—the sweetest, most mournful, most awful of the words which man may utter, or which man may hear,—the eloquence of a perishing nation. There is another eloquence, in which the national consciousness of a young or renewed and vast strength, of trust in a dazzling, certain, and limitless future, an inward glorying in victories yet to be won, sounds out as by voice of clarion, challenging to contest for the highest prize of earth; such as that in which the leader of Israel in its first days holds up to the new nation the Land of Promise; such as that which in the well imagined speeches scattered by Livy over the history of the "majestic series of victories," speaks the Roman consciousness of growing aggrandizement which should subject the world; such as that through which, at the tribunes of her revolution, in the bulletins of her rising soldier, France told to the world her dream of glory. And of this kind somewhat is ours; cheerful, hopeful, trusting, as befits youth and spring; the eloquence of a State beginning to ascend to the first class of power, eminence, and consideration, and conscious of itself. It is to no purpose that they tell you it is in bad taste; that it partakes of arrogance and vanity; that a true national good breeding would not know, or seem to know, whether the nation is old or young; whether the tides of being are in their flow or ebb; whether these coursers of the sun are sinking slowly to rest, wearied with a journey of a thousand years, or just bounding from the Orient unbreathed. Higher laws than those of taste determine the consciousness of nations. Higher laws than those of taste determine the general forms of the expression of that consciousness. Let the downward age of America find its orators and poets and artists to erect its spirit, or grace and soothe its dying; be it ours to go up with Webster to the rock, the monument, the capitol, and bid "the distant generations hail!"

In this connection remark, somewhat more generally, to how extraordinary an extent he had by his acts, words, thoughts, or the events of his life, associated himself forever in the memory of all of us, with every historical incident, or at least with every historical epoch; with every policy; with every glory; with every great name and fundamental institution, and grand or beautiful image, which are peculiarly and properly American. Look backwards to the planting of Plymouth and Jamestown; to the various scenes of colonial life in peace and war; to the opening and march and close of the revolutionary drama,—to the age of the Constitution; to Washington and Franklin and Adams and Jefferson; to the whole train of causes from the Reformation downwards, which prepared us to be Republicans; to that other train of causes which led us to be Unionists,— look round on field, workshop, and deck, and hear the music of labor rewarded, fed, and protected,—look on the bright sisterhood of the States, each singing as a seraph in her motion, yet blending in a common beam and swelling a common harmony,—and there is nothing which does not bring him by some tie to the memory of America.

We seem to see his form and hear his deep grave speech everywhere. By some felicity of his personal life; by some wise, deep, or beautiful word spoken or written; by some service of his own, or some commemoration of the services of others, it has come to pass that "our granite hills, our inland seas and prairies, and fresh, unbounded, magnificent wilderness;" our encircling ocean; the resting-place of the Pilgrims; our new-born sister of the Pacific; our popular assemblies; our free schools; all our cherished doctrines of education, and of the influence of religion, and material policy and law, and the Constitution, give us back his name. What American landscape will you look on; what subject of American interest will you study; what source of hope or of anxiety, as an American, will you acknowledge that it does not recall him?

I have reserved, until I could treat it as a separate and final topic, the consideration of the morality of Mr. Webster's public character and life. To his true fame,—to the kind and degree of influence which that large series of great actions and those embodied thoughts of great intellect are to exert on the future,—this is the all-important consideration. In the last speech which he made in the senate,—the last of those which he made, as he said, for the Constitution and the Union, and which he might have commended, as Bacon his name and memory "to men's charitable speeches, to foreign nations, and the next ages,"—yet with a better hope he asserted, "The ends I aim at shall be those of my Country, my God, and Truth." Is that praise his?

Until the seventh day of March, 1850, I think it would have been accorded to him by an almost universal acclaim, as general and as expressive of profound and intelligent conviction, and of enthusiasm, love, and trust, as ever saluted conspicuous statesmanship,—tried by many crises of affairs in a great nation, agitated ever by parties, and wholly free.

That he had admitted into his heart a desire to win, by deserving them, the highest forms of public honor, many would have said; and they who loved him most fondly, and felt the truest solicitude that he should carry a good conscience and pure fame brightening to the end, would not have feared to concede. For he was not ignorant of himself; and he therefore knew that there was nothing within the Union, Constitution, and Law, too high or too large or too difficult for him. He believed that his natural or his acquired abilities, and his policy of administration, would contribute to the true glory of America; and he held no theory of ethics which required him to disparage, to suppress, to ignore vast capacities of public service merely because they were his own. If the fleets of Greece were assembling, and her tribes buckling on their arms from Laconia to Mount Olympus, from the promontory of Sunium to the isle farthest to the west, and the great epic action was opening, it was not for him to feign insanity or idiocy, to escape the perils and the honor of command. But that all this in him had been ever in subordination to a principled and beautiful public virtue; that every sectional bias, every party tie, as well as every personal aspiring, had been uniformly held by him for nothing against the claims of country; that nothing lower than country seemed worthy enough—nothing smaller than country large enough—for that great heart, would not have been questioned by a whisper. Ah! if at any hour before that day he had died, how would then the great procession of the people of America—the great triumphal procession of the dead—have moved onward to his grave—the sublimity of national sorrow, not contrasted, not outraged by one feeble voice of calumny!

In that antecedent public life, embracing from 1812 to 1850—a period of thirty-eight years—I find grandest proofs of the genuineness and comprehensiveness of his patriotism, and the boldness and manliness of his public virtue. He began his career of politics as a Federalist. Such was his father—so beloved and revered; such his literary and professional companions; such, although by no very decisive or certain preponderance, the community in which he was bred and was to live. Under that name of party he entered congress, personally, and by connection, opposed to the war, which was thought to bear with such extreme sectional severity upon the North and East. And yet, one might almost say that the only thing he imbibed from Federalists or Federalism was love and admiration for the Constitution as the means of union. That passion he did inherit from them; that he cherished.

He came into congress, opposed, as I have said, to the war; and behold him, if you would judge of the quality of his political ethics, in opposition. Did those eloquent lips, at a time of life when vehemence and imprudence are expected, if ever, and not ungraceful, let fall ever one word of faction? Did he ever deny one power to the general government, which the soundest expositors of all creeds have allowed it? Did he ever breathe a syllable which could excite a region, a State, a family of States, against the Union,—which could hold out hope or aid to the enemy?—which sought or tended to turn back or to chill the fiery tide of a new and intense nationality, then bursting up, to flow and burn till all things appointed to America to do shall be fulfilled? These questions in their substance, he put to Mr. Calhoun, in 1838, in the senate, and that great man—one of the authors of the war—just then, only then, in relations unfriendly to Mr. Webster, and who had just insinuated a reproach on his conduct in the war, was silent. Did Mr. Webster content himself even with objecting to the details of the mode in which the administration waged the war? No, indeed. Taught by his constitutional studies that the Union was made in part for commerce, familiar with the habits of our long line of coast, knowing well how many sailors and fishermen, driven from every sea by embargo and war, burned to go to the gun-deck and avenge the long wrongs of England on the element where she had inflicted them, his opposition to the war manifested itself by teaching the nation that the deck was her field of fame. *Non illi imperium pelagi sævumque tridentum, sed nobis, sorte datum.*

But I might recall other evidence of the sterling and unusual qualities of his public virtue. Look in how manly a sort he—not merely conducted a particular argument or a particular speech, but in how manly a sort, in how high a moral tone, he uniformly dealt with the mind of his country. Politicians got an advantage of him for this while he lived; let the dead have just praise to-day. Our public life is one long electioneering, and even Burke tells you that at popular elections the most rigorous casuists will remit something of their severity. But where do you find him flattering his countrymen, indirectly or directly, for a vote? On what did he ever place himself but good counsels and useful service? His arts were manly arts, and he never saw a day of temptation when he would not rather fall than stand on any other. Who ever heard that voice cheering the people on to rapacity, to injustice, to a vain and guilty glory? Who ever saw that pencil of light hold up a picture of manifest destiny to dazzle the fancy? How anxiously rather, in season and out, by the energetic eloquence of his youth, by his counsels bequeathed on the verge of a timely grave, he preferred to teach that by all possible acquired sobriety of mind, by asking reverently of the past, by obedience to the law, by habits of patient and legitimate labor, by the culti-vation of the mind, by the fear and worship of God, we educate ourselves for the future that is revealing. Men said he did not sympathize with the masses, because his phraseology was rather of an old and simple school, rejecting the nauseous and vain repetitions of humanity and philanthropy, and progress and brotherhood, in which may lurk heresies so dreadful, of socialism or disunion; in which a selfish, hollow, and shallow ambition may mask itself,—the siren song which would lure the pilot from his course. But I say that he did sympa-thize with them; and, because he did, he came to them not with adulation, but with truth; not with words to please, but with measures to serve them; not that his popular sympathies were less, but that his personal and intellectual dignity and his public morality were greater.

And on the seventh day of March, and down to the final scene, might he not still say as ever before, that "all the ends he aimed at were his country's, his God's, and truth's." He declared, "I speak to-day for the preservation of the Union. Hear me for my cause. I speak to-day out of a solicitous and anxious heart for the restoration to the country of that quiet and harmony, which make the bless-ings of this Union so rich and so dear to us all. These are the motives and the sole motives that influence me." If in that declaration he was sincere, was he not bound in conscience to give the counsels of that day? What were they? What was the single one for which his political morality was called in question? Only that a provision of the Federal Constitution, ordaining the restitution of fugitive slaves, should be executed according to its true meaning. This only. And might he not in good conscience keep the Constitution in this part, and in all, for the preservation of the Union?

Under his oath to support it, and to support it all, and with his opinions of that duty so long held, proclaimed uniformly, in whose vindication on some great days, he had found the chief opportunity of his personal glory, might he not, in good conscience support it, and all of it, even if he could not—and no human intelligence could, certainly—know, that the extreme evil would follow, in immediate consequence, its violation? Was it so recent a doctrine of his that the Constitution was obligatory upon the national and individual conscience, that you should ascribe it to sudden and irresistible temptation? Why, what had

he, quite down to the seventh of March, that more truly individualized him?—
what had he more characteristically his own?—wherewithal had he to glory
more or other than all beside, than this very doctrine of the sacred and permanent obligation to support each and all parts of that great compact of union and
justice? Had not this been his distinction, his *speciality,*—almost the foible of his
greatness,—the darling and master passion ever? Consider that that was a sentiment which had been part of his conscious nature for more than sixty years; that
from the time he bought his first copy of the Constitution on the handkerchief,
and revered parental lips had commended it to him, with all other holy and beautiful things, along with lessons of reverence to God, and the belief and love of
His Scriptures, along with the doctrine of the catechism, the unequalled music
of Watts, the name of Washington,—there had never been an hour that he had
not held it the master work of man,—just in its ethics, consummate in its practical wisdom, paramount in its injunctions; that every year of life had deepened
the original impression; that as his mind opened, and his associations widened,
he found that every one for whom he felt respect, instructors, theological and
moral teachers, his entire party connection, the opposite party, and the whole
country, so held it, too; that its fruits of more than half a century of union, of
happiness, of renown, bore constant and clear witness to it in his mind, and that
it chanced that certain emergent and rare occasions had devolved on him to stand
forth to maintain it, to vindicate its interpretation, to vindicate its authority, to
unfold its workings and uses; that he had so acquitted himself of that opportunity as to have won the title of its Expounder and Defender, so that his proudest memories, his most prized renown, referred to it, and were entwined with
it—and say whether with such antecedents, readiness to execute, or disposition
to evade, would have been the hardest to explain; likeliest to suggest the surmise
of a new temptation! He who knows anything of man, knows that his vote for
beginning the restoration of harmony by keeping the whole Constitution, was
determined, was necessitated, by the great law of sequences,—a great law of
cause and effect, running back to his mother's arms, as resistless as the law which
moves the system about the sun,—and that he must have given it, although it
had been opened to him in vision, that within the next natural day his "eyes
should be turned to behold for the last time the sun in heaven."

To accuse him in that act of "sinning against his own conscience," is to charge
one of these things: either that no well-instructed conscience can approve and
maintain the Constitution, and each of its parts, and therefore that his, by inference, did not approve it; or that he had never employed the proper means of
instructing his conscience, and therefore its approval, if it were given, was itself

an immorality. The accuser must assert one of these propositions. He will not
deny, I take it for granted, that the conscience requires to be instructed by political teaching, in order to guide the citizen, or the public man, aright, in the matter of political duties. Will he say that the moral sentiments alone, whatever their
origin—whether factitious and derivative, or parcel of the spirit of the child
and born with it—that they alone, by force of strict and mere ethical training,
become qualified to pronounce authoritatively whether the Constitution, or any
other vast and complex civil policy, as a whole, whereby a nation is created and
preserved, ought to have been made, or ought to be executed? Will he venture
to tell you, that if your conscience approves the Union, the Constitution in all
its parts, and the law which administers it, that you are bound to obey and uphold
them; and if it disapproves, you must, according to your measure, and in your
circles of agitation, disobey and subvert them, and leave the matter there—
forgetting or designedly omitting to tell you also that you are bound, in all good
faith and diligence to resort to studies and to teachers *ab extra*—in order to determine whether the conscience *ought* to approve or disapprove the Union, the
Constitution, and the law, *in view of the whole aggregate of their nature and fruits?*
Does he not perfectly know that this moral faculty, however trained, by mere
moral institution, specifically directed to that end, to be tender, sensitive, and
peremptory, is totally unequal to decide on any action, or any thing, but the very
simplest; that which produces the most palpable and immediate result of unmixed
good, or unmixed evil; and that when it comes to judge on the great mixed cases
of the world, where the consequences are numerous, their development slow
and successive, the light and shadow of a blended and multiform good and evil
spread out on the lifetime of a nation, that then morality must borrow from history; from politics; from reason operating on history and politics, her elements
of determination? I think he must agree to this. He must agree, I think, that to
single out one provision in a political system of many parts and of elaborate interdependence, to take it all alone, exactly as it stands, and without attention to its
origin and history; the necessities, morally resistless, which prescribed its introduction into the system, the unmeasured good in other forms which its allowance
buys, the unmeasured evil in other forms which its allowance hinders—without
attention to these, to present it in all "the nakedness of a metaphysical abstraction" to the mere sensibilities; and ask if it is not inhuman, and if they answer
according to their kind, that it is, then to say that the problem is solved, and
the right of disobedience is made clear—he must agree that this is not to exalt
reason and conscience, but to outrage both. He must agree that although the
supremacy of conscience is absolute whether the decision be right or wrong, that

is, *according to the real qualities of things or not,* that there lies back of the actual conscience, and its actual decisions, the great anterior duty of having a conscience that *shall decide according to the real qualities of things;* that to this vast attainment some adequate knowledge of the real qualities of the things which are to be subjected to its inspection is indispensable; that if the matter to be judged of is any thing so large, complex, and conventional as the duty of the citizen, or the public man, to the State; the duty of preserving or destroying the order of things in which we are born; the duty of executing or violating one of the provisions of organic law which the country, having a wide and clear view before and after, had deemed a needful instrumental means for the preservation of that order; that then it is not enough to relegate the citizen, or the public man, to a higher law, and an interior illumination, and leave him there. Such discourse is "as the stars, which give so little light because they are so high." He must agree that in such case, morality itself should go to school. There must be science as well as conscience, as old Fuller has said. She must herself learn of history; she must learn of politics; she must consult the builders of the State, the living and the dead, to know its value, its aspects in the long run, on happiness and morals; its dangers; the means of its preservation; the maxims and arts imperial of its glory. To fit her to be the mistress of civil life, he will agree, that she must come out for a space from the interior round of emotions, and subjective states and contemplations, and introspection, "cloistered, unexercised, unbreathed"—and, carrying with her nothing but her tenderness, her scrupulosity, and her love of truth, survey the objective realities of the State; ponder thoughtfully on the complications, and impediments, and antagonisms which make the noblest politics but an aspiring, an approximation, a compromise, a type, a shadow of good to come, "the buying of great blessings at great prices"—and there learn civil duty *secundum subjectam materiam.* "Add to your virtue knowledge"—or it is no virtue.

And now, is he who accuses Mr. Webster of "sinning against his own conscience," quite sure that he *knows,* that that conscience,—well instructed by profoundest political studies, and thoughts of the reason; well instructed by an appropriate moral institution sedulously applied, did not commend and approve his conduct to himself? Does he know, that he had not anxiously, and maturely studied the ethics of the Constitution, and *as a question of ethics,* but of ethics applied to a stupendous problem of practical life, and had not become satisfied that they were right? Does he know that he had not done this, when his faculties were all at their best; and his motives under no suspicion? May not such an inquirer, for aught you can know, may not that great mind have verily and conscientiously thought that he had learned in that investigation many things? May he not have thought that he learned, that the duty of the inhabitants of the free States, in that day's extremity, to the republic, the duty at all events of statesmen, to the republic, is a little too large, and delicate, and difficult, to be all comprehended in the single emotion of compassion for one class of persons in the commonwealth, or in carrying out the single principle of abstract, and natural, and violent justice to one class? May he not have thought that he found there some stupendous exemplifications of what we read of, in books of casuistry, the "dialectics of conscience," as conflicts of duties; such things as the conflicts of the greater with the less; conflicts of the attainable with the visionary; conflicts of the real with the seeming; and may he not have been soothed to learn that the evil which he found in this part of the Constitution was the least of two; was unavoidable; was compensated; was justified; was commanded, as by a voice from the Mount, by a more exceeding and enduring good? May he not have thought that he had learned, that the grandest, most difficult, most pleasing to God, of the achievements of secular wisdom and philanthropy, is the building of a State; that of the first class of grandeur and difficulty, and acceptableness to Him, in this kind, was the building of our own: that unless everybody of consequence enough to be heard of in the age and generation of Washington,—unless that whole age and generation were in a conspiracy to cheat themselves, and history, and posterity, a certain policy of concession and forbearance of region to region, was indispensable to rear that master work of man; and that that same policy of concession and forbearance is as indispensable, more so, now, to afford a rational ground of hope for its preservation? May he not have thought that he had learned that the obligation, if such in any sense you may call it, of one State to allow itself to become an asylum for those flying from slavery into another State, was an obligation of benevolence, of humanity only, not of justice; that it must therefore, on ethical principles, be exercised under all the limitations which regulate and condition the benevolence of States; that therefore each is to exercise it in strict subordination to its own interests, estimated by a wise statesmanship, and a well- instructed public conscience; that benevolence itself, even its ministrations of mere good- will, is an affair of measure and of proportions; and must choose sometimes between the greater good, and the less; that if, to the highest degree, and widest diffusion of human happiness, a Union of States such as ours, some free, some not so, was necessary; and to such Union the Constitution was necessary; and to such a Constitution this clause was necessary, humanity itself prescribes it, and presides in it? May he not have thought that he learned that there are proposed to humanity in this world many fields of beneficent exertion; some larger, some smaller, some more, some less expensive and profitable to till; that among these it is always lawful, and often indispensable to make a choice; that sometimes, to acquire the right or the ability to labor in one, it is needful to covenant not to invade another; and that such covenant, in partial restraint, rather in reasonable direction of philanthropy, is good in the forum of conscience; and setting out with these very elementary maxims of practical morals, may he not have thought that he learned from the careful study of the facts of our history and opinions, that to acquire the power of advancing the dearest interests of man, through generations countless, by that unequalled security of peace and progress, the Union; the power of advancing the interest of each State, each region, each relation—the slave and the master; the power of subjecting a whole continent all astir, and on fire with the emulation of young republics; of subjecting it, through ages of household calm, to the sweet influences of Christianity, of culture, of the great, gentle, and sure reformer, time; that to enable us to do this, to enable us to grasp this boundless and ever-renewing harvest of philanthropy, it would have been a good bargain—that humanity herself would have approved it—to have bound ourselves never so much as to look across the line into the enclosure of Southern municipal slavery; certainly never to enter it; still less, still less, to

"Pluck its berries harsh and crude,
And with forced fingers rude
Shatter its leaves before the mellowing year."

Until the accuser who charges him, now that he is in his grave, with "having sinned against his conscience," will assert that the conscience of a public man may not, must not, be instructed by profound knowledge of the vast subject-matter with which public life is conversant—even as the conscience of the mariner may be and must be instructed by the knowledge of navigation; and that of the pilot by the knowledge of the depths and shallows of the coast; and that of the engineer of the boat and the train, by the knowledge of the capacities of his mechanism to achieve a proposed velocity; and will assert that he is certain that the consummate science of our great statesman, *was felt by himself to prescribe to his morality* another conduct than that which he adopted, and that he thus consciously outraged that "sense of duty which pursues us ever"—is he not inexcusable, whoever he is, that so judges another?

But it is time that this eulogy was spoken. My heart goes back into the coffin there with him, and I would pause. I went—it is a day or two since—alone, to see again the home which he so dearly loved, the chamber where he died, the grave in which they laid him—all habited as when

"His look drew audience still as night,
Or summer's noontide air,"

till the heavens be no more. Throughout that spacious and calm scene all things to the eye showed at first unchanged. The books in the library, the portraits, the table at which he wrote, the scientific culture of the land, the course of agricultural occupation, the coming- in of harvests, fruit of the seed his own hand had scattered, the animals and implements of husbandry, the trees planted by him in lines, in copses, in orchards, by thousands, the seat under the noble elm on which he used to sit to feel the southwest wind at evening, or hear the breathings of the sea, or the not less audible music of the starry heavens, all seemed at first unchanged. The sun of a bright day, from which, however, something of the fervors of mid-summer were wanting, fell temperately on them all, filled the air on all sides with the utterances of life, and gleamed on the long line of ocean. Some of those whom on earth he loved best, still were there. The great mind still seemed to preside; the great presence to be with you; you might expect to hear again the rich and playful tones of the voice of the old hospitality. Yet a moment more, and all the scene took on the aspect of one great monument, inscribed with his name, and sacred to his memory. And such it shall be in all the future of America! The sensation of desolateness, and loneliness, and darkness, with which you see it now, will pass away; the sharp grief of love and friendship will become soothed; men will repair thither as they are wont to commemorate the great days of history; the same glance shall take in, and the same emotions shall greet and bless the Harbor of the Pilgrims, and the Tomb of Webster.

Chapter XI.

ADDRESS AT THE DEDICATION
OF THE PEABODY INSTITUTE.
Delivered in South Danvers, September 29, 1854.

The Peabody Institute was an adult education foundation aimed at working men, complete with a library and various series of lectures. It sought to bridge the gap between the learning and culture of the upper classes and that of the ordinary laborer. According to Samuel Gilman Brown, it was founded "by the munificence of Geo. Peabody, Esq. of London, and from the first was regarded with great interest by Mr. Choate, who watched with sincere pleasure the prosperity of the town where he commenced his professional life, and which conferred upon him his first honors." Choate here calls on residents of Danvers to take an active part in this institution that would be "henceforth part and parcel, through its corporate existence, of the civil identity and privilege of Danvers."

I ESTEEM it a great privilege to have been allowed to unite with my former townsmen, and the friends of so many years,—by whose seasonable kindness the earliest struggles of my professional life were observed and helped,—the friends of all its periods,—so I have found them,—to unite with you in the transaction for which we are assembled. In all respects it is one of rare interest. You have come together to express anew your appreciation of the character and the objects of the giver of this splendid charity, to repeat and republish your grateful acceptance of it, and to dedicate this commodious and beautiful structure to its faithful and permanent administration. You open to-day for Danvers,—its inhabitants of this time, and all its successions,—the Lyceum of knowledge and morality. Under this dedication it shall stand while Massachusetts shall stand. This edifice will crumble, certainly, to be replaced with another; this generation of the first recipients of the gift,—the excellent giver himself,—will soon pass away; but while our social and civil system shall endure; while law shall be administered; while the sentiments of justice, gratitude, and honor, shall beat in one heart on your territory, the charity is immortal.

For every one among you it is set open equally. No fear that the religious opinions he holds sacred will be assailed, or the politics he cultivates insulted, will keep back any from his share of the diffusive good. Other places and other occasions you reserve for dissent and disputation, and struggle for mastery, and the sharp competitions of life. But here shall be peace and reconciliation. Within these walls, the knowledge and the morality, which are of no creed and no party; which are graceful and profitable for all alike,—of every creed and every party; which are true and real to every mind, as mind, and from the nature of mind,—and to every conscience, as conscience, and from the nature of conscience; and which are the same thing, therefore, in every brain and every heart,—this alone,—knowledge and morality, broad, free, as humanity itself,—is to be inculcated here.

Happy and privileged the community, beyond the measure of New England privilege even, for whom such high educational instrumentalities are thus munificently provided, and made perpetual! Happy especially, if they shall rouse themselves to improve them to their utmost capacity,—if they shall feel that they are summoned by a new motive, and by an obligation unfelt before, to an unaccustomed effort to appropriate to their hearts and their reason, all the countless good which is hidden in knowledge and a right life,—an effort to become—more than before—wise, bright, thoughtful, ingenious, good; to attain to the highest degree of learning which is compatible with the practical system of things of which they are part; to feed the immortal, spiritual nature with an ampler and higher nutrition, enriching memory with new facts, judgment with sounder thoughts, taste with more beautiful images, the moral sense with more of all things whatsoever they are lovely, honest, and of good report,—the reality of virtue, the desert of praise.

Happy, almost, above all, the noble giver, whose heart is large enough to pay, of the abundance which crowns his life,—to pay out of his single means,—the whole debt this generation owes the future. I honor and love him, not merely that his energy, sense, and integrity have raised him from a poor boy—waiting in that shop yonder—to spread a table for the entertainment of princes,—not merely because the brilliant professional career which has given him a position so commanding in the mercantile and social circles of the commercial capital of the world, has left him as completely American—the heart as wholly untravelled—as when he first stepped on the shore of England to seek his fortune, sighing to think that the ocean rolled between him and home; jealous of honor; wakeful to our interests; helping his country, not by swagger and vulgarity, but by recommending her credit; vindicating her title to be trusted on the exchange of nations; squandering himself in hospitalities to her citizens—

a man of deeds, not of words,—not for these merely I love and honor him, but because his nature is affectionate and unsophisticated still; because his memory comes over so lovingly to this sweet Argos, to the schoolroom of his childhood, to the old shop and kind master, and the graves of his father and mother; and because he has had the sagacity, and the character to indulge these unextinguished affections in a gift, not of vanity and ostentation, but of supreme and durable utility.

I have found it quite incompatible with my engagements and health, to methodize the thoughts, which have crowded on my mind in the prospect of meeting you to-day, into anything like elaborate or extended discourse; but I have certainly wished,—instead of mere topics of congratulation; or instead of diffusing myself exclusively on the easy and obvious commonplaces of the utility of knowledge, and the beauty of virtue; or instead of the mere indulgence of those trains of memory and sensibility, to which the spectacle of old friends, and of the children and grandchildren of other friends, "whom my dim eyes in vain explore," almost irrepressibly impels me,—instead of this, to submit a practical suggestion or two in regard to the true modes of turning the Lyceum to its utmost account; and then, in regard to the motives you are under to do so. These suggestions I make diffidently; and, therefore, I would not make them at all, but from the conviction that in your hands they may come to assume some little value.

I take it for granted that the declared wishes of Mr. Peabody will be considered as determining, quite peremptorily, the general mode of administering this fund. Better educational instrumentalities, indeed, no man's wisdom, in the circumstances, could have devised. Courses of lectures, then, and a library of good books, these are to form the means of the Lyceum; and the problem is, in what way can you make the most of them.

It may seem a little exaggerated at its first statement, and perhaps alarming, but it will serve at least to introduce my more particular ideas, to say that the *true view for you to take of this large provision of mental means, and of your relations to it, is to regard yourselves as having become by its bestowment permanently the members of an institution which undertakes to teach you by lectures and a library.* Herein exactly is the peculiarity of your new privilege. You are no longer, as heretofore it has been with you, merely to be indulged the opportunity of a few evenings in a year to listen, for the amusement of it, to half a dozen discourses of as many different speakers, on as many totally disconnected topics, treated possibly for ostentation, and adapted only to entertain,—but, however treated, and whatever fit, for totally forgotten in an hour; preceded, followed up, and assisted, by no preparation and no effort of the hearer; giving no direction whatever to his thoughts or readings; separated from each other, even while the lyceum season lasts, by a week of labor, devoted, even in its leisure moments, to trains of thought or snatches of reading wholly unauxiliar and irrelative, and for nine months or ten months of the year totally discontinued. Thanks to this munificence, you are come to the fruition of far other opportunities. An institution of learning, in the justest sense of the term, is provided for you. Lectures are to be delivered for you through a far larger portion of the year; a library, which will assuredly swell to thousands of volumes, is to be accumulated under your eye, from which you may derive the means of accompanying any lecturer on any subject from evening to evening; and this system of provision is permanent,—henceforth part and parcel, through its corporate existence, of the civil identity and privilege of Danvers. You enter, therefore, to-day—you may enter—a new and important school; as durably such, as truly such,—having regard to differences of circumstantial details,—as the Seminary at Andover, or the Law School at Cambridge, or the College of Medicine at Philadelphia,—all of them schools, too, and all teaching by lectures and a library.

Setting out with this idea, let me say a word on the lectures of this school,—what they should be, and how they should be heard, assisted, and turned to account by those who hear them. And I submit to the trustees of the charity to reflect, whether a succession of such discourses as I have indicated, on disconnected topics, by different speakers,—however brilliant and able the individual performer may be,—will, in the long run, yield the good, or any approximation to the good, which would be derived from courses of lectures more or less extended, like the Lowell Lectures of Boston, each by a single person, devoted to the more exact and thorough treatment of a single important subject.

Consider that the diffusion of knowledge among you is the aim of the founder. The imparting of knowledge is the task which he sets his lecturer to do; and of knowledge in any proper sense,—knowledge within the legal meaning of this charity,—how much can he impart who comes once in a year, once in a lifetime, perhaps, before his audience, a stranger, addresses it an hour, and goes his way? He can teach little, if he tries; and the chances are infinite, that to teach that little he will not try. The temptations and the tendencies of that system of exhibition are irresistible, to make him despair of conveying knowledge, and devote himself to producing effect; to select some topic mainly of emotional or imaginative capability; and even then to sacrifice the beauty which is in truth, to the counterfeit presentment which mocks it in glitter, exaggeration, ingenuity, and intensity. If he would spend his hour in picking up and explaining a shell or pebble from the shore of the ocean of knowledge, it were something; but that seems unworthy of himself, and of the expectations which await him, and up he soars, or down he sinks, to rhetoric or bathos; and when his little part is best discharged, it is not much more than the lovely song of one who hath a pleasant voice, and can play well upon an instrument.

I do not say that such lectures are hurtful. I do not deny them a certain capacity of usefulness. I do not say they are not all which you should look for in our lyceums, as ordinarily they are constituted. They are all which, for the present, you will yourselves, perhaps, be able to provide. But to an endowed and durable foundation like this, they are totally inapplicable. They would be no more nor less, after you shall be completely organized, than a gross abuse of the charity, and violation of the will, of the giver. It is not merely that they would teach no knowledge, and would not assume to do it, and that the nature and laws of that kind of composition, and the conditions of its existence, totally exclude such a function. It goes further than that. The relations between teacher and pupil, under such a system, never exist at all. The audience never think of coming before the lecturer to have the truths of the last lecture retouched, and new ones deduced or added; to have the difficulties, of which they have been thinking since they heard him before, resolved; to ask questions; to be advised what authors to read, or what experiments to undertake, on the subject he is illustrating. They carry no part of his sermon into the week with them; and he never knows or asks whether they do or not. In the nature of things, this all must be so. It is of the essential conception of knowledge, as the founder here uses the word,—knowledge as applicable to anything,—that it includes many particulars of fact or idea, arranged by method, that is, arranged according to their true relations.

Whatever it be on which knowledge is to be imparted,—whether one of the phenomena of nature, as vegetable life, or insensible motion, or the periods of the stars; or some great aspect of humanity, as the history of a renowned age or event, pregnant of a stupendous future, or a marked man of the heroic and representative type; or one of the glorious productions of mind, as a constitution of free government, or a union of states into one nationality, a great literature, or even a great poem,—whatever it be, that which makes up the consummate knowledge of it is at once so much a unity and an infinity,—it unfolds itself into so many particulars, one deduced from another by series ever progressive, one modifying another, every one requiring to be known in order that any one may be exactly known,—that if you mean to teach it by lectures at all, you must substitute a totally different system. *It must be done by courses continuously delivered, and frequently, by the same person, and having for their object to achieve the exact and exhaustive treatment of something*,—some science, some art, some age, some transaction, that changed the face of fortune and history,—something worthy to be completely known. He whom you call to labor on this foundation must understand that it is knowledge which is demanded of him. He must assure himself that he is to have his full time to impart it. He must come to the work, appreciating that he is not to be judged by the brilliancy or dulness of one passage, or one evening; but that he must stand or fall by the mass and aggregate of his teachings. He is to feel that he is an instructor, not the player of a part on a stage; that he is to teach truth, and not cut a rhetorical caper; enthusiastic in the pursuit, exact and veracious as a witness under oath in the announcement. I would have him able to say of the subject which he treats, what Cousin said of philosophy in the commencement of one of his celebrated courses, after a long interruption by the instability of the government of France: "Devoted entirely to it, after having had the honor to *suffer a little in its service,* I come to *consecrate to its illustration, unreservedly,* all that remains to me of strength and of life."

And, now, how are you to hear such courses of lectures? Essentially by placing yourselves in the relation of pupils to the lecturer. For the whole period of his course, let the subject he teaches compose the study of the hours, or fragments of hours which you give to study at all. You would read something, on some topic, every day, in all events. Let that reading, less or more, relate exclusively or mainly to the department of knowledge on which you go to hear him. If he knows his business, he will recommend all the best books pertaining to that department, and on these the first purchases for the Library will be quite likely in part to be expended. Attend the instructions of his lips by the instruction of the printed treatise. In this way only can you, by any possibility, avail yourselves at once of all that books and teachers can do. In this way only can you make one coöperate with the other. In this way only—in a larger view—can you rationally count on considerable and ever-increasing acquisitions of knowledge. Remember that your opportunities for such attainments in this school, after all, are to be few and brief. You and I are children of labor at last. The practical, importunate, ever-recurring duties of the calling to which we are assigned must have our best of life. What are your vacations, or mine, from work, for the still air of delightful studies! They are only divers infinitely minute particles of time,—half-hours before the morning or midday meal is quite ready,—days, now and then, not sick enough for the physician nor well enough for work,—a rainy afternoon,—the priceless evening, when the long task is done,—these snatches and interstitial spaces—moments literal and fleet—these are all the chances that we can borrow or create for the luxury of learning. How difficult it is to arrest these moments, to aggregate them, to till them, as it were, to make them day by day extend our knowledge, refine our tastes, accomplish our whole culture, to scatter in them the seed that shall grow up, as Jeremy Taylor has said, "to crowns and sceptres" of a true wisdom,—how difficult is this we all appreciate. To turn them to any profit at all, we must religiously methodize them. Desultory reading and desultory revery are to be forever abandoned. A page in this book, and another in that—ten minutes thought or conversation on this subject, and the next ten on that—this strenuous and specious idleness is not the way by which our intervals of labor are to open to us the portals of the crystal palace of truth. Such reading, too, and such thinking are an indulgence by which the mind loses its power—by which curiosity becomes sated, ennui supervenes, and the love of learning itself is irrevocably lost. Therefore, I say, methodize your moments. Let your reading be systematic ever, so that every interval of rest shall have its book provided for it; and during the courses of your lectures, let those books treat the topics of the course.

Let me illustrate my meaning. You are attending, I will say, a course on astronomy, consisting of two lectures in a week, for two months. Why should you not regard yourselves for these two months as students of astronomy, so far as you can study anything, or think of anything, outside of your business; and why not determine to know nothing else; but to know as much of that as you can, for all that time? Consider what this would involve, and what it might accomplish. Suppose that you, by strenuous and persistent effort, hold that one subject fully in view for so long a period; that you do your utmost to turn your thoughts and conversation on it; that you write out the lecture, from notes or memory, as soon as it is given, and rèperuse and master it before you hear the next; that you read, not on other parts of the science, but on the very parts which the lecturer has arrived at and is discussing; that you devote an hour each evening to surveying the architecture of the heavens for yourselves, seeking to learn, not merely to indulge a vague and wandering sort of curiosity, or even a grand, but indistinct and general emotion, as if listening to imaginary music of spheres, but to aspire to the science of the stars, to fix their names, to group them in classes and constellations, to trace their paths, their reciprocal influence, their courses everlasting,—suppose that thus, and by voluntary continuous exertion, you concentrate on one great subject, for so considerable a period, all the moments of time and snatches of hasty reading and opportunities of thought that otherwise would have wasted themselves everywhere, and gone off by insensible evaporation,—do you not believe that it would tell decisively upon your mental culture and your positive attainments? Would not the effort of attention so prolonged and exclusive be a discipline itself inestimable? Would not the particulars of so much well-systematized reading and thought arrange themselves in your minds in the form of science,—harder to forget than to remember? and

might you not hope to begin to feel the delicious sensations implied in growing consciously in the knowledge of truth?

I have taken for granted, in these thoughts on the best mode of administering the charity, that your own earnest purpose will be to turn it, by some mode,
to its utmost account. The gratitude and alacrity with which you accepted the
gift show quite well how you appreciate the claims of knowledge and the dignity of mental culture, and what value you set upon this rare and remarkable
appropriation to uses so lofty. I have no need, therefore, to exhort you to profit
of these opportunities; but there are one or two views on which I have formerly
reflected somewhat, and which I will briefly lay before you.

It is quite common to say, and much more common to think, without saying it aloud, that mental culture and learning, above the elements, may well
claim a high place, as luxuries and indulgence, and even a grand utility, for those
whose condition allows them a lifetime for such luxury and such indulgence,
and the appropriation of such a good; but that for labor—properly so called—
they can do little, even if labor could pause to acquire them. Not so has the
founder of this charity reasoned; nor so will you. He would say, and so do I,—
Seek for mental power, and the utmost practicable love and measure of knowledge, exactly because they will do so much for labor; first, to inform and direct
its exertions; secondly, to refine and adorn it, and disengage it from too absolute
an immersion in matter, and bring it into relation to the region of ideas and spirituality and abstraction; and, thirdly, to soothe its fatigues and relieve its burdens and compose its discontent.

True is it, of all our power, eminence, and consideration, as of our existence,
that the condition is labor. Our lot is labor. There is no reversal of the doom of
man for us. But is that a reason why we should not aspire to the love and attainment of learning, and to the bettering of the mind? For that very reason we
should do so. Does not the industry of a people at last rest upon and embody
the intellect of the people? Is not its industry as its intellect?

I say, then, forasmuch as we are children of labor, cultivate mental power.
Pointing the friends of humanity, and of America, to this charity, I say to them,
go and do likewise. Diffuse mental power. Give it to more than have it now.
Give it in a higher degree. Give it in earlier life. Think how stupendous, yet
how practicable it were to make, by an improved popular culture, the entire
laborious masses of New England more ingenious, more inventive, more prudent than now they are. How much were effected,—how much for power;
how much for enjoyment; how much for a true glory,—by this accession to the
quality of its mind. It would show itself in half a century in every acre of her

surface. In the time it would save, in the strength it would impart, in the waste it would prevent, in the more sedulous husbandry of all the gifts of God, in richer soils, created or opened; in the great coöperating forces of nature—air, water, steam, fertility—yoked in completer obedience to the car of labor; in the multiplicity of useful inventions, those unfailing exponents, as well as promoters, of popular mental activity and reach, in the aggregate of production, swelled, diversified, enriched; in the refluent wave of wealth, subsiding here and there in reservoirs, in lakes, in springs perennial, but spread, too, everywhere in rills and streamlets, and falling in the descent of dew and the dropping of the cloud,— in these things you would see the peaceful triumphs of an improved mind. Nor in these alone, or chiefly. More beautiful far, and more precious, would they beam abroad in the elevation of the standard of comfortable life; in the heightened sense of individual responsibility and respectability, and a completer individual development; in happier homes; in better appreciation of the sacredness of property, and the sovereignty of justice in the form of law; in more time found and better prized, when the tasks of the day were all well done,—more time found and better prized for the higher necessities of the intellect and soul.

I have not time to dwell now on the second reason, by which I suggested that labor should be persuaded to seek knowledge, though it would well deserve a fuller handling. You find that reason in the tendency of culture and learning to refine the work-day life, and adorn it; to disengage it from the contacts of matter, and elevate it to the sphere of ideas and abstraction and spirituality; to withdraw, as Dr. Johnson has said,—"to withdraw us from the power of our senses; to make the past, the distant, or the future predominate over the present, and thus to advance us in the dignity of thinking beings." Surely we need not add a self-inflicted curse to that which punished the fall. To earn our bread in the sweat of our brow is ordained to us certainly; but not, therefore, to forget in whose image we were made, nor to suffer all beams of the original brightness to go out. Who has doomed us, or any of us, to labor so exclusive and austere, that only half, the lower half, of our nature can survive it? The unrest of avarice, or ambition, or vanity, may do it; but no necessity of our being, and no appointment of its author. Shall we, of our own election, abase ourselves? Do you feel that the mere tasks of daily labor ever employ the whole man? Have you not a conscious nature, other and beside that which tills the earth, drives the plane, squares the stone, creates the fabric of art,—a nature intellectual, spiritual, moral, capacious of science, capacious of truth beyond the sphere of sense, with large discourse of reason, looking before and after, and taking hold on that within the veil?

What forbids that this nature shall have its daily bread also day by day? What forbids that it have time to nourish its sympathy with all kindred human blood, by studying the grand facts of universal history; to learn to look beyond the chaotic flux and reflux of mere appearances, which are the outside of the world around it, into their scientific relations and essential quality; to soar from effects to causes, and through causes to the first; to begin to recognize and to love, here and now, in waning moon or star of evening, or song of solemn bird, or fall of water, or "self-born carol of infancy," or transcendent landscape, or glorious self-sacrifice— to begin to recognize and love in these, that beauty here which shall be its dwelling-place and its vesture in the life to come; to accustom itself to discern, in all vicissitudes of things, the changed and falling leaf, the golden harvest, the angry sigh of November's wind, the storm of snow, the temporary death of nature, the opening of the chambers of the South, and the unresting round of seasons— to discern not merely the sublime circle of eternal change, but the unfailing law, flowing from the infinite Mind, and the "varied God"—filling and moving, and in all things, yet personal and apart? What forbids it to cultivate and confirm

> "The glorious habit by which sense is made
> Subservient still to moral purposes,
> Auxiliar to divine?"

What forbids that it grow

> "Accustomed to desires that feed
> On fruitage gathered from the Tree of Life?"

I do not say that every man, even in a condition of competence, can exemplify this nobler culture and this rarer knowledge. But I will say that the exactions of labor do not hinder it. Recall a familiar, though splendid and remarkable instance or two.

Burns reaped as much and as well as the duller companion by his side, and meantime was conceiving an immortal song of Scotland; and Hugh Miller was just as painstaking a stonemason and as good a workman as if he had not so husbanded his spare half-hours and moments as to become, while an apprentice and journeyman, a profound geologist and master of a clear and charming English style. But how much more a man was the poet and the geologist; how far fuller the consciousness of being; how much larger the daily draught of that admiration, hope, and love, which are the life and voice of souls!

I come to add the final reason why the working man, by whom I mean the whole brotherhood of industry, should set on mental culture and that knowledge which is wisdom a value so high—only not supreme—subordinate alone to the exercises and hopes of religion itself. And that is, that therein he shall so surely find rest from labor; succor under its burdens; forgetfulness of its cares, composure in its annoyances. It is not always that the busy day is followed by the peaceful night. It is not always that fatigue wins sleep. Often some vexation outside of the toil that has exhausted the frame, some loss in a bargain, some loss by an insolvency, some unforeseen rise or fall of prices, some triumph of a mean or fraudulent competitor,

> "The oppressor's wrong, the proud man's contumely,
> The pangs of despised love, the law's delay,
> The insolence of office, and the spurns
> That patient merit of the unworthy takes,"

some self-reproach, perhaps, follow you within the door, chill the fireside, sow the pillow with thorns, and the dark care is last in the last waking thought, and haunts the vivid dream. Happy, then, is he who has laid up in youth, and held fast in all fortune, a genuine and passionate love of reading. True balm of hurt minds; of surer and more healthful charm than "poppy or mandragora, or all the drowsy syrups of the world," by that single taste,—by that single capacity, he may bound in a moment into the still region of delightful studies, and be at rest. He recalls the annoyance that pursues him; reflects that he has done all that might become a man to avoid or bear it; he indulges in one good, long, human sigh, picks up the volume where the mark kept his place, and in about the same time that it takes the Mahometan in the Spectator to put his head in the bucket of water, and raise it out, he finds himself exploring the arrow-marked ruins of Nineveh with Layard; or worshipping at the spring-head of the stupendous Missouri, with Clark and Lewis; or watching with Columbus for the sublime moment of the rising of the curtain from before the great mystery of the sea; or looking reverentially on while Socrates—the discourse of immortality ended— refuses the offer of escape, and takes in his hand the poison to die in obedience to the unrighteous sentence of the law; or, perhaps, it is in the contemplation of some vast spectacle or phenomenon of nature that he has found his quick peace—the renewed exploration of one of her great laws—or some glimpse opened by the pencil of St. Pierre, or Humboldt, or Chateaubriand, or Wilson, of the "blessedness and glory of her own deep, calm, and mighty existence."

Let the case of a busy lawyer testify to the priceless value of the love of reading. He comes home, his temples throbbing, his nerves shattered, from a trial of a week; surprised and alarmed by the charge of the judge, and pale with anxiety about the verdict of the next morning, not at all satisfied with what he has done himself, though he does not yet see how he could have improved it; recalling with dread and self-disparagement, if not with envy, the brilliant effort of his antagonist, and tormenting himself with the vain wish that he could have replied to it—and altogether a very miserable subject, and in as unfavorable a condition to accept comfort from wife and children as poor Christian in the first three pages of the Pilgrim's Progress. With a superhuman effort he opens his book, and in the twinkling of an eye he is looking into the full "orb of Homeric or Miltonic song," or he stands in the crowd—breathless, yet swayed as forests or the sea by winds—hearing and to judge the Pleadings for the Crown; or the philosophy which soothed Cicero or Boethius in their afflictions, in exile, prison, and the contemplation of death, breathes over his petty cares like the sweet south; or Pope or Horace laughs him into good humor; or he walks with Æneas and the Sibyl in the mild light of the world of the laurelled dead; and the courthouse is as completely forgotten as the dreams of a pre-adamite life. Well may he prize that endeared charm, so effectual and safe, without which the brain had long ago been chilled by paralysis, or set on fire of insanity!

To these uses and these enjoyments, to mental culture and knowledge and morality, the guide, the grace, the solace of labor on all his fields, we dedicate this charity! May it bless you in all your successions! and may the admirable giver survive to see that the debt which he recognizes to the future is completely discharged; survive to enjoy in the gratitude and love and honor of this generation, the honor and love and gratitude with which the latest will assuredly cherish his name, and partake and transmit his benefaction!

CHAPTER XII.

SPEECH DELIVERED IN FANEUIL HALL.
October 31, 1855.

Choate gave this address before a large meeting of Whigs of the Boston area. He sets forth what will become a familiar theme of his until the end of his life: the poison introduced into the country's political life through the emergence of the Republican Party, or as he puts it, "the geographical party." "We come to protest," he declares to his audience, "with all possible emphasis and solemnity, against the inauguration, as they call it, of the party of the sections."

Like Daniel Webster, he does not hesitate to describe slavery as an evil. But, also like Webster, he considers the question impossible of solution unless both sides proceed according to the spirit of fraternal charity that must inform the relations of peoples whose fates were bound together by the ratification of the Constitution. Fanaticism and hatred on both sides must cease. In Choate's opinion, Northern radicalism has had precisely the opposite of its intended effect, tending to confirm the South in its position and to encourage it to a more aggressive posture than it might otherwise have assumed. "Is it not possible that a part of what they [the "geographical party"] call the aggressive spirit of slavery may be reaction against our own aggression?" he asks. Thus the slavery question, so fateful and portentous, is rightly a matter to be referred to statesmen rather than to radicals who possess little comprehension of the disaster that could befall the nation should an impatience with gradualism and compromise lead to the shedding of blood.

I AM gratified, beyond the power of language to express, by your kindness. By this thronging audience I am even more gratified. In this alone I hope I see the doom of the geographical party. It would have been a thing portentous and mournful, if commercial Boston had not thus poured itself into this Hall, to declare, by its ten thousand voices, against the first measure tending practically and with a real menace to a separation of the States ever yet presented, or certainly in our time presented, to the judgment or the passions of the people of America. Who should be of the earliest to discern and of the wisest to decide the true great question of the day? Did anybody suppose that your intelligence could not see what a proposition to organize the people of this country into two great geographical parties must come to if successful? Did anybody suppose that, seeing this, you would help it on, or fall asleep upon it? You, the children of the merchant princes,—you, whose profession of commerce and arts give you to know and feel, with a sort of professional consciousness and intensity, our republic to be one,—one and undivided; one and indivisible, let us say,—you, whose hearts, abroad, yet untravelled, have sometimes leaped up when you have seen the radiant flag, burning on the waste sea, along the desolate and distant coast, beneath unfamiliar constellations;—and when you have felt your country's great arm around you, were you expected to be indifferent upon a proposition to rend her into two great rabid factions, or to be cheated into a belief that there was no such proposition before the country at all?

Thank God, this sight dispels both branches of this misapprehension. The city is here, all right and straight out! Commerce is here! Commerce, in whose wants, on whose call, the Union, this Union, under this Constitution, began to be; Commerce that rocked the cradle is here,—not to follow the hearse, but to keep off the murderer; or, if they prefer it, to keep off the doctor!

The arts, the industry, of civilization, of intellect, and of the people, are here; they to which the mines and wheat-fields and cotton-grounds of a bountiful and common country supply that raw material which they give back in shapes of use and taste and beauty—they are here;—they who celebrated the establishment of the government by long processions of the trades, by music and banners, and thanksgiving to God,—singing together as morning stars over the rising ball, for the hope of a future of rewarded labor—they are here to bear witness, that the prayers of the fathers have been graciously heard, and to remember and to guard that instrumentality of constitutional union, to which, under his goodness, they owe all these things. Aye, and the charities, the philanthropy, the humanity, that dwell in these homes and hearts, are here to make their protest against the first step to moral treason—charities that love all human kind; yet are comprehended all and enfolded in the dear name of country,—philanthropy and humanity—not spasmodic, not savage, not the cold phrase of the politician, not hypocritical, not impatient, but just, wise, combining, working with—not in spite of—the will of the Highest, sowing the seed with tears, with trust, and committing the harvest to the eternal years of God—these are here. Yes, we are all here. We come to ratify the ratification. We come to say to our excellent representatives in the late Convention, again and again, Well done, good and faithful! We come to engage our hearty support and our warmest good wishes for the success of the candidates they have nominated, every man of them. We come to declare that upon trying ourselves by all the approved tests, we are perfectly satisfied that we are alive; that we are glad we are alive, since there is work to do worthy of us; that we prefer to remain for the present, Whigs! Constitutional Whigs! Massachusetts Whigs! Faneuil Hall Whigs! Daniel Webster and Henry Clay Whigs!—that we have no new party to choose to-night; that, when we have, we shall choose any other, aye, any other, than that which draws the black line of physical and social geography across the charmed surface of our native land, and finds a republic on one side to love, and nothing but an aristocracy to be "abhorred" and "avoided" on the other! Take any shape but that! We come to protest, with all possible emphasis and solemnity, against the inauguration, as they call it, of the party of the sections. We say that for any object which constitutional patriotism can approve, such a party is useless. We say, that for its own avowed objects, if it has any specific and definite objects which are constitutional and just, it is useless. We say, that if defeated in its attempt to get possession of the national government, the mere struggle will insure the triumph of that very administration on which it seems to make war; will make the fortune of certain local dealers in politics; will agitate and alienate and tend to put asunder whom God hath joined. We hold that if it should succeed in that attempt, it would be the most terrible of public calamities. I, for one, do not believe that this nation could bear it. I am not, it is true, quite of the mind of the Senator from Ohio, who dared to tell an assembly in Maine, not many days since, that there is now no union between us and the South; that the pretended Union is all meretricious; that there is no heart in it; that Russia does not hate England, nor England Russia, more than the men of the North and the men of the South hate each other. The allegation is, I think, yet untrue; the pleasure, the apparent pleasure and exultation with which he uttered it, is nothing less than awful! But yet, when we keep in view, as ever we must, the grand and unalterable conditions and peculiarities of the American national life; the capital fact lying underneath that we are historically, by constitutional law, and to a vast practical extent, a mere neighborhood of separate and sovereign States, united practically by a written league, or more accurately, by a government holding only a few great powers, and touching a few large objects; united better, perhaps, so far as united at all, by the moral ties of blood and race, a common flag, the memory of common dangers, the heritage of a common glory;—united thus, partially by that subtile essence of nationality, the consciousness of unity, the pride of unity,—itself a spirit of recent creation, requiring still to be solicited, to be reinforced, to be diffused; having regard to those instrumentalities and influences, moral and physical, which encompass us ever and endanger us, and especially to the consideration that besides the centrifugal tendencies of sovereign States, impelling them ever apart, there is a line,— a dark, dark line,—almost a fissure in the granite, whose imperfect cohesion can scarcely resist the vast weight on either side;—recollecting these things, and recollecting, too, how much more than by reason or public virtue or their true interests, men are moved by anger, pride, and force, in great civil crises,—in any way we can survey it, we cannot possibly fail to see that the process of forming such an organization, and its influence, if completely formed and fully in action, would compose a new and disturbing element in our system, which it is scarcely able to encounter, and to which no wise man and genuine Unionist would not shudder to see it exposed.

Why, look at it. Here is a stupendous fabric of architecture; a castle; a capitol; suppose the capitol at Washington. It is a fortress at once, and a temple. The great central dome swells to heaven. It rests grandly on its hill by its own weight kept steadfast, and seemingly immovable; Titan hands might have built it; it may stand to see the age of a nation pass by. But one imperfection there is; a seam in the marble; a flaw in the iron; a break scarcely visible, yet a real vertical fissure, parting by an imperceptible opening from top to foundation the whole in two. The builder saw it, and guarded against it as well as he might; those who followed, to repair, with pious and skilful hands, tried by underpinning, by lateral support, by buttress and buttress alternately, to hold the disjointed sides in contact. Practically, it was becoming less formidable; the moss was beginning to conceal it, even; and here comes a workman who proposes to knock out the well-planned lateral supports, loosen the underpinning of the ends, dig a yawning excavation under both of them, and then set on each the mountain weight of a frowning and defiant dome of its own. Down the huge pile topples in an hour. Small compensation it is that the architect of ruin finds his grave, too, beneath it!

It is to do what we may to scatter this organization in its beginnings that we are here to-night. It is for this opportunity, chiefly, that the Whigs of Massachusetts are absolutely glad that they are alive. True, we seek also to redeem Massachusetts. That last legislative year of all sorts of ignorance, and all sorts of folly, and all sorts of corruption; not dignified, but made hateful and shameful by a small and mean mimicry of treason, withal—we would blot it all out from our proud annals forever. The year which deserted Washburn, slighted the counsels of Clifford, struck a feeble but malignant blow at the judicial tenure, nullified a law of the Union, constitutional, if the Constitution is constitutional,—we would forget. Let it not come into the number of our months. In fact, let us talk of something else.

Yes, Whigs of Boston and Massachusetts! We strike at higher game. It is because the experiment is now making, whether a sectional party, merging and overriding all others, is possible; whether candidates for the presidency shall openly electioneer for that office, by advocating the formation of such a party, and not see the mantling cup of honors, to which they are reaching, dashed to their feet by the indignation of the whole country—it is because this experiment is making today that we feel that we have a duty to do. Who of us knows that it is not his last civil labor? Who of us does not feel that if it were so, our noblest labor were our last? Were it even so, what signifies it whether we personally and politically sink or swim—live or die—survive or perish! Would not that be a bright page wherein the historian, after having recorded in the former chapters of his book the long antecedents of the Whigs,—that they held the government of this good old State, with small exception, for a quarter of a century; that they held it long enough to embody their politics in official state papers; on the statute book; in public speech; through their accredited press; in the prevailing tone and maxims of public life; long enough to see those politics bear rich, practical autumnal fruits; that while they held power, popular education was improved; the instrumentalities of intercourse of all parts of the State with each other, and with the States beyond, were multiplied and perfected, and the universal industrial prosperity of the people advanced by the reforming hand, reforming wisely; that the sentiment of obedience to law, popular or unpopular, while law, of observance of order, of the supremacy of the national Constitution, within its limits over the State, and of the State constitution over the legislature; of the practicability and the necessity of reconciling and performing all political duties, not one, nor half, but *all*,—that this sentiment was taught and was practised; that liberty of conscience was held sacred; that the right to be represented equally in the government of the State was recognized, and sought to be retained in the Constitution as belonging to every human being, because such, inhabiting her soil; that they held even good laws powerless, and a government of laws impossible, if not interpreted and administered by judges as impartial as the lot of humanity will admit, and helped to be so by the tenure of independence of the ebb and flow of party; that although ever they boasted to be a branch of a national Whig connection, and as such, held a creed of national politics, combining a policy of peace with honor, industry protected by wise discrimination, improvement of the great natural agencies of intercourse, a provident and liberal and statesmanlike administration of the public domain,—a creed on which wise and good men of every State, in large numbers, sometimes by large majorities, were with them; although they held this creed of union, they yet left themselves wholly free to cherish and act on the local sentiment of slavery; that they opposed its extension by their press, by their vote, by public debate—its extension by annexation of Texas and Cuba, and by repeal of the compromise, and that their greatest and best, all who represented them, did so ever up to the limits of the Constitution and an honest statesmanship, and paused reverentially there;—would it not be a glorious page on which, after concluding this detail, he should record that their last organic act was to meet the dark wave of this tide of sectionalism on the strand, breast high, and roll it back upon its depths; aye, or to be buried under it! Would not that be higher than to follow the advice of one, once of us, who counsels the Whigs to march out of the field with all the honors? Yes, we reject the word of command. We will not march out of the field at all. We will stand just where we are, and defend those honors and add to them. Perhaps we may fall. That were better than the flight he advises; to fall, and let our recorded honors thicken on our graves. That were better than flight; but who can tell that there are not others higher to be won yet? Laurels farther up; more precious—less perishing; to be won by more heroic civil duty, and the austerer glory of more self-sacrifice. Be these ungathered laurels ours to reap!

But it occurs to me, that I have been a little too fast in assuming that your minds are already all made up not to join this geographical party. Let us then pause, and inspect the thing a little. Let us do it under a threefold dissection. See then, first, exactly what it is to be; what, if completely formed, it is to be. Second, what good it will do. And, third, what evil it will do; what evil the process of forming it will do; what evil it will do after it is formed. First, what is it to be, when formed? Exactly an organization of all the people of the free States, if they can get all, if not, majorities of all, into a political party proper, to oppose the whole people of all the slave States, organized into just such another association upon the single, but broad and fertile topic of slavery. Into this organization, on one side and the other, every other party is, if possible, to be merged; certainly by this one, every other is to be out-voted and vanquished. This promising and happy consummation, mark you, is to be a *political party proper*. It is not to be a public opinion on slavery. It is not to be a public opinion against slavery. It is not to be a mere universal personal conviction of every man which he may carry with him into all his political duties and relations, and bind up with his Democratic opinions, or Whig opinions, or Native American opinions;—that is not it, at all. It is to be, and act, as a political party properly, technically, and with tremendous emphasis so called. It is to fill office, make laws, govern great States, govern the nation; and to do this by the one single test of what is called opposition to slavery; on the one single impulse of hate and dread of the aristocracy of the South, by which slavery is maintained. To carry out this opposition, to breathe forth this hate, and this dread in action, it lives; it holds its conventions,

supports its press, selects its candidates, prescribes their creed, conducts its electioneering, and directs every act that it does and every word that it speaks. And
now, when you consider how prodigious an agency in a republic a flushed and
powerful party is at the best; when you remember what it has done to shame
and scare away liberty from her loved haunts and home by the blue Ægean, or
beneath the sunny skies of Italy; when you consider how party, as the general
fact, is sure to form and guide that public opinion which rules the world; how
it grows to be "the madness of the many for the benefit of the few;" when you
consider that to win or retain the general voice, all the ability this organization
can possibly command will be enlisted and paid; that it will offer office to the
ambitious, spoils to the greedy, the dear, delicious indulgence of his one single
idea to the zealot, strong in faith, fierce and narrow in his creed; to the sen-
timentalist and *littérateur,* the corrupting praise of a foreign press; to a distempered and unmeaning philanthropy, the cure of one evil by the creation of
ten thousand;—meditating on these things, you attain to some conception of
what this party is to be.

And now, what good is it to do? And first, what on earth is it going to do,
anyhow? It is formed, we will say. It has triumphed. It has got power in the free
States. It has got the general government. It has chosen its president. It has got
a majority in both houses of congress. The minority are a body of representatives of slaveholders. And they have met in the great chambers. What to do?
Now, it is agreed, on all hands, that in regard to what they are to do as a party,
on any subject, human or divine, *outside of slavery,* we know no more than if
they were so many men let down in so many baskets from the clouds. As a
party,—and they gained power as a party, they are to rule us as a party;—but as
a party they solemnly adjure that they hold no opinion on anything whatever,
on anything but slavery. They spread their arms wide open to every humor of
the human mind; to all the forms of sense and nonsense; to more irreconcilable
and belligerent tempers and politics than ever quarrelled in a menagerie; to men
of war and men of peace; to the friend of annexation, if he can find free soil to
annex, as you may, in Canada, and the enemy of any more area; to protection-
ists and free traders; men of strict, and men of large construction, and men of
no construction at all; temperance men and anti-temperance men; the advocate
of ten hours of labor, the advocate of twelve,—in short, they make a general
bid for every opinion on everything, with the pledge of the party to each and
all, that if they will roar with a common consent, and make a satisfactory *hulla-
baloo* on slavery, every man of them shall have a fair chance, and no privilege,
and everybody may enact everything, if he can.

And now, in the name of all common sense, in the whole history of elective government, was a free people ever called on to commit power, the whole vast enginery, the whole thunder of the State, to such a ruler as this! Slavery, they do say, they will oppose, right and left; but what other one maxim of government they will adopt, state or national; what one law, on what one subject, they will pass; what one institution, or one policy of the fathers they will spare; what one sentiment they will inculcate; what one glory they will prize; what of all that government can cause or cure, they will cause or cure or try to—we have no more to guide us than if they were an encampment of a race never seen before, poured by some populous and unknown North, from her frozen loins! How mad, how contemptible to deliver ourselves over to such a veiled enthusiast as this! Better the urn and the lot of Solon—better the fantastic chances of hereditary descent, a thousand fold.

Well, on their one single *specialty* of slavery, what are they going to do? And I say that we have not one particle more of evidence, what specific thing, or what thing in general they mean to do on slavery, than on anything else. I do say this, however, that those honest men, who, in the simplicity of their hearts, have sympathized with this new party in the hope of having the Missouri Compromise restored, have not one particle of assurance that they would do it if they could; or that if they could, they would rest there, or within half the globe of it. Loud they are in their reprobation of the repeal. So are we all! But is it a restoration they seek? No, nothing so little. When, a few days ago, a respectable Whig gentleman presented himself at one of their meetings, and being invited to speak, began by saying that they were all there to unite for the repeal of the repeal, they hissed him incontinently. Less discourteously in the manner of it, quite as unequivocally they have set forth in terms the most explicit, in the address of their convention, that the restoration of the Compromise of 1820 is not what they desire. What are they to do, then, if they win power? Either nothing at all which Whigs could not do, and would not do, if a wise and large statesmanship permit it; or they bring on a conflict which separates the States. Nothing at all which we would not do, if our fidelity to the Constitution would allow us, or that which under the Constitution cannot be done. Nothing at all, or just what their agitation from 1835 to this hour, has accomplished,—rivet the iron chains of the slave, loose the golden bands of the Union. So much for the good it will do.

But now survey the evil it would do. We cannot, of course, foreknow exactly what it would do, if it could, nor how much, exactly, it could do, if it would. We cannot know, in other words, exactly where or when or how, if it attained the whole power that it seeks, it would bring on the final strife. But one thing we know, that they cannot, by possibility, go through the process of merely and completely organizing such a party but by elaborately and carefully training the men on this side of their line to "abhor" and "avoid" the men on the other. The basis of the organization is reciprocal sectional hate. This is the sentiment at bottom. This, and nothing else. To form and heighten this; to fortify and justify it, to show that it is moral and necessary and brave, the whole vast enginery of party tactics is to be put in request. If the ingenuity of hell were tasked for a device to alienate and rend asunder our immature and artificial nationality, it could devise nothing so effectual!

I take my stand here! I resist and deprecate the mere attempt to form the party. I don't expect to live to see it succeed in its grasp at power. I am sure I hope I shall not, but I see the attempt making. I think I see the dreadful influence of such an attempt. That influence I would expose. Woe! woe! to the sower of such seed as this! It may perish where it falls. The God of our fathers may withhold the early and latter rain and the dew, and the grain may die; but woe to the hand that dares to scatter it.

Painful it is to see some of whom a higher hope might have been cherished, on motives and with views I dare say satisfactory to themselves, giving aid and comfort to such a thing. In looking anxiously out of my own absolute retirement from every form of public life, to observe how the movers of this new party mean to urge it upon the people, what topics they mean to employ, what aims they mean to propose, and, above all, what tone and spirit they mean to breathe and spread, and what influence to exert on the sectional passions or the national sentiments of our country—I have had occasion to read something of their spoken and written exhortations—this inauguration eloquence of sectionalism—and think I comprehend it. And what work do they make of it? Yes—what? With what impression of your country, your whole country—that is the true test of a party platform and a party appeal—do you rise from listening to the preachers of this new faith? What lesson of duty to all, and of the claims of all, and of love to all, has it taught you? Does not our America seem to lose her form, her color, her vesture, as you read? Does not the magic of the metamorphosis come on her?

> "Her spirits faint,
> Her blooming cheeks assume a pallid teint,
> And scarce her form remains."

Does it not seem as if one half of the map were blotted out or rolled up forever from your eye? Are you not looking with perplexity and pain, your spirits as in a dream all bound up, upon a different, another, and a smaller native land? Where do you find in this body of discourse one single recollection that North and South compose a common country, to which our most pious affections are due, and our whole service engaged? Where, beneath this logic and this rhetoric of sectionalism, do you feel one throb of a heart capacious of our whole America? The deep, full, burning tide of American feeling, so hard to counterfeit, so hard to chill, does it once gladden and glorify this inauguration oratory and these inauguration ceremonies? Is not the key-note of it all, that the slaveholders of the South are an aristocracy to be "abhorred" and "avoided;" that they are insidious and dangerous; that they are undermining our republic, and are at all hazards to be resisted? Do they not inaugurate the new party on the basis of reciprocal hate and reciprocal fear of section to section? Hear the sharp and stern logic of one of these orators:—"Aristocracy, through all hazards is to be abhorred and avoided. But a privileged class are sure to become, nay, are an aristocracy already. The local Southern law, and the national Constitution, make the slaveholders a privileged class. They are, therefore, an aristocracy to be abhorred and avoided." Such is the piercing key-note of his speech. To this he sets his whole music of discord. To this he would set the whole music of the next presidential canvass. To this, the tens of thousands of the free States are to march. "Abhor" and "avoid" the aristocracy of the South! Organize to do it the better! They are insidious and dangerous. They are undermining republican liberty. March to defend it! Aye, march, were it over the burning marl, or by the light which the tossing wave of the lake casts pale and dreadful.

"I might show," the same orator proceeds, "that the Constitution is wrong in thus conceding to a privileged class. I might show, *a priori,* that such a class would be dangerous. I choose rather to teach you so to read the history of America, that you shall find its one great lesson will be hatred and dread of the aristocracy of the South, for its conduct even more than for its privileges." And so he unrolls the map, and opens the record. He traces the miraculous story; he traces the miraculous growth from the birthday of the Constitution, and from the straitened margin of the old thirteen States, through all the series of expansion,—the acquisition of Louisiana, and the adoption of that State into the Union; the successive adoption, also, of Kentucky, Tennessee, Mississippi, Alabama and Missouri; the annexation of Florida and Texas, and California,— a growth in fifty years, from a narrow heritage between the Atlantic and Alleghany, and the spring-heads of the Connecticut and the mouth of the St. Mary's in Georgia, to the dimensions of Roman, of Russian, of Asiatic boundlessness—this he traces across the Alleghanies, across the imperial valley and the

Father of Rivers, through the opened portals of the Rocky Mountains to the shores of the great tranquil sea—aye, and beyond these shores to richer dominion over the commerce of the East, to which it opens a new and nearer way—this majestic series, our glory, our shame, he runs over; and the one single lesson he gathers and preaches from it is, that the aristocracy of the South is as insidious and dangerous and undermining in practice as it is threatening *a priori;* that we should "abhor" and "avoid" it, for what it has done, as well as for what the Constitution and the laws secure to it. This is the lesson of the History of America. As he studies the map and reads the history, so is the new party to do it; so are the fathers, and so are the children of the free States all to read it; it is to teach them all one dull lesson, and to sound in their ears one single, dreary, and monotonous warning. The annexation of Louisiana, the master-work of Jefferson, unless you say the Declaration of Independence is his master-work; the annexation of Florida, by treaty, for which John Quincy Adams acquired so just a fame, and which stipulates for the incorporation of its inhabitants into the Union; the victories of Palo Alto, Monterey, Buena Vista, and Contreras, which crowned the arms of America with a lustre imperishable, although they could not vindicate to justice and history, the administration or the politics which brought on the war, nor the Free Soilers of New York, whose tactics caused the election of that administration; this expansion, so stupendous—this motion, silent and resistless, of all the currents of national being towards the setting sun—like that of our astronomical system itself, towards the distant constellation; this all is to kindle no emotion, to inspire no duty, to inculcate no truth, but to "abhor" and "avoid" the aristocracy, whose rapacious use or insidious fabrication of opportunity, so strikingly illustrates the folly of the Constitution.

Oh! how soothing and elevating to turn from this to the meridian brightness, the descending orb, the whole clear day, of our immortal Webster! How sweet, how instructive to hang again on the lips now mute, still speaking, whose eloquence, whose wisdom, were all given ever to his whole America! How grand to feel again the beat of the great heart which could enfold us all! He saw, too, and he deplored the spread of slavery. He marked, and he resisted the frenzy of the politics by which the then administration gave it so vast an impulse by annexing Texas and making war with Mexico. He had surveyed—no man had so deeply done it—the growth of his country from the rock of Plymouth and the peninsula of Jameston to the western sea. But did he think it just to trace it all to the aggressive spirit of the aristocracy who hold slaves? Could his balanced and gigantic intelligence and his genuine patriotism have been brought to believe and to teach that the single desire to find a new field for slavery to till, has in fifty years transformed a strip of sea coast into a national domain larger than Europe?

Is nothing to be ascribed to the necessities of national situation and the opportunities of national glory; nothing to the sober, collective judgment of the people of all the sections; nothing to the foresight of some great men—like Jefferson and John Quincy Adams—who loved not slavery, nor the expansion of the area of slavery, but who did love their country dearly and wisely, and knew that that evil would be more than compensated by the exceeding good; nothing to a diffused, vehement nationality, brave, ambitious, conscious of a mighty strength, burning to try itself against the resistance of foreign contact, and finding on its West and South-west border no equal force to hold it back; nothing to the blindness of mere party tactics and the power of a popular administration; nothing to the love of glory, and contention, and danger which flames and revels in the adolescent national heart? Is it all mere and sheer negro-breeding and negro-selling that has done this? More. Is nothing to be ascribed to the influence of Northern aggression against slavery, provoking by an eternal law a Southern rally for its defence and propagation? Have these great readers of our history forgotten that as far back as 1805, as 1801, the press, some influential portions of the press of a large political party at the North, began to denounce the election and reëlection of Jefferson as a triumph of the slave power; the acquisition of Louisiana, that absolute necessity of our peace, how much more of our greatness, as another triumph of the slave power; that this form of sectionalism already assailed the slave representation of the Constitution, and tried to strike it out; that it bore its part, a large part, in inflaming New England to the measure of the Hartford Convention; that, hushed to silence by the fervid flood of nationality which swept the country at the close of a war, breathing into us the full first inspiration of American life, it awoke again on the application of Missouri for admission; that, silenced once more by that adjustment, a few years later it took on the more virulent type of abolitionism; and from that moment, helped on by the general progress of the age, it has never ceased for an hour to make war on the institutions of the South, to assail the motives, and arraign the conscience of the slave-holder; to teach to "abhor" and to "avoid" him, and denounce the Union as a compact with hell? Is it not possible that a part of what they call the aggressive spirit of slavery may be reäction against our own aggression? May it not be, that in this recrimination of the sections, and in the judgment of history, there may be blows to take as well as blows to give? That great man whose name I have spoken, could see, and he dared to admit, the errors of both sections. In those errors, in this very hate and this very dread which the new party would organize, he saw the supreme danger of his country. To correct those errors, to allay that dread, to turn that hate to love, was the sublime aim of his last and noblest labor. "I am looking out," he said, "not for my own security or safety, for I am looking out for no fragment on which to float away from the wreck, if wreck there must be, but for the good of the whole, and the preservation of all. I speak to-day for the Union! Hear me, for my cause!" He could not have abandoned himself, he never saw an hour in which he could have any more abandoned himself to this gloomy enterprise of sectionalism, than Washington could have done it, stooping from the pathos and grandeur and parental love of the Farewell Address; than the leader of Israel could have done it, as he stood in that last hour on Pisgah and surveyed in vision, the widespread tents of the kindred tribes, rejoicing together in the peace and in the light of their nation's God. O, for an hour of such a life, and all were not yet lost.

Chapter XIII.

SPEECH "ON THE POLITICAL TOPICS NOW PROMINENT BEFORE THE COUNTRY."
Delivered at Lowell, Mass., October 28, 1856.

As a good Whig, Choate was a strong Union man, and few political matters filled him with greater dread than the prospect of its dissolution. In this speech he builds on the sentiments he had expressed several months before in a letter to the Whig State Central Committee of Maine:

"The first duty, then, of Whigs, not merely as patriots and as citizens—loving, with a large and equal love our whole native land—but as Whigs, and because we are Whigs, is to unite with some organization of our countrymen, to defeat and dissolve the new geographical party, calling itself Republican. This is our first duty. It would more exactly express my opinion to say that at this moment it is our only duty. Certainly, at least, it comprehends and suspends all others; and in my judgment, the question for each and every one of us is, not whether this candidate or that candidate would be our first choice—not whether there is some good talk in the worst platform—not whether this man's ambition, or that man's servility or boldness or fanaticism or violence, is responsible for putting the wild waters in this uproar—but just this—by what vote can I do most to prevent the madness of the times from working its maddest act—the very ecstasy of its madness—the permanent formation and the actual present triumph of a party which knows one half of America only to hate and dread it—from whose unconsecrated and revolutionary banner fifteen stars are erased or have fallen. . . . To this duty, to this question, all others seem to me to stand for the present postponed and secondary.

"And why? Because, according to our creed, it is only the united America which can peacefully, gradually, safely, improve, lift up, and bless, with all social and personal and civil blessings, all the races and all the conditions which compose our vast and various family—it is such an America, only, whose arm can guard our flag, develop our resources, extend our trade, and fill the measure of our glory; and because, according to our convictions, the triumph of such a party puts the Union in danger. That is my reason. And for you and for me and for all of us, in whose regards the Union possesses such

a value, and to whose fears it seems menaced by such a danger, it is reason enough. Believing the noble Ship of State to be within a half cable's length of a lee shore of rock, in a gale of wind, our first business is to put her about, and crowd her off into the deep, open sea. That done, we can regulate the stowage of her lower tier of powder, and select her cruising ground, and bring her officers to court-martial at our leisure."

For these opinions, Josiah Quincy accused Choate of speaking in favor of "upholding the slaveholders' dynasty," but in fact Choate was saying simply that before the issue of slavery could be brought to a satisfactory resolution, sectional hatreds had to cease. It was a cautionary note that would be drowned out amid the excitement of the late 1850s.

I HAVE accepted your invitation to this hall with pleasure—although it is pleasure not unattended by pain.

To meet you, Fellow-citizens of Lowell and of Middlesex, between whom, the larger number of whom, and myself, I may hope from the terms of the call under which you assemble, there is some sympathy of opinion and feeling on the "political topics now prominent before the community;" to meet and confer, however briefly and imperfectly, on the condition of our country, and the duties of those who aspire only to be good citizens, and are inquiring anxiously what in that humble yet responsible character they have to do—to meet thus, and here—not as politicians, not as partisans, not as time-servers, not as office-seekers, not as followers of a multitude because it is a multitude, not as sectionalists, but as sons and daughters of our united and inherited America; who love her, filially and fervently for herself; our own—the beautiful, the endeared, the bounteous; the imperial and general Parent!—and whose hearts' desire and prayer to God is only to know how we shall serve her best,—this is a pleasure and a privilege for which I shall be very long and very deeply in your debt.

And this pleasure, there is here and now nothing to alloy. Differing as we have done, some of us, through half our lives; differing as now we do, and shall hereafter do, on means, on details, on causes of the evil, on men, on non-essentials—non-essentials I would say in so far as the demands of these most rugged and eventful times are concerned—I think that on the question, what is the true issue before us and the capital danger we have to meet; on this, and on all the larger ideas, in all the nobler emotions which ought to swell the heart and guide the votes of true men to-day—through this one sharp and dark hour we shall stand together, shoulder to shoulder, though we have never done so before, and may never do so again.

I infer this from the language of your invitation. The welcome with which you have met me, allows me to expect so much. The place we meet in gives assurance of it.

If there is one spot of New England earth rather than another, on whose ear that strange music of discords to which they are rallying the files—a little scattered and a little flinching, thank God!—of their Geographical party—must fall like a fire bell in the night, it is here; it is in Middlesex; it is in Lowell!

If this attempt at combining States against States for the possession of the government has no danger in it for anybody, well and good. Let all then sleep on, and take their rest. If it has danger for anybody, for you, Fellow-citizens of Lowell, more than for any of New England or as much, it has that danger. Who needs the Union, if you do not? Who should have brain and heart enough to comprehend and employ the means of keeping it, if not you? Others may be Unionists by chance; by fits and starts; on the lips; Unionists when nothing more exciting, or more showy, or more profitable, casts up. You are Unionists by profession; Unionists by necessity; Unionists always. Others may find Vermont, or Massachusetts, or New Hampshire, or Rhode Island, large enough for them. You need the whole United Continent over which the flag waves to-day, and you need it governed, within the limits of the actual Constitution, by one supreme will. To secure that vast, and that indispensable market at home; to command in the least degree a steady, uniform, or even occasional protection against the redundant capital, matured skill, pauper labor, and ebbing and falling prices of the Old World at peace; to enable the looms of America to clothe the teeming millions of America;—you need a regulation of commerce, uniform, one, the work of one united mind, which shall draw along our illimitable coast of sea and lake, between the universal American race on one side, and all the rest of mankind on the other, a line, not of seclusion, not of prohibition, but a line of security, and discrimination—discrimination between the raw material at least and the competing product—a line of social and industrial boundary behind which our infancy may grow to manhood; our weakness to strength; our "prentice hand" to that skill which shall hang out the lamp of beauty on the high places of our wealth, and our power, and our liberty!

Yes, this you need; and you know how, and where, you can have it.

How perfectly our springing and yet immature manufacturing and mechanical interests in 1788 discerned this need, and with what deep, reasonable, passionate enthusiasm they celebrated the adoption of the Constitution which held out the promise of meeting it! I know very well that all good men; all far-seeing men; all large-brained and large-hearted men were glad that day. I recall that grand and exultant exclamation of one of them: "It is done; we have become a nation." But even then it seemed to some, more than to others, the dawn of a day of good things to come. If you turn to that procession and that pageant of industry, in Philadelphia, on the 4th of July, 1788,—that grand and affecting dramatic action through which, on that magnificent stage as in a theatre, there were represented the sublime joy, and the sublime hopes with which the bosom of Pennsylvania was throbbing,—then and thus I think you seem to see, that while the Constitution promised glory and happiness to all our America, it was to the labor of America the very breath of life. We hear it said that it was for trade—foreign and domestic, largely—that the new and more perfect union was formed, and that is true. Very fit it was that in that gorgeous day of national emblems, the silver Delaware should have shown forth prominently—decorated and festive—to announce and welcome from all her mast-heads the rising orb of American commerce. Yet was there one piece in the performance opening a still wider glimpse of its immense utilities and touching the heart with a finer emotion. That large "stage borne on the carriage of the Manufacturing Society, thirty feet in length, on which carding machines, and spinning machines, and weaving machines were displaying the various manufacture of cotton, was viewed," says an eye-witness, "with astonishment and delight by every specta-tor." "On that stage was carried the emblem of the future wealth and indepen-dence of our country." In that precious form of industry in which the harvest of Southern suns and the labor of Northern hands and brains may meet to pro-duce a fabric for all nations to put on,—the industry of reason, and of the people,— "in that," says he, "is a bond of union more powerful than any one clause of the Constitution." In the motto on that carriage, "May the Union government pro-tect the manufactures of America," read the hopes and the necessities of this labor. Such still is your prayer; such your right; as with the fathers so with the children! May that same Pennsylvania which so celebrated the adoption of the Constitu-tion perpetuate it to-day! Wheresoever else the earth may shake, and the keepers and pillars of the house may tremble and bow themselves, let the keystone of the national arch, intrusted to hold it against the sky, stand fast in its place of strength and beauty forever!

Pardon me if I have seemed to find in the *mere interests* of Lowell a reason why, if there is a danger, you should be the first to discern and first to meet it. I turn from the interests of Lowell to the *memories* of Middlesex; and I find in them at least assurance that if there is a danger, your eye will see it and your ear catch it as far and as quick as the old Minutemen saw the midnight signals in the belfrys, and caught the low midnight drum-beat. Surely, surely, that immortal boast of Webster will be yours, "Where American liberty raised its first voice, and where its youth was nurtured and sustained, there it still lives, in the strength of its manhood and full of its original spirit. If discord and disunion shall wound it, if party strife and blind ambition shall hawk at and tear it, if folly and mad-ness, if uneasiness under salutary and necessary restraint, shall succeed in separating it from the Union—by which alone its existence is made sure—it will stand, in the end, by the side of that cradle in which its infancy was rocked; it will stretch forth its arm with whatever of vigor it may still retain over the friends who gather around it; and it will fall at last, if fall it must, amidst the proudest monuments of its own glory, and on the very spot of its origin." Yes, it was here, that the American people began to be, and the American nation was born in a day. There, on the 19th of April; there, on the 17th of June; on that narrow green; beyond that little bridge; on those heights of glory; there,—even as the cloud of battle parted and the blood of your fathers was sinking into the ground—the form and faces of the old thirteen colonies passed away, and the young Republic lifted his forehead from the "baptism of fire;" the old provincial flags were rolled up and disappeared as a scroll, and the radiant banner by which the united America is known, and shall be, for a thousand years of history, known to all the world as one, was handed down from the sky. Here at least shall not the dismemberment of that nation begin. Here at least the first star shall not be erased from that banner!

No, Fellow-citizens of Middlesex. They may persuade you that there is no danger in what they are doing; they may persuade you that a combination of sixteen States to wrest the possession of the government from the other fifteen, is all right, all safe, and all necessary. But if they fail in this; if they fail to show that whatever they wish or mean to do, they are not subjecting the Union of America, and the peace and honor of America, to a trial which may exceed its strength, then tell them they had better try that case in *some other county*. Tell them that while the summit of that monument catches the rays of the rising and descending sun, and the returning or departing sailor greets it from his mast-head, it shall stand the *colossal image of a whole country;* and the flag that floats from it to-day shall float there while the earth bears a plant, or the sea rolls a wave!

I meet you for these reasons with pleasure. But I said and feel that that pleasure is attended close by pain. Some of you will partake of that with me also. All will comprehend it. I do not disguise that I look on the occasion with too anxious an interest, with too many fond memories of the past, with too keen a sense of the contrast of the present with the past, with too much thought of the possible future, for unmixed pleasure even here. I will not call this presidential election in advance a peril or a crisis, for that might be to beg the question, but I will venture in advance to say, that the best wish a patriot could make for his country is that she may never undergo such another. The first desire of my heart, at least, is that I may never see such another. To this desire, personal considerations do not at all contribute. I should be ashamed of myself if they did, although I cannot but wonder at that discriminating injustice and insolence of dictation which claims freedom of thought and purity of motive for itself, and allows them to others, and denies them to me. But this is nothing. Is there no one here who shares with me the wish, that his country, that himself, might never see another such a crisis as this? Is there no one here,—are there not hundreds here,— who, recalling the presidential elections they have assisted in, and contrasting their safe and their noble stimulations; their sublime moments; their admirable influences, as a training to a closer union, and a truer and intenser American feeling and life, with this one; does not confess some anxiety, some bewilderment, some loathing, some fear? Those generous, animated, fraternal contendings of the American people for a choice of the successor of Washington; conducted in the name and under the control of two great parties; running, both of them, through and through the Union, into every State and every vicinage, every congressional district, and every school district, and every parish; and binding Texas to Maine, Georgia to New Hampshire, Missouri to Massachusetts, by a new, artificial, and vehement cohesion,—a tie, not mystic, by which you greeted, every man greeted, a brother and an ally, "*idem sentientem de republica*"; everywhere that careful, just, and constitutional recognition on every party banner; by every party creed and code; in every party speech, and song, and procession of torchlight,—the recognition of an equal title to love, regard, honor, equality, in each and every state and region; that studious and that admirable exclusion of all things sectional; all things which supposed the existence of a conflict of sections; all opinions, all theories of policy, all enterprises of philanthropy, all aims of all sorts in which his geographical and social position could prevent any one American from sharing alike; those platforms broad as our continent; equal as our Constitution; comprehensive as our liberty; those mighty minglings of minds and hearts, in which Webster could address Virginians in the Capitol Square at Richmond, and Berrien and Bell and Leigh and Johnson could feel and heighten the inspiration of Faneuil Hall and Bunker Hill,—all everywhere at home;—those presidential contests which left our Union stronger, our mutual acquaintance and respect closer and deeper, our country a dearer and fairer and grander ideal, hastening forward the growth of our nationality almost as much as a foreign war, without its blood, its crime, and its cost,—is there no one, are there not hundreds here, who recall and regret them? Contrasted with them and their day, does not this one, and this time, seem more a dream than a reality? Can we avoid the vain wish that it was only and all a dream? Does this attempt to weave and plait the two North wings of the old national parties into a single Northern one, and cut the Southern wing off altogether, strike you to be quite as far-sighted and safe as it is new and bold? In the temporary and local success which seemed a little while ago to attend it here, and which led certain small editors, little speakers on low stumps, writers of bad novels and forgotten poems, preachers of Pantheism and revilers of Jefferson, and excellent gentlemen, so moral and religious that they could not rejoice at their country's victories over England,—led these people to suppose they had all at once become your masters and mine; in that temporary and local success did you see nothing but rose colors and the dawn of the Millennium? To combine States against States, in such a system as ours, has it been generally held a very happy device towards forming a more perfect union and insuring domestic tranquility? To combine them thus against each other geographically, to take the whole vast range of the free States, lying together, sixteen out of thirty-one, seventeen millions out of five or six and twenty millions,—the most populous, the strongest, the most advancing,—and form them in battalion against the fewer numbers and slower growth, and waning relative power on the other side; to bring this sectional majority under party drill and stimulus of pay and rations; to offer to it as a party the government of our country, its most coveted honors, its largest salaries, all its sweets of patronage and place; to penetrate and fire so mighty and so compact a mass with the still more delicious idea that they are moving for human rights and the equality of man; to call out their clergy from the pulpit, the library, the bedside of the dying, the chair of the anxious inquirer, the hearth of the bereaved, to bless such a crusade; to put in requisition every species of rhetoric and sophistry, to impress on the general mind that the end justifies the means; that the end here to be attained is to give Kansas to freedom; to stanch her blood and put out her fires; and then to execute the sublime and impressive dogma that all men are born free and equal; and that such a Geographical party is a well-adapted means to that end,—does this strike you as altogether in the spirit of Washington, and Franklin, and the Preamble to the Constitution, and the Farewell Address? Does it strike you that if carried out it will prove to be a mere summer excursion to Moscow? Will there be no bivouac in the snow; no avenging winter hanging on retreat? No Leipsic; no Waterloo?

Fellow-citizens, if the formation and growth of this faction of Northern States against the South has impressed us at all alike, you appreciate why I said that I meet you with pain. It was the pain of anxiety; the pain of fear. Relieved as I am from that in a great degree by the late decisive demonstrations from Pennsylvania and Indiana, we yet feel together that we have a duty to perform or to attempt still. That which we cannot hinder here, we may at least deplore and expose. That which we cannot do for ourselves, New Hampshire, Connecticut, the great, calm, central mass of States may do for us. Against that which locally and temporarily is too strong for our strength here, we may at least protest.

With courtesy then; with justice to those from whom we differ; in the fear of God; in the love of our whole America; in all singleness of heart; appealing from the new men to the old; to the sober second thought of Massachusetts and New England; to their judgment; to their patriotism,—after some generations, perhaps some days, have passed,—let us put on record our reasons for deliberate and inextinguishable opposition to this Geographical party.

You see, Fellow-citizens, already what I regard as the issue we have to try. In their mode of stating that issue, I take leave totally to differ from some of the organs of this movement here. The question to-day is not as they would frame it and force it on us, whether we would have Kansas free soil or slave soil, any more than whether we worship an "anti-slavery God and believe in an anti-slavery Bible." The question is this: Shall slavery be permitted, through the agency of extreme Northern or extreme Southern opinions, to combine and array the sixteen States in which it does not exist, and the fifteen States in which it does exist, into two political parties, separated by a physical and social boundary, for the election of president, for the constituting of the two houses of congress, and the possession of the government? Much trouble it has caused us; much evil it has done. It is the one stupendous trial and peril of our national life. But shall it bear this, the deadliest fruit of all?

I say, Not so; never; but certainly not yet. This is the issue.

And now addressing myself to this issue, the first thing I have to say is, such a party is absolutely useless for every one of its own objects which it dares avow. For every one which it avows it is useless. Every one of them it is certain to endanger or to postpone.

But here let me submit a preliminary thought or two.

In trying the question whether the exigencies of the times demand such a tremendous organization as this, or whether we are bound to oppose it, I hold it to be time worse than wasted to get up a disputation in advance as to what party, or what section is most to blame for the occurrences of the last two years. This is all well enough for politicians. To you and to me it is trifling and it is criminal. If a resort to this stupendous innovation is necessary and is safe; if it will work great, certain, and needful good, and will not formidably and probably endanger the domestic tranquility and the more perfect union of the States,—form it, and triumph in it. If such a resort is unnecessary; if it will work no certain and great good; if it will disturb our peace and endanger our existence, let it be condemned and punished as moral treason, and there an end. Try it, and judge it by itself.

What is it to you or me; what is it to the vast, innocent, and quiet body of our countrymen, North or South, whose folly, whose violence, whose distrust, whose fanaticism for slavery or against slavery, whose ambition low or high, is responsible for the past or present? Leave this to them whose trade is politics, whose trade is agitation, and let us meet the practical measure they present us, and pass on that. I know very well there are faults on both sides, faults South, faults North, faults of parties, faults of administration. We should not have voted for the repeal of the Compromise. We would have voted, when that thing was done and its restoration was seen to be impossible, to secure to Kansas the opportunity, uninvaded, unawed, uninfluenced, to grow to the measure of a State, to choose her own institutions, and then come to join the "Grand Equality." As she is to-day, at rest, at peace,—in some fair measure so,—revived, respiring, so ought she ever to have been, if freedom and slavery were to be allowed to meet breast to breast upon her surface at all. Herein is fault. Herein is wrong. Beyond, far back of all this, years before that Compromise, years before that repeal, the historian of sectional antagonisms might gather up more matter of reciprocal crimination. Either region might draw out a specious manifesto enough on which to appeal to the reason and justice of the world and to the God of nations, and to the God of battle for that matter, if that were all.

But to this great question, thus forced on us, Shall the States of the North be organized for the purpose of *possessing the government* upon the basis of this party, what are all these things to the purpose? Because there has been violence and blame, are you therefore to fly on a remedy ten thousand times worse than the disease? We should like to see slavery cease from the earth; but should we like to see black regiments from the West Indies landing at Charleston or New Orleans to help on emancipation? We would like to see Kansas grow up to freedom; but should we like to see the bayonets that stormed the Redan and the Malakoff glittering there to effect it? This glorifying him who does his own work, and this denunciation of him who holds a slave; this singing of noisy songs, and this preaching of Sharpe's rifle sermons; these lingering lamentations about the spread of the cotton plant, about the annexing of Louisiana by Jefferson, and of Florida by John Quincy Adams, do not touch the question before the nation. That question is about the new party. That question is on combining the North against the South on slavery to win the government. Shall that party, shall that attempt triumph, or shall it perish under the condemnation of your patriotism?

Is that needful? Is that just? Is that prudent? That is the question; and to that hold up its orators, and poets, and preachers; and let the sound and calm judgment of America decide it.

Something else when that is decided, as it seems now likely to be, we shall have to do. Some changes of administrative politics must be and will be had. But in the mean time, and in the first place, the question is, Shall your Geographical party live or die?

I have said, then, for my first reason of opposition, that for any and every one of the objects this new party dares to avow, it is absolutely useless. It is no more needed for any object it dares to avow, than thirty thousand of Marshal Pelissier's Zouaves are needed in Kansas to-day.

And on this question of necessity is not the burden of proof on him who undertakes to introduce into our political order and experience so tremendous a novelty as this? Is not the presumption in the *first* instance altogether against getting up a Geographical party on slavery for possession of the government? Considering that such a thing, if not necessarily and inevitably poison, is, however, extreme medicine at the best; that it has been down to this hour admitted to be and proclaimed to be the one great peril of our system by all who have loved it best and studied it most deeply; that every first-class intelligence and character in our history of whatever type of politics, and what is quite as important, the sound and sober general mind and heart, has held and taught this, is it too much to say that he whose act outrages our oldest, and most fixed, and most implicit habits of thought and most cherished traditions on this subject; who mocks at what we have supposed our most salutary and most reasonable fears; who laughs at a danger to the American confederacy, at which the firmness of Washington, the courage of Hamilton, and the hopeful and trusting philanthropy and philosophy of Jefferson, confident always of his countrymen, at which these men trembled,—is it too much to tell the propounder of this project that he shall make out its necessity, or he shall be nonsuited on his own case? I say to him, then, Pray confine yourself in the first instance to the point of *necessity*. Do not evade that question. Don't mix others with it. Tell us exactly what you really propose to do about slavery, without phrases, and then show us that if it ought to be done it is necessary to combine the Northern States against the South on a presidential election in order to do it. Speak to this. Don't tell us how provoked you are, or how provoked the Rev. Mr. This, or the Hon. Mr. That, has come to be against the South; how passionately one Southern member spoke, or another Southern member acted; how wicked it was in Washington to hold slaves, and what a covenant with hell a Constitution is which returns the fugitive to the master. Don't exasperate yourself irrelevantly. Don't mystify or trick us with figures to prove that the seventeen millions of people in the Northern States contribute three fourths of the whole aggregate of $4,500,000,000 of annual industrial production. This, if it were true, or were not true, might beget vanity, and the lust of sectional dominion, and contempt; but it is nothing at all to the purpose. Don't say you want to teach the South this thing or that thing. Don't say you want to avenge on a section to-day the annexation of Louisiana or Florida or Texas. Don't keep coming down on the South; just condescend to come down on the question. What are your objects precisely; and how comes this new and dangerous combination of States necessary to accomplish them?

What, then, first, are the objects of the Geographical party, and is such a party necessary for such objects? I ask now for *its measures*. What would it do if it could?

To find out these to reasonable perfection, for me, at least, has not been easy. It is not easy to know where to look for the authentic evidence of them. The Philadelphia platform and Colonel Fremont's letter of acceptance are part of that evidence. They are not all—they are not the most important part. You must go elsewhere for it. The actual creed and the real objects must be sought in the tone and spirit of their electioneering; in the topics of their leaders; in the aggregate of the impression their whole appeal is calculated to make on the public mind and the collective feelings of the North. These speak the aims, these make up the life, these accomplish the mission of a party. By these together judge it.

Much meditating on this evidence, I arrive at two results. I find one object distinctly propounded; one of great interest to the Northern sentiment, and one which you and I and all should rejoice to see constitutionally and safely accomplished at the right time and in the right way,—and that is the accession of Kansas as a free State to the Union. This is one. Beyond, behind this, more or less dim, more or less frowning, more or less glittering, more or less constitutional, there looms another range or another show of objects, swelling and subsiding and changing as you look,—"in many a frozen, many a fiery Alp,"—cloud-land, to dazzle one man's eye, to disappear altogether before the gaze of another, as the showman pleases. These are their other objects.

Turn first, then, to that one single practical and specific measure which they present to the North, and on which they boast themselves by eminence and excellence the friends of Kansas,—the admission of that territory as a free State.

And now if this is all, will any sane and honest man, uncommitted, tell you that there is a necessity for this tremendous experiment of an organization and precipitation of North on South to achieve it? Have you, has one of you, has one human being north of the line of geographical separation, a particle of doubt that if Kansas has peace under the reign of law for two years, for twelve months, the energies of liberty, acting through unforced, unchecked, and normal free-soil immigration, would fill her with freedom, and the institutions of freedom, as the waters fill the sea? What more than such peace under such rule of law do you want? What more does Mr. Speaker Banks think you want? Legislation of anybody? No. Interference by anybody? No. Hear him:—

"Now for this (the repeal of the Compromise) we have a remedy. It is not that we shall legislate against the South on the subject of slavery. It is not that we shall raise the question whether in future territories slavery shall be permitted or not. We lay aside all these questions, and stand distinctly and simply on the proposition that that which gave peace to the country in 1820, that which consummated the peace of the country in 1850, ought to be made good by the government of the United States, and with the consent of the American people. (Applause.) That is all. No more, no less—no better, no worse. That is all we ask—that the acts of 1820 and 1850 shall be made good, in the place of conflagration, and murder, and civil war for the year 1856—by the voice of the American people, South, let me say, as well as North. (Applause.) Now, to do that no legislation is required. It is not necessary that the halls of congress should be opened again to agitation. We desire the election of a man to the presidency of the United States of simple views and of determined will,—a man who will exert the influence of this government in that portion of the territory of the United States, so as to allow its people to settle the question for themselves there."

What is this but to say, Put out the conflagration, stop the reign of violence, give peace, law, and order to rule, and Kansas will have freedom, if she does not prefer slavery, as certainly she will not. And such, I take it, is the all but universal judgment of the North.

Well; but do they answer, Oh, very true; but we cannot have this peace unless the North gets possession of the government. Mr. Buchanan's administration will not insure it. Mr. Fillmore's administration will not insure it.

I might content myself with replying that the condition of Kansas at this hour gives this extravagance to the winds. I will not say that territory to-day is as quiet as Middlesex; but I will say that before the next President takes his seat it will be as free as Middlesex. It has a majority for freedom, and it is increasing. Of a population of about thirty thousand, some five thousand only are from the slave States.

I will not leave it on that reply. With what color of justice, I choose to add, do the leaders of this party assume to tell you that they alone desire to give or are able to insure Kansas her only chance to be free? With what justice do they tell you that the Democratic party, or the Fillmore party, refuse to give her peace, and all the practical opportunities of liberty? Do they suppose that we have not read the record of the last two months of the last congress? We, whose sons and brothers are on that disturbed and sad soil; we, who deplore the repeal of the Compromise quite as much as they do; we, who should see with exultation and thanksgiving to God the peaceful victories of freedom in that frontier; we, who hate and dread the gamblings of politicians, and the selfish and low tactics of party, but should rejoice unspeakably to see the statesmanship of our country securing the government of that territory to its own free will,—do they suppose that we did not read, or could not understand, or cannot remember how the leaders and the members of every party in congress dealt with this great subject? Republicans the only helpers of Kansas to freedom, indeed! How did they propose to reach the object? By making some twenty-five thousand people into a sovereign State, and bringing it, just as it was, into the Union under the Topeka constitution! Yes, you would have made them a State *extempore*. You would have given to these twenty-five thousand people, organized as absolutely without law and against law as if two thousand should get together on Boston Common and make a government, the same voice in the Senate of the United States which the Constitution gives to New York, to Pennsylvania, to Virginia, to Massachusetts; the power to turn the scale and decide the vote on a debate of war and peace, or a treaty of boundary, or of commerce, or a nomination to the highest judicial or diplomatic office in the Constitution.

This they would have done—a measure of passion; an act for which the file affords no precedent; revolutionary almost; almost a crime in the name of liberty.

Defeated in this, they would do nothing. They would allow nobody else to do anything. They passed Mr. Dunn's bill to be sure,—the first one in the history of this government which legislated human beings directly into a state of slavery; but as they engrafted the restoration of the Missouri Compromise into it, they knew it could not become a law, and that goes for nothing. There they stuck; and had they not repeatedly an opportunity to unite in putting out the fires, and stanching the blood, and hushing the shrieks of Kansas; in giving her a chance to revive and respire; in giving her a chance to choose herself of the fruit of the tree of liberty and live? Yes; repeatedly. Did they avail themselves of it? No. Did they allow others to do so? No. No! Did not Mr. Toombs present a bill, and did not the Senate pass it and send it to the House? Did not this bill propose an early admission of Kansas,—in so far just what the Republicans wanted? Did it not annul the more obnoxious part of the obnoxious laws of the territorial legislature? Did it not provide for registration of voters, commissioners to take census of inhabitants, and an interval of ample sufficiency for those whom violence had expelled to return and assert their rights? Did not Mr. Hale of New Hampshire say of this:—

> "I take this occasion to say that the bill, as a whole, does great credit to the magnanimity, to the patriotism, and to the sense of justice of the honorable Senator who introduced it. It is a much fairer bill than I expected from that latitude. I say so because I am always willing and determined, when I have occasion to speak anything, to do ample justice. I THINK THE BILL IS ALMOST UNEXCEPTIONABLE."

Did the Republicans—when they found that the Missouri Compromise could not be restored, nor Kansas be admitted instantly under the Topeka constitution—in order to stanch the blood, and to silence the cry of the territory, the crime against which they assumed to prosecute and avenge—give ground *an inch?* Would they take a single step towards temporary truce even, or a time to breathe? Not one,—Mr. Clayton, Mr. Crittenden in the Senate, and Mr. Haven in the House, held up successively the olive-branch, tempted and entreated them, by eloquence, and reason, and feeling, to do something, if they could not do all, or what they wished, to close the feast of horrors!—but not a finger would they lift. Cold and motionless as the marble columns about them—the 25,000 men and the Topeka constitution should come in a State—as they knew it would not—or murder, arson, and rapine might waste Kansas, and electioneer for the Geographical party.

I do not say they intended that the reign of terror should continue in Kansas; all of them could not have so intended, I do not say that any of them did. I say that if it had continued, a full share of the responsibility had been theirs. I say that it is no thanks to them that it has ceased. I say that it does not lie in their mouths to tell the calm, just, and reasonable men of the North that they are the only party, and a combination of States against States the only means, of giving to Kansas the freedom we all desire for her.

Easy it were in my judgment to demonstrate or afford the highest degree of probability that their triumph would defeat, or postpone, or impair and profane the consummation which they seek. But I am confined to the question of the necessity of their measures, for the attainment of our ends.

So much for this function of the new party, the admission of Kansas as a free State. To this end it is no more needed than sixteen black regiments from the Leeward Islands.

Beyond this, what are its objects? With anxious and curious desire to comprehend the whole of this extraordinary phenomenon, I have extreme difficulty in making these ulterior objects out. Some of them are unavowed, I suppose—some of them are avowed in one place and denied in another; some of the speakers have one—some have another. If you tell them their aims are dangerous, unconstitutional, revolutionary, Mr. Banks shall reply, "Not a bit of it; we don't mean to legislate against the South on slavery at all; we don't mean to say that future territories shall not have slavery if they like it, to their heart's content. We want nothing and nobody but a President of 'simple views and determined will,' who will allow the 'people of Kansas to settle the question for themselves there.'" If thereupon you answer, Well, if this is all, there really seems to be no great need of evoking such a tremendous spirit as the combination of North against South to reach it; less force, less fire, less steam, less wear and tear of machinery would do the business one would think; up rises another, more fervid, more gloomy, better informed, or not so cunning, and exclaims, "No, that is not all! that is hardly the beginning. We sing and hear a strain of far higher mood than that; we have the tide of slavery to roll back; the annexation of Louisiana and Texas to avenge or compensate; we too would taste the sweets of power, and we will have power; it is a new order of the ages we bring on; our place of worship (such is Governor Seward's expression) is neither in this mountain, nor yet in Jerusalem; our mission is equality and freedom to all men."

To seek, through all this Babel of contradictory and irresponsible declarations, what they really design to do, were vain and idle. To maintain the necessity of organizing a party like this, to accomplish no mortal can tell us what, seems pretty bold dealing with the intelligence of the country. That which it is impossible to state, it is not apparently needful to try to do. If there is no perplexity of plot to be unravelled, why is such a divinity invoked? If there is one, will they show us what it is?

I must not forget in this search for their objects, outside of Kansas, that they have been much in the habit of sending us to the Declaration of Independence to find them. Their platform does so; their orators are said to do so. If I understand Governor Seward, in his first speech in Detroit, he does so. Reverend teachers of Republicanism do so. They are the party of the Declaration of Independence, and not a Geographical party. Here are two of their resolutions:—

"*Resolved,* That the maintenance of the principles promulgated *in the Declaration of Independence, and embodied* in the Federal Constitution, are essential to the preservation of our republican institutions; and that the Federal Constitution, the rights of the States, and the union of the States, shall be preserved.

"*Resolved,* That, with our republican fathers, we hold it to be self-evident truth that all men are endowed with inalienable right to 'life, liberty, and the pursuit of happiness,' and that the *primary object* and *ulterior design* of our Federal Government were to secure these rights *to all persons* within its exclusive jurisdiction; that as our republican fathers, when they had abolished slavery in all our national territory, ordained that no *person* should be deprived of 'life, liberty, or property,' without due process of law, it becomes our duty to maintain this provision of the Constitution against all attempts to violate it, for the purpose of establishing slavery in the territories of the United States, by positive legislation prohibiting its existence or extension therein. That we deny the authority of congress, of a territorial legislature, or any individual or *association of individuals,* to give legal assistance to slavery in any territory of the United States, while the present Constitution *shall be maintained.*"

And yet what information does this afford about the object of the new party? How do we know what they mean to do, and whether it ought to be done, and whether a combination of free States to do it is fit and is necessary any the more for this? It is a thing so extraordinary for a political party to put forward the Declaration of Independence as its platform, or as a prominent and distinguishing part of its platform, and to solicit the votes of a section of the States of this Union by the boast that it claims some special and characteristic relation to that immortal act and composition; that it means to put it to some use, and derive from it some power, or some rule of interpretation, or some motive to governmental action which are new and peculiar to itself,—that we pause on it with wonder, and perplexity, and alarm.

If a newly organized political party should announce that its principles were the principles of the Bible, and its spirit and aims the spirit and aims of the Bible; should put this ostentatiously in its platform, write it on its flags, carry it about by torchlight, thunder it from its pulpits and from the stands of its mass-meeting speakers, lay or clerical; should you not feel some small or some considerable confusion, perplexity, misgiving, mirth, and fear in view of such demonstration? If you did not, or if you did, think it a poor, arrogant, impious, and hypocritical method of electioneering, would you not wish to know with a trifle more of precision and fulness what were these principles, and that spirit, and those aims of the Bible thus suddenly adopted into the creed of a party? If they told you they meant those principles and that spirit "promulgated in the Bible" and "embodied in the Constitution," should you feel that you knew much more than you did before? So here. What do these mean by this adoption of the Declaration of Independence into their creed? What are *"those principles promulgated"* in *it, and "embodied in the Constitution?"* The Declaration announces all men to be born free and equal, and to have certain inalienable rights, among which is the right to liberty. The Constitution sends back the fugitive slave to his master. Is this a case of a principle *promulgated* in one, and *embodied* in the other? If not, how does their platform deal with it? What are the "principles so *embodied?*" In what article, in what word, are they so? Which do they go for, the "promulgation," or the "embodiment?" What practical legislation, or administration, are they supposed to prescribe or warrant? Nay—come a little closer; what do they intend to say they get from the Declaration, or do by means of the Declaration, more than anybody else gets from it, and does by means of it? Would they venture the proposition that the Federal Government derives any powers, any one power from that source? Certainly not; or if so, it is the most dangerous and most revolutionary heresy ever yet promulgated. Would they say that they call in the Declaration to interpret the *language* of the Constitution? I suppose not; for, that the meaning of those who constructed that consummate frame of government, and weighed, measured, and stamped its words of gold, and drew, or sought to draw, with so much precision and certainty, the delicate line which parts the powers given to the Union from those retained to the States or the people, and therein ordained that all powers not delegated to the United States, or prohibited to the States, are reserved respectively to the States or the people,—that this language, in this instrument of 1787, can be *interpreted,* enlarged or narrowed, darkened or illustrated by the language of that other instrument, not less renowned, penned in 1776, in a time and for a purpose so different,—that thrilling appeal to the reason and justice of nations, in which a people assume to vindicate upon grounds of natural right their claim to take their place in the great equality of States, and then announce their sublime decision to make their claim good by revolution and battle—composed to engage the sympathies of mankind for the new nation, and to lift up its own spirit to the demands of the great crisis,—that the latter of these papers, in point of time, is to be interpreted by the former in any sense, of which any jurist, or any reader of his mother-tongue, can form conception, is a proposition too extravagant to be imputed to the author of the platform.

Well, then, if they do not use the Declaration as a source of power, nor as a help to construction, what do they mean to do with, or do by it? How profiteth it them any more than others? than us? Why, they would say they were going to execute their constitutional powers "in the *spirit* of the Declaration." That is it, is it? They are to take the constitutional powers as they exist—to find them as you find them, and as all find them, by just and legitimate interpretation. But the difference between you and them is, they "are going to *execute* them in the spirit of the Declaration." Well, now, what does even this mean? What sort of execution is this to insure? How do you apply your rule? Nay—what is the rule? What is the spirit of the Declaration in this behalf? Is it anything more than its meaning? It is what the framers of it, the congress of 1776, then *meant,* by their language, is it not? Did they mean then to assert that slaves had an inalienable right to liberty? Did they mean to make any assertion at all upon the subject of master and slave? Was that application of this generality of natural right in their contemplation in any, the least degree? Were they consciously and intentionally conceding and proclaiming that it was a sin to hold a slave and a duty to emancipate?

How the student of the history of that act may answer this inquiry is not now to the purpose. The question is not now on the actual principles of the Declaration as its framers understood and limited and applied them. It is on the meaning of the framers of the Republican platform. What is *their* "spirit of the Declaration," and how do they mean to use it; and what do they mean to draw from it in executing the Constitution? If they will point out one single object they can or design to accomplish through it, which other parties have not accomplished and cannot accomplish, by administering the government upon these principles of equal and exact justice to all the States and all the sections, in the purpose of promoting internal tranquility and a more perfect Union, which have heretofore constituted the recognized creed of American statesmanship, we can then judge whether this parade of that instrument and that act in their platform has any meaning at all, and if so whether what is meant is needful or safe. We can then judge whether they have used a form of language intended to lead the passionate and unthinking to believe they intended something, and yet to leave themselves at liberty to protest when examined on it that they intended nothing. We can then judge whether this language of their creed is revolutionary and dangerous, or whether it merely.

> "Palters with us in a double sense;
> That keeps the word of promise to our ear,
> And breaks it to our hope."

Holding then, Fellow-citizens, the clear and settled conviction that this combination of Northern States against the South is totally unnecessary for any purpose, I record my protest against the attempt to form it and give it power. No interest of freedom requires or will be helped by it. No aspects of slavery justify it. It will not give liberty to an acre, or to a man, one hour sooner than they will have it without. It will not shorten or lighten the rule or limit the spread of slavery in the least degree.

And is not this enough to deter you from an innovation so vast, an experiment so untried, an agency of influences so incapable to be calculated?

But what if, more than novel and more than needless, it proves only an enormous evil? What if it proves, of all the fruits that slavery has borne yet, the deadliest?

To many I know the bare imagination of such fear is matter of mirth. Seeing farther than I can see, or more sanguine, or more bold, for them it seems without terror; or promises only good, or a preponderance of good, or to be a necessary evil and a risk worth taking at the worst. Let me dare to avow that which I assuredly believe and deeply feel. To me, to many thoughtful men whose opinions are far more important than mine, there is occasion for the wisdom of fear.

The grounds and the particulars of the apprehension with which such men may regard this party, there is no need here and now to open at large.

We have come so near to the time when practical consequences are to take the place of our conjectures,—or to be scattered to the winds forever or for a space, if this party is defeated,—that I may forbear to display them in detail. I compress my convictions upon the whole subject of the proposed organization in a brief, articulate enumeration, and deliver them to your judgment.

They are:—

That in the exact sense in which the language has been used, and the thing been held out for warning in the Farewell Address, and by all the illustrious men of both schools of our politics, of Washington and of Jefferson, whom heretofore the American people has regarded as its safest and most sagacious councillors,— but on a scale more gigantic and swayed by passions far more incapable of control or measure than they have any of them feared,—it is a *Geographical party,*— confined exclusively in fact and in the nature of things to one of the two great regions into which the American States are distributed; seeking objects, resting on principles, cultivating dispositions, and exerting an aggregate of influence and impressions calculated to unite all on one side of the line which parts the two regions against all on the other, upon the single subject on which, without the utmost exercise of forbearance, sense, and virtue, they cannot live at peace;

but for which they could not fail to be one people forever; by reason of which their disruption is possible at all times.

That in the sense of the language heretofore employed in American politics and history to describe this kind of thing there is not now and there never has been another Geographical party; that both the other two which now divide or now unite the people,—extending through every State North and South, professing political and industrial creeds, seeking objects, breathing a spirit and presenting candidates which every region may own alike, exerting each an aggregate of influence and impression calculated to foster an American feeling and not a sectional animosity;—that both these—whatever else may be alleged against them—are national parties.

That the Geographical party, in its nature and spirit and immediate object of taking possession of the government, is founded in essential injustice to the section which it excludes; that in ethics and reason these States are partners, and stockholders, and contractors each with all,—a partnership, an incorporation for all the good and glory and progress to which national life may aspire; that therefore, although the will of the majority is the law of the mighty concern, yet that that requires a will obedient to justice; and it is not just that a section, or a class of partners should associate among themselves by that organization called a party, to appropriate, to the practical exclusion of the rest, the government, and all the honor, profit, and power which belongs to its possession and administration, for an indefinite period, or for a presidential term, forasmuch as it violates or deserts the great implied agreement of the society—implied in the act of coming into the federal tie—that a property, a privilege, a power, a glory so large, so desirable, as the possession and administration of the government, shall pass about by a just and equitable rotation, and every section shall at all times have its share:

That if the manner in which the South has performed its duties to the Union and to the Northern section of States be regarded as a whole, from the adoption of the Constitution to this day, it affords no justification of the attempt to take possession of the government, to the exclusion of that section of States; that her federal obligations, as such, have been discharged as the general fact; that she has set no example of such sectional exclusion as this; that her federal life and activities have been exerted in and through national parties, and as a branch or wing thereof; that she has supplied her proportionate share of capacity and valor to the service of the whole country, and that the bad language, and violent acts, and treasonable devices of her bad men create no case for the injustice here meditated:

That the repeal of the Missouri Compromise, and the disposition of the South to form Kansas into a slave State, while we condemn and deplore the former, and demand that the free-will of all its people shall be permitted to disappoint the latter, creating no necessity for the Geographical party, afford no excuse for the injustice meditated:

That such a party is dangerous to the internal tranquillity and general welfare of the United States, and that it tends by probable and natural consequence less or more remote to their separation.

Such was once, was ever, until to-day, the universal judgment of wise and honest men and true patriots; and by their counsels it is safe, moral, and respectable to abide.

That such a party, militant or triumphant, electioneering for the administration or in possession of it, must exert influences of wide and various evil, even whether they do or do not reach to the overthrow of our system; that it accustoms the people of each section to turn from contemplating that fair and grand ideal, the whole America, and to find their country in one of its fragments; a revolution of the public affections, and a substitution of a new public life; that it accustoms them to exaggerate, intensify, and put forward into everything the one element of discord and diversity, and to neglect the cultivation of the less energetic elements of resemblance and union; that, in fixing their attention on a single subject, and that one appealing simply to passion and emotion, to pride, to fear, to moral sensibilities, it exasperates and embitters the general temper, and sows the seeds of sentiments which we did not inherit, but which we may transmit,—sentiments of the vehement and energetic class which form and unform nations; that it has to an extraordinary degree changed the tone of political discussion in this its own section, and made it intolerant, immoral, abusive and insolent to those who differ, to an extent to which our party disputes have before afforded no example; that it tends to place moderate men and national men, North and South, in a false position, by presenting to them the alternative of treason to the whole or treason to the section,—thus putting moderate counsels to shame, and destroying the influence which might help to restore the good temper and generous affection of the parts and the whole.

That while it is organized on the single basis of resistance to what it calls the slave power, it misconceives or disregards the true duties of the patriotism, philanthropy, and Christianity of the Free States in the matter of slavery; that it excites hatred of the master, but no prudent, nor reasonable, nor useful love of the slave; that to hinder the mere extension of that relation over more area, although one good thing, is not the only one demanded; that even that may be rendered worse than useless by the mode of seeking to effect it; that whatsoever else we do or attempt, in whatsoever else our power comes short of our wishes in this regard, we are bound to know that discords and animosity on this subject between North and South, however promoted, do but retard the training for freedom and postpone the day of its gradual and peaceful attainment. If ye so hate the master, or so fear him, or so contend with him, that ye rivet the fetters of the slave or lengthen the term of his slavery, what reward have ye or has he?

With these opinions, Fellow-citizens, I aim, in this election, at one single object; I feel but one single hope, and one single fear. To me, all of you, all men who aim at that object and share that hope and that fear, seem allies, brothers, partners of a great toil, a great duty, and a common fate. For the hour, opinions upon other things, old party creeds adapted for quiet times, old party names and symbols and squabbles and differences about details of administration, seem to me hushed, suspended, irrelevant, trifling,—the small cares of a master of ceremonies in the palace on the morning of the revolution, about red heels, smallclothes, and buckles in the shoe, within an hour of the final storm. I care no more now whether my co-worker is a Democrat, or an American, or an old Whig, a Northern man or a California man, than you should care if a fire fell on your city in winter and was devouring your workshops and streets one after another, and houseless women and children and old men and sick were seen hovering on the side of the river in the snow, whether he who passed or received your buckets was rocked in his cradle on this side of the sea or the other; whether he was an Arminian or Calvinist; a ten-hours' labor man or a twenty-four hours' labor man. The election once over, we are our several selves again. "If we get well," the sick man said, when with difficulty reconciled to his enemy, both being supposed dying, "if we get well, it all goes for nothing."

Certainly somewhat there is in the position of all of us a little trying,—ties of years, which knit some of us together, are broken; cold regards are turned on us, and bitter language and slander, cruel as the grave, is ours.

> "I cannot but remember such things were,
> That were most precious to me."

You have decided, Fellow Whigs, that you can best contribute to the grand end we all seek, by a vote for Mr. Fillmore. I, a Whig all my life, a Whig in all things, and, as regards all other names, a Whig to-day, have thought I could discharge my duty most effectually by voting for Mr. Buchanan and Mr. Breckenridge; and I shall do it. The justice I am but too happy in rendering you, will you deny to me? In doing this, I neither join the Democratic party, nor retract any opinion on the details of its policy, nor acquit it of its share of blame in bringing on the agitations of the hour. But there are traits, there are sentiments, there are specialties of capacity and of function, that make a party as they make a man, which fit it in an extraordinary degree for special service in special crises,—to meet particular forms of danger by exactly adapted resistance—to fight fire with fire—to encounter by a sharper, more energetic, and more pro-nounced antagonism the precise type of evil which assails the State. In this way every great party successively becomes the saviour of the Constitution. There was never an election contest that in denouncing the particulars of its policy I did not admit that the characteristic of the Democratic party was this: that it had burned ever with that great master-passion this hour demands—a youthful, vehement, exultant, and progressive nationality. Through some errors, into some perils, it has been led by it; it may be so again; we may require to temper and restrain it, but to-day we need it all, we need it all!—the hopes—the boasts—the pride—the universal tolerance—the gay and festive defiance of foreign dictation—the flag—the music—all the emotions—all the traits—all the energies, that have won their victories of war, and their miracles of national advancement,—the country needs them all now to win a victory of peace. That done, I will pass again, happy and content, into that minority of conservatism in which I have passed my life.

To some, no doubt, the purport and tone of much that I have said may seem to be the utterance and the spirit of fear. Professors among their classes, preach-ers to implicit congregations, the men and women of emotion and sentiment, will mock at such apprehensions. I wish them joy of their discernment; of the depth of their readings of history; of the soundness of their nerves. Let me excuse myself in the words of an English statesman, then and ever conspicuous for spirit and courage, the present prime minister of England, in a crisis of En-gland far less urgent than this. "Tell me not that this is the language of intimida-tion; tell me not that I am appealing to the fears instead of to the reason of the House. In matters of such high concern, which involve not personal and indi-vidual considerations, but the welfare of one's country, no man ought to be ashamed of being counselled by his fears. But the fears to which I appeal are the fears which the brave may acknowledge, and the wise need not blush to own. The fear to which I appeal is that early and provident fear which Mr. Burke so beautifully describes as being the mother of safety. 'Early and provident fear,' says Mr. Burke, 'is the mother of safety, for in that state of things the mind is firm and collected, and the judgment unembarrassed; but when fear and the thing feared come on together and press upon us at once, even deliberation, which at other times saves us, becomes our ruin, because it delays decision; and when the peril is instant, decision should be instant too.' To this fear I am not ashamed of appealing; by this fear legislators and statesmen ought ever to be ruled; and he who will not listen to this fear, and refuses to be guided by its counsel, may go and break his lances against windmills, but the court of chancery should enjoin him to abstain from meddling with public affairs."

They taunt you with being "Union-savers." I never thought that a sarcasm of the first magnitude, but as men can but do their best, let it go for what they think it worth. I take for granted, Fellow-citizens, that you, that all of us, despise cant and hypocrisy in all things,—the feigning a fear not felt, the cry of peril not believed to exist, all meanness and all wickedness of falsehood in our dealings with the mind of the people. But I take it for granted, too, that we are above the cowardice and immorality of suppressing our sense of a danger, threatening precious interests and possible to be averted, from the dread of jokers of jokes; and that we are above the folly of yielding that vast advantage which deep convictions give to earnest men in the dissensions of the Republic. Think what a thing it were to win the proud and sounding name in reality which they bestow in decision! Suppose, only suppose it so for the argument, that there is danger, over-estimated perhaps by the solicitude of filial love, but real or probable and less or more remote,—suppose, merely for the supposition, that Washington had reason to leave that warning against this kind of geographical combinations, *under all pretexts,* and that this one comes within the spirit and the terms of that warning,— suppose it to be so that we are right; that vehement passions, eager philanthropy, moral emotions not patient nor comprehensive of the indispensable limitations of political duty; that anger, pride, ambition, the lust of sectional power, the jealousy of sectional aggression, the pursuit even of ends just and desirable by means disproportioned and needless and exasperating—the excess and outbreak of virtues, by which more surely than by vices a country may be undone,—that these all working in an unusual conjuncture of affairs and state of public temper, have exposed and are exposing this Union to danger less or more remote,—and then suppose that by some word seasonably uttered, some vote openly and courageously given, some sincere conviction plainly expressed, we could do something to earn the reality of the praise which they give us in jest,—something for the safety, something for the peace, of this holy and beautiful house of our fathers,— something, were it ever so little,—would not this be compensation for the laughter of fools; aye! for alienated friendships, averted faces, and the serpent tooth of slander,—a thing worth dying for, and even worth having lived for?

CHAPTER XIV.

THE ELOQUENCE OF REVOLUTIONARY PERIODS.
A LECTURE DELIVERED BEFORE THE MECHANIC APPRENTICE'S LIBRARY ASSOCIATION, February 19, 1857.

One of Choate's later addresses, "The Eloquence of Revolutionary Periods" places the American War for Independence in the context of other great turning points in the history of Western civilization. All these events, Choate explains, in which the destinies of nations are decided, call forth from great men heights of eloquence unmatched in more eirenic times.

Samuel Gilman Brown writes that the speech "is full of high thoughts, and raises one by its beauty and magnanimity. Its eloquent defense of Cicero was harshly criticized— one hardly knows why—by some who accept the later theories of Cicero's life; but was received with rare satisfaction by the lovers of the patriotic Roman—nearly the most eloquent of the ancients." It can come as no surprise to students of Choate that his address should conclude by comparing Daniel Webster, one of the great orators in Massachusetts history, to the greatest speakers of antiquity, even going so far as to speculate on whether Webster might have slowed the decay of ancient Greece.

IF YOU consider deliberative eloquence, in its highest forms and noblest exertion, to be the utterances of men of genius practised, earnest, and sincere, according to a rule of art, in presence of large assemblies, in great conjunctures of public affairs, *to persuade a People,* it is quite plain that those largest of all conjunctures, which you properly call times of revolution, must demand and supply a deliberative eloquence *all their own.*

All kinds of genius,—I mean of that genius whose organ is art or language, and whose witness, hearer, and judge is the eye, ear, imagination, and heart of cultivated humanity,—if cast on a marked and stormy age, an age lifted above and out of the even, general flow of prescriptive life, by great changes, new ideas, and strong passions, extraordinary abilities and enterprises, some grand visible revelation of the death-throes, birth-times, in which an old creation passes away and a new one comes to light,—all kinds of such genius, cast on such an age, are tinged and moulded by it. None so hardy, none so spiritual, none so individualized, none so self-nourished, none so immersed in its own consciousness, subjectivity, and self-admiration, as not to own and bow to the omnipresent manifested spirit of the time. Goethe, Byron, Alfieri, the far mightier Milton, are ready illustrations of this. Between them and that crisis of the nations, and of the race in which they lived, on which they looked fascinated, entranced, how influencive and inevitable the sympathy! Into that bright or dim dream of enchantment, invention, ideality, in which was their poet-life, how are the shapes of this outward world projected, how its cries of despair or triumph reëcho there, that new heaven and new earth, their dwelling-place; how they give back the cloud and storm, and sunshine and waning moon; how they breathe the gales, and laugh with the flowers, and sadden with the wastes, of our earth and sky! Topics, treatment, thoughts, characters, moods,—how they all but imitate and reproduce the real in the ideal, life in immortality. Take the extraordinary instance of Milton. That England of the great Civil War, the England of the Commonwealth and Cromwell, that England which saw the king discrowned and beheaded, the House of Lords abolished, Puritanism triumphant on the bloody days of Worcester and Dunbar, the deliberations of the Long Parliament, the Westminster Assembly constructing and promulgating its creed on the awful mysteries,—how does the presence and influence of that England seem to haunt you in "Samson Agonistes," in "Paradise Lost," in "Paradise Regained,"—a memory, a sense of earth revived in the peace of the world beyond the grave, ages after death! Milton's soul, if ever mortal spirit did so, "was a star, and dwelt apart." Yet everywhere, almost,—in the dubious war on the plains of heaven; in the debates of the synod of fallen demigods; in the tremendous conception of that pride and will and self-trust, which rose in the Archangel ruined against the Highest; in those dogmas and those speculations of theology which wander unresting, unanswered, through eternity; in that tone of austere independence and indignant insubordination, obedient, however, to a higher law and a diviner vision; in that contempt of other human judgments, and defiant enunciation of its own,—everywhere you seem to meet the Puritan, the Republican, the defender of the claim of the people of England to be free; the apologist, the advocate of the execution of kings; the champion in all lands and all ages of the liberty of conscience, of speech, of the press; the secretary, the counsellor of Cromwell; the child, organ, memorial of the age. That heroic individuality, what was it but the product of a hard, unaccommodating, original, mighty nature, moulded and tinged by the tragic and sharp realities of national revolution? and it seems to go with him, partaking of its mixed original, whithersoever the song wanders, soars, or sinks,—in the paths of Eden, on the "perilous edge of

battle" waged for the throne of God, in reporting the counsels of the Infinite in
the past eternity, in hailing the Holy Light on which those orbs, overplied, as he
consoled himself, in liberty's defence, were closed forever.

So, too, of the lesser but yet resplendent names of Goethe, Byron, Alfieri:
the spirit of the time was as vehement in them as it was in the young Napoleon.
They shared its fire, its perturbed and towering mind, its longings, its free thinking, its passion of strong sensations, its deep insights, its lust of power and of
change, and all its dark unrest, as fully as he did; and they uttered its voices in
those troubled, unequalled songs, as *he* uttered them first at Marengo and Lodi
by the cannon of his victories.

Sometimes the blessedness of that great calm which follows the exhausted
tempest of the moral heaven, in which the winds go down and the billows rock
themselves to sleep, is imaged in the poems of an age. That most consummate
effort of the finer genius of Rome,—the Georgics of Virgil, for example,—that
decorated, abundant, and contented Italy that smiles there; the cattle, larger and
smaller, on so many hills; the holidays of vintage; the murmur of bees; the happy
husbandman; the old, golden age of Saturn returning,—what is all that but the
long sigh of the people of Rome, the sigh of Italy, the sigh of the world, breathed
through that unequalled harmony and sensibility, for peace,—peace under its
vine and fig-tree,—peace, rest, after a hundred years of insecurity, convulsion,
and blood?

Now, if that form of genius,—genius in art, in poetry, whose end is delight,
whose wanderings

> "are where the Muses haunt
> Clear spring, or shady green, or sunny hill,"

whose nourishment is

> "Of thoughts that voluntary move harmonious numbers,"

—if that kind,—solitary, introspective, the creature of the element,—takes a bias
and a tincture from a strongly agitated time, how much truer must this be of that
genius whose office, whose art, it is, by speech, by deep feelings and earnest convictions overflowing in eloquent speech, to communicate with the people of
such a time directly upon the emotions it excites, the hopes it inspires, the duties
it imposes, the tremendous alternative it holds out? How inevitable that the eloquence of revolutions should be all compact of the passing hour! How inevitable
that the audiences such seasons assemble, the crises hurried onward as the sea its

succession of billows, the great passions they set on fire, the pity, the terror they justify, the mighty interests they place at stake, the expansive and gorgeous ideas on which they roll, the simplicity, definiteness, and prominence of the objects which they set before all men's eyes, the concussion, the stimulation which they give to the whole meditative as well as emotional faculties of a generation,— how inevitable that such a conjunctive age and revolution should create its own style and tone and form of public speech!

For, what is a revolution? I shall call it that agony through which, by which,— the accustomed course, the accustomed and normal ebb and flow, of the life of the State, being violently suspended, from causes in part internal,—a new nation is born, or an old nation dies, or by which, without losing its identity, a nation puts off its constitution of tyranny and becomes free, self-governed, or is despoiled of its constitution of freedom and becomes enslaved, the slave of its own government. Such a change as either of these,—such a birth, such a dying, such emancipation, such enslavement,—such a change,—vast, violent, compressed within some comparatively brief time, palpable to all sense and all consciousness, so that thousands, millions, feel together that the spell of a great historical hour is upon them all at once,—such an one I call a revolution. And these are they which are transacted on the high places of the world, and make up the epic and the tragic matter of the story of nations.

Illustrations of all these kinds will readily occur to you. Of one class, of a revolution in which a national life expired, internal causes co-working with force from without, you see an instance, grand, sad, memorable in that day, when in the downward age of Greece, that once radiant brow was struck by Philip, and by the successors of Alexander, forever to the earth. Of a revolution in which a nation, keeping its life, its identity, exchanged a government of freedom for a government of tyranny, you have an instance, not less grand and memorable, bloodier and fuller of terror in its incidents and instrumentalities, in that time when republican Rome became the Rome of the Cæsars, and the dignity of the Senate unrobed itself, and the proud and noble voice of the people in the forum died away in the presence of the purple and the guard. Of that type of revolution in which a nation, still keeping its life and identity, exchanges her constitution of slavery for one of freedom, or seems to do so, or rises to do so, you will recall the example of the France of 1789. Of that other type of revolution in which a nation begins, or seems to begin, to be, there are examples in Ireland in 1782, in America in 1776. These, and such as these, if other such there are, I call revolutions.

In some things,—in causes, incidents, issues, lessons, distinguished from one another by some traits of the eloquence they demand and supply,—there is a certain common character to them all; and there are certain common peculiarities by which the eloquence of them all is sure to be unlike, essentially, the whole public speech of times quieter, happier, less crowded, less glorious.

Glance first at the common characteristics of all the deliberative eloquence of all the classes of revolutions, as I have defined revolution.

If you bear in mind that the aim of deliberative eloquence is *to persuade to an action,* and that to persuade to an action it must be shown that to perform it will gratify some one of the desires or affections or sentiments,—you may call them, altogether, *passions,*—which are the springs of all action, some love of our own happiness, some love of our country, some love of man, some love of honor, some approval of our own conscience, some fear or some love of God, you see *that* eloquence will be characterized,—first, by the nature of the actions to which it persuades; secondly, by the nature of the desire or affection or sentiment,—the nature of the passion, in other words,—by appeal to which it seeks to persuade to the action; and then, I say, that the capital peculiarity of the eloquence of all times of revolution, as I have described revolution, is that the actions it persuades to are the highest and most heroic which men can do, and the passions it would inspire, in order to persuade to them, are the most lofty which man can feel. "High actions and high passions,"—such are Milton's words,—high actions through and by high passions; these are the end and these the means of the orator of the revolution.

Hence are his topics large, simple, intelligible, affecting. Hence are his views broad, impressive, popular; no trivial details, no wire-woven developments, no subtle distinctions and drawing of fine lines about the boundaries of ideas, no speculation, no ingenuity; all is elemental, comprehensive, intense, practical, unqualified, undoubting. It is not of the small things of minor and instrumental politics he comes to speak, or men come to hear. It is not to speak or to hear about permitting an Athenian citizen to change his tribe; about permitting the Roman Knights to have jurisdiction of trials equally with the Senate; it is not about allowing a £10 householder to vote for a member of Parliament; about duties on indigo, or onion-seed, or even tea.

"That strain you hear is of an higher mood."

It is the rallying cry of patriotism, of liberty, in the sublimest crisis of the State,— of man. It is a deliberation of empire of glory, of existence on which they come together. To be or not to be,—that is the question. Shall the children of the men of Marathon become slaves of Philip? Shall the majesty of the senate and people of Rome stoop to wear the chains forging by the military executors of the will of Julius Cæsar? Shall the assembled representatives of France, just waking from her sleep of ages to claim the rights of man,—shall they disperse, their work undone, their work just commencing; and shall they disperse at the order of the king? or shall the messenger be bid to go, in the thunder-tones of Mirabeau,—and tell his master that "we sit here to do the will of our constituents, and that we will not be moved from these seats but by the point of the bayonet"? Shall Ireland bound upward from her long prostration, and cast from her the last link of the British chain, and shall she advance "from injuries to arms, from arms to liberty," from liberty to glory?

Shall the thirteen Colonies become, and be, free and independent States, and come unabashed, unterrified, an equal, into the majestic assembly of the nations? These are the thoughts with which all bosoms are distended and oppressed. Filled with these, with these flashing in every eye, swelling every heart, pervading electric all ages, all orders, like a visitation, "an unquenchable public fire," men come together,—the thousands of Athens around the Bema, or in the Temple of Dionysus,—the people of Rome in the forum, the Senate in that council-chamber of the world,—the masses of France, as the spring-tide, into her gardens of the Tuileries, her clubrooms, her hall of the convention,—the representatives, the genius, the grace, the beauty of Ireland into the Tuscan Gallery of her House of Commons,—the delegates of the Colonies into the Hall of Independence at Philadelphia,—thus men come, in an hour of revolution, to hang upon the lips from which they hope, they need, they demand, to hear the things which belong to their national salvation, hungering for the bread of life.

And then and thus comes the orator of that time, kindling with their fire; sympathizing with that great beating heart; penetrated, not subdued; lifted up rather by a sublime and rare moment of history made real to his consciousness; charged with the very mission of life, yet unassured whether they will hear or will forbear; transcendent good within their grasp, yet a possibility that the fatal and critical opportunity of salvation will be wasted; the last evil of nations and of men overhanging, yet the siren song of peace—peace when there is no peace—chanted madly by some voice of sloth or fear,—there and thus the orators of revolutions come to work their work! And what then is demanded, and how it is to be done, you all see; and that in some of the characteristics of their eloquence they must all be alike. *Actions,* not law or policy, whose growth and fruits are to be slowly evolved by time and calm; actions daring, doubtful but instant; the new things of a new world,—these are what the speaker counsels; large, elementary, gorgeous ideas of right, of equality, of independence, of liberty, of progress through convulsion,—these are the principles from which he reasons, *when he reasons,*—these are the pinions of the thought on which he soars and stays; and then the primeval and indestructible sentiments of the breast of man,—his sense of right, his estimation of himself, his sense of honor, his love of fame, his triumph and his joy in the dear name of country, the trophies that tell of the past, the hopes that gild and herald her dawn,—these are the springs of action to which he appeals,— these are the chords his fingers sweep, and from which he draws out the troubled music, "solemn as death, serene as the undying confidence of patriotism," to which he would have the battalions of the people march! Directness, plainness, a narrow range of topics, few details, few but grand ideas, a headlong tide of sentiment and feeling; vehement, indignant, and reproachful reasonings,— winged general maxims of wisdom and life; an example from Plutarch; a pregnant sentence of Tacitus; thoughts going forth as ministers of nature in robes of light, and with arms in their hands; thoughts that breathe and words that burn,— these vaguely, approximately, express the general type of all this speech.

I have spoken of some characteristics common to the eloquence of all revolutions. But they differ from one another; and their eloquence differs too.

Take first that instance—sad, grand, and memorable forever—in which Greece, prepared for it by causes acting within, perished at last by the gold and the phalanx of Macedon. The orator of that time is the first name in the ancient eloquence, in some respects—in the transcendent opportunity of his life and death at least—the first name in *all* eloquence,—Demosthenes.

Begin with him,—the orator of the nation which is expiring. The most Athenian of the Athenians, the most Greek of all the Greeks, it was his mission to utter the last and noblest protest of Grecian independence, and to pour out the whole gathered, traditional, passionate patriotism of the freest and most country-loving of all the races of man, in one final strain of higher mood than the world before or since has heard. The scheme of politics, the ethics, the public service, the eloquence, the whole life, of this man have all the unity and consistency of parts,—all the simplicity and rapid and transparent flow of a masterpiece of Attic art. That dying hour in the Temple of Neptune brought the long tragic action with a befitting grandeur and terror and pity to its close. At the moment when he became of age to take on him the first duties of Athenian citizenship, he saw soonest of his countrymen, with keenest and justest discernment, that the independence of Athens—the independence of the whole old historical Greece—was directly and formidably assailed by the arms and the gold of a rising, half-barbarous military monarchy on its northern frontier. If that Philip—if that Alexander—succeeded in the design so transparent to his eye,— so transparent to ours now, though some good men and wise men could not yet see it so,—the Greece of his birth, pride, and love,—that fair, kindred group of States, not straitly united by a constitution, yet to him, by language, by blood, by culture, by institutions, by tradition, by trophies,—"the descent and con-catenation and distribution of glory,"—by disdain of masters abroad and tyrants at home, seeming to him a beautiful identity,—that Greece would perish for evermore. To frustrate that design, was the *one single* effort of the public life of Demosthenes of thirty years. To devise, to organize and apply, the means of doing so, was the one single task of all his statesmanship, all his diplomacy, all his plans of finance, all his political combinations, all his matchless eloquence.

Whatsoever of usefulness, or goodness, or grandeur there is in patriotism,—that patriotism which is employed in keeping its country alive,—all this praise is his. Some there were in that downward age—some ponderous historians of Greece there are now—who said and say that a Macedonian conquest was not so bad a thing; that it was not so much a dying of Greece as a new life in another body, a higher being, a mere transmutation of matter, a mere diffusion of the race and language, the fountain merely sinking into the earth in Attica to rise in Syria, to rise in Alexandria. All these metaphysics of history were lost on him. He felt like a Greek who was a Greek. He felt that the identity of Greek polit-ical life consisted in this: that it owned no foreign master, and that it acknowl-edged no despotic single will at home. Independence of all the world without; self-government; the rule and the obedience of law self-imposed; rights and obligations reciprocally due,—due from man to man within the city, under the constitution,—this was in essence Grecian public life—Grecian life. Love of beauty and of glory, faultless taste, subtilty and fancy in supreme degree, over-flowing in an art, a poetry, a speculative philosophy, an eloquence, a whole literature,—making up so large a part of our manifold and immortal inheri-tance from the past,—this was greatness too, certainly. But it is in her pride of independence, and in her tempestuous internal freedom; it is in Marathon or Thermopylæ and the games of the Olympia—and that stormy, quick-witted, wilful and passionate people—that he recognized, that we recognize the true and nobler individuality.

To keep all this against the gold and the spear of that half civilized military despotism—in the first rising strength of a new national life—was the mission, say rather the high endeavor of Demosthenes. To this for a lifetime he gave himself,—he abandoned himself,—nor rested till all was over; and a little poi-son in a ring was all the dying mother could leave her child to help him escape her murderers and his; death by poison in the temple on the island,—praise, tears, and admiration through all time.

You see at once, in the singleness and simplicity, yet difficulty and grandeur, of the work he had to work, an explanation of many of the characteristics of his eloquence usually dwelt on,—its directness, its perspicuity, its disdain of ornament, its freedom from dissertation, and refining, and detail, and wearisome development,—the fewness of its topics, the limited range of its ideas,—*its harmony and unity of spirit and effect,*—the whole speech of three hours seeming but one blow of a thunderbolt, by which a tower, a furlong of a city-wall, might tumble down,—its austere, almost fierce, gloomy intensity and earnestness,— its rapidity and vehemence,—the indignation, the grief, the wonder, the love which seem to cry out, "Why will ye die?"

But this brings me to say that there are other characteristics less spoken of: here and there through these grand exhortations there breathes another tone, for which you must seek another solution. That spirit—so vehement, so enthusiastic, so hopeful, so bold—was clear-sighted too; and he could not fail to discern in all things around him but too much cause to fear that he had come on the last times of Greece. Yes, he might well see and feel that it was his to be the orator of the expiring nation!

The old public life of Greece was in its decay. The outward, visible Athens seemed unchanged. There she sat, as in the foretime, on her citadel rock, in sight of her auxiliar sea, crowned, garlanded, wanton, with all beauty, all glory, and all delight. Yet all was changed! There stood the walls of Themistocles; but the men of Marathon, where were they? Instead—vanity, effeminacy, sensual self-indulgence, sordid avarice, distrust of the gods,—the theatre, the banquet, the garland dripping with Samian wine!

The second childhood had come. Like their own grasshoppers, they would make their old age an ungraceful infancy, an evening revel, and sing their fill. Gleams of the once matchless race and time broke through here and there, and played on the surface, as the sun setting on Salamis; but the summer was ending; the day was far spent; the bright consummate flower that never might in other climate grow, was fain to bow to the dread decree of eternal change!

The great statesman was himself unchanged. His whole public life, therefore, was a contention. It was one long breathing, one long trust, one long prayer that these dry bones might live.

Therefore, also, ever, there seems to me through all that fire, sublimity, and confidence, a certain—I know not what I should call it—a half-indulged, half-repressed consciousness that all is lost, and all is vain! It is as if the orator were a prophet too, and the vision he saw confronted and saddened the speech he uttered. There is the expostulation, the reproach, the anger, the choking grief of a patriot who has his whole country, literally, within the sound of his voice, among the scenes of all their glory, who knows—who thinks he knows—as well as he knows his own existence, that if they WILL, they SHALL be free,—who cannot let go the dear and sweetest error, if it is so, of salvation possible to the State, and yet, when the pause of exhaustion comes, and the vision his wishes had sketched shows less palpably, and the glow of the spirit sinks, almost owns to himself that the hope he felt was but the resolution of despair.

"I see a hand you cannot see,
I hear a voice you cannot hear!"

Three days of this man's life stand out to the imagination from its grand, sad, general tenor.

First of these was that in his thirtieth year when he pronounced his first oration against Philip of Macedon. That day—without office, without even call by the people, without waiting for the veteran haranguers and advisers of the city toward whom the assembly was looking to hear, when the sacrifices had been performed, and the herald had made proclamation—he went up to counsel his countrymen; and when he had concluded, he, the son of the sword manufacturer,— a young man, in the yet early flush and enthusiasm of public virtue,—had practically, without formal suffrage, elevated himself to the chief magistracy of Athens for all the future lifetime of Athenian freedom. He sprung up that day by one bound to this height so dazzling, and there he stood till the eye of Greece was closed forever. As he came down from that stage on which Pericles had spoken to a former generation, not unconscious of the actual triumph, some feeling of the greater future in the instant,—a grave expectation on that stern, melancholy face, that the midnight studies in the cave by the sea had loosed the tongue of the stammerer; that the closed lips had been touched by fire, and the deep miraculous fountain of eloquence been unsealed,—I can imagine him to say, "And these applauses I have won by no flattery of the people; no sophistries; no rhetoric; no counsels of self-indulgence; no siren song transforming to beasts! As I have won let me keep them. Be mine to avow that without regenerated Athens Greece already has her master. Be mine to open my country's eye to the whole danger and the single remedy; to turn these States away from their idle fears of Persia and their senseless jealousy of each other, and fix their apprehensions on their true enemy, perhaps their destroyer, this soldier of Macedon. Be mine to persuade old men and rich men to give, and young men, spurning away the aid of mercenaries, themselves to strike for Greece by sea and land as in her heroic time. Be mine to lift up the heart of this Athens; to erect the spirit of this downward age; to reënthrone the sentiment of duty for its own sake,—the glory of effort, the glory of self-sacrifice and of suffering,—to reënthrone these fading sentiments in the soul of my people,—or all is lost—is lost!"

And as these thoughts which embody his exact whole public life came on him, I can imagine him turning away from the applauses of an audience that had found by a sure instinct in that essay of an hour its mightiest orator in that young man,—turning the sight up from the Salamis and the busy city beneath, and pausing to stay his spirit by the cheerful and fair religions of the Acropolis,— that temple, that fortress, that gallery of the arts,—serene and steadfast as the floor of Olympus,—and then descending homewards to begin his great trust of guiding the public life of expiring Greece.

Turn to his next great day. Twelve years have passed, and the liberties of Greece have been cloven down at Chæronea forever. Philip is dead, and the young Alexander is master. And now, in this hour of her humiliation, he who had advised and directed the long series of her unavailing warfare; to whose eloquence, to whose fond dream, to whose activity, to whose desperate fidelity incorrupt, she owed it, that she had fallen as became the mother of the men of Marathon,—he is arraigned for this whole public life, and rises before an audience gathered of all Greece—gathered of all the lettered world, to vindicate his title to the crown.

The youthful orator has grown to be a man of fifty-two. For him, for Greece, the future now is indeed a dream. Some possible chance, some god, some oracle, may give to strike another blow; but for the present all is over—is over! It is the glory or the shame of the past which is to be appreciated now. It is the dead for freedom for whom he is to give account. It is for a perished nation that he comes there and then to be judged. Others have laid down the trust of public life at the close of splendid successes. His administration saw liberty and the State expire. Others could point the nation they had been conducting to some land of promise beyond the river; to some new field and new age of greatness; "to future sons and daughters yet unborn," and so challenge the farewell applauses of their time. He and his Athens had lost all things,—independence, national life, hope, all things but honor; and how should he answer, in that day, for his share in contributing to a calamity so accomplished? How he answered all men know. In the noblest deliberative discourse ever uttered by mortal lips, there, in their presence who had seen his outgoings and incomings for his whole public life, who had known his purity, his wisdom, his civil courage; who had sympathized, had trembled, had kindled with all his emotions of a lifetime; in whose half-extinguished virtue he had lighted up the fire of a better age, he reviewed that grand and melancholy story; he gave them to see through that pictured retrospect how it had been appointed to them to act in the final extremity of Greece; what dignity, what responsibleness, what tragic and pathetic interest, had belonged to their place and fortunes; how they had been singled out to strike the last blow for the noblest cause; and how gloriously they had been minded, without calculation of the chances of success or failure, to stand or fall in the passes of the dear mother land! All that Greece had in her of the historical past—all of letters, refinement, renowned grace and liberty—all was represented by you, and nobly have ye striven to defend it all! Grandly ye resolved; grandly ye have resisted; grandly have ye fallen!

That day he read his history in a nation's eyes. The still just, stricken heart of the people of Athens folded the orator-statesman to its love, nod set on his head forever the crown of gold!

One day more was wanting to that high tragic part, and how that was discharged Plutarch and Lucian have imagined strikingly. If it were a death self-inflicted, our moral judgments must deeply deplore and condemn. Some uncertainty attends the act; and from the Grecian stand-point, we may admit its pathos and own its grandeur.

Sixteen years had now passed since the fatal battle of Chæronea,—eight since the pleading for the crown. He was now in the sixtieth year of his life. In that time the final struggle of Greece was attempted,—another attempt,—and all was over. In August, three hundred and twenty-two years before Christ, a decisive victory of the Macedonians had scattered the hasty levies of the Greeks,—the Macedonian conqueror came near to Athens; stationed a garrison of her conquerors above the harbor to command it; abolished the democratical constitution, and decreed the banishment of twelve thousand Athenian citizens. One thing more was wanting to attest that Athens, that Greece had completely perished at length—and that was the surrender of the orator to atone by death for the resistance which he had so long persuaded his countrymen to attempt against her ultimate destroyer. This surrender the conqueror demanded. He had no longer a country to protect him by arms. Could she do it by her gods? He withdrew to an island some miles from Athens, and there sought an asylum in the temple of Neptune. The exile hunter came with his Thracians to the door, and would have persuaded him to commit himself to what he called the clemency of the king of Macedon. I give the rest in a free translation from Lucien.

"I dread the clemency which you offer me," he answered, "more than the torture and death for which I had been looking; for I cannot bear that it be reported that the king has corrupted me by the promise of life to desert the ranks of Greece, and stand in those of Macedon. Glorious and beautiful I should have thought it, if that life could have been guarded by my country; by the fleet; by the walls which I have builded for her; by the treasury I have filled; by her constitution of popular liberty; by her assemblies of freemen; by her ancestral glory; by the love of my countrymen who have crowned me so often; by Greece which I have saved hitherto. But since this may not be, if it is thus that this island, this sea, this temple of Neptune, these altars, these sanctities of religion cannot keep me from the court of the king of Macedon, a spectacle,—a slave,—I, Demosthenes, whom nature never formed for disgrace,—I, who have drunk in from Xenophon, from Plato, the hope of immortality,—I, for the honor of Athens, prefer death to slavery, and wrap myself thus about with liberty, the fairest winding sheet!" And so he drew the poison from his ring, and smiled and bade the tyrant farewell, and died, snatched opportunely away by some god, his attendant reported,—great unconquered soul; and the voice of Greece was hushed forever.

Next for instruction and impressiveness to the revolution by which a nation dies, is that in which, preserving its life, it is compelled to exchange a constitution of freedom for the government of tyranny. And in this class the grandest, most bloody, memorable, and instructive in the history of man, is that by which republican Rome became the Rome of the Cæsars; and senate, consul, knights, tribune, people, the occasional dictator, all were brought down on a wide equality of servitude before the emperor and the army. Of the aspect of such a revolution in eloquence, you have an illustration of extraordinary interest and splendor in the instance of Cicero, that greatest name by far of the whole Roman mental and lettered culture,—the most consummate production of the Latin type of genius,—the one immortal voice of the Latin speech, by universal consent; teacher, consoler, benefactor of all ages,—in whom Augustine and Erasmus could find and love a kind of anticipated approximative Christianity. Turning from all he wrote, spoke, did, and suffered beside, all his other studies, all his other praise, fix your eye on him now, as the the orator of the expiring liberty of the commonwealth.

He was murdered, in the sixty-fourth year of his life, by the triumvirate of soldiers, Augustus, Lepidus, and Mark Antony, who had just consummated the overthrow of that republic, extinguished the hopes the death of Julius Cæsar had excited, and were in the act to set up the frowning arch of the ranged empire. His death not only closed the prescription, as Antony said, but it did more; it closed and crowned, with a large, tragic interest, that most stupendous of revolutions which, beginning years before, (he is a wise man who can tell you when it began), transformed at length republican Rome into the Rome of Augustus, of Tiberius, and passed the dominion of the world, from the senate and people of the one Eternal City, to an Emperor and his legions. With his life the light of freedom went out. Till that voice was hushed the triumph of despotism seemed insecure; it was fit, her grandest themes and her diviner nourishment of liberty forbidden, that eloquence should die.

No great man's life had ever a grander close. The stream of the revolution in which the republic was to perish had swept all Rome along, him with the rest, unsympathizing, resisting. It seemed to have consummated the downfall of the constitution when it made Julius Cæsar perpetual dictator. But he was slain by the conspirators in March of the forty-fourth year before Christ; and with this event, though he had not been of the conspiracy, the hopes of Cicero to stay the bloody and dark tide, and to reëstablish and reform the constitution of the republic, revived at once; and thenceforward, with scarcely the intermission of sleep, he gave himself to the last—they proved to be last—proud and sad offices of Roman liberty, until all such hopes were quenched in his blood. In that interval of not quite two years, I rejoice to say that no worshipper of the Cæsars of that day or this, no envier and sneerer at transcendent and prescriptive reputations, no laborious pedant judging of high souls by his own small one, and loving his own crotchet better than the fame of the truly great departed,—no Appian, nor Dion Cassius, nor Dr. Hooke, nor Merivale, nor Drumann,—not one of them in those last two years pretends to find by his microscope fitted into the end of his telescope, one spot on the sun going down. In all things and in all places of duty, by wise counsels given freely, by correspondence with the generals of the republic in arms, by personal intercourse with patriots at Rome, by universal activity and effective influence, by courage, by contempt of death, by eloquence, ringing sweeter and nobler in the senate-house and in the meetings of the people, each strain sweeter and nobler than the former till the last,—he shone out, last and greatest of Romans. "For myself," he said, in one of the fourteen immortal discourses in the senate, "I make this profession. I defended the Commonwealth when I was young. I will not desert her now that I am old. I despised the swords of Catiline; shall I tremble at those of Antony? Nay, joyfully rather would I yield this frame to a bloody death, if so I might win back freedom to the State." That lofty profession he held fast—to the end. That death it was his to welcome! It could not give to Rome the freedom for which she was no longer fit; yet had he "the consolation, the joy, the triumph" not to survive it, and to leave an example, which is of the lessons of liberty and glory unblamed, to-day and forever.

I know very well that there is a theory of history, and rather a taking theory too, which would bereave him, and all the other great names of the last ages of the republic, of their wreath, and set it on the brow of the first Cæsar and the second, of Julius Cæsar and Cæsar Augustus. There is a theory, that it was time the republic should end, and the empire begin. Liberty, they say, had failed splendidly. It had grown an obsolete idea. It was behind the age. In the long, fatal flow of that stream of development and necessity, which they say represents the history of man, the hour was reached in which it was fit that one despotic will and one standing army should rule the world. That hour, they tell you, Cicero ought to have recognized; that will he ought piously to have hailed in the person of Cæsar, and the person of Antony. And so he mistook the time; and died contending vainly and ungracefully with destiny, and built his monument on sands over which, he should have seen, the tide of the ages was rising already.

But is not such a theory as this, in such an application of personal disparagement as this, about as poor, shallow, heartless, and arrogant a pedantry as any in the whole history of the follies of learning! This judgment of a man's actions, soul, genius, prudence, by the light of events that reveal themselves five hundred or one hundred years after he is in his grave—how long has that been thought just? Because now we are able to see that the struggle of liberty against mailed despotism,—of the senate and people of Rome against the spirit of Cæsar in arms, say rather the spirit of the age, was unavailing,—shall we pronounce in our closets, that a patriot-senator, a man, made consul from the people according to the constitution, bred in the traditions, bathed in the spirit proud of that high, Roman fashion, of freedom, was a child not to have foreseen it as well? Because he ought to have foreseen it, and did so, was it, therefore, not nobler to die for liberty than to survive her? Is *success* all at once to stand for the test of the excellency of dignity, and the excellency of honor! Be it, that to an intelligence that can take in the ages of time and eternity and the greatest good of a universe of being, the republic might seem to have fulfilled its office, and that it was better the empire should take its place, as the seed cannot quicken except it die; does it follow that we are to love and honor the unconscious human instruments of the dread change more than those who courageously withstood it,—Julius Cæsar, the atheist and traitor; Augustus, the hypocrite; Antony, the bloody and luxurious, who conquered the constitution,—better than Cato or Catullus, or Brutus or Cicero, who stood round it in its last gasp? Because offences must come, shall not the moral judgments of men denounce the woe against him by whom they come? Easy is it, and tempting for the Merivales and Congreves (I am sorry to see De Quincey in such company) to say the senate

and people of Rome were unfit to rule the world they had overrun; and, therefore, it was needful for an emperor and his guard and his legions to step in; easy
and tempting is such a speculation, because nobody can disprove it, and it
sounds of philosophy, seems to be new. But when they pursue it so far as to see
no grandeur in the struggle of free-will with circumstance, and of virtue and
conscience with force, and feel no sympathy with the resistance which patriotism desperately attempts against treason, I reject and hoot it incredulously.

How soothing and elevating to turn from such philosophy, falsely so called,
to the grand and stirring music of that eloquence—those last fourteen pleadings
of Cicero, which he who has not studied knows nothing of the orator, nothing
of the patriot—in which the Roman liberty breathed its last. From that purer
eloquence, from that nobler orator, the great trial of fire and blood through
which the spirit of Rome was passing had burned and purged away all things
light, all things gross; the purple robe, the superb attitude and action, the splendid commonplaces of a festal rhetoric, are all laid by; the ungraceful, occasional
vanity of adulation, the elaborate speech of the abundant, happy mind, at its
ease, all disappear; and instead, what directness, what plainness, what rapidity,
what fire, what abnegation of himself, what disdain, what hate of the usurper
and the usurpation, what grand, swelling sentiments, what fine raptures of liberty, roll and revel there. How there rise above and from out that impetuous
torrent of speech, rushing fervidly, audibly, distinctly, between the peals of that
thunder with which, like a guardian divinity, he seems to keep the senate-house,
and the forum where the people assembled, unprofaned by the impending
tyranny,—how there rise, here and there, those tones, so sweet, so mournful,
boding and prophetic of the end. Almost you expect,—when the sublime expostulation is ended, and the fathers of the republic rise all together from their seats
to answer the appeal by a shout in the spirit of the time of Tarquin the Proud,
and the Second Punic War, and the ten thousand voices of the multitude are calling the orator to come out from the senate-house and speak to them in the forum,
out of doors, to them, also, of the perils and the chances of their freedom,—
almost you expect to hear, in the air, as above the temple of the doomed
Jerusalem, the awful, distant cry, Let us go hence! let us go hence! The alternative of his own certain death, if the republic fell resisting—what pathos, what
dignity, what sincerity, what merit intrinsical, it gives to his brave counsels of
resistance!

"Lay hold on this opportunity of our salvation, Conscript Fathers,—by the
Immortal Gods I conjure you!—and remember that you are the foremost men
here, in the council chamber of the whole earth. Give one sign to the Roman

people that even as now they pledge their valor—so you pledge your wisdom to the crisis of the State. But what need that I exhort you? Is there one so insensate as not to understand that if we sleep over an occasion such as this, it is ours to bow our necks to a tyranny not proud and cruel only, but ignominious—but sinful? Do ye not know this Antony? Do ye not know his companions? Do ye not know his whole house—insolent—impure—gamesters—drunkards? To be slaves to such as he, to such as these, were it not the fullest measure of misery, conjoined with the fullest measure of disgrace? If it be so—may the gods avert the omen—that the supreme hour of the republic has come, let us, the rulers of the world, rather fall with honor, than serve with infamy! Born to glory and to liberty, let us hold these bright distinctions fast, or let us greatly die! Be it, Romans, our first resolve to strike down the tyrant and the tyranny. Be it our second to endure all things for the honor and liberty of our country. To submit to infamy for the love of life can never come within the contemplation of a Roman soul! For you, the people of Rome—you whom the gods have appointed to rule the world—for you to own a master, is impious.

"You are in the last crisis of nations. To be free or to be slaves—that is the question of the hour. By every obligation of man or States it behooves you in this extremity to conquer—as your devotion to the Gods and your concord among yourselves encourage you to hope—or to bear all things but slavery. Other nations may bend to servitude; the birthright and the distinction of the people of Rome is liberty."

Turn, now, to another form of revolution altogether. Turn to a revolution in which a people, who were not yet a nation, became a nation,—one of the great, creative efforts of history, her rarest, her grandest, one of her marked and widely separated geological periods, in which she gathers up the formless and wandering elements of a preëxisting nature, and shapes them into a new world, over whose rising the morning stars might sing again. And these revolutions have an eloquence of their own, also; but how unlike that other,—exultant, trustful, reasonable, courageous. The cheerful and confident voice of young, giant strength rings through it,—the silver clarion of his hope that sounds to an awakening, to an onset, to a festival of glory, preparing! preparing!—his look of fire now fixed on the ground, now straining towards the distant goal; his heart assured and high, yet throbbing with the heightened, irregular pulsations of a new consciousness, beating unwontedly,—the first, delicious, strange feeling of national life.

Twice within a century men have heard that eloquence. They heard it once when, in 1782, Ireland, in arms, had extorted—in part from the humiliation and necessities of England, in part from the justice of a new administration—the independence of her parliament and her judiciary,

> "That one lucid interval snatched from the gloom
> And the madness of ages, when filled with one soul,
> A nation o'erleaped the dark bounds of her doom,
> And for one sacred instant touched liberty's goal,"—

and Mr. Grattan, rising slowly in her house of commons, said: "I am now to address a free people; ages have passed away, and this is the first moment in which you could be distinguished by that appellation. I found Ireland on her knees; I watched over her with an eternal solicitude. I have traced her progress from injuries to arms, from arms to liberty, Spirit of Swift, spirit of Molyneux, your genius has prevailed! Ireland is now a nation. In that character, I hail her; and, bowing to her august presence, I say, Live Forever!"

Men heard that eloquence in 1776, in that manifold and mighty appeal by the genius and wisdom of that new America, to persuade the people to take on the name of nation, and begin its life. By how many pens and tongues that great pleading was conducted; through how many months, before the date of the actual Declaration, it went on, day after day; in how many forms, before how many assemblies, from the village newspaper, the more careful pamphlet, the private conversation, the town-meeting, the legislative bodies of particular colonies, up to the Hall of the immortal old Congress, and the master intelligences of lion heart and eagle eye, that ennobled it,—all this you know. But the leader in that great argument was John Adams, of Massachusetts. He, by concession of all men, was the orator of that revolution,—the revolution in which a nation was born. Other and renowned names, by written or spoken eloquence, coöperated effectively, splendidly, to the grand result,—Samuel Adams, Samuel Chase, Jefferson, Henry, James Otis in an earlier stage. Each of these, and a hundred more, within circles of influence wider or narrower, sent forth, scattering broadcast, the seed of life in the ready, virgin soil. Each brought some specialty of gift to the work; Jefferson, the magic of style, and the habit and the power of delicious dalliance with those large, fair ideas of freedom and equality, so dear to man, so irresistible in that day; Henry, the indescribable and lost spell of the speech of the emotions, which fills the eye, chills the blood, turns the cheek pale,—the lyric phase of eloquence, the "fire-water," as Lamartine has said, of the revolution, instilling into the sense and the soul the sweet madness of battle; Samuel Chase, the tones of anger, confidence, and pride, and the art to inspire them. John Adams's eloquence alone seemed to have met every demand of the time; as a question of right, as a question of prudence, as a question of immediate opportunity, as a question of feeling, as a question of conscience, as a question of historical and durable and innocent glory, he knew it all, through and through; and in that mighty debate, which, beginning in Congress as far back as March or February, 1776, had its close on the second and on the fourth of July, he presented it in all its aspects, to every passion and affection,—to the burning sense of wrong, exasperated at length beyond control by the shedding of blood; to grief, anger, self-respect; to the desire of happiness and of safety; to the sense of moral obligation, commanding that the duties of life are more than life; to courage, which fears God, and knows no other fear; to the craving of the colonial heart, of all hearts, for the reality and the ideal of country, and which cannot be filled unless the dear native land comes to be breathed on by the grace, clad in the robes, armed with the thunders, admitted an equal to the assembly, of the nations; to that large and heroical ambition which would build States, that imperial philanthropy which would open to liberty an asylum here, and give to the sick heart, hard fare, fettered conscience of the children of the Old World, healing, plenty, and freedom to worship God,—to these passions, and these ideas, he presented the appeal for months, day after day, until, on the third of July, 1776, he could record the result, writing thus to his wife: "Yesterday the greatest question was decided which ever was debated in America; and a greater, perhaps, never was, nor will be, among men."

Of that series of spoken eloquence all is perished; not one reported sentence has come down to us. The voice through which the rising spirit of a young nation sounded out its dream of life is hushed. The great spokesman, of an age unto an age, is dead.

And yet, of those lost words is not our whole America one immortal record and reporter? Do ye not read them, deep cut, defying the tooth of time, on all the marble of our greatness? How they blaze on the pillars of our Union! How is their deep sense unfolded and interpreted by every passing hour! how do they come to life, and grow audible, as it were, in the brightening rays of the light he foresaw, as the fabled invisible harp gave out its music to the morning!

Yes, in one sense, they are perished. No parchment manuscript, no embalming printed page, no certain traditions of living or dead, have kept them. Yet, from out, and from off, all things around us,—our laughing harvests, our songs of labor, our commerce on all the seas, our secure homes, our school-houses and churches, our happy people, our radiant and stainless flag,—how they come pealing, pealing, Independence now, and Independence forever!

And now, on a review of this series of the most eloquent of the eloquent, and of these opportunities of their renown, does our love deceive us, or have we not ourselves seen and heard, and followed mourning to the grave, one man, who, called to act in a time so troubled and high, would have enacted a part of equal splendor, and won a fame as historical? Our Webster—was there ever yet a cause to be pleaded to an assembly of men on earth to which he would not have approved himself equal? Consider that he was cast on a quiet, civil age, an age, a land, of order, of law, of contentment, of art, of progress by natural growth, of beautiful and healthful material prosperity, resting on an achieved and stable freedom. We saw that ocean only in its calm. But what if the stern north-east had blown on that ocean, or the hurricane of the tropics had vexed its unsounded depths? That mighty reason, that sovereign brow and eye, that majestic port, that fountain of eloquent feeling, of passion, of imagination,— which seems to me to have been in him never completely opened, fathomless as a sea, and like that demanding the breaking up of the monsoon, or the attraction of those vast bodies the lights of the world, to give it to flow, rise, and ebb,—what triumph of eloquence the ages ever witnessed was beyond those marvellous faculties, in their utmost excitement, to achieve?

Assisted by that unequalled organ of speech, the Greek language of Demosthenes, might he not have rolled an equal thunder, and darted an equal flame?— might he not have breathed virtue into the decay of Greece, and turned back for a space the inevitable hour?

The shaken pillars of the old constitution of Roman liberty, the old grand traditions dishonored, the dignity of the senate, the privilege of the people assailed,— would not their last great champion have acknowledged in him an ally worthy of the glorious, falling cause?

And when the transcendent question of our Independence was to be debated, was he not the very man to stand by Adams, and second the motion which has made the illustrious mover immortal? The rights of the colonies in point of law on their charters; the violations of these rights; the larger rights of man,—the right to liberty and the pursuit of happiness; the right—the conditions, the occasions, of the right—to the national life,—would not he, too, have set these to view transparent, exact, clear as a sunbeam? When reason has convinced, and conscience has instructed, would not that hand, too, have swept with as all-commanding power the chords of the greater passions,—grief, indignation, pride, hope, self-sacrifice,—whose music is at once the inspirer and the utterance of the sublimest moments of history, through which the first voices of the sense and the love of country are breathed?

And then, as the vision of independent America gleamed through the future, would he not already, with a soul as trustful, a trumpet-tone as confident, a voice of prophecy as sure as on that later, festal day, from the Rock of the Pilgrims, bid the distant generations hail? And yet, in that want of grandest opportunities for the effort of his powers, had he large compensation, happier, nor less glorious, when he rose and shone and set on that unclouded sky, and on that wide, deep calm of moral nature, than in soaring, as he would have soared, on all its storms, and wielding, as he would have wielded, all its thunders.

Chapter XV.

AMERICAN NATIONALITY.

An Oration Delivered in Boston on the Eighty-Second
Anniversary of American Independence, July 5, 1858.

*Choate delivered this address to the Boston Democratic Club on the occasion of the
eighty-second anniversary of American independence. The sense of crisis that haunted
the United States during the late 1850s is all too evident in this plea for moderation
and Union.*

*Choate spoke these words the year before his death, and eyewitness testimony reports
that although his physical weakness was evident to all, his eloquence and dedication to
the Union were as inspiring as ever. Dartmouth College professor Samuel Gilman Brown
describes the scene:*

*"He was received with wild and tumultuous applause, and heard with profound inter-
est and sympathy by the multitudes which crowded the Tremont Temple; but many were
pained to perceive the marks of physical weakness and exhaustion. He spoke with difficulty, and could hardly be heard throughout the large hall. But there was an earnestness
and almost solemnity in his words which sunk deep into the hearts of the audience. It was
a plea for the nation, in view of a peril which he thought he foresaw, as a necessary result
of rash counsels, of a false political philosophy, and of wild theories of political morality.
He never again addressed his fellow-citizens on questions of general political interest, and
his last public words may be said to have been spoken in behalf of that Union which he so
warmly loved—that one nation whose grand march across the continent, whose unrivaled
increase in all the elements of power so stimulated and gratified his patriotic ambition."*

It is well that in our year, so busy, so secular, so discordant, there comes one
day when the word is, and when the emotion is, "Our country, our whole
country, and nothing but our country." It is well that law, our only sovereign
on earth; duty, not less the daughter of God, not less within her sphere supreme;
custom, not old alone, but honored and useful; memories; our hearts,—have
set a time in which,—scythe, loom, and anvil stilled, shops shut, wharves silent,

the flag,—our flag unrent,—the flag of our glory and commemoration waving on mast-head, steeple, and highland, we may come together and walk hand in hand, thoughtful, admiring, through these galleries of civil greatness; when we may own together the spell of one hour of our history upon us all; when faults may be forgotten, kindnesses revived, virtues remembered and sketched unblamed; when the arrogance of reform, the excesses of reform, the strifes of parties, the rivalries of regions, shall give place to a wider, warmer, and juster sentiment; when turning from the corners and dark places of offensiveness, if such the candle lighted by malignity, or envy, or censoriousness, or truth, has revealed anywhere,—when, turning from these, we may go up together to the serene and secret mountain-top and there pause, and there unite in the reverent exclamation, and in the exultant prayer, "How beautiful at last are thy tabernacles! What people at last is like unto thee! Peace be within thy palaces, and joy within thy gates! The high places are thine, and there shalt thou stand proudly, and innocently, and securely."

Happy, if such a day shall not be desecrated by our service! Happy, if for us that descending sun shall look out on a more loving, more elevated, more united America! These, no less, no narrower, be the aims of our celebration. These always were the true aims of this celebration. In its origin, a recital or defence of the grounds and principles of the Revolution, now demanding and permitting no defence, all taken for granted, and all had by heart; then sometimes wasted in a parade of vainglory, cheap and vulgar, sometimes profaned by the attack and repulse of partisan and local rhetoricians; its great work, its distinctive character, and its chief lessons remain and vindicate themselves, and will do so while the eye of the fighting or the dying shall yet read on the stainless, ample folds the superscription blazing still in light, "Liberty and Union, now and forever, one and inseparable."

I have wished, therefore, as it was my duty, in doing myself the honor to join you in this act, to give some direction to your thoughts and feelings, suited at once to the nation's holiday, and seasonable and useful in itself. How difficult this may be, I know. To try, however, to try to do anything, is easy, and it is American also. Your candor will make it doubly easy, and to your candor I commit myself.

The birthday of a nation, old or young, and certainly if young, is a time to think of the means of keeping alive the nation. I do not mean to say, however, because I do not believe, that there is but one way to this, the direct and the didactic. For at last it is the spirit of the day which we would cherish. It is our great annual national love-feast which we keep; and if we rise from it with hearts larger, beating fuller, with feeling purer and warmer for America, what signifies it how frugally, or how richly, or how it was spread; or whether it was a strain on the organ, the trumpet tones of the Declaration, the prayer of the good man, the sympathy of the hour, or what it was, which wrought to that end?

I do not, therefore, say that such an anniversary is not a time for thanksgiving to God, for gratitude to men, the living and the dead, for tears and thoughts too deep for tears, for eulogy, for exultation, for all the memories and for all the contrasts which soften and lift up the general mind. I do not say, for example, that to dwell on that one image of progress which is our history; that image so grand, so dazzling, so constant; that stream now flowing so far and swelling into so immense a flood, but which burst out a small, choked, uncertain spring from the ground at first; that transition from the Rock at Plymouth, from the unfortified peninsula at Jamestown, to this America which lays a hand on both the oceans,—from that heroic yet feeble folk whose allowance to a man by the day was five kernels of corn, for three months no corn, or a piece of fish, or a moulded remainder biscuit, or a limb of a wild bird; to whom a drought in spring was a fear and a judgment, and a call for humiliation before God; who held their breath when a flight of arrows or a war-cry broke the innocent sleep or startled the brave watching,—from that handful, and that want, to these millions, whose area is a continent, whose harvests might load the board of famishing nations, for whom a world in arms has no terror;—to trace the long series of causes which connected these two contrasted conditions, the Providences which ordained and guided a growth so stupendous; the dominant race, sober, earnest, constructive,—changed, but not degenerate here; the influx of other races, assimilating, eloquent, and brave; the fusion of all into a new one; the sweet stimulations of liberty; the removal by the whole width of oceans from the establishments of Europe, shaken, tyrannical, or burdened; the healthful virgin world; the universal progress of reason and art,— universal as civilization; the aspect of revolutions on the human mind; the expansion of discovery and trade; the developing sentiment of independence; the needful baptism of wars; the brave men, the wise men; the Constitution, the Union; the national life and the feeling of union which have grown with our growth and strengthened with our strength,—I do not say that meditations such as these might not teach or deepen the lesson of the day. All these things, so holy and beautiful, all things American, may afford certainly the means to keep America alive. That vast panorama unrolled by our general history, or unrolling; that eulogy, so just, so fervent, so splendid, so approved; that electric, seasonable memory of Washington; that purchase and that dedication of the dwelling and the tomb, the work of woman and of the orator of the age; that record of his generals; that visit to battle-fields; that reverent wiping away of dust from great urns; that speculation, that dream of her past, present, and future; every ship builded on lake or ocean; every treaty concluded; every acre of territory annexed; every cannon cast; every machine invented; every mile of new railroad and telegraph undertaken; every dollar added to the aggregate of national or individual wealth,—these all as subjects of thought, as motives to pride and care, as teachers of wisdom, as agencies for probable good, may work, may insure, that earthly immortality of love and glory for which this celebration was ordained.

My way, however, shall be less ambitious and less indirect. Think, then, for a moment, on AMERICAN NATIONALITY itself; the outward national life, and the inward national sentiment; think on this; *its nature, and some of its conditions and some of its ethics*—I would say, too, some of its dangers, but there shall be no expression of evil omen in this stage of the discourse, and to-day, at least, the word is safety, or hope.

To know the nature of American nationality, examine it first by contrast, and then examine it in itself.

In some of the elemental characteristics of political opinion, the American people are one. These they can no more renounce for substance than the highest summit of the highest of the White Hills, than the peak of the Alleghanies, than the Rocky Mountains can bow and cast themselves into the sea. Through all their history, from the dawn of the colonial life to the brightness of this rising, they have spoken them, they have written them, they have acted them, they have run over with them. In all stages, in all agonies, through all report, good and evil,—some learning from the golden times of ancient and mediæval freedom, Greece and Italy and Geneva, from Aristotle, from Cicero and Bodinus, and Machiavel and Calvin; or later, from Harrington and Sidney and Rousseau; some learning, all reinforcing it directly from nature and nature's God,—all have held and felt that every man was equal to every other man; that every man had a right to life, liberty, and the pursuit of happiness, and a conscience unfettered; that the people were the source of power, and the good of the people was the political object of society itself. This creed, so grand, so broad,—in its general and duly qualified, so true,—planted the colonies, led them through the desert and the sea of ante-revolutionary life, rallied them all together to resist the attacks of a king and a minister, sharpened and pointed the bayonets of all their battles, burst forth from a million lips, beamed in a million eyes, burned in a million bosoms, sounded out in their revolutionary eloquence of fire and in the Declaration, awoke the thunders and gleamed in the lightning of the deathless words of Otis, Henry, and Adams, was graved forever on the general mind by the pen of Jefferson and Paine, survived the excitements of war and the necessities of order, penetrated and tinged all our constitutional composition and policy, and all our party organizations and nomenclature, and stands to-day, radiant, defiant, jocund, tiptoe, on the summits of our greatness, one authoritative and louder proclamation to humanity by Freedom, the guardian and the avenger.

But in some traits of our politics we are not one. In some traits we differ from one another, and we change from ourselves. You may say these are subordinate, executory, instrumental traits. Let us not cavil about names, but find the essences of things. Our object is to know the nature of American nationality, and we are attempting to do so, first, by contrasting it with its antagonisms.

There are two great existences, then, in our civil life, which have this in common, though they have nothing else in common, that they may come in conflict with the nationality which I describe; one of them constant in its operation, constitutional, healthful, auxiliary, even; the other rarer, illegitimate, abnormal, terrible; one of them a force under law; the other a violence and a phenomenon above law and against law.

It is first the capital peculiarity of our system, now a commonplace in our politics, that the affections which we give to country we give to a divided object, the States in which we live and the Union by which we are enfolded. We serve two masters. Our hearts own two loves. We live in two countries at once, and are commanded to be capacious of both. How easy it is to reconcile these duties in theory; how reciprocally, more than compatible, how helpful and independent they are in theory; how in this respect our system's difference makes our system's peace, and from these blended colors, and this action and counteraction, how marvellous a beauty, and how grand a harmony we draw out, you all know. Practically you know, too, the adjustment has not been quite so simple. How the Constitution attempts it is plain enough. There it is; *litera scripta manet,* and heaven and earth shall pass before one jot or one tittle of that Scripture shall fail of fulfilment. So we all say, and yet how men have divided on it. How they divided in the great convention itself, and in the very presence of Washington. How the people divided on it. How it has created parties, lost and given power, bestowed great reputations and taken them away, and colored and shaken the universal course of our public life! But have you ever considered that in the nature of things this must be so? Have you ever considered that it was a federative system we had to adopt, and that in such a system a conflict of head and members is in some form and to some extent a result of course? There the States were when we became a nation. There they had been for one hundred and fifty years—for one hundred and seventy years. Some power, it was agreed on all hands, we must delegate to the new government. Of some thunder, some insignia, some beams, some means of kindling pride, winning gratitude, attracting honor, love, obedience, friends, all men knew they must be bereaved, and they were so. But when this was done, there were the States still. In the scheme of every statesman they remained a component part, unannihilated, indestructible. In the scheme of the Constitution, of compromise itself, they remained a component part, indestructible. In the theories of all publicists and all speculators they were retained, and they were valued for it, to hinder and to disarm that centralization which had been found to be the danger and the weakness of federal liberty. And then when you bear in mind that they are sovereignties, *quasi,* but sovereignties still; that one of the most dread and transcendent prerogatives of sovereignties, the prerogative to take life and liberty for crime, is theirs without dispute; that in the theories of some schools they may claim to be parties to the great compact, and as such may, and that any of them may, secede from that compact when by their corporate judgment they deem it to be broken fundamentally by the others, and that from such a judgment there is no appeal to a common peaceful umpire; that in the theories of some schools they may call out their young men and their old men under the pains of death to defy the sword point of the federal arm; that they can pour around even the gallows and the tomb of him who died for treason to the Union, honor, opinion, tears, and thus sustain the last untimely hour, and soothe the disembodied, complaining shade; that every one, by name, by line of boundary, by jurisdiction, is distinct from every other, and every one from the nation; that within their inviolate borders lie our farms, our homes, our meeting-houses, our graves; that their laws, their courts, their militia, their police, to so vast an extent protect our persons from violence, and our houses from plunder; that their heaven ripens our harvests; their schools form our children's mental and moral nature; their charities or their taxes feed our poor; their hospitals cure or shelter our insane; that their image, their opinions, their literature, their morality are around us ever, a presence, a monument, an atmosphere—when you consider this you feel how practical and how inevitable is that antagonism to a single national life, and how true it is that we "buy all our blessings at a price."

But there is another antagonism to such a national life, less constant, less legitimate, less compensated, more terrible, to which I must refer,—not for reprobation, not for warning, not even for grief, but that we may know by contrast, nationality itself,—and that is, the element of sections. This, too, is old; older than the States, old as the Colonies, old as the churches that planted them, old as Jamestown, old as Plymouth. A thousand forms disguise and express it, and in all of them it is hideous. *Candidum seu nigrum hoc tu Romane caveto.* Black or white, as you are Americans, dread it, shun it! Springing from many causes and fed by many stimulations; springing from that diversity of climate, business, institutions, accomplishment, and morality, which comes of our greatness, and compels and should constitute our order and our agreement, but which only makes their difficulty and their merit; from that self-love and self-preference which are their own standard, exclusive, intolerant, and censorious of what is wise and holy; from the fear of ignorance, the jealousy of ignorance, the narrowness of ignorance; from incapacity to abstract, combine, and grasp a complex and various object, and thus rise to the dignity of concession and forbearance and compromise; from the frame of our civil polity, the necessities of our public life and the nature of our ambition, which forces all men not great men,—the minister in his parish, the politician on the stump on election day, the editor of the party newspaper,—to take his rise or his patronage from an intense local opinion, and therefore to do his best to create or reinforce it; from our federative government; from our good traits, bad traits, and foolish traits; from that vain and vulgar hankering for European reputation and respect for European opinion, which forgets that one may know Aristophanes, and Geography, and the Cosmical Unity and Telluric influences, and the smaller morals of life, and all the sounding pretensions of philanthropy, and yet not know America; from that philosophy, falsely so called, which boasts emptily of progress, renounces traditions, denies God and worships itself; from an arrogant and flashy literature which mistakes a new phrase for a new thought, and old nonsense for new truth, and is glad to exchange for the fame of drawing-rooms and parlor windows, and the side-lights of a car in motion, the approval of time and the world; from philanthropy which is short-sighted, impatient and spasmodic, and cannot be made to appreciate that its grandest and surest agent, in His eye whose lifetime is Eternity, and whose periods are ages, is a nation and a sober public opinion, and a safe and silent advancement, reforming by time; from that spirit which would rule or ruin, and would reign in hell rather than serve in heaven; springing from these causes and stimulated thus, there is an element of regions antagonistic to nationality. Always I have said, there was one; always there will be. It lifted its shriek sometimes even above the silver clarion tone that called millions to unite for independence. It resisted the nomination of Washington to command our armies; made his new levies hate one another; assisted the caballings of Gates and Conway; mocked his retreats, and threw its damp passing cloud for a moment over his exceeding glory; opposed the adoption of any constitution; and perverted by construction and denounced as a covenant with hell the actual Constitution when it was adopted; brought into our vocabulary and discussions the hateful and ill-omened words North and South, Atlantic and Western, which the grave warnings of the Farewell

Address expose and rebuke; transformed the floor of congress into a battle field of contending local policy; convened its conventions at Abbeville and Hartford; rent asunder conferences and synods; turned stated assemblies of grave clergymen and grave laymen into shows of gladiators or of the beasts of gladiators; checked the holy effort of missions, and set back the shadow on the dial-plate of a certain amelioration and ultimate probable emancipation, many degrees. Some might say it culminated later in an enterprise even more daring still; but others might deny it. The ashes upon that fire are not yet cold, and we will not tread upon them. But all will unite in prayer to Almighty God that we may never see, nor our children, nor their children to the thousandth generation may ever see it culminate in a Geographical party, banded to elect a Geographical President, and inaugurate a Geographical policy.

"Take any shape but that, and thou art welcome!"

But now, by the side of this and all antagonisms, higher than they, stronger than they, there rises colossal the fine sweet spirit of nationality, the nationality of America! See there the pillar of fire which God has kindled and lifted and moved for our hosts and our ages. Gaze on that, worship that, worship the highest in that. Between that light and our eyes a cloud for a time may seem to gather; chariots, armed men on foot, the troops of kings may march on us, and our fears may make us for a moment turn from it; a sea may spread before us, and waves seem to hedge us up; dark idolatries may alienate some hearts for a season from that worship; revolt, rebellion, may break out in the camp, and the waters of our springs may run bitter to the taste and mock it; between us and that Canaan a great river may seem to be rolling; but beneath that high guidance our way is onward, ever onward; those waters shall part, and stand on either hand in heaps; that idolatry shall repent; that rebellion shall be crushed; that stream shall be sweetened; that overflowing river shall be passed on foot dry shod, in harvest time; and from that promised land of flocks, fields, tents, mountains, coasts and ships, from North and South, and East and West, there shall swell one cry yet, of victory, peace, and thanksgiving!

But we were seeking the nature of the spirit of nationality, and we pass in this inquiry from contrast to analysis. You may call it, subjectively regarded, a mode of contemplating the nation in its essence, and so far it is an intellectual conception, and you may call it a feeling, towards the nation thus contemplated, and so far it is an emotion. In the intellectual exercise it contemplates the nation as it is one, and as it is distinguished from all other nations, and in the emotional exercise it loves it, and is proud of it as thus it is contemplated. This you may call its ultimate analysis. But how much more is included in it! How much flows from it! How cold and inadequate is such a description, if we leave it there! Think of it first as a state of consciousness, as a spring of feeling, as a motive to exertion, as blessing your country, and as reacting on you. Think of it as it fills your mind and quickens your heart, and as it fills the mind and quickens the heart of millions around you. Instantly, under such an influence, you ascend above the smoke and stir of this small local strife; you tread upon the high places of the earth and of history; you think and feel as an American for America; her power, her eminence, her consideration, her honor, are yours; your competitors, like hers, are kings; your home, like hers, is the world; your path, like hers, is on the highway of empires; our charge, her charge, is of generations and ages; your record, her record, is of treaties, battles, voyages, beneath all the constellations; her image, one, immortal, golden, rises on your eye as our western star at evening rises on the traveller from his home; no lowering cloud, no angry river, no lingering spring, no broken crevasse, no inundated city or plantation, no tracts of sand, arid and burning, on that surface, but all blended and softened into one beam of kindred rays, the image, harbinger, and promise of love, hope, and a brighter day!

Think of it next, as an active virtue. Is not all history a recital of the achievements of nationality, and an exponent of its historical and imperial nature? Even under systems far less perfect, and influences far less auspicious than ours, has it not lifted itself up for a time above all things meaner, vindicating itself by action, by the sublimity of a brave daring, successful or unsuccessful, by the sublimity of a working hope? How loose, for example, and how perfidious, was that union of the States of Greece in all times! How distinct were the nations of Attica, of Laconia, of Thessaly, of Bootia, and how utterly insufficient the oracle, the Amphyctionic Assembly, the games, the great first epic, to restrain Athens and Sparta and Thebes from contending, by diplomacy, by fraud, by battle, for the mastery! And yet even in the historical age, when the storm of Eastern invasion swept that blue sea, and those laughing islands, and iron-bound coast, over, above, grander and more useful than the fear and policy which counselled temporary union,—were there not some, were there not many, on whose perturbed and towering motives came the thought of that great, common, Greek name; that race, kindred at last, though policy, though mines of marble, though ages had parted them,—that golden, ancient, polished speech, that inherited ancestral glory, that national Olympus, that inviolated, sterile and separate earth, that fame of camps, that fire of camps which put out the ancient life of the Troy of Asia; and was it not such memories as these that burn and revel in the pages of Herodotus? Did not Sparta and Athens hate one another and fight one another habitually, and yet when those Lacedæmonian levies gazed so steadfastly on the faces of the fallen at Marathon, did they not give Greek tears to Athens and Greek curses to Persia, and in the hour of Platæa did they not stand together against the barbarian?

What else formed the secret of the brief spell of Rienzi's power, and burned and sparkled in the poetry and rhetoric of his friend Petrarch, and soothed the dark hour of the grander soul of Machiavel, loathing that Italy, and recalling that other day when "eight hundred thousand men sprang to arms at the rumor of a Gallic invasion?"

Is not Prussia afraid of Austria, and Saxony of Bavaria, and Frankfort jealous of Dresden, and so through the twenty-seven or eight or thirty States, great and small; and yet the dear, common fatherland, the old German tongue, the legend of Hermann, the native and titular Rhine flowing rapid, deep, and majestic, like the life of a hero of antiquity—do not these spectacles and these traditions sometimes wake the nationality of Germany to action, as well as to life and hope?

But if you would contemplate nationality as an active virtue, look around you. Is not our own history one witness and one record of what it can do? This day and all which it stands for,—did it not give us these? This glory of the fields of that war, this eloquence of that revolution, this wide one sheet of flame which wrapped tyrant and tyranny and swept all that escaped from it away, forever and forever; the courage to fight, to retreat, to rally, to advance, to guard the young flag by the young arm and the young heart's blood, to hold up and hold on till the magnificent consummation crowned the work—were not all these imparted as inspired by this imperial sentiment? Has it not here begun the master-work of man, the creation of a national life? Did it not call out that prodigious development of wisdom, the wisdom of constructiveness which illustrated the years after the war, and the framing and adopting of the Constitution? Has it not, in the general, contributed to the administering of that government wisely and well since? Look at it! It has kindled us to no aims of conquest. It has involved us in no entangling alliances. It has kept our neutrality dignified and just. The victories of peace have been our prized victories. But the larger and truer grandeur of the nations, for which they are created and for which they must one day, before some tribunal give account, what a measure of these it has enabled us already to fulfil! It has lifted us to the throne and has set on our brow the name of the great Republic. It has taught us to demand nothing wrong, and to submit to nothing wrong; it has made our diplomacy sagacious, wary, and accomplished; it has opened the iron gate of the mountain, and planted our ensign on the great, tranquil sea; it has made the desert to bud and blossom as the rose; it has quickened to life the giant brood of useful arts; it has whitened lake and ocean with the sails of a daring, new and lawful trade; it has extended to exiles, flying as clouds, the asylum of our better liberty; it has kept us at rest within all our borders; it has repressed without blood the intemperance of local insubordination; it has scattered the seeds of liberty, under law and under order, broadcast; it has seen and helped American feeling to swell into a fuller flood; from many a field and many a deck, though it seeks not war, makes not war, and fears not war, it has borne the radiant flag all unstained; it has opened our age of lettered glory; it has opened and honored the age of the industry of the people!

We have done with the nature of American nationality, with its contrasts, analysis and fruits. I have less pleasure to remind you that it has conditions also, and ethics. And what are some of these? This is our next consideration.

And the first of these is that this national existence is, to an extraordinary degree, not a growth, but a production; that it has origin in the will and the reason, and that the will and the reason must keep it alive, or it can bear no life. I do not forget that a power above man's power, a wisdom above man's wisdom, a reason above man's reason, may be traced without the presumptuousness of fanaticism in the fortunes of America. I do not forget that God has been in our history. Beyond that dazzling progress of art, society, thought, which is of His ordaining, although it may seem to a false philosophy a fatal and inevitable flow under law—beyond this I do not forget that there have been, and there may be again interpositions, providential, exceptional, and direct, of that Supreme Agency without which no sparrow falleth. That condition of mind and of opinion in Europe, and more than anywhere else, in England, which marked the period of emigration, and bore flower, fruit and seed after its kind in the new world; that conflict and upheaval and fermenting in the age of Charles the First, and the Long Parliament, and Cromwell, and Milton—violated nature asserting herself; that disappearance of the old races here, wasting so mysteriously and so seasonably— that drear death giving place as in nature to a better life; that long colonial growth in shade and storm and neglect, sheltered imperfectly by our relations to the mother country, and not yet exposed to the tempest and lightning of the high places of political independence; burdened and poor, but yet evolving, germinant, prophetic; that insane common attack of one tyranny on so many charters; that succession of incompetent English commanders and English tactics against us in the war; that one soul breathed in a moment into a continent; the

Declaration so timely, and so full of tone; the name, the services, the influence of Washington—these are "parts of His ways," and we may understand and adore them.

I do not forget either that in the great first step we had to take—that difficulty so stupendous, of beginning to mould the colonies into a nation, to overcome the prejudices of habit and ignorance, the petty cavils of the petty, the envy, the jealousy, the ambition, the fears of great men and little men; to take away partition walls, roll away provincial flags and hush provincial drums, and give to the young Republic *E Pluribus Unum,* to set out onward and upward on her Zodiac path,—I do not forget that in this, too, there were helps of circumstances for which no philosophy and no pride can make us unthankful.

Take one. Have you ever considered, speculating on the mysteries of our national being, how providentially the colonial life itself, in one respect, qualified for Union, and how providentially it came to pass that independence and nationality were born in one day? Suppose that from the times when they were planted respectively, these colonies had been independent of one another, and of every one—suppose this had been so for one hundred and fifty years, for one hundred and seventy years; that in the eye of public law they had through all that time ranked with England, with France; that through all that time they had made war, concluded peace, negotiated treaties of commerce and of alliance, received and sent ministers, coined money, superintended trade, "done all other things which independent States of right may do;" and then that a single foreign power had sought to reduce them. I do not say that that power would have reduced them. I do not say that necessity, that prudence, which is civil necessity, would not have taught them to assist one another, and that in one sense, and that a just one, they would have fought and triumphed together. But when that victory was won and the cloud rolled off seaward, would these victors have flown quite so easily into a common embrace and become a single people? This long antecedent several independence; this long antecedent national life—would it not have indurated them and separated them? These old high actions and high passions flowing diverse; these opposed banners of old fields; this music of hostile marches; these memories of an unshared past; this history of a glory in which one only had part,—do you think they could have been melted, softened, and beaten quite so easily into the unity of a common life? Might not the world have seen here, instead, another Attica, and Achaia and Lacedæmonia, and Messina, and Naples and Florence and Saxony? Did not that colonial life, in its nature—that long winter and lingering spring—discipline and prepare men for the future of their civil life, as an April snow enriches the earth it seems to bury? Did it not keep back the growths which might otherwise have shot up into impracticable ranknesses and diversities? Did it not divert men from themselves to one another—from Massachusetts and Virginia and New York, to the forming or the possible America? Instead of stunting and enfeebling, did it not enlarge and strengthen? And when all that host flocked together, to taste together the first waters of independent life, and one high, common, proud feeling pervaded their ranks, lifted up all hearts, softened all hearts at once—and a Rhode Island General was seen to fight at the Eutaws; and a New Yorker, or one well beloved of Massachusetts, at Saratoga; and a Virginian to guide the common war, and a united army to win the victory for all—was not the transition, in a moment so sublime, more natural, less violent, more easy to the transcendent conception of nationality itself?

I do not deny, too, that some things subordinate and executory are a little easier than at first; that the friction of the machine is less somewhat; that mere administration has grown simpler; that organizations have been effected which may move of themselves; that departments have been created and set going, which can go alone; that the Constitution has been construed authoritatively; that a course, a routine has been established in which things—some things— may go on as now, without your thought or mind. Bold he is, moreover, I admit, not wise, who would undertake to determine what chance, or what Providence may do, and what man may do in the sustentation of national life. But remember, that is a false philosophy and that is no religion which absolves from duty. That is impiety which boasts of a will of God, and forgets the business of man. Will and reason created, will and reason must keep. Every day, still, we are in committee of the whole on the question of the Constitution or no Constitution. Eternal vigilance is the condition of union, as they say it is of liberty. I have heard that if the same Omnipotence which formed the universe at first should suspend its care for a day, primeval chaos were come again. Dare we risk such a speculation in politics and act on it? Consider how new is this America of yours! Some there are yet alive who saw this infant rocked in the cradle. Some there are yet alive who beheld the first inauguration of Washington; many that felt how the tidings of his death smote on the general heart. Some now alive saw the deep broad trench first excavated, the stone drawn from the mountainside, the mortar mingled, the Cyclopean foundation laid, the tears, the anthems, the thanksgiving of the dedication day. That unknown, therefore magnified, therefore magnificent original; that august tradition of a mixed human and Divine; that hidden fountain; the long, half-hidden flow glancing uncertain and infrequent through the opening of the old forest, spreading out, at last, after leagues, after centuries, into the clear daylight of history; the authoritative prescription; the legend, the fable, the tones of uncertain harps, the acquiescence of generations, rising in a long line to life as to a gift,—where for us are they? On all this architecture of utility and reason, where has Time laid a finger? What angularity has it rounded; what stone has it covered with moss; on what salient or what pendant coigne of vantage has it built its nest; on what deformity has its moonlight and twilight fallen? What enables us then to withhold for a moment the sustaining hand? The counsel of philosophy and history, of Cicero, of Machiavel, of Montesquieu, to turn to the first principles, to reproduce and reconstruct the ancient freedom, the masculine virtues, the plain wisdom of the original—is it not seasonable counsel eminently for you? Remember, your reason, your will, may keep, must keep what reason and will builded. Yours is the responsibility, yours, to country, to man, unshared, unconcealed.

I do not know that I need to say next that such a spirit of nationality reposing on will and reason, or, however produced, not spontaneous, and therefore to some extent artificial, demands a specific culture to develop it and to make it intense, sure and constant. I need not say this, because it is so plain; but it is important as well as plain. There is a love of country which comes uncalled for, one knows not how. It comes in with the very air, the eye, the ear, the instincts, the first taste of the mother's milk, the first beatings of the heart. The faces of brothers and sisters, and the loved father and mother,—the laugh of playmates, the old willow-tree, and well, and school-house, the bees at work in the spring, the note of the robin at evening, the lullaby, the cows coming home, the singing-book, the catechism, the visits of neighbors, the general training,—all things which make childhood happy, begin it; and then as the age of the passions and the age of the reason draw on, and love and the sense of home and security and of property under law, come to life;—and as the story goes round, and as the book or the newspaper relates the less favored lots of other lands, and the public and the private sense of a man is forming and formed, there is a type of patriotism already. Thus they had imbibed it who stood that charge at Concord, and they who hung deadly on the retreat, and they who threw up the hasty and imperfect redoubt on Bunker Hill by night, set on it the blood-red provincial flag, and passed so calmly with Prescott and Putnam and Warren through the experiences of the first fire.

But now to direct this spontaneous sentiment of hearts to the Union, to raise it high, to make it broad and deep, to instruct it, to educate it, is in some things harder, some things easier; but it may be done; it must be done. She, too, has her spectacles; she, too, has her great names; she, too, has her food for patriotism, for childhood, for man. "Americans," said an orator of France, "begin with the infant in the cradle. Let the first word he lisps be Washington." Hang on his neck on that birth-day, and that day of his death at Mount Vernon, the Medal of Congress, by its dark ribbon; tell him the story of the flag, as it passes glittering along the road; bid him listen to that plain, old fashioned, stirring music of the Union; lead him when school is out at evening to the grave of his great-grandfather, the old soldier of the war; bid him, like Hannibal, at nine years old, lay the little hand on that Constitution and swear reverently to observe it; lift him up and lift yourselves up to the height of American feeling; open to him, and think for yourselves, on the relation of America to the States; show him upon the map the area to which she has extended herself; the climates that come into the number of her months; the silver paths of her trade, wide as the world; tell him of her contributions to humanity, and her protests for free government; keep with him the glad and solemn feasts of her appointment; bury her great names in his heart, and into your hearts; contemplate habitually, lovingly, intelligently, this grand abstraction, this vast reality of good; and such an institution may do somewhat to transform this surpassing beauty into a national life, which shall last while sun and moon endure.

But there is another condition of our nationality of which I must say something, and that is that it rests on compromise. America, the Constitution, practicable policy, all of it, are a compromise. Our public is possible—it can draw its breath for a day—only by compromise.

There is a cant of shallowness and fanaticism which misunderstands and denies this. There is a distempered and ambitious morality which says civil prudence is no virtue. There is a philanthropy,—so it calls itself,—pedantry, arrogance, folly, cruelty, impiousness, I call it, fit enough for a pulpit, totally unfit for a people; fit enough for a preacher, totally unfit for a statesman;—which, confounding large things with little things, ends with means, subordinate ends with chief ends, one man's sphere of responsibility with another man's sphere of responsibility, seed-time with harvest, one science with another science, one truth with another truth, one jurisdiction with another jurisdiction, the span-long day of life with the duration of States, generals with universals, the principle with the practice, the Anglo-Celtic-Saxon of America with the pavers of Paris, cutting down the half-grown tree to snatch the unripe fruit—there is a philanthropy which scolds at this even, and calls it names.

To such a spirit I have nothing to say, but I have something to say to you. It is remarked by a very leading writer of our times, Lord Macaulay—ennobled less by title than by genius and fame,—"that compromise is the essence of politics."

That which every man of sense admits to be so true, as to have become a common-place of all politics, is peculiarly true of our national politics. Our history is a record of compromises; and this freedom and this glory attest their wisdom and bear their fruits. But can these compromises stand the higher test of morality? Concessions for the sake of the nation; concessions for what the general opinion of America has pronounced concessions for America; concessions in measures; concessions in spirit for such an end;—are they a virtue?

I hope it is worth something, in the first place, that the judgment of civilization, collected from all its expression and all its exponents, has ranked concession for the keeping and well-being of the nation, among the whiter virtues. Starting with the grand central sentiment that patriotism is the noblest practical limitation of universal philanthropy, and reserving its enthusiasm, its tears, for the martyred patriot, and deeming his death the most glorious of deaths, it has given ever the first place to him whose firmness, wisdom, and moderation have built the State, and whose firmness, wisdom, and moderation keep the State. These traits it has stamped as virtues. These traits it has stamped as great virtues. Poetry, art, history, biography, the funeral discourse, the utterance of that judgment, how universally have they so stamped them! He whose harp, they said, attracted and fused savage natures; he who gave to his people, not the best government, but the best that they would bear; he who by timely adaptations elevated an inferior class to equality with a superior class, and made two nations into one; he whose tolerance and comprehension put out the fires of persecution; and placed all opinions and religions on one plane before the law; he whose healing counsels composed the distractions of a various empire,—he is the great good man of civilization. Ambition might have been his aim to some extent, but the result is a country, a power, a law. On that single title, it raised his statue, hung on it the garland that cannot die, kept his birthday by the firing of cannons, and ringing of bells, and processions, and thanks to God Almighty. He may not have been fortunate in war; he may not have been foremost among men of genius; but what Luxembourg, what Eugene, what Marlborough heaped on his ashes such a monument, as the wise, just, cold, Dutch deliverer of England? What Gates, what Lee, what Alexander, what Napoleon, won such honor, such love, such sacred and warm-felt approval as our civil father, Washington? Does that judgment, the judgment of civilization, condemn Demosthenes, who would have invited Persia to help against Macedon; or Cicero, who praised and soothed the young Octavius, to win him from Anthony; or the Calvinist William, who invited the papal Austria to fight with him against Louis XIV.? Does it dream of branding such an act as hypocrisy, or apostacy? Does it not recognize it rather as wisdom, patriotism, and virtue, masculine and intelligent? Does it not rather give him all honor and thanks, who could forego the sweets of revenge, rise above the cowardice of selfishness and the narrow memory of personal inapplicable antecedents, and for the love of Athens, of Rome, of England, of liberty, could magnanimously grasp the solid glory of great souls?

But this judgment of civilization, I maintain next, is a sound moral judgment. It is founded on a theory of duty which makes the highest utility to man the grandest achievement of man. It thinks that it discerns that the national life is the true useful human life. It thinks that it discerns that the greater includes the less; that beneath that order, that government, that law, that power, reform is easy and reform is safe—reform of the man, reform of the nation. It ventures to hold that a nation is the grandest of the instrumentalities of morals and religion. It holds that under that wing, beneath that lightning, there is room, there is capacity, for humbly imitating His plan who sits in the circle of eternity, and with whom a thousand years are as one day; room, motive, capacity for labor, for culture, for preparation, for the preaching of the gospel of peace to all, for elevating by slow, sure, and quiet gradations down to its depths, down to its chains, society itself. Concession to keep such an agent is concession to promote such ends.

Do you remember what a great moralist and a great man, Archbishop Whately, said on this subject in the House of Lords? He was advocating concession to Catholics; and see how much stronger was truth than the hatred of theologians. The biographer of Peel calls the speech a splendid piece of reasoning; and it decided the vote:—

"So great is the outcry which it has been the fashion among some persons for several years past to raise against *expediency,* that the very word has become almost an illomened sound. It seems to be thought by many a sufficient ground of condemnation of any legislator to say that he is guided by views of expediency. And some seem even to be ashamed of acknowledging that they are, in any degree, so guided. I, for one, however, am content to submit to the imputation of being a votary of expediency. And what is more, I do not see what right any one who is not so has to sit in Parliament, or to take any part in public affairs. Any one who may choose to acknowledge that the measures he opposes are expedient, or that those he recommends are inexpedient, ought manifestly to have no seat in a deliberative assembly, which is constituted for the express and sole purpose of considering what measures are *conducive to the public good;*—in other words, 'expedient.' I say, the *'public* good,' because, of course, by 'expediency' we mean, not that which may benefit some individual, or some party or class of men, at the expense of the public, but what conduces to the good of the nation. Now this, it is evident, is the very object for which deliberative assemblies are constituted. And so far is this from being regarded, by our Church at least, as something at variance with religious duty, that we have a prayer specially appointed to be offered up during the sitting of the Houses of Parliament, that their consultations may be 'directed and prospered for the *safety*, *honor*, and *welfare* of our sovereign and her dominions.' Now, if this be not the very definition of political expediency, let any one say what is."

I have no doubt, however, that this judgment of civilization rests in part on the difficulty and the rarity of the virtue which it praises. We prize the difficult and the rare because they are difficult and rare; and when you consider how easy and how tempting it is to fall in with and float with the stream on which so many swim; how easy is that broad road and how sweet that approved strain; how easy and how tempting it is to please an assenting congregation, or circle of readers, or local public; how easy and how tempting to compound for sins which an influential man "is not inclined to, by damning those he has no mind to;" how easy to please those we see, and forget those out of sight; what courage, what love of truth are demanded to dissent; how hard it is to rise to the vast and varied conception, and to the one idea, which grasps and adjusts all the ideas; how easy it is for the little man to become great, the shallow man to become profound; the coward out of danger to be brave; the free-state man to be an anti-slavery man, and to write tracts which his friends alone read; when you think that even the laughter of fools and children and madmen, little ministers, little editors, and little politicians, can inflict the mosquito bite, not deep, but stinging;—who wonders that the serener and the calmer judgment allots "to patient continuance in well doing," to resistance of the parts, to contention for the whole, to counsels of moderation and concession, "glory, honor, and immortality?"

"What nothing earthly gives or can destroy,
The soul's calm sunshine, and the heartfelt joy."

But this judgment of civilization is the judgment of religion too. You believe with the Bible, with Cicero, with the teachings of history, that God wills the national life. He wills civilization, therefore society, therefore law, therefore government, therefore nations. How do we know this? Always, from the birth of the historical time, civilized man led the national life. Therein always the nature God has given him has swelled to all its perfection, and has rendered the worthiest praise to the Giver of the gift. He who wills the end wills the indispensable means; he wills the means which his teachers, nature and experience, have ascertained to be indispensable. Then he wills these means, concession, compromise, love, forbearance, help, because his teachers, nature and experience, have revealed them to be indispensable. Then he wills our national life. Then he wills the spirit which made it and which keeps it. Do you dare to say, with President Davies, that you believe that Providence raised up that young man, Washington, for some great public service,—with the spectator of that first inauguration, that you believe the Supreme Being looked down with complacency on that act,—with that Senate which thanked God that he had conducted to the tomb a fame whiter than it was brilliant; and yet dare to say that the spirit of Washington ought not to be your spirit, his counsels your guide, his Farewell Address your scripture of political religion? But what does he say? I need not repeat it, for you have it by heart; but what said a greater than he? "Render unto Cæsar the things which are Cæsar's." Render under Cæsar the things that are Cæsar's, and thus, to that extent, you "render unto God the things which are God's." Be these words our answer and our defence. When they press us with the common-places of anti- slavery, be these words of wisdom our answer. Say to them, "Yes, I thank God I keep no slaves. I am sorry there is one on earth; I am sorry even that there is need of law, of subordination, of order, of government, of the discipline of the schools, of prisons, of the gallows; I wonder at such a system of things; piously I would reform it; but beneath that same system I am an American citizen; beneath that system, this country it is my post to keep; while I keep her there is hope for all men, for the evil man, for the intemperate man, for slaves, for free, for all; that hope your rash and hasty hand would prostrate; that hope my patience would advance." Have they done? Are they answered?

There are other conditions and other laws of our nationality on which there needs to be said something if there were time. That it is not and that it cannot come to good, that it cannot achieve its destiny, that it cannot live even, unless it rests on the understanding of the State, you know. How gloriously this is anticipated by our own Constitution, you remember. How well said Washington— who said all things as he did all things, well—"that in proportion as governments rest on public opinion, that opinion must be enlightened." There must then be intelligence at the foundation. But what intelligence? Not that which puffeth up, I fancy, not flippancy, not smartness, not sciolism, whose fruits, whose expression are vanity, restlessness, insubordination, hate, irreverence, unbelief, incapacity to combine ideas, and great capacity to overwork a single one. Not quite this. This is that little intelligence and little learning which are dangerous.

These are the characteristics, I have read, which pave the way for the downfall of States; not those on which a long glory and a long strength have towered. These, more than the general of Macedon, gave the poison to Demosthenes in the Island Temple. These, not the triumvirate alone, closed the eloquent lips of Cicero. These, before the populous North had done it, spread beneath Gibraltar to the Lybian sands in the downward age. These, not Christianity, not Goth, not Lombard, nor Norman, rent that fair one Italy asunder, and turned the garden and the mistress of the earth into a school, into a hiding place, of assassins— of spies from Austria, of spies from France, with gold to buy and ears to catch and punish the dreams of liberty whispered in sleep, and shamed the memories and hopes of Machiavel and Mazzini, and gave for that joy and that beauty, mourning and heaviness. This is not the intelligence our Constitution means, Washington meant, and our country needs. It is intelligence which, however it begins, ends with belief, with humility, with obedience, with veneration, with admiration, with truth; which recognizes and then learns and then teaches the duties of a comprehensive citizenship; which hopes for a future on earth and beyond earth, but turns habitually, reverently, thoughtfully to the old paths, the great men, the hallowed graves of the fathers; which binds in one bundle of love the kindred and mighty legend of revolution and liberty, the life of Christ in the Evangelists, and the Constitution in its plain text; which can read with Lord Chatham, Thucydides and the stories of master States of antiquity, yet holds with him that the papers of the Congress of 1776 were better; whose patriotism grows warm at Marathon, but warmer at Monmouth, at Yorktown, at Bunker Hill, at Saratoga; which reforms by preserving, serves by standing and waiting, fears God and honors America.

I had something to say more directly still on the ethics of nationality, on the duty of instructing the conscience; on the crimes of treason, and slander, and fraud; that are committed around us in its name; on the shallowness and stupidity of the doctrine that the mere moral sentiments, trained by a mere moral discipline, may safely guide the complex civil life; of the teachers and studies which they need to fit them for so precious, difficult, and delicate a dominion; of the high place in the scale of duties, which, thus fitted, they assign to nationality; of the judgment which, thus fitted they would apply to one or two of the common-places and practices of the time. But I pass it all to say only that these ethics teach the true subordination, and the true reconciliation of apparently incompatible duties. These only are the casuists, or the safest casuists for us. Learn from them how to adjust this conflict between patriotism and philanthropy. To us, indeed, there seems to be no such conflict, for we are philanthropists in proportion as we are unionists. Our philanthropy, we venture to say, is a just philanthropy. That is all. It loves all men, it helps all men, it respects all rights, keeps all compacts, recognizes all dangers, pities all suffering, ignores no fact, master and slave it enfolds alike. It happens thus that it contracts the sphere of our duty somewhat, and changes not the nature, but the time, the place, the mode of performing it. It does not make our love cold, but it makes it safe; it naturalizes it, it baptizes it into our life; it circumscribes it within our capacities and our necessities; it sets on it the great national public seal. If you say that thus our patriotism limits our philanthropy, I answer that ours is American philanthropy. Be this the virtue we boast, and this the name by which we know it. In this name, in this quality, find the standard and the utterance of the virtue itself. By this, not by broad phylacteries and chief seats, the keener hate, the gloomier fanaticism, the louder cry, judge, compare, subordinate. Do they think that nobody is a philanthropist but themselves? We, too, look up the long vista and gaze, rapt, at the dazzling ascent; we, too, see towers rising, crowned, imperial, and the tribes coming to bend in the opening of a latter day. But we see peace, order, reconciliation of rights along that brightening future. We trace all along that succession of reform, the presiding instrumentalities of national life. We see our morality working itself clearer and clearer; one historical and conventional right or wrong, after another, falling peacefully and still; we hear the chain breaking, but there is no blood on it, none of his whom it bound, none of his who put it on him; we hear the swelling chorus of the free, but master and slave unite in that chorus, and there is no discordant shriek above the harmony; we see and we hail the blending of our own glory with the eternal light of God, but we see, too, shapes of love and beauty ascending and descending there as in the old vision!

Hold fast this hope; distrust the philanthropy, distrust the ethics which would, which must, turn it into shame. Do no evil that good may come. Perform your share, for you have a share, in the abolition of slavery; perform your share, for you have a share, in the noble and generous strife of the sections— but perform it by keeping, by transmitting, a UNITED, LOVING AND CHRISTIAN AMERICA.

But why, at last, do I exhort, and why do I seem to fear, on such a day as this? Is it not the nation's birthday? Is it not this country of our love and hopes, which celebrates it? This music of the glad march, these banners of pride and beauty, these memories so fragrant, these resolutions of patriotism so thoughtful, these hands pressed, these congratulations and huzzaings and tears, this great heart throbbing audibly,—are they not hers, and do they not assure us? These forests of masts, these singing workshops of labor, these fields and plantations whitening for the harvest, this peace and plenty, this sleeping thunder, these bolts in the closed, strong talon, do not they tell us of her health, her strength, and her future? This shadow that flits across our grasses and is gone, this shallow ripple that darkens the surface of our broad and widening stream, and passes away, this little perturbation which our telescopes cannot find, and which our science can hardly find, but which we know cannot change the course or hasten the doom of one star; have these any terror for us? And He who slumbers not, nor sleeps, who keeps watchfully the city of his love, on whose will the life of nations is suspended, and to whom all the shields of the earth belong, our fathers' God, is he not our God, and of whom, then, and of what shall we be afraid?

Chapter XVI.

SPEECH ON THE BIRTHDAY OF DANIEL WEBSTER.
January 21, 1859.

When in 1859 Choate rose to deliver his "Speech on the Birthday of Daniel Webster," the increasingly vitriolic state of political discourse in the United States obviously weighed heavily on his mind. He concludes his speech by noting that Webster's birthday is best celebrated by a renewed commitment to what the great figure so cherished— "our country, our whole country, our united country."

[The seventy-seventh anniversary of the birthday of Daniel Webster was commemorated by a banquet at the Revere House. At the conclusion of the feast, and after the opening address by the president of the day, Hon. Caleb Cushing, Mr. Choate, being called upon, spoke as follows:]

I WOULD not have it supposed for a moment that I design to make any eulogy, or any speech, concerning the great man whose birthday we have met to observe. I hasten to assure you that I shall attempt to do no such thing. There is no longer need of it, or fitness for it, for any purpose. Times have been when such a thing might have been done with propriety. While he was yet personally among us,—while he was yet walking in his strength in the paths or ascending the heights of active public life, or standing upon them,—and so many of the good and wise, so many of the wisest and best of our country, from all parts of it, thought he had title to the great office of our system, and would have had him formally presented for it, it was fit that those who loved and honored him should publicly,—with effort, with passion, with argument, with contention,—recall the series of his services, his life of elevated labors, finished and unfinished, display his large qualities of character and mind, and compare him, somewhat, in all these things, with the great men, his competitors for the great prize. Then was there a battle to be fought, and it was needful to fight it.

And so, again, in a later day, while our hearts were yet bleeding with the sense of recent loss, and he lay newly dead in his chamber, and the bells were tolling, and his grave was open, and the sunlight of an autumn day was falling on that long funeral train, I do not say it was fit only, it was unavoidable, that we all, in some choked utterance and some imperfect, sincere expression, should, if we could not praise the patriot, lament the man.

But these times have gone by. The race of honor and duty is for him all run. The high endeavor is made, and it is finished. The monument is builded. He is entered into his glory. The day of hope, of pride, of grief, has been followed by the long rest; and the sentiments of grief, pride, and hope, are all merged in the sentiment of calm and implicit veneration. We have buried him in our hearts. That is enough to say. Our estimation of him is part of our creed. We have no argument to make or hear upon it. We enter into no dispute about him. We permit no longer any man to question us as to what he was, what he had done, how much we loved him, how much the country loved him, and how well he deserved it. We admire, we love, and we are still. Be this enough for us to say.

Is it not enough that we just stand silent on the deck of the bark fast flying from the shore, and turn and see, as the line of coast disappears, and the headlands and hills and all the land go down, and the islands are swallowed up, the great mountain standing there in its strength and majesty, supreme and still—to see how it swells away up from the subject and fading vale? to see that, though clouds and tempests, and the noise of waves, and the yelping of curs, may be at its feet, eternal sunshine has settled upon its head?

There is another reason why I should not trust myself to say much more of him to-night. It does so happen that you cannot praise Mr. Webster for that which really characterized and identified him as a public man, but that you seem to be composing *a tract for the times*.

It does so happen that the influence of his whole public life and position was so *pronounced*—so to speak—so defined, sharp, salient; the spirit of his mind, the tone of his mind, was so unmistakable and so peculiar; the nature of the public man was so transparent and so recognized everywhere,—that you cannot speak of him without seeming to grow polemical, without seeming to make an attack upon other men, upon organizations, upon policy, upon tendencies. You cannot say of him what is true, and what you know to be true, but you are thought to be disparaging or refuting somebody else.

In this way there comes to be mingled with our service of the heart something of the discordant, incongruous, and temporary. So it is everywhere. They could not keep the birthday of Charles James Fox, but they were supposed to attack the grave of Pitt, and aim at a Whig administration and a reform bill. An historian can hardly admire the architecture of the age of Pericles, or find some palliation of the trial of Socrates, but they say he is a Democrat, a Chartist, or a friend of the secret ballot. The marvellous eloquence, and noble, patriotic enterprise of our Everett, can scarcely escape such misconstruction of small jealousy.

Yes; sad it is, but true, that you cannot say here to-night what you think, what you know, what you thank God for, about the Union-loving heart, the Constitution-defending brain, the moderation-breathing spirit, the American nature of the great man,—our friend,—but they call out you are thinking of them! So powerful is the suggestion of contrast, and such cowards does conscience make of all bad men!

I feel the effect of this embarrassment. I protest against such an application of anything I say. But I feel, also, that it will be better than such a protest, to sum up in the briefest and plainest and soberest expression, what I deem will be the record of history,—let me hope, with the immunities of history,—concerning this man, as a public man.

He was, then, let me say, of the very foremost of great American Statesmen. This is the class of greatness in which he is to be ranked. As such, always, he is to be judged. What he would have been in another department of thought; how high he would have risen under other institutions; what he could have done if politics had not turned him from calm philosophy aside; whether he were really made for mankind, and to America gave up what was meant for mankind; how his mere naked intellectual ability compared with this man's or that,—is a needless and vain speculation.

I may, however, be allowed to say that, although I have seen him act, and heard him speak, and give counsel, in very high and very sharp and difficult crises, I always felt that if more had been needed more would have been done, and that half his strength or all his strength he put not forth. I never saw him make what is called an effort without feeling that, let the occasion be what it would, he would have swelled out to its limits. There was always a reservoir of power of which you never sounded the depths, certainly never saw the bottom; and I cannot well imagine any great historical and civil occasion to which he would not have brought, and to which he would not be acknowledged to have brought, an adequate ability. He had wisdom to have guided the counsels of Austria as Metternich did, if he had loved absolutism as well; skill enough and eloquence enough to have saved the life of Louis the Sixteenth, if skill and eloquence could have done it; learning, services, character, and dignity enough for a Lord Chancellor of England, if wisdom in counsel and eloquence in debate would have been titles to so proud a distinction.

But his class is that of American Statesmen. In that class he is to find his true magnitude. As he stood there he is to take his place forever in our system. To that constellation he has gone up, to that our telescopes or our naked eye are to be directed, and there I think he shines with a large and unalterable glory.

In every work regard the writer's end. In every life regard the actor's end.

In saying this I do not mean to ignore or disparage his rank, also, in the profession of the law. In that profession he labored, by that he lived, of that he was proud, to that he brought vast ability and exquisite judgment, and in that he rose at last to the leadership of the bar. But I regard that, rather, as a superinduced, collateral, accessional fame, a necessity of greatness,—a transcendent greatness, certainly; but it was not the labor he most loved, it was not the fame which attracts so many pilgrims to his tomb, and stirs so many hearts when his name is sounded. There have been Bacons, and Clarendons, and one Cicero, and one Demosthenes, who were lawyers. But they are not the Bacons, the Clarendons, they are not the Cicero and the Demosthenes of historical fame.

It is a noble and a useful profession; but it was not large enough for the whole of Webster.

In that class, then, let me say next,—which is the class of American statesmen,—of foremost American statesmen,—it happened to him to be thrown on our third American age. This ever must be regarded when we would do him justice, or understand him, or compare him with others.

It is easy to say and to see that if his lot had made him a member of the Revolutionary Congress, he would have stood by the side of Washington and Jefferson, Adams and Chase, and that from his tongue, too, Independence would have thundered. It is easy to say and see that it would not have been that his lips were frozen and his arm palsied; that the cabals of Gates, of Conway, could have gone undetected there; that a foolish fear of long enlistments would have delayed the great strife; that so many retreats, pinched winter-quarters, blood traced on the snow by the naked feet of bleeding men, would have proved that the want of funds and the fear of unpopularity were too strong for the sentiment of Liberty!

It is easy to say, too, and to see that if he had been thrown on the constitutional age he would have been found with Hamilton, Jay, and Madison; that his pen, too, and his tongue would have leaped to impress that generation with the nature and necessity of that great work; that he would have risen to the utmost height of the great argument, and that on the pillars, on the foundation-stones of that Constitution which he first read on the little pocket-handkerchief, his name, his wisdom, too, would now be found chiselled deeply. But he was cast on the third age of our history, and how was his part acted there?

In this class, then, let me say further, of the foremost of great American statesmen, I say there was never one, of any one of our periods,—I shall not except the highest of the first period,—of a more ardent love of our *America, and of the whole of it;* of a truer, deeper, broader sense of what the Farewell Address calls the Unity of Government,—its nature, spring, necessity,—and the means of securing it; or who said more, and did more to sink it deep in the American heart. Of the relations of the States to our system,—of their powers, their rights, their quasi sovereignty,—he said less, not because he thought less or knew less, but because he saw there was less necessity for it. But the Union, the Constitution, the national federal life, the American name,—*E Pluribus Unum,*—these filled his heart, these dwelt in his habitual speech.

This, I think, exactly, was his specialty. To this master passion and master sentiment his whole life was subordinated carefully. He was *totus in illis.* He began his public course in opposition to the party which had the general government; and he dearly loved New England; but he "had nothing to do with the Hartford Convention." He drew his first breath in a Northern State and a Northern region; his opinions were shaped and colored by that birth-place and by that place of residence; the local interests he powerfully advocated; for that advocacy he has even been taunted and distrusted. But it was because he thought he saw, and just so far as he saw, that the local interest was identical with the national interest, and that that advocacy was advocacy for the whole, and that policy was American policy, that he espoused it.

Some aged clergyman has been reported to have said, that the sermon—whatever the theology, whatever the ability—was essentially defective, if it did not leave on the hearer the impression that the preacher loved his soul, and that God and the Saviour loved it. I never heard him make a speech,—a great speech,—whatever were the topic, or the time, that did not leave the impression that he loved nothing, desired nothing, so much as the good and glory of America; that he knew no North and no South; that he did not seem to summon around him the whole brotherhood of States and men, and hold them all to his heart! This gave freshness and energy to all his speech. This set the tune to the universal harmony. Even his studies revealed this passion. He knew American history by heart, as a statesman, not as an antiquary, should know it; the plain, noble men, the high aims, and hard fortunes of the colonial time; the agony and the glory of the Revolutionary War, and of the age of the Constitution, were all familiar to him; but chiefly he loved to mark how the spirit of national life was evolving itself all the while; how the colonies grew to regard one another as the children of the same mother, and therefore, fraternally; how the common danger, the common oppression, of the ante-revolutionary and revolutionary period served to fuse them into one; how the Constitution made them formally one; and how the grand and sweet and imperial sentiment of a united national life came at last to penetrate and warm that whole vast and various mass, and move it as a soul.

"Spiritus intus alit, totamque infusa per artus
Mens agitat molem, et magno se corpore miscet."

In this master sentiment I *find the key* to all his earlier and all his later policy and opinions. Through his whole lifetime, this is the central principle that runs through all, accounts for all, reconciles all.

In the department of a mere adventurous and originating policy, I do not think he desired to distinguish himself. In the department of a restless and arrogant and clamorous reform, I know he did not wish to distinguish himself. The general tendency of his mind, the general scope of his politics, were towards conservation.

This rested on a deep conviction that, if the government continued to exist, and this national life continued to be kept, and if these States were held in peace together, the growth of it, the splendid future of it, were as certain as the courses of the seasons. He thought it wiser, therefore, always, that we should grow great under the Union, than that we should be forced to grow great by legislation. He thought it wiser, therefore, at first,—local opinion may have, or may not have, a little influenced this,—to let America grow into a manufacturing people, than that she should be forced to become so. But when that policy was adopted, and millions had been invested under it, and a vast, delicate, and precious interest had grown up, then it seemed to him that just so much had been added to our American life, that for so much we had gone forward in our giant course, and he would guard it and keep it.

He did not favor a premature and unprincipled expansion of territory; though he saw and rejoiced to see, if America continued just, and continued brave, and the Union lasted, how widely—to what Pacific and tropic seas—she must spread,—and how conspicuous a fame of extent was spread out before her. But when the annexation was made and the line drawn and the treaty signed, then he went for her, however "butted and bounded;" then he kept steady to the compact of annexation; then there was no date so small, no line so remote, that he would not plant on it the ensign all radiant, that no foreign aggression might come! *Here you have the Websterianism of Webster.*

I cannot trace this great central principle and this master sentiment and trait which is the characteristic of his whole politics, through the last years of his life, without awakening feelings, some feelings unsuited to the time. I believe, you believe, the country and history will believe, that all he said and all he did, he said and did out of a "full heart for the Constitution," and that the "austere glory" of that crisis of his America and of himself will shine his brightest glory. When some years have passed away, if not yet, that civil courage, that wisdom which combines, constructs, and reconciles; which discerns that in the political world, in our political world especially, no theory and no idea may be pressed to its extreme, and that common sense, good temper, good nature, and not the pedantry of logical abstraction, and the clamor of intemperate sectional partisanships, are the true guides of life; and that deemed a gloomy foolishness, refuted by our whole history, that because in this cluster of States there are different institutions, a different type of industry, different moral estimates, they cannot live together and grow together to a common nationality by forbearance and reason; that an honest, just, and well-principled patriotism is a higher moral virtue than a virulent and noisy philanthropy; and that to build and keep this nation is the true way to serve God and serve man—these traits and these opinions will be remembered as the noblest specimen of the genius and wisdom of Webster. Better than any other passage, or any other catastrophe, these will be thought most happily to have "concluded the great epic of his life." I refer you for them all to his immortal volumes; lasting as the granite of our mountains, lasting as the pillars of our capitol and our Constitution.

They say he was ambitious! Yes; as Ames said of Hamilton, "there is no doubt that he desired glory; and that, feeling his own force, he longed to deck his brow with the wreath of immortality." But I believe he would have yielded his arm, his frame to be burned, before he would have sought to grasp the highest prize of earth by any means, by any organization, by any tactics, by any speech, which in the least degree endangered the harmony of the system.

They say, too, he loved New England! He loved New Hampshire—that old granite world—the crystal hills, gray and cloud-topped; the river, whose murmur lulled his cradle; the old hearth-stone; the grave of father and mother. He loved Massachusetts, which adopted and honored him—that sounding sea-shore, that charmed elm-tree seat, that reclaimed farm, that choice herd, that smell of earth, that dear library, those dearer friends; but the "sphere of his duties was his true country." Dearly he loved you, for he was grateful for the open arms with which you welcomed the stranger and sent him onwards and upwards.

But when the crisis came, and the winds were all let loose, and that sea of March "wrought and was tempestuous," then you saw that he knew even you only as you were, American citizens; then you saw him rise to the true nature and stature of American citizenship; then you read on his brow only what he thought of the whole Republic; then you saw him fold the robes of his habitual patriotism around him, and counsel for all—for all.

So then he served you—"to be pleased with his service was your affair, not his."

And now what would he do, what would he be if he were here to-day? I do not presume to know. But what a loss we have in him.

I have read that in some hard battle, when the tide was running against him, and his ranks were breaking, some one in the agony of a need of generalship exclaimed, "Oh for an hour of Dundee!"

> "So say I, Oh for an hour of Webster now!
> Oh for one more roll of that thunder inimitable!
> One more peal of that clarion!
> One more grave and bold counsel of moderation!
> One more throb of American feeling!"

One more Farewell Address! And then might he ascend unhindered to the bosom of his Father and his God.

But this is a vain wish, and I can only offer you this sentiment—

The birth-day of Webster—Then best, then only well celebrated—when it is given as he gave that marvellous brain, that large heart, and that glorious life, to our country, our whole country, our united country.

APPENDIX I.

ADDRESS AT THE FUNERAL OF HON. RUFUS CHOATE.
IN THE ESSEX STREET MEETING-HOUSE.*
BOSTON, July 23, 1859.
BY NEHEMIAH ADAMS, D.D., PASTOR OF THE ESSEX STREET CHURCH.

"THE BEAUTY of Israel is slain upon thy high places." And can this be he? Is he dead? "All ye that are about him bemoan him; and all ye that know his name say, How is the strong staff broken, and the beautiful rod!" Could no judge be found who, in this cause, would rule at his motion? Was there no jury whom he could persuade, or at least divide? Alas! would not even the executioner pay him courtesy?

As the apple-tree among the trees of the wood, so was he among the sons. The whirlwind passed by; the fruit-tree, loaded with fragrant fruit, lies as low as the withered tree.

In the halls of Congress he rose to speak, and one and another who did not care to listen, and were departing, caught the first tones of his voice, paused, turned back, and became enchained by his eloquence. He was to speak before some institute, and an assembly came together which was never surpassed, and their tribute to his power over them was as rich a chaplet as ever descended on the brows of orators. The merchant princes laid their questions before him, and his counsels gave them almost the assurance of a verdict. Men bound him to their service as soon as they anticipated trouble, or they bought his promise not to appear against them. The profession were assembled, and to the stranger it was a chief object of interest that he was there. His illustrious friend and yours is dying at Marshfield; many are round about him; but whose is that well-proportioned form, in the front of the picture, with that lithe, graceful carriage of the body, that striking head, marked throughout with genius, that face bending toward the dying man with an expression in which great thoughtfulness and great love

---

* Nehemiah Adams, D. D. *Address at the Funeral of Hon. Rufus Choate in the Essex Street Meeting-House, July 23, 1859.* Boston: 1859 [Ed.].

mingle? And has all come to this? Weep, cities and villages! Weep, halls of learning, halls of legislation, halls of justice! Weep, forum, bar, pulpit! He who commanded so great reverence and love is dead. In that beautiful idiom of the tongue in which he was lord, he is "no more." Now, like the common dead, he waits upon the Christian minister for the funeral service, and then "the clods of the valley shall be sweet unto him; and every man shall draw after him, as there are innumerable before him."

Has all that rich, gathered harvest of learning and knowledge, all that wisdom and prudence in affairs, all that acquaintance with the master-spirits of his race, and that power to apply their beautiful creations and inventions, perished? That tongue should never long be silent which wrought with such magic. That mind is just the representative of a world of fancy and imagination which we need, to teach us how to invest the commonplace and literal with the spell of beauty and originality. How can we do without him? No one else can satisfy our want. In the closing words of his speech at a recent celebration of Webster's birthday, we shall often say,—as we listen to orators, or try, perchance, ourselves to be such,—"O for one hour of" Choate! But is he "no more"? What error does that pathetic phrase contain! If he fulfilled the purpose for which his Creator made him a free agent, he is all that he ever was, and will be infinitely more. For he who looks on that coffin and continues to be a materialist, and says that that great soul perished with the body, must not accuse others of credulity. We decline to argue with him.

How gentle he was in his intercourse with you. He gave you a chair as no one else would do it. He persuaded you at his table to receive something from him, in a way that nothing so gross as language can describe. He treated every man as though he were a gentleman; and he treated every gentleman almost as he would a lady. His playfulness was so wise that you would as much admire as smile. One word would often drop from him of such comprehensive, picturesque meaning and beauty, that the whole company would sit in smiles and think about it, as before a picture, till he skilfully turned the conversation. Then again, how inquiring, how docile he seemed as he sat and listened to you! His intense desire to know everything about a subject led him to ask simple questions, to express a childlike wonder, to press you further,—all which was the musing mood of his own mind, though it seemed like simplicity. I have seen him as earnest in having one tell him how the tenor, alto, and soprano stood, relatively, on the score, and why, as though it were a point in jurisprudence. He made you feel that you were teaching him; and you forgot for the moment how much wiser your information made him than it had ever made you.

It will not be deemed unsuitable if his pastor should, "now and here," as he himself would say, open to you a slight view of him as a parishioner. The intervals were not long between some expression or token of his remembrance,—all the more grateful as they were oftentimes delicate and simple; though now and then the valuable contribution to the pastor's library of the work in sixteen volumes, or in six, or in four, or two, reflected as much honor upon the giver, who showed his own power to appreciate and select such books, as it made the receiver feel the obligation to raise his own standard of acquirements. It was the man himself appearing before you in his tokens of remembrance which gave them their principal value. If he is at Washington, he must needs tell a minister at home, in his letter, how "the Sabbath bells do not a little aggravate homesickness." See, once for all, in a note accompanying a royal octavo edition of Wordsworth, the man, original and peculiar in his kindness to a pastor as he was in all other qualities;—for there is little risk in supposing that very few men ever wrote just such a letter as the following under the same circumstances:—

"My dear Sir,—Having had a child born within a few days, I have thought I could do no honester thing than to send my minister a volume of poetry,—a volume, as Wordsworth might say. I shall be sorry if you happen to own the edition.

I am most truly,
Your friend and servant,
R. CHOATE."
October 2, 18—.

Had he been an angel, could any Christian pastor ever have feared for his own sake to preach before him, knowing that such a heart was in his bosom? No, the only pain was in the intenseness of the desire to say or do any thing which might be to the spiritual benefit of such a man.

I have kneeled with him in prayer when a great sorrow was upon his heart. I have stood with him as he leaned against the door and wept. Yes, I have seen him weep. And when wept, you will believe that it was to me, and would be to any man, "a great mourning; as the mourning of Hadadrimmon."

A very short time before he was to deliver his address before the New England Society of New York, I asked him if he had yet written it. "Not the seventhousandth part of a word," was his idiomatic answer. "But," said he, "I believe that I shall appropriate a speech made at Park Street Church the other evening."

It was a charge at the ordination of a young friend from Geneva, who was to labor as an evangelist in Canada. Coming as the candidate did from Geneva, it was natural for any one who addressed him to speak of the Puritans in their connection with Geneva. The few, unambitious words on that topic, on that occasion, reported in a newspaper, were an accidental spark which entered the furnace-chamber of his great mind, and kindled it for a performance which will not soon be forgotten. It was like him thus to recognize one who had done him a service even unintentionally; nor did he fear the imputation of plagiarism; for his taking of another man's thoughts was as when the sun plagiarizes the waters, and turns them into showers, and rainbows, and gorgeous sunsets, and harvest, and grass upon the mountains and herbs for the service of man.

His love of nature had a most interesting property, which, theoretically, one might be tempted, without knowing the man, to say was not agreeable to the highest reach of sentiment. He loved Nature chiefly in her utility. He was, in his own sphere, creator, and he loved things not only for themselves, but as creating. The ocean must have its ships and commerce to please him; it must report to him how it fills harbors and estuaries, that he may love it supremely. Nothing was more poetical to him than that which he so often speaks of in his addresses,— "the hum of labor." A mechanic was with him Homeric. The ringing of an anvil, the whirring of a planing-machine, the factory bells, and wheels, and looms, were all of them to his mind impersonations of beauty. He would, perhaps, be more imaginative over a great wheat-field, than in the solemn woods, so far was his mind from anything dreamy, or from being sentimental for its own sake. Yet when he was a boy, and drove his father's cow, and cut his switch, as no boy in that capacity must fail to do who would drive well, he has said that more than once, when he had thrown away his switch, he has returned to find it, and has carried it back and thrown it under the tree from which he took it, for, he said, "Perhaps there is, after all, some yearning of nature between them still." He had not walked far one morning, a few years ago, he said, and he gave as a reason, that his attention was taken by a company of those large, creeping things which lie on their backs in the paths as soon as the light strikes them. "But of what use was it for you to help them over with your cane, knowing that they would become supine again?" "I gave them a fair start in life," he said, "and my responsibility was at an end." He has probably helped to place more people on their feet than otherwise; and no one has enjoyed it more than he.

Let us unite and do him honor, in view of his decision of character in connection with political affairs. I am not to intrude them here, nor is it important for my purpose to say, or to know, of what school or party he was at any time a member; for had it been science, or religion, or business, in which he had shown the decision of which I speak, it would have served my purpose as well.

If there ever was a party or class of men who had reason to be proud of their position and relationship to each other, it was those old, conservative, very respectable Federalists, many of whom bore so close a resemblance to the old school of English gentlemen. With such men the idea and the name of Democrat were exactly opposite to all their instincts and associations of ideas. Nowhere was this more true than of the Federalists of Essex County in this State, where Mr. Choate had his birth, and where he entered into professional life. Remembering that these deep-seated associations of ideas have been, till quite recently, transmitted from Federalists to old Whigs, it has seemed to me that in Mr. Choate's alliance, through the force of conviction, with the party with which he has of late sympathized, we have an illustration of decision of character for which all men, irrespective of their creeds, must do him honor. He had no political interest of his own to promote by it; he was conscious of seeming to forsake, not only his old associates, but some of his long-cherished associations of ideas, which, in a man of his mental structure, did greater violence to his feelings than anything else.

You will perceive that my remarks have no reference to the correctness or incorrectness of his political opinions, at one time or another; but meeting around him, as you do to-day, with your party banners trailed, and with reversed arms, you will all confess that in such a change as he made in his political relationships, and for the way in which he sustained himself in it, he is worthy of honor and love, for manliness of character, for moral courage, for noble daring, for self-reliance, and for his power to give a reason of the hope that was in him.

He was no changeling in anything. He carried heavy anchorage. Wherever he dropped it, there he rode, tides, winds, tempests, notwithstanding, and, more than all, with gallant barks around him more prudently retiring from the roadsteads till the weather should be fair.

He was not insensible to animadversions upon him. He loved the good opinion of his fellow-men, because he loved them, and he was very sorry when those whom he wished to respect blamed him.

A minister, who took a deep interest in political affairs, once said severe and sharp things about him. His friends were moved with resentment; but Mr. Choate said, with evident grief, and like a child, "I am disposed to write him a letter, and tell him that he is mistaken." Few things in him have ever touched me more than this incident, in view of all the circumstances of the case.

It may seem remarkable to some, that a man of his nervous temperament, and subject to such great and frequent demands upon it, should not have fallen into the habitual use of some powerful narcotic. Had he done so, it would have plainly manifested itself in one so constantly before the public as he. Exaltation of spirits by a powerful narcotic is inevitably followed by a corresponding depression, unfitting its miserable subject for continuous mental labor. But we all know how consecutive he was in his mental efforts. When he had performed one great service, he was ready for another of a different but equally laborious kind, or for his daily work.

Some have been interested to inquire whether he had the artificial aid here referred to, in his mental efforts. The highly respected physician who has been his medical attendant for twenty years places this, by his denial of it, beyond a question. He would have known it if it were so. On the contrary, he says that he could ordinarily put him to sleep with a Dover's powder. Once, at home, using laudanum in a tooth, it produced a sickness which showed that his system was a stranger to such a narcotic.[1]

He made the impression upon those who witnessed his daily life, that he was as pure and upright in his private history, as he was honorable and noble in his intercourse with men. He therefore needs no vindication here, nor elsewhere; and in this respect he is fortunate above many who have been much in public life, or have in any way become pre-eminent. Tempted, of course, as we are, if, like us, he sinned, he needed repentance, and the blood that cleanseth from sin. Without holiness no man shall see the Lord. If he was mortal, he was a sinner; and if he was not mortal, why is he there? Whether he did or did not experience that new birth, without which no man can see the kingdom of God, we are not called upon to decide. There are things which make us hope. He knew what he must do to be saved. He was speaking with a Christian friend, in his recent sickness, about his feelings under the preaching of the Gospel. He said, "Any man who goes to perdition under that preaching, goes on his own responsibility."

---

1. Since this Address was delivered, a gentleman of the highest respectability has called upon me to say, that, to his personal knowledge, a friend, a few years since, told Mr. Choate of a prevailing belief that he used opium, and that Mr. Choate replied, in the most emphatic manner, The perfect confutation of this charge, which even charitable men feared might have confirmation in the corrugated, worn look occasioned by intense efforts, should be an admonition to us; while, no doubt, it will awaken, in many, that stronger love which comes to a generous mind with the regret at having entertained an injurious suspicion.

He spoke at that time of Mr. Webster's last hours, and he discussed the question of that great man's probable relation to his God and Saviour. He emphatically said, with deep emotion: "I believe he was right; he comprehended the scheme";—and he repeated the words, "he comprehended the scheme." Mr. Choate could say, as Mr. Webster once said on the causeway between Somerville and Medford: "My father and my mother are in heaven; their faith is good enough for me; I have never wavered as to my confidence in it."

Where there is a clear perception of the way to be saved through Christ,—where one "comprehended the scheme," the only question which remains is, Did the heart yield to it? Did, at least, the certain and near approach of death, by the grace of God, (for even death is, of itself, without power to change the heart,) constrain the soul to accept the provisions of the Gospel? The rule of the Gospel is, that a man who knows the truth shall confess Christ before men.

In the absence of the highest kind of evidence, we are permitted to remember, that the last public effort of this friend of ours was made on a platform over the very spot where he, at this moment, sleeps in death, and that that effort was a testimony to the Gospel of our Lord Jesus Christ, and an appeal to its ministers to make full proof of their ministry. One thing is certain, that for this he to-day has a reward; for what an assembly is this! met here on that spot where he lifted up his voice and gave that which proved to be his dying testimony to the religion of Jesus. God says: "Them that honor me I will honor."

O how easy it is for Christian love to hope that the mercy which removes our transgressions from us, may have made him one of its trophies, and that, through a peril and hazard the thought of which should be a warning to us amidst the cares of this life and the temptations of our respective callings, his soul was led to comply with the conditions of peace which God has revealed! "We must think more of that Great Country," he said to his son the day before he died.

On board the steamer he said to me, "I am going to the Isle of Wight." I believe that he expected there to find his grave. He knew that it was only a question of time with regard to the issue of his disease. He had as great a dread of bodily suffering, and of its effect upon those who witnessed it, as I ever knew.

It was, therefore, one of the many marks of extraordinary power in this man, that he was willing to die far from home, rather than know that those whom he loved were enduring the pangs which his protracted sufferings might occasion.

He once said, speaking of sudden death: "I agree with De Quincey on that subject."[2] "The prayer," said Mr. Choate, " 'From sudden death, good Lord,

2. *Miscellaneous Essays,* Ticknor and Fields's edition, p. 168.

deliver us,' must mean, as the expression is also rendered. Otherwise I protest against it." His wish was not granted.

But death prepared for by means of any sufferings, is followed by a far more exceeding and eternal weight of glory. He may have been led about in the dark wilderness of sickness and pain, to humble him and to prove him, and that he might know what was in his heart, and whether he would love the Lord his God, or no.

The words of parting are nearly all said, but we shrink from this separation. "Then said Thomas, which is called Didymus, unto his fellow-disciples, Let us also go, that we may die with him." We would keep him here; we would be in his company. Seldom did love mingle in greater proportions with the honor paid to the illustrious dead, than is everywhere the case in the tributes which he receives.

How true it is that we are spontaneously treated as we have treated others, and that in this respect, "with what measure ye mete, it shall be measured to you again." He fills the thoughts of those who knew him, much like a deceased and loved relative; you would almost believe that he is bone of your bone and flesh of your flesh.

The future is, to my mind, filled with him. I think of heaven: is he there? I think of the spirits of just men made perfect: is he among them? The Son of Man will come in the clouds of heaven: I think, his eyes will see Him. There shall be a resurrection of the dead; his form will partake of it. There is a day of judgment at the end of the world; he will stand and be judged. Eternity! it will be for him!

Great Work of God! Great Ornament of human kind! Great Friend! If such be the will of God, one great joy in heaven will be to meet you there, to mark your radiant beauty and glory, to hear your new song to redeeming love, to learn forever your wondrous history among the ransomed, and with the angels that excel in strength.

Appendix II.

AN ADDRESS DELIVERED AT THE UNVEILING OF THE STATUE OF RUFUS CHOATE.*
In the Court House in Boston, October 15, 1898,
By Joseph H. Choate.

I deem it a very great honor to have been invited by the Suffolk Bar Association to take part on this occasion in honor of him who still stands as one of the most brilliant ornaments of the American Bar in its annals of two centuries. Bearing his name and lineage, and owing to him, as I do, more than to any other man or men—to his example and inspiration, to his sympathy and helping hand—whatever success has attended my own professional efforts, I could not refuse the invitation to come here to-day to the dedication of this statue, which shall stand for centuries to come, and convey to the generations who knew him not some idea of the figure and the features of Rufus Choate. Neither bronze nor marble can do him justice. Not Rembrandt himself could reproduce the man as we knew and loved him—for until he lay upon his death-bed he was all action, the "noble, divine, godlike action" of the orator—and the still life of art could never really represent him as he was.

I am authorized, at the outset, to express for the surviving children of Mr. Choate their deep sense of gratitude to the generous donor of this statue of their honored father, and their complete appreciation of the sentiment which has inspired the city and the court to accept it as a public treasure, and to give it a permanent home at the very gates of the Temple of Justice, at whose shrine he worshipped. They desire also to express publicly on this occasion their admiration of the statue itself, as a work of art, and a faithful portrait, in form and feature, of the living man as he abides in their loving memory. The City of Boston is certainly indebted to Mr. French for his signal skill in thus adding a central figure to that group of great orators whom its elder citizens once heard with delight—Webster, Choate, Everett, Mann, Sumner and Garrison. In life,

* Joseph H. Choate, *An Address Delivered at the Unveiling of the Statue of Rufus Choate in the Court House in Boston, October 15, 1898.* Boston: 1898 [Ed.].

they divided the sentiments and applause of her people. In death, they share the honors of her Pantheon.

It is forty years since he strode these ancient streets with his majestic step—forty years since the marvellous music of his voice was heard by the living ear—and those of us who, as students and youthful disciples, followed his footsteps, and listened to his eloquence, and almost worshipped his presence, whose ideal and idol he was, are already many years older than he lived to be; but there must be a few still living, and present here to-day, who were in the admiring crowds that hung with rapture on his lips—in the courts of justice, in the densely packed assembly, in the Senate, in the Constitutional Convention, or in Faneuil Hall consecrated to Freedom—and who can still recall, among life's most cherished memories, the tones of that matchless voice, that pallid face illuminated with rare intelligence, the flashing glance of his dark eye, and the light of his bewitching smile. But, in a decade or two more, these lingering witnesses of his glory and his triumphs will have passed on, and to the next generation he will be but a name and a statue, enshrined in fame's temple with Cicero and Burke, with Otis and Hamilton and Webster, with Pinkney and Wirt, whose words and thoughts he loved to study and to master.

Many a noted orator, many a great lawyer, has been lost in oblivion in forty years after the grave closed over him, but I venture to believe that the Bar of Suffolk, aye, the whole Bar of America, and the people of Massachusetts, have kept the memory of no other man alive and green so long, so vividly and so lovingly, as that of Rufus Choate. Many of his characteristic utterances have become proverbial, and the flashes of his wit, the play of his fancy and the gorgeous pictures of his imagination are the constant themes of reminiscence, wherever American lawyers assemble for social converse. What Mr. Dana so well said over his bier is still true to-day: "When as lawyers we meet together in tedious hours and seek to entertain ourselves, we find we do better with anecdotes of Mr. Choate, than on our own original resources." The admirable biography of Professor Brown, and his arguments, so far as they have been preserved, are text books in the profession—and so the influence of his genius, character and conduct is still potent and far reaching in the land.

You will not expect me, upon such an occasion, to enter upon any narrative of his illustrious career, so familiar to you all, or to undertake any analysis of those remarkable powers which made it possible. All that has been done already by many appreciative admirers, and has become a part of American literature. I can only attempt, in a most imperfect manner, to present a few of the leading traits of that marvellous personality, which we hope that this striking statue will help to transmit to the students, lawyers and citizens who, in the coming years, shall throng these portals.

How it was that such an exotic nature, so ardent and tropical in all its manifestations, so truly southern and Italian in its impulses, and at the same time so robust and sturdy in its strength, could have been produced upon the bleak and barren soil of our northern cape, and nurtured under the chilling blasts of its east winds, is a mystery insoluble. Truly, "this is the Lord's doing, and it is marvellous in our eyes." In one of his speeches in the Senate, he draws the distinction between "the cool and slow New England men, and the mercurial children of the sun, who sat down side by side in the presence of Washington, to form our more perfect union." If ever there was a mercurial child of the sun, it was himself most happily described. I am one of those who believe that the stuff that a man is made of has more to do with his career than any education or environment. The greatness that is achieved, or is thrust upon some men, dwindles before that of him who is born great. His horoscope was propitious. The stars in their courses fought for him. The birthmark of genius, distinct and ineffaceable, was on his brow. He came of a long line of pious and devout ancestors, whose living was as plain as their thinking was high. It was from father and mother that he derived the flame of intellect, the glow of spirit and the beauty of temperament that were so unique.

And his nurture to manhood was worthy of the child. It was "the nurture and admonition of the Lord." From that rough pine cradle, which is still preserved in the room where he was born, to his premature grave at the age of fifty-nine, it was one long course of training and discipline of mind and character, without pause or rest. It began with that well-thumbed and dog's-eared Bible from Hog Island, its leaves actually worn away by the pious hands that had turned them, read daily in the family from January to December, in at Genesis and out at Revelations every two years; and when a new child was born in the household, the only celebration, the only festivity, was to turn back to the first chapter, and read once more how "in the beginning God created the heaven and the earth," and all that in them is. This Book, so early absorbed and never forgotten, saturated his mind and spirit more than any other, more than all other books combined. It was at his tongue's end, at his fingers' ends—always close at hand until those last languid hours at Halifax, when it solaced his dying meditations. You can hardly find speech, argument or lecture of his, from first to last, that is not sprinkled and studded with biblical ideas and pictures, and biblical words and phrases. To him the book of Job was a sublime poem. He knew the Psalms by heart, and dearly loved the prophets, and above all Isaiah, upon whose gorgeous imagery he made copious drafts. He pondered every word, read with most subtle keenness, and applied with happiest effect. One day coming into the Crawford House, cold and shivering—and you remember how he could shiver—he caught sight of the blaze in the great fireplace, and was instantly warm before the rays could reach him, exclaiming, "Do you remember that verse in Isaiah, 'Aha! I am warm. I have the fire'?" and so his daily conversation was marked.

And upon this solid rock of the Scriptures he built a magnificent structure of knowledge and acquirement, to which few men in America have ever attained. History, philosophy, poetry, fiction, all came as grist to his mental mill. But with him, time was too precious to read any trash; he could winnow the wheat from the chaff at sight, almost by touch. He sought knowledge, ideas, for their own sake, and for the language in which they were conveyed. I have heard a most learned jurist gloat over the purchase of the last sensational novel, and have seen a most distinguished bishop greedily devouring the stories of Gaboriau one after another, but Mr. Choate seemed to need no such counter-irritant or blister, to draw the pain from his hurt mind. Business, company, family, sickness—nothing could rob him of his one hour each day in the company of illustrious writers of all ages. How his whole course of thought was tinged and embellished with the reflected light of the great Greek orators, historians and poets; how Roman history, fresh in his mind as the events of yesterday, supplied him with illustrations and supports for his own glowing thoughts and arguments, all of you who have either heard him or read him know.

But it was to the great domain of English literature that he daily turned for fireside companions, and really kindred spirits. As he said in a letter to Sumner, with whom his literary fraternity was at one time very close: "Mind that Burke is the fourth Englishman,—Shakspeare, Bacon, Milton, Burke": and then in one of those dashing outbursts of playful extravagance, which were so characteristic of him, fearing that Sumner, in his proposed review, might fail to do full justice to the great ideal of both, he adds: "Out of Burke might be cut 50 Mackintoshes, 175 Macaulays, 40 Jeffreys and 250 Sir Robert Peels, and leave him greater than Pitt and Fox together." In the constant company of these great thinkers and writers he revelled, and made their thoughts his own; and his insatiable memory seemed to store up all things committed to it, as the books not in daily use are stacked away in your public library, so that at any moment, with notice or without, he could lay his hand straightway upon them. What was once imbedded in the gray matter of his brain did not lie buried there, as with most of us, but grew and flourished and bore fruit. What he once read he seemed never to forget.

This love of study became a ruling passion in his earliest youth. To it he sacrificed all that the youth of our day—even the best of them—consider indispensable, and especially the culture and training of the body; and when we recall his pale face, worn and lined as it was in his later years, one of his most pathetic utterances is found in a letter to his son at school: "I hope that you are well and studious, and among the best scholars. If this is so, I am willing you should play every day till the blood is ready to burst from your cheeks. Love the studies that will make you wise, useful and happy when there shall be no blood at all to be seen in your cheeks or lips." He never rested from his delightful labors—and that is the pity of it—he took no vacations. Except for one short trip to Europe, when warned of a possible breakdown in 1850, an occasional day at Essex, a three days' journey to the White Mountains was all that he allowed himself. Returning from such an outing in the summer of 1854, on which it was my great privilege to accompany him, he said "That is my entire holiday for this year." So that when he told Judge Warren so playfully that "The lawyer's vacation is the space between the question put to a witness and his answer," it was of himself almost literally true. Would that he had realized his constant dream of an ideal cottage in the old walnut grove in Essex, where he might spend whole summers with his books, his children and his thoughts.

His splendid and blazing intellect, fed and enriched by constant study of the best thoughts of the great minds of the race, his all-persuasive eloquence, his teeming and radiant imagination, whirling his hearers along with it, and sometimes overpowering himself, his brilliant and sportive fancy, lighting up the most arid subjects with the glow of sunrise, his prodigious and never-failing memory, and his playful wit, always bursting forth with irresistible impulse, have been the subject of scores of essays and criticisms, all struggling with the vain effort to describe and crystallize the fascinating and magical charm of his speech and his influence.

But the occasion and the place remind me that here to-day we have chiefly to do with him as the lawyer and the advocate, and all that I shall presume very briefly to suggest is, what this statue will mean to the coming generations of lawyers and citizens.

And first, and far above his splendid talents and his triumphant eloquence, I would place the character of the man—pure, honest, delivered absolutely from all the temptations of sordid and mercenary things, aspiring daily to what was higher and better, loathing all that was vulgar and of low repute, simple as a child, and tender and sympathetic as a woman. Emerson most truly says that character is far above intellect, and this man's character surpassed even his exalted intellect, and, controlling all his great endowments, made the consummate beauty of his life. I know of no greater tribute ever paid to a successful lawyer, than that which he received from Chief Justice Shaw—himself an august and serene personality, absolutely familiar with his daily walk and conversation—in his account of the effort that was made to induce Mr. Choate to give up his active and exhausting practice, and to take the place of Professor in the Harvard Law School, made vacant by the death of Mr. Justice Story—an effort of which the Chief Justice, as a member of the corporation of Harvard, was the principal promoter. After referring to him then, in 1847, as "the leader of the Bar in every department of forensic eloquence," and dwelling upon the great advantages which would accrue to the school from the profound legal learning which he possessed, he said: "In the case of Mr. Choate, it was considered quite indispensable that he should reside in Cambridge, on account of the influence which his genial manners, his habitual presence, and the would be likely to exert over the young men, drawn from every part of the United States to listen to his instructions."

What richer tribute could there be to personal and professional worth, than such words from such lips? He was the fit man to mould the characters of the youth, not of the city or the State only, but of the whole nation. So let the statue stand as notice to all who seek to enter here, that the first requisite of all true renown in our noble profession—renown not for a day or a life only, but for generations—is Character.

And next I would point to it as a monument to self discipline; and here he was indeed without a rival. You may search the biographies of all the great lawyers of the world, and you will find none that surpassed, I think none that approached him, in this rare quality and power. The advocate who would control others must first, last and always control himself. "Every educated man," he once said, "should remember that 'great parts are a great trust,'" and, conscious of his talents and powers, he surely never forgot that. You may be certain that after his distinguished college career at Dartmouth—first always where there was none second—after all that the law school, and a year spent under the tuition of William Wirt, then at the zenith of his fame, could lend to his equipment, and after the five years of patient study in his office at Danvers, where he was the only lawyer, he brought to the subsequent actual practice of his profession an outfit of learning, of skill and research, which most of us would have thought sufficient for a lifetime; but with him it was only the beginning. His power of labor was inexhaustible, and down to the last hour of his professional life he never relaxed the most acute and searching study, not of the case in hand only, but of the whole body of the law, and of everything in history, poetry, philosophy and literature that could lend anything of strength or lustre to the performance of his professional duties. His hand, his head, his heart, his imagination were never out of training. Think of a man already walking the giddy heights of assured success, already a Senator of the United States from Massachusetts, or even years afterwards, when the end of his professional labors was already in sight, schooling himself to daily tasks in law, in rhetoric, in oratory, seeking always for the actual truth, and for the "best language" in which to embody it—the "precisely one right word" by which to utter it—think of such a man, with all his ardent taste for the beautiful in every domain of human life, going through the grinding work of taking each successive volume of the Massachusetts Reports as they came out, down to the last year of his practice, and making a brief in every case in which he had not been himself engaged, with new researches to see how he might have presented it, and thus to keep up with the procession of the law. Verily, "all things are full of labor; man cannot utter it: the eye is not satisfied with seeing, nor the ear filled with hearing."

So let no man seek to follow in his footsteps, unless he is ready to demonstrate, in his own person, that infinite work is the only touchstone of the highest standing in the law, and that the sluggard and the slothful who enter here must leave all hope behind.

Again we hail this statue, which shall stand here as long as bronze shall endure, as the fit representative of one who was the perfect embodiment of absolute loyalty to his profession, in the highest and largest and noblest sense; and, if I might presume to speak for the whole American Bar, I would say that in its universal judgment he stands in this regard pre-eminent, yes, foremost still. Truly, he did that pious homage to the Law which Hooker exacted for her from all things in Heaven and Earth, and was governed by that ever-present sense of debt and duty to the profession of which Lord Bacon spoke. He entered her Courts as a High Priest, arrayed and equipped for the most sacred offices of the Temple. He belonged to the heroic age of the Bar, and, after the retirement of Webster, he was chief among its heroes. He was the centre of a group of lawyers and advocates, the ablest and the strongest we have known, by whose aid the chief tribunal of this ancient commonwealth administered justice so as to give law to the whole country. Such tributes as Loring and Curtis and Dana lavished upon his grave can never wither. Each one of them had been his constant antagonist in the great arena, and each could say with authority:

—"*experto credite, quantus*
In clypeum assurgat, quo turbine torqueat hastam."

One after the other, they portrayed in words not to be forgotten his fidelity to the Court, to the client and to the law, his profound learning, his invincible logic, his rare scholarship and his persuasive eloquence, his uniform deference to the Court and to his adversaries—and more and better than all these—what those specially interested in his memory cherish as a priceless treasure—his marvellous sweetness of temper, which neither triumph nor defeat nor disease could ruffle, his great and tender and sympathetic heart, which made them, and the whole bench and bar, love him in life, and love him still.

He magnified his calling with all the might of his indomitable powers. Following the law as a profession, or, as Judge Sprague so justly said, "as a science, and also as an art," he aimed always at perfection for its own sake, and no thought of money, or of any mercenary consideration, ever touched his generous and aspiring spirit, or chilled or stimulated his ardor. He espoused the cause of the poorest client, about the most meagre subject of controversy, with the same fidelity and enthusiasm as when millions were at stake, and sovereign States the combatants. No love of money ever planted the least root of evil in his soul; and this should not fail to be said in remembrance of him, in days when money rules the world.

His theory of advocacy was the only possible theory consistent with the sound and wholesome administration of justice—that, with all loyalty to truth and honor, he must devote his best talents and attainments, all that he was, and all that he could, to the support and enforcement of the cause committed to his trust. It is right here to repeat the words of Mr. Justice Curtis, speaking for himself and for the whole Bar, that "Great injustice would be done to this great and eloquent advocate, by attributing to him any want of loyalty to truth, or any deference to wrong, because he employed all his great powers and attainments, and used to the utmost his consummate skill and eloquence, in exhibiting and enforcing the comparative merits of one side of the cases in which he acted. In doing so he but did his duty. If other people did theirs, the administration of justice was secure."

His name will ever be identified with trial by jury, the department of the profession in which he was absolutely supreme. He cherished with tenacious affection and interest its origin, its history and its great fundamental maxims— that the citizen charged with crime shall be presumed innocent until his guilt shall be established beyond all reasonable doubt; that no man shall be deprived by the law of property or reputation until his right to retain it is disproved by a clear preponderance of evidence to the satisfaction of all the twelve; that every suitor shall be confronted with the proofs by which he shall stand or fall; that only after a fair hearing, with full right of cross-examination, and the observance of the vital rules of evidence, shall he forfeit life, liberty or property, and then only by the judgment of his peers.

Regarding these cardinal principles of Anglo-Saxon justice and policy as essential to the maintenance of liberty and of civil society, he stood as their champion "with spear in rest and heart on flame," sheated in the panoply of genius.

To-day, when we have seen a great sister republic on the verge of collapse for the violation of these first canons of Freedom, we may justly honor such a champion.

But he displayed his undying loyalty to the profession on a still higher and grander scale, when he viewed and presented it as one of the great and indispensable departments of Government, as an instrumentality for the well-being and conservation of the State. *"Pro clientibus saepe; pro lege, pro republica semper."*

I regard the magnificent argument which he made on the judicial tenure in the Constitutional Convention of 1853 as the greatest single service which he ever rendered to the profession, and to the Commonwealth, of which he was so proud. You will observe, if you read it, that it differs radically in kind, rather than in degree, from all his other speeches, arguments and addresses.

Discarding all ornament, restraining with careful guard all tendency to flights of rhetoric, in clear and pellucid language, plain and unadorned, laying bare the very nerve of his thought, as if he were addressing, as no doubt he meant to address and convince, not alone his fellow delegates assembled in the Convention, but the fishermen of Essex, the manufacturers of Worcester and Hampden, and the farmers of Berkshire—all the men and women of the Commonwealth, of that day and of all days to come—he pleads for the continuance of an appointed judiciary, and for the judicial tenure during good behavior, as the only safe foundations of justice and of liberty.

He draws the picture of "a good judge profoundly learned in all the learning of the law;" "not merely upright and well intentioned;" "but the man who will not respect persons in judgment;" standing only for justice, "though the thunder should light upon his brow," while he holds the balance even, to protect the humblest and most odious individual against all the powers and the people of the Commonwealth; and "possessing at all times the perfect confidence of the community, that he bear not the sword in vain." He stands for the existing system which had been devised and handed down by the Founders of the State, and appeals to its uniform success in producing just that kind of a judge; to the experience and example of England since 1688; to the Federal system which had furnished to the people of the Union such illustrious magistrates; and finally to the noble line of great and good judges who had from the beginning presided in your courts. He then takes up and disposes of all objections and arguments drawn from other States, which had adopted an elective judiciary and shortened terms, and conclusively demonstrates that to abide by the existing constitution of your judicial system was the only way to secure to Massachusetts forever "a government of laws and not of men."

It was on one of the red-letter days of my youth that I listened to that matchless argument, and, when it ended, and the last echoes of his voice died away as he retired from the old Hall of the House of Representatives, leaning heavily upon the arm of Henry Wilson, all crumpled, dishevelled and exhausted, I said to myself that some virtue had gone out of him—indeed some virtue did go out of him with every great effort—but that day it went to dignify and ennoble our profession, and to enrich and sustain the very marrow of the Commonwealth. If ever again that question should be raised within her borders, let that argument be read in every assembly, every church and every school-house. Let all the people hear it. It is as potent and unanswerable to-day, and will be for centuries to come, as it was nearly half a century ago when it fell from his lips. Cling to your ancient system, which has made your Courts models of jurisprudence to all the world until this hour. Cling to it, and freedom shall reign here until the sunlight shall melt this bronze, and justice shall be done in Massachusetts, though the skies fall.

And now, in conclusion, let me speak of his patriotism. I have always believed that Mr. Webster, more than any other one man, was entitled to the credit of that grand and universal outburst of devotion, with which the whole North sprang to arms in defense of the Constitution and the Union, many years after his death, when the first shot at Fort Sumter, like a fire bell in the night, roused them from their slumber, and convinced them that the great citadel of their liberties was in actual danger. Differ as we may and must as to his final course in his declining years, the one great fact can never be blotted out, that the great work of his grand and noble life was the defense of the Constitution—so that he came to be known of all men as its one Defender—that for thirty years he preached to the listening nation the crusade of nationality, and fired New England and the whole North with its spirit. He inspired them to believe that to uphold and preserve the Union, against every foe, was the first duty of the citizen; that if the Union was saved, all was saved; that if that was lost, all was lost. He moulded better even than he knew. It was his great brain that designed, his flaming heart that forged, his sublime eloquence that welded the sword, which was at last, when he was dust, to consummate his life's work, and make Liberty and Union one and inseparable forever.

And so, in large measure, it was with Mr. Choate. His glowing heart went out to his country with the passionate ardor of a lover. He believed that the first duty of the lawyer, orator, scholar was to her. His best thoughts, his noblest words, were always for her. Seven of the best years of his life, in the Senate and House of Representatives, at the greatest personal sacrifice, he gave absolutely to her service. On every important question that arose, he made, with infinite study and research, one of the great speeches of the debate. He commanded the affectionate regard of his fellows, and of the watchful and listening nation. He was a profound and constant student of her history, and revelled in tracing her growth and progress from Plymouth Rock and Salem Harbor, until she filled the continent from sea to sea. He loved to trace the advance of the Puritan spirit, with which he was himself deeply imbued, from Winthrop and Endicott, and Carver and Standish, through all the heroic periods and events of colonial and revolutionary and national life, until, in his own last years, it dominated and guided all of Free America. He knew full well, and displayed in his many splendid speeches and addresses, that one unerring purpose of freedom and of Union ran through her whole history; that there was no accident in it all; that all the generations, from the Mayflower down, marched to one measure and followed one flag; that all the struggles, all the self-sacrifice, all the prayers and the tears, all the fear of God, all the soul-trials, all the yearnings for national life, of more than two centuries, had contributed to make the country that he served and loved. He, too, preached, in season and out of season, the gospel of Nationality. He was the faithful disciple of Webster, while that great Master lived, and, after his death, he bore aloft the same standard and maintained the same cause. Mr. Everett spoke nothing more than the truth, when he said in Faneuil Hall, while all the bells were tolling, at the moment when the vessel bringing home the dead body of his lifelong friend cast anchor in Boston Harbor: "If ever there was a truly disinterested patriot, Rufus Choate was that man. In his political career there was no shade of selfishness. Had he been willing to purchase advancement at the price often paid for it, there was never a moment, from the time he first made himself felt and known, that he could not have commanded anything that any party had to bestow. But he desired none of the rewards or honors of success."

He foresaw clearly that the division of the country into geographical parties must end in civil war. What he could not see was, that there was no other way—that only by cutting out slavery by the sword, could America secure Liberty and Union too—but to the last drop of his blood, and the last fibre of his being, he prayed and pleaded for the life of the nation, according to his light. Neither of these great patriots lived to see the fearful spectacle which they had so eloquently deprecated. But when at last the dread day came, and our young heroes marched forth to bleed and die for their country—their own sons among the foremost—they carried in their hearts the lessons which both had taught, and all Massachusetts, all New England, from the beginning, marched behind them, "carrying the flag and keeping step to the music of the Union," as he had bade them, and so I say, let us award to them both their due share of the glory.

Thus to-day we consign this noble statue to the keeping of posterity, to remind them of "the patriot, jurist, orator, scholar, citizen and friend," whom we are proud to have known and loved.

INDEX

NOTE ON THE EDITORS

Thomas E. Woods, Jr., holds a bachelor's degree in history from Harvard and his Ph.D. from Columbia University. He is currently assistant professor of history at Suffolk Community College, a unit of the State University of New York, in Brentwood, New York.

Conservative Leadership Series editor Christopher B. Briggs holds degrees from Bowdoin College (summa cum laude) and The Catholic University of America. Assistant editor of *Humanitas,* a journal of the humanities published in Washington, D.C., he lives in northern Virginia.